Burke Aaron Hinsdale

The Old Northwest

With a View of the Thirteen Colonies as Constituted by the Royal Charters

Burke Aaron Hinsdale

The Old Northwest
With a View of the Thirteen Colonies as Constituted by the Royal Charters

ISBN/EAN: 9783337039097

Printed in Europe, USA, Canada, Australia, Japan

Cover: Foto ©ninafisch / pixelio.de

More available books at **www.hansebooks.com**

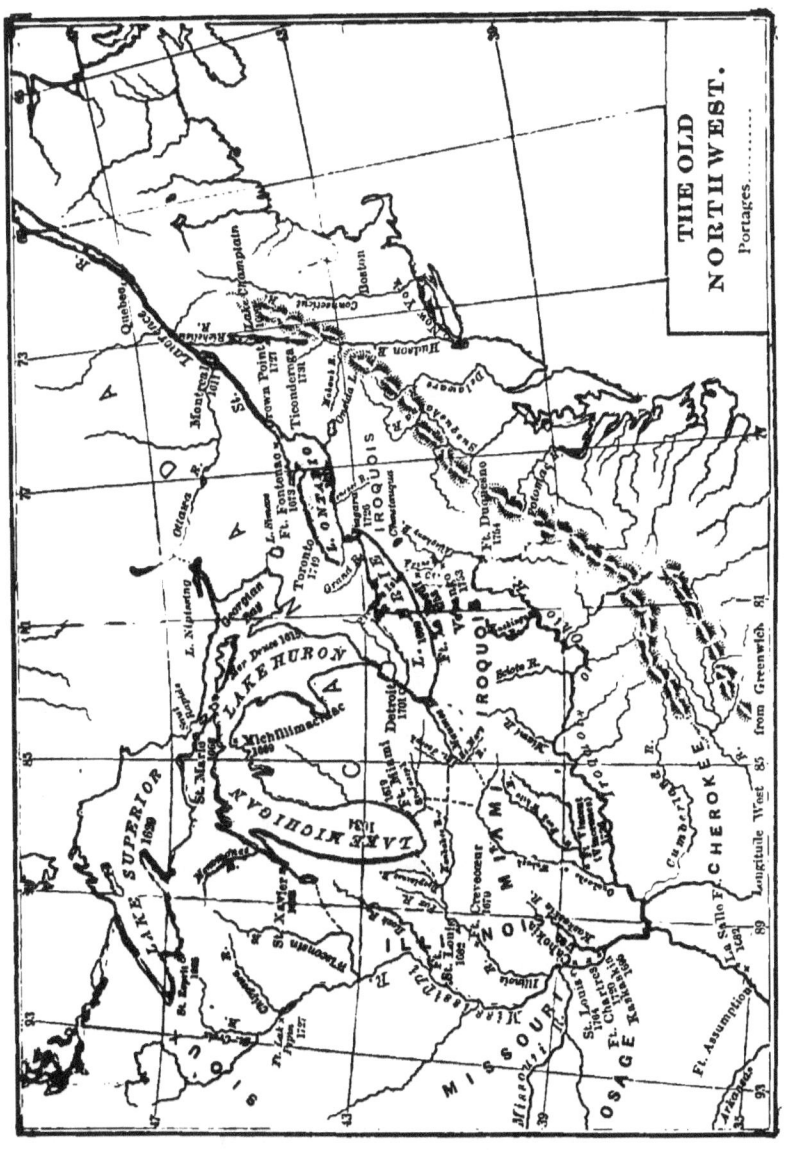

THE
OLD NORTHWEST

WITH A VIEW OF THE THIRTEEN COLONIES AS CONSTITUTED BY THE ROYAL CHARTERS

BY

B. A. HINSDALE, Ph.D.

PROFESSOR OF THE SCIENCE AND ART OF TEACHING, UNIVERSITY OF MICHIGAN; AUTHOR OF "SCHOOLS AND STUDIES," AND EDITOR OF "THE WORKS OF JAMES ABRAM GARFIELD"

"Religion, morality, and knowledge being necessary to good government and the happiness of mankind, schools and the means of education shall forever be encouraged."
—*Ordinance* of 1787.

"No colony in America was ever settled under such favorable auspices as that which has just commenced at the Muskingum."—WASHINGTON.

"We look to you of the Northwest to finally decide whether this is to be a land of slavery or freedom. The people of the Northwest are to be the arbiters of its destiny."
—SEWARD.

NEW YORK
TOWNSEND MAC COUN
1888

F
479
H 58

PREFACE.

SAVE New England alone, there is no section of the United States embracing several States that is so distinct an historical unit, and that so readily yields to historical treatment, as the Old Northwest. It is the part of the Great West first discovered and colonized by the French. It was the occasion of the final struggle for dominion between France and England in North America. It was the theatre of one of the most brilliant and far-reaching military exploits of the Revolution. The disposition to be made of it at the close of the Revolution is the most important territorial question treated in the history of American diplomacy. After the war, the Northwest began to assume a constantly increasing importance in the national history. It is the original public domain, and the part of the West first colonized under the authority of the National Government. It was the first and the most important Territory ever organized by Congress. It is the only part of the United States ever under a secondary constitution like the Ordinance of 1787. No other equal part of the Union has made in one hundred years such progress along the characteristic lines of American development. Moreover, the Northwest has stood in very important relations to questions of great national and international importance, as the use and ownership of the Mississippi River, and the territorial growth and integrity of the Union. To portray those features of this region that make it an historical unit is the central purpose of this book. But as the Northwest is intimately dependent upon the Atlantic Plain, a view of the Thirteen Colonies as Constituted by the Royal Charters has also been given. No previous writer has covered the ground, and the work is wholly new in conception.

Dr. Edward A. Freeman insists " that the most ingenious and eloquent of modern historical discourses can, after all, be nothing more than a comment on a text." Historical texts are not history, but even ingenious and eloquent comments often suffer from lack of a sufficiency of the text that they are written to elucidate. In this work, liberal quotations from original documents will be found, accompanied by the necessary discussion. The subjects treated in Chapters VI., VII., XI., XII., and XIII., in particular, cannot be satisfactorily handled in any other way. Furthermore, while these documents are in no sense rare, they do not lie in the way of the common reader or of the ordinary student or teacher of history. This feature of the work, it is believed, will be highly appreciated by all these classes, and especially by the student and the teacher.

B. A. HINSDALE.

UNIVERSITY OF MICHIGAN,
   ANN ARBOR, March 1, 1888.

CONTENTS.

		PAGE
I.	NORTH AMERICA IN OUTLINE,	1
II.	THE FIRST DIVISION OF NORTH AMERICA,	6
III.	THE FRENCH DISCOVER THE NORTHWEST,	21
IV.	THE FRENCH COLONIZE THE NORTHWEST,	38
V.	ENGLAND WRESTS THE NORTHWEST FROM FRANCE: THE FIRST TREATY OF PARIS,	55
VI.	THE THIRTEEN COLONIES AS CONSTITUTED BY THE ROYAL CHARTERS (I.),	70
VII.	THE THIRTEEN COLONIES AS CONSTITUTED BY THE ROYAL CHARTERS (II.),	98
VIII.	THE WESTERN LAND POLICY OF THE BRITISH GOVERNMENT FROM 1763 TO 1775,	120
IX.	THE NORTHWEST IN THE REVOLUTION,	147
X.	THE UNITED STATES WREST THE NORTHWEST FROM ENGLAND: THE SECOND TREATY OF PARIS,	162
XI.	THE NORTHWESTERN LAND-CLAIMS,	192
XII.	THE NORTHWESTERN CESSIONS (I.),	203
XIII.	THE NORTHWESTERN CESSIONS (II.),	224

CONTENTS.

		PAGE
XIV.	THE LAND-ORDINANCE OF 1785,	255
XV.	THE ORDINANCE OF 1787,	263
XVI.	THE TERRITORY OF THE UNITED STATES NORTHWEST OF THE RIVER OHIO,	280
XVII.	THE ADMISSION OF THE NORTHWESTERN STATES TO THE UNION,	317
XVIII.	SLAVERY IN THE NORTHWEST,	345
XIX.	THE CONNECTICUT WESTERN RESERVE,	368
XX.	A CENTURY OF PROGRESS,	393

LIST OF MAPS.

I.	THE OLD NORTHWEST,	*Frontispiece.*
		PAGE
II.	DRAINAGE FEATURES OF THE UNITED STATES,	2
III.	FRENCH EXPLORATIONS AND POSTS IN THE OLD NORTHWEST,	38
IV.	TERRITORY OF THE PRESENT UNITED STATES, 1755 TO 1763,	62
V.	TERRITORY OF THE PRESENT UNITED STATES AFTER FEBRUARY 10, 1763,	68
VI.	PROPOSAL OF THE COURT OF FRANCE AT THE SECOND TREATY OF PARIS,	176
VII.	BOUNDARY-LINES PROPOSED AT THE SECOND TREATY OF PARIS,	180
VIII.	TERRITORY OF THE PRESENT UNITED STATES AFTER SEPTEMBER 3, 1783,	188
IX.	TERRITORY OF THE THIRTEEN ORIGINAL STATES,	200
X.	MAP OF OHIO SURVEYS,	291
XI.	THE OLD NORTHWEST IN 1888,	393

THE OLD NORTHWEST.

I.

NORTH AMERICA IN OUTLINE.

NORTH AMERICA is easily separable into three very plainly marked physical divisions. The Pacific Highlands, which are a vast plateau surmounted by the Rocky and Sierra Nevada Mountain systems, extend from the Arctic Ocean to the Isthmus of Panama, and form the primary feature of the continent. The Atlantic Highlands, consisting of the Labrador Plateau and the Appalachian Mountain system, with the adjacent eastern slope, extend from Labrador almost to the Gulf of Mexico; and form the secondary feature. Between the Pacific Highlands and the Atlantic Highlands, extending from the southern Gulf to the northern Ocean, 5,000 miles in length by 2,000 in breadth at the widest part, and opening out like a fan to the north, is the Central Plain.

The Central Plain is also easily separable into three parts. First, the Arctic Plain descends by easy slopes from the wavy elevation called the Height of Land, north and northeast to the Arctic Ocean and Hudson Bay. Secondly, south of the Height of Land and a second similar elevation that takes off from it, near the head of Lake Superior, and sweeps southeast and northeast until it unites with the Appalachian Mountains in Northern New York, the Mississippi Valley falls away gently to the Gulf of Mexico. Thirdly, between the Arctic Plain and the Mississippi Valley lies the Basin of the Great Lakes, that is lengthened eastward in the St. Lawrence Valley.

The two sides of the continent, as divided by the eastern ranges of the Rocky Mountains, present the strongest contrasts. The western side consists of great mountain chains, attaining high elevations, with short and abrupt descents to the Pacific Ocean; the eastern side is a vast plain, descending to the Arctic and Atlantic Oceans and the Gulf of Mexico, by long and easy lines, save in the southeast, where it is interrupted by the moderate elevation of the Appalachian Mountains. Straight lines can be drawn from the Arctic Ocean to the Gulf of Mexico, from the southern shore of Lake Ontario to the Rio Grande, and from the source of the Ohio to the source of the Kansas, that will at no point rise 2,000 feet above the level of the sea. In fact, the geographer passes over whole States without finding any elevations of surface that he need represent upon a map intended for common purposes.

On the one side, and particularly south of 49° north latitude, the coast line is remarkably regular; on the other side, remarkably irregular.

On the west, few rivers descend to the sea, and not one of these cuts through the mountain masses and reaches the interior; on the east, every subdivision of the Central Plain is traversed by a great natural water-way. Hudson Strait, Hudson Bay, and the Nelson-Winnipeg River system together reach the very foot-hills of the Rocky Mountains. The noble St. Lawrence, cutting through the Appalachian Mountains, opens a channel for the Great Lakes to discharge their floods, and for man to ascend to the central parts of the continent. The Mississippi—Father of Waters—with his 35,000 miles of navigable affluents, gives ready means of access to every part of the great valley that bears his name. If three men should ascend these three water-ways to their farthest sources, they would find themselves in the heart of North America, and, so to speak, within a stone's-throw of one another. One of these water-ways has played hitherto no considerable part in the affairs of civilized men; but the

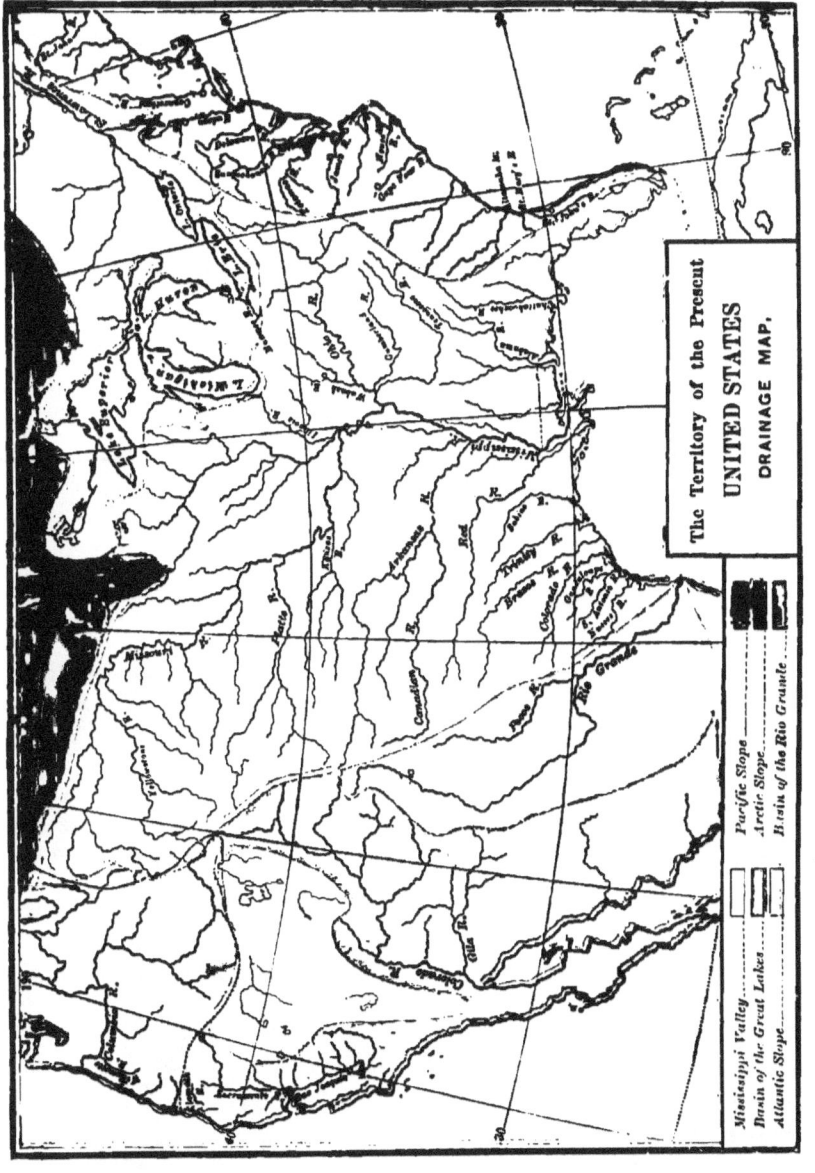

other two are as prominent in the history of America as they are in its geography.

The world scarcely offers a parallel to the ease and celerity with which the passage can be made from the upper waters of any one of these great water-ways to either of the others. "The Great Lakes occupy an elevated plateau, the summit, in fact, of the vast expanse of land which spreads out between the Alleghanies and the Rocky Mountains; no large streams flow into them, and they drain limited areas;"[1] and their basins are separated from the regions north and south by water-sheds that in no point rise to the dignity of mountains. Lake Superior is 900 feet above the Gulf of St. Lawrence; Lake Itasca, Pittsburg, and Cairo are 1650, 700, and 300 feet respectively above the Gulf of Mexico. From Omaha west along the Platte River, the Union Pacific Railroad ascends by a grade of five feet to the mile; while from St. Paul northwest to the Yellowstone, the ascent is but two feet to the mile. In Ohio, Indiana, Illinois, and Wisconsin the streams flowing in opposite directions often head in the same swamps; and in times of high water it would almost be possible to push a flat-bottomed boat from the Lake Basin into the Mississippi Valley. The highest level of the Ohio Canal is 395 feet, the highest level of the Miami Canal, 380 feet, above Lake Erie. A simple pump suffices to carry the sewage of Chicago to a level where gravitation takes it to the Mississippi. Lake Michigan once had an outlet to the Gulf of Mexico, and should the "Hennepin Canal" ever be built, it will be an artificial outlet.

In the days when the Northwest was discovered and explored, and again in the days when it was settled, the short and easy portages between the northern and southern streams, scattered all the way from Western New York to Minnesota, were of very great importance.

The Appalachian system consists of several chains or

---

[1] Hubbard: Memorials of a Half Century, 3.

ranges, and the valleys lying between them. To the explorer or pioneer attempting to reach the interior, they opposed a continuous mountain-wall from 3,500 to 7,000 feet in height, a slight obstacle, indeed, as compared with the mountains on the other side of the continent, but still considerable, and playing no unimportant part in history. The Atlantic Plain, as the slope east of these mountains is called, is coursed by many rivers that furnish excellent harbors at their mouths and render the whole region readily accessible from the sea. Five of these rivers, the Hudson, the Delaware, the Susquehanna, the Potomac, and the James, cut through the mountain-wall. The valleys of these rivers to-day are roadways for great lines of travel and transportation leading to the West; but when the country was in a state of nature, only one of them offered an easy passage from the Atlantic Plain to the Mississippi Valley. Geologists tell us that once Lake Ontario had an outlet to New York Bay; and certain it is that by the Hudson and Mohawk, the streams flowing to the Lakes whose sources are intertwined with those of the Mohawk, and the short and easy portages between them, the explorer and the colonist could readily have reached the interior but for a formidable obstacle that will receive attention in another place. Despite this obstacle, the site of Oswego was visited by Englishmen before the site of Pittsburg; while it was through the Mohawk Valley that the first canal and railroad were built connecting the East and the West. From New York Bay to the St. Lawrence extends a deep valley that cuts the mountains asunder; Hudson River fills the southern half, Lake Champlain and the River Richelieu the northern half, of this valley; and these waters, together with the easy "divide" between them, have played a very important part in American history from the very first.

These geographical features of our continent have been boldly sketched, because they have had the greatest influence upon the course of American, and particularly of Western-American, history. Had some convulsion of nature lowered the Appalachian Mountains to the level of the country east and west at the time the first English colonies were founded on the Atlantic slope, or thrown up a system of mountains as high as the Appalachians along the low water-sheds that separate the Lake Basin and the Arctic Plain from the Mississippi Valley when the first French settlements in Canada were planted, no one can tell in what different lines history would have run. Nor can one rightly estimate the prodigious influence upon the Northwest of the fact that it lies partly within the Lake Basin and partly within the Mississippi Valley, and that it holds in its bosom all the rivers flowing to the Lakes on the south, and to the Mississippi on the west, from the Ohio to the head of Lake Superior.

Speaking relatively, North America has an open and a closed side; and fortunately it is the open side that faces Europe.

II.

THE FIRST DIVISION OF NORTH AMERICA.

FOR two hundred years after its discovery, North America had no independent life and history. The seeds of future American questions were being thickly planted, but for the time no such questions appeared. The continent was the theatre of European ambition, strife, and endeavor. Three great nations played each an important part in the drama—Spain, France, and England. We are now to see how the country was first divided among them.

I. THE SPANIARDS IN THE GULF OF MEXICO.

The Spaniards had not firmly established themselves in the West Indies before they plunged into the Caribbean Sea and the Gulf of Mexico. Columbus himself was on the coast of South America in 1498, and on the coast of Central America in 1502 and 1503. Balboa crossed the Isthmus of Darien, and discovered and named the South Sea, in 1513. Cortez began the conquest of Mexico in 1519, and Pizarro that of Peru in 1526. In 1512 Ponce de Leon discovered and named Florida. Miruelo ran along the western side of the peninsula as far as Pensacola in 1516. In 1519 Pineda coasted the northern shore of the Gulf as far as Pánuco, in Mexico, and on his return discovered the Mississippi River, which was first called "The River of the Holy Spirit." In 1520 Ayllon sailed to the coast of Georgia and South Carolina; and five years later he continued his explorations as far as Virginia, where he planted an ill-fated settlement on the future site of Jamestown. In 1527 De Narvaez conducted an unfortunate expedition to the northern shore of the Gulf. He lost his life while crossing the stream of the Mississippi out at sea, but De Vaca, one of his lieutenants, and a few others, survived the perils of the deep and of the land, to tell in after-years one of the most romantic tales to be found in the history of American exploration. Hernando de Soto, Governor of Cuba, having obtained from Charles V. a grant of the country from Florida to the River of Palms, landed at Tampa Bay in 1539 with a large and well-appointed command. He hoped to find a rich Indian kingdom, such as Pizarro had found in Peru and Cortez in Mexico. After two years' marching in the interior, De Soto, disappointed in his search, found himself in latitude 35° north, on the eastern bank of the Mississippi. Crossing the river, he continued his march many hundreds of miles to the northwest; but, still disappointed, he returned the next year to the river, his command greatly reduced by battle, disease, and famine, and himself wasted in body and broken in spirit, where he died. In the sonorous language of Bancroft: "His soldiers pronounced his eulogy by grieving for their loss; the priests chanted over his body the first requiems that were ever heard on the waters of the Mississippi. To conceal his death, his body was wrapped in a mantle, and in the stillness of midnight was silently sunk in the middle of the stream. The wanderer had crossed a large part of the continent in his search for gold, and found nothing so remarkable as his burial-place."[1] His surviving companions fled down the river to the Gulf, and made their way to their countrymen in Mexico. At the same time that De Soto was seeking his imaginary El Dorado in the region south of the Missouri, Coronado, who had come overland from Mexico, was searching in the same region for the fabled "Seven cities of Cibola." The two commands were so near each other "that an Indian runner, in a few days, might have carried tidings between them;" in fact, "Coronado actually heard of his

---

[1] History: 6-volume edition, 1876, I., 50.

countryman, and sent him a letter, but his messenger failed to find De Soto's party."[1] Spaniards had now virtually met in the centre of the Mississippi Valley, coming from points as distant as Tampa Bay and the Gulf of California; they had found no El Dorado or Cibola, and they gave over the attempt at exploration and conquest in these regions.

In no important sense did the Spanish discoveries make known the Mississippi to the world. Holding the shore line from Florida to Mexico, Spain, in the sixteenth century, had the finest opportunity ever offered any nation to explore, occupy, and possess the Mississippi Valley; the Appalachicola, the Mobile, the Colorado, and, above all, the Mississippi itself, invited her to ascend them and people their banks. No powerful Indian nation was on the soil to oppose her, no European rival was present to deny her right. Why did she not do so? The answer is one of the exploded theories of political economy. In that age Europeans generally, and Spaniards particularly, held to the "Bullion Theory:" The precious metals are the only form of wealth. Not finding them in the region visited by De Soto, Spain fixed her attention on regions where she had already found them; and so intent was she on the mines of Mexico and South America, that her gallions ploughed the waters of the Gulf for one hundred years, ignorant or regardless of the fact that they were crossing and recrossing before a portal that stood always open to admit them to the richest valley in the world. So indifferent was Spain to her opportunity that in the next century she allowed the Mississippi to slip from her hands to those of France, without serious protest. When another century had gone, she awoke from her indifference, and made strenuous efforts to recall the mistake. Unfortunately for her, but fortunately for the world, it was too late. Fortunately for the world: for what greater calamity could have befallen civilization on this continent than a South America or a Mexico

---

[1] Narrative and Critical History of America, II., 292.

planted between the Alleghany and the Rocky Mountains? Still, Spain, in the sixteenth century, founded two settlements within the present limits of the United States. Santa Fé, hidden away, in 1582, in one of the upper valleys of the Rio Grande, never played any part in history until our own times. But to hold Florida against all comers was to Spain a simple necessity. The peninsula offered an excellent base for attacking the fleets that bore the spoil of the East Indies, Mexico, and Peru from Vera Cruz and Carthagena to Spain, as well as for menacing the islands at the entrance of the Gulf; and "the hurricanes of the tropics had already strewn the Florida coast with the fragments of Spanish wrecks."[1] Hence the savage vigor with which she expelled the Huguenot colonies from Northern Florida, and the persistence with which she held the English colonists on the north at bay down to 1763, when she surrendered the peninsula as the price of the Queen of the Antilles. St. Augustine, founded in 1565, a castle rather than a colony, was the key to the positions of Spain in the Gulf and in the East India seas.

II. THE FRENCH IN THE VALLEY OF THE ST. LAWRENCE.

Verrazzano in 1524 led the first French official exploring expedition to North America. He sailed along the coast from latitude 32° to Newfoundland, landing at many places, and visiting New York Bay, and then returned to France. This voyage, which added considerably to contemporary knowledge of America, and led to other and more important voyages, gave color to the claim that France afterward made to the whole coast within the extreme points that Verrazzano touched. James Cartier, also with a French commission, made three voyages to the northern parts of the continent in 1534, 1535, and 1540. In 1534 he explored the coast of Newfoundland and the shores of the Gulf of St. Lawrence, visited Labrador, and discovered the St. Lawrence River. Hoping

---

[1] Narrative and Critical History of America, II., 254.

that this river was the long-sought passage to Cathay, Cartier sailed up its current to Stadeconna, the Indian name of Quebec. Leaving here his ships, he pushed on with two or three boats and a few companions to Hochelaga, an Indian town on the present site of Montreal. It was the month of September; the northern forests were putting on their gorgeous autumn garments, and the Frenchmen could not sufficiently admire the beauty of the country. Cartier visited Stadeconna and Hochelaga again in 1540, when he took possession of Canada, as the Indians called the country, in the name of his royal master, by raising a cross surmounted by the *fleur-de-lis*, and emblazoned with the legend: FRANCISCUS PRIMUS, DEI GRATIA FRANCORUM REX REGNAT. Attempts to colonize the valley were immediately made, but they ended in failure.

Samuel de Champlain was the father of Canada. He came to America with Pontgravé, in 1603. Sent up the St. Lawrence to Hochelaga, he was filled, like Cartier, with admiration as he viewed the country, and was at once convinced that this valley, and not Acadia, must be the seat of the future French-American Empire. Deeply patriotic and fervently religious, Champlain longed to plant among the forests and waters of the north a colony that should shed lustre on the arms of France and extend the bounds of the Catholic Church. The forests and waters abounded in the valuable furs that, next to gold and silver, were the prime object of search to the first American colonists; they would shield a colony from its enemies; while the great river that was lost in unknown regions of mystery would probably lead on to the lands of Marco Polo. He returned to France burning with desire to carry out this purpose. His coveted opportunity soon came; in 1608 he had the great happiness to plant, under the rock of Quebec, the first permanent French settlement in Canada. The next year he plunged into the wilds of Northern New York, where, near the head of Lake Champlain, he met a war party of Mohawk Indians. Although he destroyed the party,

Champlain was so much impressed by their courage, and by what he heard of the formidable confederacy to which they belonged, that on returning to Canada he directed his attention to the north and west, where he found man, if not nature, more tractable.

The Gulf and River St. Lawrence, and the streams that fall into the river on the north, gave the French easy entrance to the interior of the great continent. Ascending to the head of Lake Huron by the Ottawa, Lake Nipissing, and Georgian Bay, they were at the foot of Lakes Michigan and Superior, that stand to the Northwest in some such relation as the lung-lobes to the human body. Ascending the St. Lawrence to the southern shore of Lake Ontario, they had turned the left flank of the Appalachian Mountains, and gained the edge of that vast plain which stretches away to the Gulf of Mexico and the Rio Grande. The use that they made of these advantages will form the subject of a future chapter.

It was most fortunate that Champlain concluded not to invade the seats of the Iroquois, but to lay the foundations of New France farther to the north. Had he persisted in his first purpose, and been successful, he would have made the region in which the Genesee and the Richelieu, the Hudson and the Delaware, the Susquehanna and the Ohio take their rise French territory, and so have given the French the advantage of a position that two great generals have called the key to the eastern half of the United States.[1] As it was, Champlain fully won the title accorded him: "Father of New France." The planting of Quebec was the most important event that had taken place in North America since its discovery, save only the planting of Jamestown the previous year.

---

[1] "General Scott, standing on the field of Bemus Heights, declared this Commonwealth [New York] to hold the military key of the continent east of the Mississippi, and on the same spot, General Grant confirmed the judgment." Roberts: New York, in Commonwealth Series, I., 124.

III. THE ENGLISH ON THE ATLANTIC PLAIN.

John Cabot, sailing with a commission from Henry VII. of England, discovered North America in 1497. His son Sebastian visited it again in 1498. How much of the coast these navigators skirted, is matter of controversy; some say the whole coast from 36° to 67° north latitude. But it is certain that the elder Cabot made his landfall a year and more before Columbus touched the shore of the sister continent. Both the Cabots took possession of the country in the name of the English king, and English historians, statesmen, and jurists have always based on these voyages England's claim to that portion of North America which fell to her at the first apportionment.

For a long time, owing to her unwillingness to offend Spain, to her absorption in attempts to find the northeast and northwest passages, to her domestic troubles, and to her indifference, England took little interest in the new empire that the Cabots had given her; but toward the close of the sixteenth century she began to awake to her opportunity, and to take an interest in western planting. Her first colony was Jamestown, planted in 1607; and between that date and 1733 she had absorbed the Dutch and the Swedes on the Hudson and the Delaware, and divided the whole coast, often by boundary lines that ran to the Pacific Ocean, into thirteen colonies.

Both in respect to character and geographical position, the colonists of the Atlantic Plain present strong points of contrast to those on the Gulf coast and those in the St. Lawrence Valley. They were not adventurers thirsting for gold and conquest, like the Spaniards; nor were they trappers, traders in furs, *voyageurs*, and priests intent on Indian evangelization, like the French. There was, indeed, in most of the thirteen colonies a considerable infusion of adventure, but it took the direction of business rather than of conquest. Nearly all the

English colonists were interested in industry, trade, and politics; and many of them, as the New Englanders and Marylanders, came seeking in the wilderness those religious and civil rights that were denied them at home. They were not blind to the advantage of the fur trade, nor wholly indifferent to the religious state of the Indians; but Indian trade was the smaller part of their commerce, and their religious zeal took the direction of establishing a new church where they could themselves live at peace rather than of converting the savages to the old one. Accordingly, they were more than content to plant their settlements by the sea.

Then the English seem to have been more thoroughly than either the French or the Spaniards under the influence of those false ideas of the North American continent that did so much to shape the course of history.

To the imagination of Europe, America was first an archipelago. The explanation of this belief is due to several circumstances: to Columbus's expectation that he would first come to the outlying Asiatic islands; to his belief that the West Indies were the islands that he expected to find; and to the fact that the early voyagers to North America touched the coast at widely separated parts, which geographers were unable for a long time properly to connect. In 1660 Endicott called New England "this Patmos," and as late as 1740 the Duke of Newcastle directed letters to the "Island of New England."

Navigators and geographers next conceived of our continent as a long and narrow strip of land running north and south, cut by water-ways that connected the two oceans. Most evident signs that a great continent lay behind the shore that seamen touched at points as remote as Labrador and Mexico, such as the great rivers that came down to the sea, were constantly disregarded. "A Mapp of Virginia" sold in London in 1651 lays down Hudson River as communicating by "a mighty great lake" with "the sea of China and the Indies," and carries a legend running along the shore of California, "whose happy shores (in ten days' march with fifty foot and thirty horsemen from the head of James River, over those hills and through the rich adjacent valleys beautifyed with as proffitable rivers which necessarily must run into that peacefull Indian sea) may be discovered to the exceeding benefit of Great Britain and joye of all true English."[1] An official map of Maryland, published in 1670, and certified by a competent authority to be by " no means a bad one," represents the Alleghanies above the Cumberland Mountains, and gives this description of them: "These mighty high and great Mountaines, trending N.E. and S.W. and W.S.W., is supposed to be the very middle ridg of Northern America and the only Natural cause of the fierceness and extreame stormy cold winds that come northwest from thence all over this continent and makes frost."[2] This conception of North America explains the endeavors of Smith, Hudson, and Cartier to find the India road in the rivers that they explored. It explains also the fact that Captain Newport, in 1608, brought over from England a barge so constructed that it could be taken to pieces and then put together, with which he and his company were instructed to ascend the James River as far as the falls, then to carry their barge beyond the falls and descend to the south sea, "being ordered not to return without a lump of gold as a certainty of the said sea." This persistent misconception of North America was due to that mental prepossession which prevented men seeing any insuperable obstacle to their finding a western sea-road to the Indies, and to the fact that Balboa, Drake, and others, from the mountains of Darien, had seen the two oceans that wash its shores. It is well to illustrate this false notion thus at length, because evidences of its influence in history are abundant.

Shut out from the Gulf of Mexico by the Spaniards, and from the River St. Lawrence by the French; not caring to

---

[1] Narrative and Critical History, III., 465.
[2] Browne: Maryland, in the Commonwealth Series, 100.

venture far from the coast inland, and actually confined to it by a great physical cause, the English were much slower than their rivals in seeing in North America a vast continent.

Then, when the English colonists ascended from one to two hundred miles the rivers coursing the Atlantic Plain they found themselves confronted by the Appalachian wall and their further progress arrested. Accustomed to pass and repass these mountains in a few hours' time at a dozen points, it is difficult for us to conceive how, at that day, they impressed the imaginations of men and retarded the spread of settlements to the West. The southern Indians called them the "Endless Mountains," the English, sometimes, "the Great Mountains."

The memorials of the first emigrants to Ohio, although the best natural roads had now been discovered and improved, and all obstruction from the Indians had ceased, tell us how difficult of passage they found these mountain ridges. In fact, at the close of the last century, the safest, easiest, and quickest line of travel from Philadelphia or Baltimore to Central Kentucky, or even to Fort Hamilton, that stood on the present site of Cincinnati, led to Wadkins' Ferry on the Potomac; thence up the Shenandoah Valley, through Martinsburg, Winchester, and Staunton; thence over the "divide" to New River and on to Cumberland Gap—the "Wilderness Road" of early Western emigration, the "Valley Road" of recent warfare—and thence by Crab Orchard and Lexington to the Ohio.[1]

At the north, Nature had indeed prepared a highway to the West; but the Mohawk Valley was exposed to attack from Canada, as the burning of Schenectady shows, while the people of the Long House blocked the Englishman's way to the Lake Basin almost as effectually as they blocked the Frenchman's way to the sources of the Delaware and the Susquehanna. The Iroquois were generally friendly to the

---

[1] Speed: The Wilderness Road, 12, 23.

English and hostile to the French; but that haughty, jealous race were but little more disposed to see their ancestral seats invaded by their friends than by their foes.

The facts now presented account for the extreme tardiness of the English colonists in entering the country west of the Appalachian Mountains. It is related that one Colonel Abraham Wood, who dwelt at the falls of the Appomattox, with a party of hunters and traders, crossed the Blue Ridge and discovered New River in 1654. It is said that a Captain Henry Batte, in 1666, coming also from Appomattox, crossed the mountains, and followed for some distance a stream flowing westward. It is further related that a Captain Bolton reached the Mississippi in 1670; that a party of New Englanders, in 1677, made their way overland to New Mexico, and on their return told their story to the Boston authorities; and that Virginians were at the falls of the Kanawha in 1671. To find authority for these reports, or any of them, seems a hopeless undertaking. Parkman says neither the Wood nor the Bolton tale is "sustained by sufficient authority," and he pronounces the Boston story "without proof and improbable."[1]

The tenacity with which the English colonists clung to the coast, their meagre ideas of the continent behind them, and the lack of romantic elements in their life, are well illustrated in Governor Spotswood's famous adventure to the Shenandoah Valley in August and September, 1716. We have the authority of the governor for saying that a company of Virginians ascended the Blue Ridge Mountains, "Tho' they had hitherto been thought to be unpassable," in 1610; but he himself was the first to lead the way into the valley beyond. Attended by some members of his staff, Spotswood proceeded in his coach from Williamsburg to the frontier. Here he was joined by some Virginia gentlemen and their retainers, a company of rangers, and four Indians, fifty persons in all.

---

[1] La Salle and the Discovery of the Great West. Introduction.

Taking to horse, the gay company took their westward way by the upper Rappahannock. On the thirty-sixth day from Williamsburg they scaled the mountains, and saw the valley beyond that has commanded so much admiration. After drinking the king's health, they descended the western slope to the river, which they crossed and named the "Euphrates." The governor took formal possession of the region for George I. of England. Much light is thrown upon the convivial habits of Virginians at that time by an entry found in the diary of the chronicler. "We got all the men together and loaded their arms, and we drank the king's health in champagne and fired a volley, the princess' health in Burgundy and fired a volley, and all the rest of the royal family in claret and a volley; we drank the governor's health and fired another volley. We had several sorts of liquors: viz., Virginia red wine and white wine, Irish usquebaugh, brandy, shrub, two sorts of rum, champagne, canary, cherry punch, cider, etc." The lapse of eight weeks and the distance of 440 miles travelled, going and coming, brought Spotswood back to Williamsburg. He now celebrated the hardships of the journey by creating the "Knights of the Golden Horseshoe." To ascend the mountains the horses had been shod with iron, which was unnecessary in tide-water Virginia; and the governor caused small golden horseshoes, set with jewels and inscribed with the legend, *Sic juvat transcendere montes*, to be made in London and distributed among his companions. This expedition was important in results, but its most noticeable feature is its date, 1716. This was one hundred and nine years after the landing at Jamestown, and thirty-four years after La Salle had navigated the Mississippi from the Illinois to the Gulf. Spotswood's main object was to study the relation of the Virginia frontier to the French in the Lake country. How little advantage he derived from his observations and inquiries of the Indians is well told in this paragraph from one of his letters, written in 1718:

"The chief aim of my expedition over the great mountains, in 1716, was to satisfy myself whether it was practicable to come at the Lakes. Having on that occasion found an easy passage over that great ridge of mountains w'ch before were judged impassable, I also discovered, by the relation of Indians who frequent those parts, that from the pass where I was it is but three days' march to a great nation of Indians living on a river w'ch discharges itself in the Lake Erie; that from ye western side of one of the small mountains w'ch I saw that lake is very visible, and cannot, therefore, be above five days' march from the pass aforementioned, and that the way thither is also very practicable, the mountains to the westward of the great ridge being smaller than those I passed on the eastern side, w'ch shews how easy a matter it is to gain possession of those lakes."[1]

Who the first Englishmen were to pass the Great Mountains and descend the streams flowing to the setting sun, can never be known. They undoubtedly belonged to that class of Indian hunters who, following every stream to its headspring, and entering every gap in the mountain ranges, discovered the path leading from the Potomac by Wills' Creek to the Ohio in 1748, and who, a little later, "gave names to the streams and ridges of Tennessee, annually passed the Cumberland Gap, and chased game in the basin of the Cumberland River."[2] They are men who have no individuality, as have the French discoverers in the north and west. The influence of the Colonial character in confining the English to the sea-shore has been pointed out; the reflex of that confinement upon the Colonial character and life will receive attention in another place; but here the observation may be dropped that the colonists were a long time developing the

---

[1] Cooke, Virginia, in the Commonwealth Series, 314, 315, and Waddell, Annals of Augusta County, 6–9, give accounts of the Spotswood expedition. The passages quoted are from Waddell.
[2] Bancroft: History, IL, 362; IIL, 63.

typical Indian hunter and fighter. Such men as Boone and Kenton and Wetzel belong to the country west of the mountains.

By a sort of tacit agreement, the three powers adopted priority of discovery as the rule for dividing and appropriating North America. Spain was at first disposed to claim the whole continent under the papal bull of 1493; but the maritime enterprise, military and naval power, and diplomatic force of England and France compelled her to admit them to a share of the spoil. The Spanish navigators and explorers from Columbus to De Soto gave the Gulf region to Spain; Cartier gave the St. Lawrence to France; the Cabots, the Atlantic Plain to England.

The adjustment of territorial claims and rights was a long and difficult process; and it was only as the principle of use and settlement, and even the sword, was brought in to help out discovery that points of dispute were ever settled. The recognition by Spain of discovery as the ground of title left unanswered the question where the boundary line should be drawn between Florida and Georgia and the Carolinas, and the question was never put at rest until she yielded the whole peninsula in 1763. France at first claimed the Atlantic coast south of Nova Scotia under the voyage of Verrazzano; but the failure of the Huguenot colonies in Carolina and Florida, and the resolution of England in insisting upon the Cabot title, led France to yield that shore, and to content her ambition with the north. The Cabots discovered the northeastern coast years before the first French navigator crossed the ocean; but as England did not follow up discovery with settlement, and as the French made greater discoveries in that quarter, a vast region that might have been England's fell to France. Henry IV. of France, in the patent that he gave to De Monts, carried the southern boundary of Acadia to the latitude of Philadelphia; and the English kings lapped their charters over upon the French, as we shall soon see. Again, under the rule of priority Spain was entitled to the Mississippi Valley; but, like England on the northeast coast, she did not follow discovery with occupation, and so the valley fell to France, who entered it from the north. This brought France and England into collision along the western side of the Alleghanies, as well as in the northeast and north. In general, the disputes as to the rightful ownership of a given region of territory grew out of one or both of two circumstances: a disagreement as to who the first discoverer was, or a disagreement as to how far the rights resulting from his discovery extended. Every one of the powers admitted that the others had territorial rights, but their quarrels never ended until France retired from the continent.

The remark should be added that it is impossible to represent correctly these facts on maps. The names "Acadia," "Virginia," and "Florida" stand for very different things at different times; and at no particular time, for a full century following Jamestown, were their boundary lines defined. The lines of delimitation, drawn on the most carefully constructed maps, answer but a vague general purpose. The French included Plymouth and New Amsterdam in Acadia, and Spanish maps of the seventeenth century sometimes carry Florida beyond Quebec. But more absurd than this, some sixteenth-century geographers, and notably the Dutch, "out of spite to the Spaniards," include the whole of both North and South America in New France.[1]

---

[1] Parkman: Pioneers of France in the New World, 183, 184, note.

III.

THE FRENCH DISCOVER THE NORTHWEST.

WHAT ready access to the heart of North America the Saint Lawrence gave the French, was pointed out in the first and second chapters. We are now to see what use they made of their opportunity.

The advantages of the position harmonized admirably with the French character, particularly as developed under the new conditions, and with the great ideas that underlay New France. These northern colonists shrunk from a life of material development like that of their southern neighbors; they had some agriculture, but they were not such tillers of the soil as the Puritans of Massachusetts Bay, the Dutch of Hudson River, the Quakers of the Delaware, and still less the Virginia or Carolina planters; they cared for no trade but that in furs and peltries; they were indifferent to civil and religious freedom, and had no share in that passion for political and religious progress that characterized the British colonists; and, so far from desiring a State without a king and a Church without a bishop, they could not even conceive of State and Church without them. They never developed a self-reliant colonial character, but were more than content to go on as they began—the children of patronage and power. But they desired to enlarge the borders of France and increase her glory; they loved the fur trade; and they longed to plant the emblems of the true faith beside all the unknown rivers and hidden lakes of the wilderness. Not only did the bolder minds burn to penetrate the secrets of the continent, but the majority, now hunters or farmers, and now soldiers or *voy-*

ageurs, loved the free and picturesque life of the forests and waters that made the history of Canada one long adventure. Dominion, evangelization of the Indians, and the fur trade were the three ideas on which the colony rested. The soldier, the priest, and the trader are the three types of character that are never out of our sight. In one marked feature the French plan of colonization differed from that of the English. The English found no place whatever, not even the smallest, for the Indians: the French made them the very centre and heart of their whole scheme. Sympathetic, social, pliable to new conditions, the French revealed a genius for getting on with the savages that is rather confirmed than disproved by their sore experience with the Iroquois. With such ideas as these, under leaders who combined adventure, religious zeal, and far-reaching policy, they gained the rear and northern flank of the English settlements, and, almost before the latter, absorbed with their farms and shops, fishing and trade, churches and politics, were aware of what was going on, well-nigh confined them to the narrow slope between the mountains and the sea. There is no reason to think that Champlain saw the final end; but he marked out the general plan, and was himself the first to put it in practice.

In 1611 Champlain made the rude beginnings of the city of Montreal. Here he and the French traders met the wild warriors and hunters as they descended the St. Lawrence and the Ottawa: he to win influence over the Indians and to gain knowledge of their country, they to buy the Indian catch of beaver-skins. In 1613, following two pioneers whom he had sent to winter with the Indians, he ascended the Ottawa, and thus began the first survey of the route by which the Canadian Pacific Railway passes from the valley of the St. Lawrence to the region of the Upper Lakes. Trusting the false tale of one of the two pioneers, he expected to reach a great northern sea that would bear him on to the regions of the East, which Columbus had sought in the western waters. Disappointed in this endeavor, he still reached the Isle des Allumettes, the

Indian half-way house to Lake Huron, before returning to Quebec. In this vast primeval forest, six years after Smith landed on the shore of the James, but seven years before the foot of Miles Standish touched Plymouth Rock, Champlain won the respect of the Indian tribes and displayed the emblems of his religion.

In the month of May, 1615, four Récollet friars, a branch of the great Franciscan order, landed at Quebec. They came by the procurement of Champlain to carry forward the work of Indian conversions. Having celebrated the first mass ever heard in Canada, they distributed to each a province of the wilderness empire of Satan. To Le Caron the Hurons were assigned; and soon the priest was on his way to their distant villages. As well the heroic temper of the man as his religious outlook is shown by a single sentence from one of his letters to a friend: "I must needs tell you what abundant consolation I found under all my troubles; for when one sees so many infidels needing nothing but a drop of water to make them children of God, he feels an inexpressible ardor to labor for their conversion, and sacrifice to it his repose and his life."[1] Soon the soldier followed the priest. Ascending the Ottawa and the Mattawan, crossing the portage to Lake Nipissing, and then descending French River and Georgian Bay, Champlain found his way to the "Mer Douce" of the French maps, the Lake Huron of ours. Striking inland from Thunder Bay, he found Le Caron already established in the country of the Hurons.

The savages were all expectation; for the white chief whose prowess on the battle-field they had already learned, had promised to lead them against the Iroquois. The attack upon the Senecas in Central New York proved a failure, and Champlain returned with the Hurons to their villages, where he spent the winter. In the spring he returned to his colony, where he had been given up for dead; and the first French

---

[1] Parkman: Pioneers of France, 363, 364.

exploration undertaken with a settled plan was at an end. Three or four important things had been accomplished. The two early routes to Lake Huron had been discovered—one by the Ottawa and Nipissing, the other by the Trent and Lake Simcoe; "Mer Douce" and Lake Ontario, the first two of the five lakes seen by white men, had been found; French influence over the mind of the savages had been felt in a wider sphere; and, finally, the scene of the future Huron Mission had been visited. It was Champlain's last and greatest achievement as an explorer; it was the first step toward the French possession of the old Northwest, and also the first in that long march which more than a hundred years later brought Frenchmen and Englishmen together in deadly strife beyond the Great Mountains.

Were we sketching the broader subject, we should now turn aside to watch the experiment of Indian evangelization tried by the Jesuits, who had succeeded the Récollets, among the Hurons. Mr. Parkman has told that story with his accustomed learning and eloquence. Here two facts will suffice. Just as the Jesuits were thanking God for what seemed an assured success—the conversion of a savage nation to the Cross —the Iroquois fell upon them, and scattered the Hurons in a storm of blood and fire. Secondly, the destruction of this mission, rather the truculent fury of the "Romans of the West" that caused it, was an important element in great questions. Mr. Parkman tells us that, could the French have brought the haughty Iroquois within the circle of their full influence, American history would still have reached its destined goal, but by somewhat different paths. Tamed savages ruled by priests would have been scattered through the valleys of the Lakes and the Mississippi; slaughter would have been repressed and agriculture developed; the Indian population would not have declined, if it did not increase; and the fur trade would have enriched Canada. France would have filled "the West with traders, settlers, and garrisons, and cut up the virgin wilderness into fiefs, while as yet the colonies of

England were but a weak and broken line along the shore of the Atlantic; and when at last the great conflict came, England and Liberty would have been confronted, not by a depleted antagonist, still feeble from the exhaustion of a starved and persecuted infancy, but by an athletic champion of the principles of Richelieu and Loyola." While the Iroquois blocked the Englishman's way to the West, they also turned the Frenchman aside from the St. Lawrence and the Lower Lakes to the Ottawa and Nipissing; they ruined the fur trade "which was the life-blood of New France;" they "made all her early years a misery and a terror;" they retarded the growth of Absolutism until Liberty was equal to the final struggle; and they influence our national history to this day, since "populations formed in the ideas and habits of a feudal monarchy, and controlled by a hierarchy profoundly hostile to freedom of thought, would have remained a hindrance and a stumbling-block in the way of that majestic experiment of which America is the field."[1]

Etienne Brulé, who had served Champlain as an interpreter in his journey to the "Mer Douce," was the first to penetrate the region beyond that body of water. This he did before 1629, bringing back with him an ingot of copper and a description of a lake that well fits Lake Superior, its size, length, and the rapids by which it discharges its waters.

In 1634 Jean Nicollet, a hardy explorer and trained woodsman, passed through the Straits of Mackinaw, discovered Lake Michigan, and made his way to Green Bay. He remained in this region a year, during which time he heard much of a "great water" to the west that he took to be the sea, but which was really the Mississippi River. He appears to have been on the Wisconsin, for he says if he had paddled three days more he should have reached the sea.

In 1641 Fathers Jogues and Raymbault preached to two

---

[1] The Jesuits in North America, 446-449.

thousand Indians, Ojibwas and others, at the Saut Sainte Marie.

In 1659–1660 Grosselliers and Radisson reached the head of the great Lake, and visited Indians dwelling among the streams and lakes of Western Wisconsin and Eastern Minnesota. They also visited the country beyond Lake Superior, and were the first to give the world information of those formidable tribes, the Sioux.

In 1661 Father Ménard and Jean Guerin penetrated the Upper Peninsula of Michigan, leaving Lake Superior at Keweenaw Bay. Their lines of travel are lost in history, as their footsteps are in the wilderness, but some writers suppose that they actually found the Mississippi.

The French had now discovered, and in this order, four of the Great Lakes: Huron, Ontario, Superior, and Michigan. From the day that he found the "Mer Douce," Champlain probably conjectured that its waters mingled with those of the Ottawa under the rock of Quebec; but years elapsed before the connection was thoroughly established. The Father of New France laid down a connection on his map of 1632, representing Lake Erie as a widened river; but on some maps of later date the Upper and Lower Lakes are wholly disconnected. In fact, the Susquehanna was once thought to be an outlet of Lake Erie. This lake was the very last to be discovered, as well as the very last to be thoroughly explored. It was known to the French as early as 1640, but we have no certain information of its navigation, nor of the river connecting it with Lake Huron, until 1669. In that year Louis Joliet, who ranks as an explorer next to Champlain and La Salle, returning from Lake Superior, where he had gone in quest of copper, made the passage and sailed along the northern shore to the eastward. At least, in September of that year we find Joliet, La Salle, and two Sulpitian priests in the woods of Grand River, between Lakes Erie and Ontario, discussing geography, trade, and Indian conversions. Adopting Joilet's advice, the Sulpitians concluded to go by the new

THE FRENCH DISCOVER THE NORTHWEST.   27

route to the far-distant Pottawatomies. In 1670 they ascended the Strait, stopping on the site of Detroit, and made their way to the Saut Sainte Marie. These priests were Galinée and Dollier, the first of whom made the earliest map of the Upper Lakes now known to exist.

Thus, from 1615 to 1670, while the English colonists were treading the paths of their hard practical life, making farms and towns, fighting the Indians, and contending with the home government for rights and privileges, the French were laying open the northwestern lands and waters, but making no use of Lake Erie in carrying on their hardy operations. The reasons of this are essential to the meaning of our story. Le Caron and Champlain had found Lake Huron by ascending the Ottawa, and had thus set the direction of northwestern travel. Later, however, the route by Lake Simcoe was more frequently used by the Jesuits and fur traders. The base of the great triangle forming Southwestern Canada was shorter than the two sides. Moreover, the Ottawa route was not much harder than the one by the lake. The *voyageur* or the priest made his way along either route in a birch-bark canoe, and carrying over the portages, or around the rapids, while more laborious than paddling, still broke the monotony of what was at best a wearisome life. But more than all the rest, the northern route was far less dangerous. It lay through the country of the friendly Algonquins and Hurons, while the hostile Iroquois wholly barred or made very perilous the portage of the Niagara. Had it not been for the great river that discharges its floods into the St. Lawrence opposite the island of Montreal, northwestern discovery would have been retarded for half a century. The site of Detroit, the best on the Lakes for the purposes of the French, owing to its water-transportation, its relations to the Indians, and its neighborhood to the beaver-grounds, was not known until 1669, and not occupied until 1701; and then the finder and the founder came from Canada by the Ottawa and Lake Huron.

The same facts explain another curious surprise in the

early history of this region. The territory comprised within the present State of Ohio was the last portion of the Northwest to be explored and claimed by the French. French maps that lay down the far northern waters with much correctness, leave us almost wholly ignorant of the size and configuration of Lake Erie. Maps that correctly figure the rivers of Canada and of Illinois make the Ohio and the Wabash one stream, called "Wabash or Ohio," flowing from its source almost due west, and thus nearly obliterating the State of Ohio. Sometimes Lake Erie runs south far toward the Gulf of Mexico; and later its course is due east and west. Charlevoix's map of 1744 bears on the southern side of the lake the words, "this shore is almost unknown," and Celoron's map of 1750 repeats the legend. Evans's and Mitchell's maps, both published in 1755, give the lake an almost east and west trend. It was at this time that the rivers of Ohio made their first appearance in cartography. The similar streams of Illinois and Wisconsin had long been known and mapped. "The great geographer, D'Anville of France, in 1755, lays down the Beaver, with the Mahoning from the west, rising in a lake, all very incorrectly, with Lake Erie rising to the northeast like a pair of stairs, and the Ohio nearly parallel to it."[1] Last of all, when the Connecticut Land Company sent its surveyors to Ohio, in 1796, it found, to its surprise and financial loss, that the Connecticut Western Reserve contained a million acres less land than had been supposed. The company should have charged the shortage to the Alleghany Mountains and the Iroquois: the mountains blocked the Englishman's path to the West, while the Iroquois, who exterminated the Eries about 1660, and whose hunting and war parties long roamed the waste that they had made, rendered the farthest extreme of the Northwest much safer ground than Ohio for the *voyageurs*, traders, and missionaries of France. Besides, the shorter

---

[1] Hon. C. C. Baldwin, from whose tracts, published by the Western Reserve Historical Society, these facts are mainly gathered.

distance by the northern shore drew the travel to that side of the Lake.

Wherever they went the French took prudent thought for the morrow. June 14, 1671, Saint-Lusson, who had been sent from Canada for that very purpose, standing amid a throng of savages and a cluster of Frenchmen, by a white cross and a cedar post bearing the royal arms, that had been raised at the foot of the Saut Rapids, holding a sword in one hand and a clod of earth in the other, with religious and civil ceremonies, took possession of the Saut, the Lakes Huron and Superior, with all the countries, rivers, lakes, and islands contiguous and adjacent thereto, both those already discovered and those yet to be discovered, bounded on the one side by the seas of the north and west, and on the other by the South Sea, in the name of the High, Mighty, and Redoubtable Monarch, Louis XIV., the Most Christian King of France and Navarre. All that "now remains of the sovereignty thus pompously proclaimed," says Mr. Parkman, is "now and then the accents of France on the lips of some straggling boatman or vagabond half-breed—this, and nothing more."[1]

Meantime, the Jesuits, not cast down by the loss of the Huron Mission, were busy planting missions in the country beyond "Mer Douce."

The two most important of these missions, standing to the wilderness in some such relation as that of the early Christian monasteries of Western Europe to the surrounding heathenism, were those of Saut Sainte Marie and Saint-Esprit, the latter near the head of Lake Superior. The common rallying-points of Indians and Frenchmen alike, these missions became centres of real geographical information as well as of idle rumor and vague conjecture. Only a man who has brought his imagination to bear on the facts of wilderness life can conceive what was then going on. At any given time, some French discoverer might be paddling his canoe along

---

[1] La Salle and the Discovery of the Great West, 42–44.

some unknown river, or toiling through some unknown forest, hundreds of miles from the nearest settlement or mission; and report of what he saw or did might be many months in finding its way to his countrymen. The yearly reports of the Jesuit missions, called "Relations," now that the Jesuits have become more secular and less spiritual, abound in natural knowledge,[1] which shows that the priests were grappling with the new questions that thronged upon the dullest minds, and which the brightest could not answer. Father Marquette had been stationed at Saint-Esprit, where he heard much of the mysterious river to find which had become the ambition of every ambitious Frenchman in New France.

La Salle came out to Canada at the age of twenty-three in 1666, burning with the great passion of the Age of Maritime Discovery—the thought of finding a western road to the riches of the East. Of all the men who shed lustre upon French discovery in New France, La Salle alone ranks beside Champlain. A band of Seneca Indians who wintered with him at his seigniory of La Chine, on the shore of Lake St. Louis, in one of the lulls of savage warfare, told him of a river called the Ohio that rose in their country and, at a distance of an eight moons' journey, emptied into the sea. Responding to that prepossession which leads men of ardent temper to interpret facts in the light of favorite theories and cherished purposes, he concluded that this river must flow to the Gulf of California. He had started with the Sulpitian priests on a journey to the Ohio, resolved to put this theory to the test, when by accident he met Joliet in the wilderness of Grand River. One of the questions that the little company discussed was that of a road to the great river of which the French were now hearing so much, from tribes as distant as the Senecas and the Sioux. Joliet, who had become familiar with the reports that floated to the missions of the Upper Lakes, contended that the road should be sought in

---

[1] Parkman: La Salle, 29.

the northwest; La Salle, who was fresh from his conference with the Senecas, contended as earnestly for the southwest. Joliet went on his way to Montreal. Galinée and Dollier, turned from their former purpose by his arguments, ascended the Strait of Detroit. La Salle, with his few followers, was left alone in the wilderness—alone, but not shaken in his purpose. Owing to the lack of original documents, and to the confusion of second-hand reports, the next two or three years of his life are wrapped in much obscurity, and are the subject of much vehement debate; but it is now generally held that in those years La Salle discovered the Ohio, descending it to the Falls at Louisville, perhaps even to the Mississippi. But this conclusion, while no doubt sound, is reached by cautious criticism of fragmentary documents. La Salle's discovery in no sense made the Ohio known to the world, and the region between the lake and the river remained to be explored as late as the year 1750. There is some evidence going to show that in this obscure passage of his life La Salle descended the Illinois to the Mississippi. But History has adjudged the honor of discovering the great river to others, and she is not likely to change her verdict.

Plainly, the time had come for the Mississippi to be discovered; and in 1672 Frontenac, the French governor, commissioned Joliet to make the discovery. At Mackinaw the intrepid explorer met the intrepid priest whose name will ever be associated with his own in Western annals. At the outset Marquette placed the enterprise under the patronage of the Immaculate Virgin, promising that if she granted them success the river should be named "The Conception." This pledge he strove to keep; but an Indian word, the very meaning of which has been disputed, is its designation. Ascending the Fox River, crossing the portage to the Wisconsin, one of the most remote from Canada of the many portages uniting the two systems of waters, and then descending the Wisconsin, on June 17, 1673, they found themselves, probably first of white men since De Soto's companions fled from the midnight burial of their chief, on the bosom of the Father of Waters. We shall not follow them as they descend the mighty flood to a point below the mouth of the Arkansas. Having satisfied themselves that the river did not flow to the sea of Virginia or to the Gulf of California, but to the Gulf of Mexico, they turned back toward the north, and, by way of the Illinois River, the Chicago portage, and Lake Michigan, returned to Green Bay, having paddled their canoes, in four months, two thousand five hundred miles. Joliet lived many years to encounter new perils, among them a journey by the Saguenay to Hudson Bay; but Marquette, worn out by labors and vigils, soon after died on the lonely eastern shore of Lake Michigan.

La Salle's ambition became more ardent the longer it was fed by his glowing imagination. But the triumph of Joliet and Marquette changed the current of his thoughts. Asia was no longer the vision that he saw in the west, but the Mississippi Valley. Spain had discovered the Mississippi, but had failed to take possession: he would fortify its mouth and hold the river against the world. England had planted her colonies on the Atlantic shore, claiming the whole continent behind them: he would gain their rear and shut the gateways of the West against them forever. In a word, he would change the seat of the French-American empire from the St. Lawrence to the Mississippi. It was La Salle who first distinctly conceived the policy that led on to Fort Duquesne, Braddock's defeat, and Forbes's march to the Forks of the Ohio.

Early in the year 1679, he built, near the foot of Lake Erie, the Griffin, a vessel of sixty tons burden, to be used in the prosecution of his plans. Money was needed, and he must supply it by trading in furs. August 7th the Griffin spread her sails for the northern waters. She was the first craft other than an Indian canoe or a boat propelled by oars that ever sailed our inland seas above Lake Ontario. On the 12th of that month she had reached the expansion of the Strait that lies just above the city of Detroit. Unlike the Protestant explorers, the Catholic drew largely upon the Saints' calendar for geographical names ; and the school-boy of to-day, as he pores over the map of North America, finds in the names of rivers, lakes, and capes valuable hints of early exploration. Of this we have an excellent example in the naming of Lake Sainte-Claire.

" The saint whose name was really bestowed, and whose day is August 12th, is the female 'Sainte Claire,' the foundress of the order of Franciscan nuns of the thirteenth century, known as ' Poor Claires.' Clara d'Assisi was the beautiful daughter of a nobleman of great wealth, who early dedicated herself to a religious life and went to St. Francis to ask for advice. On Palm Sunday she went to church with her family, dressed in rich attire, where St. Francis cut off her long hair with his own hands and threw over her the coarse penitential robes of the order. She entered the convent of San Damiano in spite of the opposition of her family and friends. It is related of her that on one occasion, when the Saracens came to ravage the convent, she arose from her bed, where she had been long confined, and placing the pyx, which contained the host, upon the threshold, she knelt down and began to sing, whereupon the infidels threw down their arms and fled. Sancta Clara is a favorite saint all over Europe, and her fame in the New World ought not to be spoiled—like the record of the dead in a battle gazette—by a misspelt name.

" F. Way, in his work on Rome, published in 1875, says: ' Sancta Clara has her tomb at the Minerva, and she dwelt between the Pantheon and the Thermæ of Agrippa. The tenement she occupied at the time of her decease still exists, but is not well known. In a little triangular place on or near Via Tor. Argentina lodged the first convent of the Clarisses. If, crossing the gate-way, you turn to the left of the court, you will face two windows of a slightly raised ground-floor. It was there Innocent IV. visited her, and there, on August 12, 1253, listening to the reading of the Passion, in the midst of her weeping nuns, died the first abbess of the Clarisses and the founder of 4,000 religious houses.'"[1]

The lake named, the Griffin went on her way. From Green Bay, La Salle sent her on the return voyage loaded with furs. She was never heard of again, to La Salle's most bitter disappointment. What was her fate will always be a matter of conjecture.

Who were the first white men to penetrate the territory of Illinois, probably can never be told with certainty. It is clear that the Illinois River had been visited by white men before Joliet and Marquette ascended it on their way northward in 1673. At least, there is a map in existence of earlier date on which the upper parts of the river are laid down.[2] Perhaps the readiest answer to the question that this map suggests is, that La Salle actually discovered the Illinois in 1672. Marquette returned to the Indian town of Kaskaskia after his first visit, to establish the mission of the Immaculate Conception, but his stay was of short duration. La Salle's eye was on the Illinois when he ascended the Lakes in 1679. Part of the Griffin's cargo was rigging and anchors for a vessel to be built on that river, with which he expected to sail down the Mississippi and make the West Indies. When he parted with his vessel at Green Bay, he ascended the western shore of Lower Michigan, and built Fort Miamis at the mouth of the St. Joseph River. Ascending this river to the Kankakee portage, in December, he crossed to that stream, and launched his eight canoes, containing thirty-three men, himself, Tonty, and Hennepin included, on its current. Passing places soon to become memorable in western annals, as "Starved Rock" and Peoria Lake, he finally stopped at a point just below the lake and began a fortification. He gave to this fort a name that, better than anything else, marks the desperate condition of his affairs. Hitherto he had refused to believe that the

---

[1] Hubbard : Memorials of a Half Century, 164-166.
[2] Parkman : La Salle, 23.

Griffin was lost—the vessel that he had strained his resources to build, and freighted with his fortunes; somewhere on the Lakes she must be afloat, perhaps driven by the storm into some sheltering bay, perhaps aground on some hidden bar. But as hope of her safety grew faint, he named his fort *Crèvecœur*—" Broken Heart." Neither his ardent temper nor the state of his affairs would permit him to stand still. Having put a vessel on the stocks, and despatched Hennepin to the Upper Mississippi, he left Tonty in command of the post, and started on a winter journey to Canada to procure material for her construction. Here fresh disappointments met him, and he returned to his Illinois fort to find that he had named it even better than he knew: the fort had been plundered and was deserted.

In the autumn of 1681, La Salle once more travelled the long road leading from the St. Lawrence to the head of the " Lake of the Illinois," as he called Lake Michigan. The winter following, he dragged his canoes on sledges to the Illinois River, and then launched them on its stream. On February 6, 1682, he found himself on the river that he had so long sought, and which fate seemed to have decreed that he should never reach. April 9th following, he and his little party stood just above the mouth of the Mississippi, beside a column bearing the arms of France, with an appropriate inscription, and a cross, with a leaden plate, also appropriately inscribed, buried near. Some hymns having been chanted, amid volleys of musketry and shouts of " Long live the King " La Salle took formal possession, for his royal master King Louis XIV. of France and Navarre, of the country of Louisiana, from the mouth of the Ohio along the Mississippi and the rivers which flow into it from its source beyond the country of the Sioux to its mouth at the sea, and also to the mouth of the River of Palms. Another hymn was chanted, and renewed shouts of " Live the King ! " completed the transaction.

This act was far more significant than the similar one performed by Saint-Lusson at the Saut, eleven years before. It closed the Mississippi to the Spaniards for one hundred years; it led to a French colony in Louisiana; it made necessary that chain of wilderness posts which Braddock sought to pierce at the Forks of the Ohio in 1755. That the Mississippi Valley was laid open to the eyes of the world by a *voyageur* who came overland from Canada, and not by a *voyageur* who ploughed through the Atlantic and the Gulf of Mexico from Spain, is a fact of far-reaching import. The first Louisiana was the whole valley; this and the Lake-St. Lawrence Basin made up the second New France. How the two blended and supplemented each other geographically, as well as their first historical relations, have been indicated. Before we lose sight of the act that La Salle performed that April day we should mark the date that fixes its relation to the English colonies —1682, the year that Penn laid out the squares of Philadelphia, but thirty-four years before Spotswood and his retinue drank their wine on the banks of the Shenandoah.

Our present theme is the discovery of the Northwest. Other matters have been introduced only as they lead up to that grand result. But French ambition was not absorbed by the Mississippi problem. Frenchmen pushed into the great forests and plains beyond the sources of that river. In the seventeenth century, they knew the "thousand lakes" of Minnesota better than Americans knew them fifty years ago. Du Lhut, for whom the terminus of the Northern Pacific Railroad is named, before the year 1700 explored much of the region through which that railroad runs. Nor have we attempted more than an outline map of the earliest history of the old Northwest. Having done so much—having indicated how the French, long before the English reached the foot-hills of the Alleghanies, had crossed and threaded the great western valley, we are ready to attempt a similar map of early Northwestern colonization.

But before essaying that task, a word concerning the enchanting tale of French discovery in North America. As we read that tale, we seem, for the time, to be looking out of the wondering eyes with which the French first surveyed this new northern and western world—the eyes of Cartier as he sailed up the St. Lawrence; of Champlain as he paddled his bark canoe up the current of the Richelieu or shouldered it around the rapids of the Ottawa; of Nicollet as he steered through the Straits of Mackinaw into the expanse of Lake Michigan; of Joliet as he rowed beneath the cliffs of the Saguenay—the eyes of Brulé at the Saut, of Hennepin at Niagara, of Marquette on the River of Conception, of Du Lhut in the country of the Dakotas—the eyes of La Salle as he descended the Ohio, followed the Indian trails of Illinois and Arkansas, or pronounced that sounding formula at the mouth of the Mississippi—we seem to look out of their eyes upon this virgin world of forest and stream, of prairie and lake, of buffalo and elk, of natural beauty and human ugliness. But, after all, our impressions are faint compared with theirs. Ideal presence is not real presence. Even if we could follow them on their old paths, we could not undo the great changes that civilized man has wrought. Nor can we recall the innocency of their eyes any more than we can renew the devotion of their hearts to King and Church. All that is possible for us is a pale picture of as grand a panorama of natural beauty and sublimity as was ever unrolled to the vision of explorers. To men like Champlain, Marquette, and La Salle, exploring New France was a poem whose splendor almost made them forget the hardships and perils of the exploration.

IV.

THE FRENCH COLONIZE THE NORTHWEST.

THE English colonies in America began with villages and outlying farms; the French colonies, with missionary stations, fortified posts, or trading houses, or with the three combined. The triple alliance of priest, soldier, and trader continued through the period of colonization. Often, but not always, settlements grew up around these missions or posts; and these settlements constituted the colonies of New France.

Immediately following the visit of Le Caron and Champlain to the "Mer Douce," in 1615, the Récollet Fathers established missions on its eastern side, which, however, soon passed into the hands of the Jesuits. These missions were stepping-stones to the regions beyond. The reader who has followed the narrative thus far will not be surprised to learn that the French beginnings in the Northwest were within the Upper Peninsula of Michigan. Some of these beginnings long ago disappeared, others became permanent settlements. Saint-Esprit, at La Pointe, planted by Allouez in 1665, is one example of the first; Saut Ste. Marie, planted by Marquette in 1668, of the second. This village is the oldest town in the Northwest—fourteen years older than Philadelphia, and one hundred and twenty years older than Marietta, O. A mission was planted on the island of Michilimackinac within a year of that at the Saut. This establishment was soon removed to Pointe St. Ignace, on the mainland, to the north and west, and afterward to the northern point of the Southern Peninsula. But we are not able to trace a continuous

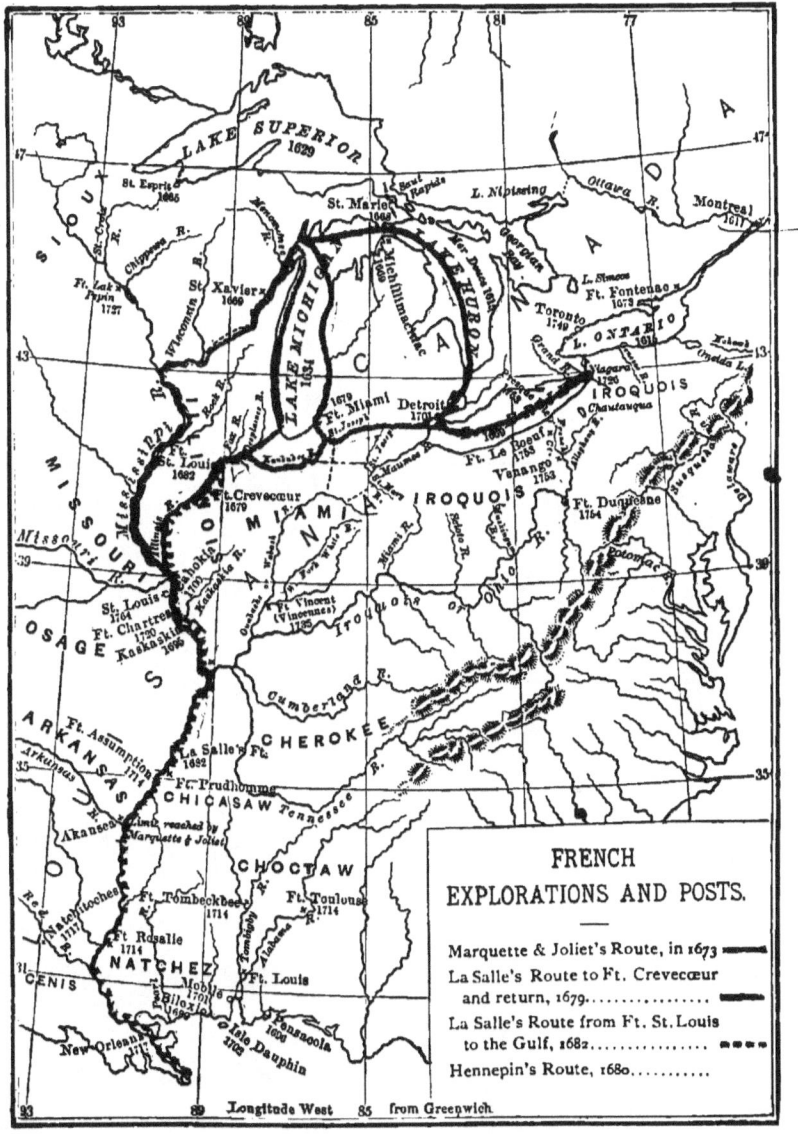

history from the mission to the Mackinaw of the fisherman and tourist of to-day.

The beginnings made in Lower Michigan bear such important relations to facts of larger moment that time must be taken to point them out.

In previous chapters I have spoken of the English colonists as contented with their prosaic life, and as not seeking to enter the regions beyond the Mountains and the Lakes. This requires some qualification. Within the State of New York are the Hudson and the Mohawk Rivers. The Dutch, having a passion for beaver equal to that of the French themselves, early occupied the confluence of the two streams, and then began throwing out advanced settlements along the line of the smaller one. The English conquest of the Dutch colony did not at once change its character. Furs long continued the leading staple of its commerce. The two rivers presented the readiest means of reaching the west found south of the St. Lawrence. From the very first, the people of New York cultivated good feeling and commercial relations with their neighbors of the "Long House;" and these, whether in peace or war, were able to influence all the tribes to the very sources of the Mississippi. After they had crushed the Hurons, these intractable warriors claimed Southwestern Canada as their own; and after their western conquests they set up a claim to all the lands to the Mississippi, south of the southern boundary of Michigan. No nation was ever more jealous than the Six Nations; but the skilful diplomatists of New York succeeded in winning from them many valuable concessions, some of which they did and some of which they did not understand. These will be more fully noticed in another place; but here it is important to remark that after the colony had passed into English hands, they sometimes permitted the New York traders to pass through their country to the Lakes. Once on the shore of Lake Erie, the traders were but a few days' paddling from the best beaver-grounds in the whole Northwest—those of the lower Michigan Peninsula.

"The region between Lake Erie and Saginaw was one of the great beaver-trapping grounds. The Huron, the Chippewas, the Ottawas, and even the Iroquois, from beyond Ontario, by turns sought this region in large parties for the capture of this game, from the earliest historic times. It is a region peculiarly adapted to the wants of this animal. To a great extent level, it is intersected by numerous water-courses, which have but moderate flow. At the head-waters and small inlets of these streams the beaver established his colonies. Here he dammed the streams, setting back the water over the flat lands, and creating ponds, in which were his habitations. Not one or two, but a series of such dams, were constructed along each stream, so that very extensive surfaces became thus covered permanently with the flood. The trees were killed, and the land was converted into a chain of ponds and marshes, with intervening dry ridges. In time, by nature's recuperative process —the annual growth and decay of grasses and aquatic plants— these filled with muck or peat, with occasional deposits of boglime, and the ponds and swales became dry again.

"Illustrations of this beaver-made country are numerous enough in our immediate vicinity. In a semicircle of twelve miles around Detroit, having the river for base, and embracing about one hundred thousand acres, fully one-fifth part consists of marshy tracts or prairies, which had their origin in the work of the beaver. A little farther west, nearly one whole township, in Wayne County, is of this character."[1]

Such temptation as this the Dutch and English traders could not be expected to resist. When Denonville came to Canada as governor, in 1685, he found New France beset on either side. The English of Hudson Bay were seeking to draw the trade of the Northwestern tribes to those northern waters; the English of New York were seeking to draw it to Hudson River. The competition threatened to become too keen; for the Englishman offered cheaper goods, and the Indians liked his rum as well as they did the Frenchman's brandy.

---

[1] Hubbard: Memorials of a Half Century, 362–363.

THE FRENCH COLONIZE THE NORTHWEST.

But more than this, Governor Dongan of New York had divined the ideas of La Salle, and had begun to counterwork them. He proposed that the English should enter the west, exclude the French, and limit them to the St. Lawrence. It was a war of ideas. It was at this time that New York obtained from the Iroquois the first of those concessions that afterward played so important a part in English policy, and became the basis of the New York claim to the western country. The two mother countries were at peace; but Denonville and Dongan conducted a long correspondence growing out of the rival claims, often angry, sometimes bitter. The French governor sometimes despaired of his cause, although he triumphed in the end. The Iroquois were never friendly to the French, and often hostile; and they now strove to alienate the Northwestern tribes from them. But Denonville had some great advantages over his rival. He was absolute in Canada, and was thoroughly supported by his king, while Dongan was wholly unsupported. The English king was a creature of Louis XIV.'s, and the colonies other than New York, although Dongan was upholding their common cause, were wholly indifferent to the issue. But he might have won but for one force that he was powerless to overcome: he had no weapon that he could oppose to the French *coureurs des bois*. These redoubtable bush-rangers, always proud of their French blood and language, and always impatient of French authority; devoted to the King, but caring nothing for his law; leading a life picturesque and reckless; with the bravery and generosity of the traditional outlaw; familiar with every stream and at home in every forest; delighting in illicit trade; often under the ban of the governor; ready to confess themselves or quick to shed blood; rapidly succumbing to the hardships and dangers of their irregular life, but still more rapidly recruited from the settlements—the *coureurs des bois* now rendered to New France one of their greatest services. They had become so numerous that every family in Canada was said to have a member in the bush. They had great influence with the Indians; they hated the English; and they were often envied by their countrymen who followed more orderly lives. They had their own leaders, some of whom could bring together five or six hundred men. Du Lhut was the most celebrated of these, and in this first crisis of Northwestern history he played a conspicuous part. He built a fort on the northern side of Lake Superior, to control the road from the Upper Lakes to Hudson Bay. He also pointed out to Denonville the importance of closing the gate-way of Detroit. The governor gave him a commission to close it, which Du Lhut hastened to execute. In 1686 he built Fort St. Joseph, at the head of the Strait, near where Fort Gratiot afterward stood. St. Joseph was abandoned and destroyed soon after, but not until a fort had been built on the site of Detroit. This action had not been taken a moment too soon, for immediately we hear of men from New York on their way to Mackinaw. In 1686 and 1687 strong parties of English and Dutch traders, escorted by Iroquois warriors, made this attempt; the first of these had actually passed St. Joseph before it was discovered and captured, the second was stopped on Lake Erie. Nor did the English then give over the attempt to penetrate the upper country; we hear afterward of New York traders at various places, and notably in the neighborhood of Fort Miamis, on the St. Joseph, in 1694. But building and garrisoning forts were only a part of the services rendered in this trying time by the *coureurs des bois*. They placated the Indians, and patrolled the forests and lakes for stray Englishmen. So competent an authority as Judge Campbell expresses the opinion that but for them the Michigan region would have fallen into English hands before the close of the seventeenth century.[1] But before the Strait of Detroit was occupied by the French, plantings had already been made farther to the west.

From the time of La Salle's visit in 1679, we can trace a

---

[1] Political History of Michigan, 40.

THE FRENCH COLONIZE THE NORTHWEST. 43

continuous French occupation of Illinois. After La Salle had navigated the great river to the Gulf, he had a double-headed scheme. First, he would plant a colony on the Illinois to hold the country against the Six Nations, who extended their forays to the Mississippi, to protect the western Indians, and to gather furs. A second colony, planted at the mouth of the Mississippi, would command Lower Louisiana and receive and ship to France the furs gathered on the upper waters. He would bind together the two colonies by a chain of fortified posts, which should also be continued through the Lake country to the settlements on the St. Lawrence. He now changed the scene of his northern operations. He planted his citadel of St. Louis on the summit of "Starved Rock," proposing to make that the centre of his colony. This undertaking well under way, he started for France to carry out the second part of his programme. Further we shall not follow this indomitable explorer, except to say that in 1687, while seeking, by an overland journey to Canada, to save from destruction his southern colony, that, either by mistake or treachery, had been landed in Texas rather than at the mouth of the Mississippi, he was slain by an assassin of his own party, just one hundred years before Anglo-American institutions were established in the territory that he had called his own. La Salle was the father of Illinois. At first his colony was exceedingly feeble, but it was never discontinued. "Joutel found a garrison at Fort St. Louis . . . in 1687, and in 1689 La Hontan bears testimony that it still continued. In 1696 a public document proves its existence; and when Tonty, in 1700, again descended the Mississippi, he was attended by twenty Canadians, residents on the Illinois."[1] Even while the wars named after King William and Queen Anne were going on, the French settlements were growing in numbers and increasing in size; those wars over, they made still more rapid progress. Missions grew into settlements and parishes.

---

[1] Monette: History of the Mississippi Valley, i., 153, 154.

Old Kaskaskia was begun in what La Salle called the "terrestrial paradise" before the close of the seventeenth century.

The Wabash Valley was occupied about 1700, the first settlers entering it by the portage leading from the Kankakee. Later the *voyageurs* found a shorter route to the fertile valley. Ascending the Maumee, then called "The Miami of the Lake," whose heads are interlaced with those of the Wabash, and crossing the short portage leading to that stream, they could descend to the Ohio. As the Frenchmen found their way to the confluence of the two streams by the Wabash, and as they knew little of the Ohio, then called "the River of the Iroquois," they took the Wabash for the main stream. Post Vincents, the Vincennes of our maps, was planted in 1735, and became the principal of a long but thin line of settlements.

The nearest road from Canada to the Mississippi lies through the State of Ohio, the most remote through the State of Wisconsin; the Ohio portages were the last to be travelled by the French, that of the Fox and the Wisconsin was the first. The Iroquois long excluded the French from Ohio, and the remoteness of Wisconsin, aided perhaps by the rigor of the climate, tended to a similar result. Still, the Jesuits planted several missions in the latter State. That of St. Francis Xavier, planted by Claude Allouez, the founder of Saint-Esprit, at Green Bay, in 1669, was the most important, and became, in course of time, the nucleus of a small French settlement. Mention may also be made of Prairie du Chien and of the post on Lake Pepin.

The French located their principal missions and posts with admirable judgment. There is not one of them in which we cannot see the wisdom of the priest, of the soldier, and the trader combined. The triple alliance worked for an immediate end, but the sites that they chose are as important to-day as they were when they chose them. The fact is, nature had decided all these questions ages before the soil of the New World had been pressed by the white man's foot. Marquette called the Straits of Mackinaw "the key, and, as it were, the gate for all the tribes from the South as the Saut is for those of the North, there being in this section of the country only these two passages by water, for a great number of nations have to go by one or other of these channels in order to reach the French settlements. This presents a peculiarly favorable opportunity both for instructing those who pass here and also for obtaining easy access and conveyance to their places of abode." The straits were called the "home of the fishes." " Elsewhere, although they exist in large numbers," says Marquette, "it is not properly their home, which is in the neighborhood of Michilimackinac. It is this attraction which has heretofore drawn to a point so advantageous the greater part of the savages in this country, driven away by fear of the Iroquois."[1] . La Salle's colony of St. Louis was planted in one of the gardens of the world, in the midst of a numerous Indian population, on the great line of travel between Lake Michigan and the Mississippi River. Kaskaskia and the neighboring settlements held the centre of the long line extending from Canada to Louisiana. The Wabash colony commanded that valley and the Lower Ohio. Detroit was a position so important that, securely held by the French, it practically banished from the English mind for fifty years the thought of acquiring the Northwest. The Indians and the beavers have long since disappeared from the region lying between the lakes and the Mississippi; that region has twice changed hands since those early days; the whole country has been transformed by the hand of man; but the Saut Canal, the Mackinaw shipping, and the cities of Chicago, St. Louis, and Detroit show us how geography conditions history, as well as that the savage and the civilized man have much in common. Then how unerringly were the French guided to the carrying places between the Northern and the Southern waters, viz., Green Bay, Fox River, and

---

[1] Cooley: Michigan, in Commonwealth Series, 11.

the Wisconsin; the Chicago River and the Illinois; the St. Joseph and the Kankakee; the St. Joseph and the Wabash; the Maumee and the Wabash; and, later, on the eve of the war that gave New France to England, the Chautauqua and French Creek routes from Lake Erie to the Ohio.

Much of this work was done while hostilities were in progress. About the time that King William's War began, in 1689, Governors Dongan and Denonville were both recalled. No English governor or commander succeeded to Dongan's ideas, while Count Frontenac vigorously prosecuted the policy of La Salle. In America the advantage of the war lay decidedly with the French. The Iroquois never recovered from the blows that Frontenac dealt them. The Northwestern Indians were more completely wedded to the French interest. Louisiana was colonized. Posts and settlements connecting the mouths of the St. Lawrence and the Mississippi were established. The Strait of Detroit was guarded by a fortified post. The Treaty of Ryswick, that will be more fully characterized in another place, left all colonial disputes to future wars. The English challenge to the discoverers of the West was hurled back beyond the mountains, there to lie until renewed a half-century later. But the challenge had been given, and was sure to be renewed; and it is very probable that, if a statesman having the genius of William Pitt had then directed British counsels, British ascendancy in the Western country would have been established during the progress of King William's War.

Still New York did not at once resign her Western plans and aspirations. In 1701 the Iroquois conveyed to King William III. all their claims to the country formerly occupied by the Hurons. These were the lands bounded by Lakes Ontario, Huron, and Erie, "containing in length about 800 miles, and in breadth 400 miles, including the country where beavers and all sorts of wild game keeps."[1] The Iro-

---

[1] Campbell: Political History of Michigan, 57.

quois did not lay claim to the Lower Peninsula of Michigan, but this grant nevertheless covered Detroit or "Fort De Tret," as the deed calls it. Nor did the French feel altogether easy. La Motte Cadillac, afterward governor of Louisiana, who had for some time seen that the fort at Detroit was no longer adequate, recommended a settlement. Receiving little encouragement in Canada, he carried his plan across the ocean. He returned with authority from the minister Ponchartrain to carry it out. Cadillac came to the spot, July 24, 1701, with fifty soldiers and fifty artisans and tradesmen, a Jesuit missionary, and a Récollet chaplain. He built a fort, which he named Ponchartrain, for the French minister, and began the settlement of Detroit. This settlement marks the real beginning of civil and political history within the present limits of Michigan.

In due time the French began to establish themselves on the Northern frontier of the British colonies. They built Fort Niagara in 1726, four years after the English built Fort Oswego. Following the early footsteps of Champlain, they ascended to the head of the lake that bears his name, where they fortified Crown Point in 1727, and Ticonderoga in 1731. Presque Isle, the present site of the city of Erie, was occupied about the time that Vincennes was founded in the Wabash Valley. Finally, just on the eve of the last struggle between England and France, the French pressed into the valleys of the Alleghany and the Ohio, at the same time that the English also began to enter them.

Writers like Monette, with a strong French bias, speak admiringly of the growth of the French settlements in the West.[1] This was more rapid than the early growth of the Canadian settlements, but very slow as measured by the English colonies, not to speak of the Western settlements of the United States.

In 1712 old Kaskaskia was the capital of Illinois. In 1721

---

[1] History of the Mississippi Valley, Book II., Chaps. III, IV.

it was the seat of a college and a monastery. Fort Chartres, founded in 1720, was the later capital, and one of the most formidable fortresses on the continent. A report of the population of the Mississippi settlements in 1766 assigns sixty-five permanent families to Kaskaskia, forty-five to Cahokia, sixteen to St. Philip, twelve to Prairie du Rocher, and forty to Fort Chartres. These villages, with the outlying farms, probably represented a population of twenty-five hundred souls. But this was after the English domination began, and the decline may have already begun. Monette claims a population of two or three thousand for Kaskaskia when it was at its best estate. He also asserts that, in 1730, the settlements on the Illinois embraced one hundred and forty families, besides about six hundred converted Indians, many traders, *voyageurs*, and *coureurs des bois*. In 1765 Croghan, the Indian agent, found about one hundred families at Vincennes and Ouiatenon, and no doubt there were others scattered along the river thus he did not see. The same year Rogers, the redoubtable partisan soldier, found eighty or one hundred families, and about six hundred souls, within the stockade at Detroit, and about twenty-five hundred in the settlement, which extended up and down the river, on both sides, some eight miles. Judge Walker estimates the total white population between the lakes and the two rivers at ten thousand, at the close of the war that transferred the sovereignty to England, and the estimate would seem a liberal one.[1]

Surely this is a poor showing for three quarters of a century of growth in the garden of the West. But we must remember the ideas upon which New France was builded. The trader was opposed to settlements because they meant the destruction of his trade. The Jesuit was opposed to them because they meant the destruction of his mission-field. The *voyageur* and the *coureur des bois* were opposed to them be-

---

[1] The Northwest during the Revolution, in Michigan Pioneer Collections, III., 12 et seq.

cause they meant the destruction of their favorite modes of life. Only the soldier was left, and his business was not colonization. Then the French people, dearly attached to their native country, have no real genius for colonies. In the seventeenth century the French Protestants would have been only too glad to plant colonies in America that would have shed lustre upon the name of France; but the same spirit that made them desirous of removing to America made it impossible for them to do so. Great pains were taken to protect the colonies against dangerous ideas. The strength that comes from freedom and self-dependence was resolutely suppressed; colonial initiative in business or politics was not permitted; trade, and particularly the fur-trade, was kept in the hands of grinding monopolies; there was no politics, no printing press, no independent intellectual or religious life; the throne was the seat of power as well as the fountain of honor; in a word, New France was protected to death. The Old Régime crushed the life out of Canada, but no Frenchmen in the world were more devoted to the Old Régime than the Canadians. The king expended great sums of money on the colony, but corruption in Quebec, if possible, was ranker than corruption in Paris. A colony without colonists is an impossibility, but this the home government did not seem to understand. Some of the more far-seeing governors called for agriculturists and artisans, and notably Jonquière, who wanted ten thousand peasants sent over to people the Ohio Valley; but these calls made little impression, and led to no change of policy.

In 1765 Croghan reported the *habitants* of the Wabash as "an idle, lazy people, a parcel of renegades from Canada," "much worse than the Indians," and those of the Detroit as "generally poor wretches, a lazy, idle people depending chiefly on the savages for subsistence," "whose manners and customs they have certainly adopted." Judge Walker supposes that these descriptions apply to the *voyageurs* and *coureurs des bois*, who flocked into the settlements in great numbers in periods of idleness, rather than to the active and substantial traders and farmers, "many of them respectable, and some of noble birth and connections."[1] No doubt this is perfectly true, but it is also true that the French settlements produced these classes in great numbers. In fact, one reason why the Frenchman got on so happily with the Indians was that he readily became an Indian himself. This peculiar development of wilderness-life is pertinent to Dr. Ellis's pregnant remark, that for every Indian converted to Christianity hundreds of white men have fallen to the level of barbarism. Besides, Croghan visited the Wabash and the Detroit soon after the close of the war, when the population was no doubt much demoralized.

The industries of the Western settlements were furs, peltries, and agriculture. Twenty thousand hides and skins are said to have been shipped from the Wabash in 1705. The towns on the Mississippi were peculiarly well situated to carry on the fur-trade, since they could reach the whole upper country to the very sources of the river. The settlers early began to cultivate the soil. Besides growing maize and the vegetables of the New World, they introduced the European grains, vegetables, and fruits. In 1746 the Wabash country shipped six hundred barrels of flour to New Orleans, besides large quantities of hides, peltry, tallow, and bees-wax. The Detroit *habitants* also cultivated the soil, but that settlement drew large quantities of supplies from the Illinois. Describing the trade that sprung up between the Illinois country and Lower Louisiana, Monette says, furs, peltries, grain, flour, etc., were sent down the Mississippi to Mobile, and thence to the West Indies and to Europe; "and in return, the luxuries and refinements of European capitals were carried to the banks of the Illinois and Kaskaskia Rivers." Chartres was "the centre of life and fashion in the West." "The Jesuit College at Kaskaskia continued to

---

[1] Michigan Pioneer Collections, III., 12 et seq.

flourish until the irruption of hostilities with Great Britain." The same writer finds "six distinct settlements, with their respective villages," on the Mississippi in 1731, extending from Cahokia, five miles below the present site of St. Louis, to Kaskaskia on the river of that name, five miles above its mouth.

While conceding such decided advantages to the French in their competition with the English that he expresses surprise that their grip of the St. Lawrence and the Mississippi was ever loosened, Professor Shaler still holds that they had some disadvantages. Canada is covered with drift, which is commonly fitted for cultivation at great cost of labor, and is north of the corn and pumpkin belt. After describing the American method of tilling the corn and the pumpkin, by which two crops are produced on the same land in one year, while the girdled trees are still standing, Professor Shaler remarks: "It is hardly too much to say that, but for these American plants and the American method of tilling them, it would have been decidedly more difficult to have fixed the early colonies on this shore."[1] The point is well taken as to Canada, but not as to the West, where the two plants were thoroughly native to the soil.

The first Louisiana, in a geographical sense, is that of Franquelin's great map, 1684. On the Gulf it extends from Mobile to the mouth of the Rio Grande; on the north, the line runs along the shore of Lake Erie, and then northwest by the sources of the streams flowing into Lake Michigan until lost in the far North. East and west, it takes in the drainage of the Mississippi, and the Gulf streams beyond as far as the Rio Grande.[2] The first political Louisiana was the grant made to Anthony Crozat, in 1712: "The River St. Louis, heretofore called the Mississippi, from the edge of the sea as far as the Illinois, together with the River of St. Philip, here-

---
[1] The Physiography of North America: Introduction to Narrative and Critical History of America, IV.
[2] Parkman: La Salle, 289, note.

tofore called the Missouri, and of the St. Jerome, heretofore called the Ouabache, with all the countries, territories, lakes within land, and the rivers which fall directly or indirectly into that part of the river St. Louis."[1] Crozat's Louisiana was a separate colony, but not wholly independent of Canada. In 1717 Illinois, with limits not very different from those of the present State, was made a separate government, but still dependent upon Louisiana. Still later the Wabash country was separated from Illinois. It is foreign to our own purpose to describe the machinery by which these governments were carried on. But they were personal governments—governments of officers not of laws. The governor and the intendant commonly quarrelled, as the king no doubt expected and desired them to do. What constant pains were taken to smother the very germs of political life is well shown by a letter that Colbert wrote to Frontenac in 1672.

"It is well for you to observe that you are always to follow in the government of Canada the forms in use here; and since our kings have long regarded it as good for their service not to convoke the states of the kingdom, in order, perhaps, to abolish insensibly this ancient usage, you on your part should very rarely, or, to speak more correctly, never give a corporate form to the inhabitants of Canada. You should even, as the colony strengthens, suppress gradually the office of the syndic who presents petitions in the name of the inhabitants; for it is well that each should speak for himself and none for all."[2]

Such a letter as this prepares us for the fact that "on politics and the affairs of the nation, they [the Illinois inhabitants] never suffered their minds to feel a moment's anxiety, believing implicitly that France ruled the world and all must be right." Major Stoddard, writing about the year 1804, says that the people of Louisiana "did not relish at first the change in the administration of justice when they came under the juris-

---

[1] Narrative and Critical History, V., 28.   [2] Cooley: Michigan, 9, 10.

diction of the United States. The delays and the uncertainty attendant on trial by jury, and the multifarious technicalities of our jurisprudence, they could not well comprehend, either as to its import or its utility, and it is not strange that they should have preferred the more prompt and less expensive decisions of the Spanish tribunals."[1]

The French colonists were utterly indifferent to what Americans call political rights. They could no more comprehend the men trained in the English colonial school than such men could comprehend them. What fervent appeals the Continental Congress made to the Canadians to join in the war against Great Britain! What sacrifices the States made to break the British power in Canada! And what a very meagre response was made to the appeals and sacrifices alike! Some of the Canadians cast in their lot with the States: the Western *habitants* were generally friendly to the patriot cause, but this was owing to their hostility to England rather than to any conception that they had of what was involved in the contest. There is, perhaps, no better measure of the provincialism of the Revolutionary Fathers than their quiet assumption that the Canadians, steeped to the lips in *ancien régime*, had political sentiments and aspirations like their own. Possibly the national pride of a few Canadians was touched when the Congress of 1774, in the address to the people of Canada, invoked the shade of "the immortal Montesquieu;" but that was all. The incapacity of the Canadians to manage representative institutions and the jury system was urged as a reason for restoring the French system of laws, when the Quebec bill was before Parliament; and it is impossible to deny force to the argument. In fact, the want of political ideas and habits, on the part of the *habitants* of Illinois, was a serious inconvenience when the time came to organize society on an Anglo-Saxon basis.

Finally, the cruel oppression of the monopolies, and the

---

[1] Monette: History of the Valley of the Mississippi, i., 191, 194.

restrictive policy of the government, had much to do with driving the young men of Canada from regular industry into the woods; and the remoteness of the Illinois settlements from Quebec and New Orleans helps to explain their comparative prosperity.

Turgot was right when he compared colonies to fruit that falls to the ground when ripe, but colonies never ripen under such a regimen as this.

V.

ENGLAND WRESTS THE NORTHWEST FROM FRANCE:

THE FIRST TREATY OF PARIS.

THIS contest was the culmination of the long and bitter struggle of England and France for supremacy in the New World. I shall rapidly review the main facts leading up to this culmination, and then assign to the West its place in the controversy.

Professor J. R. Seeley has attempted to show that "Expansion" is the key to English history in the seventeenth and eighteenth centuries; that the wars of England and France grew out of their colonial rivalries; and that the explanation of the policies of the two powers must be sought in Asia, the Indies, and America.[1] There is a considerable measure of truth in the propositions that the English professor expounds with so much eloquence and learning; but there is an unmistakable difference between the first four Anglo-French wars in America and the last one of the series. The very names that three of them bear indicate their origin and nature: they were wars of kings and queens. These wars began in Europe; they grew out of Old World quarrels, and the treaties of peace that ended them were mainly concerned with Old World matters. The colonies fought because the mother countries fought. The fifth and last of these wars began in America; it was waged here two years before it was declared

---

[1] The Expansion of England.

in Europe; it involved a distinct and most important American question; and the terms of peace affected the welfare and destiny of America more than of any other part of the globe.

In 1629, when the colonies of both powers were in their very infancy, David Kirk captured Quebec and sent the garrison to Europe; but, on the conclusion of peace, the conquest was given up to France, and the life of the colony began again.

King William's War, 1689-97, was but the extension to America of the great European contest growing out of the ascension of William and Mary to the throne of England. The most striking features of this war are the massacres of Schenectady, Salmon Falls, the seizure and plunder of Port Royal, and the two unsuccessful attempts to invade and reduce Canada, one made by way of Lake Champlain and the other by the Lower St. Lawrence. Peace came with the Treaty of Ryswick in 1697, each belligerent surrendering all countries, islands, forts, and colonies, wherever situated, that he had captured, belonging to the other at the opening of hostilities.

Queen Anne's War, 1702-13, was a prolongation of the one that preceded it. It is the American phase of the war of the Spanish succession. Again the English colonists captured Port Royal, thenceforth called Annapolis, and again they vainly attempted, both by the Champlain and the St. Lawrence routes, the reduction of Canada. America is much more prominent in the Treaty of Utrecht than in the Treaty of Ryswick. Newfoundland and the adjacent islands, and Nova Scotia, or Acadia, "with its ancient boundaries," were ceded to the English Crown. The treaty also restored to Great Britain the Hudson Bay region, which had fallen into French hands, and contained an agreement, " on both sides, to determine within a year, by commissaries to be chosen forthwith, named by each party, the limits which are to be fixed between the said Bay of Hudson and the places appertaining to France." Another stipulation of the treaty was the springing point of bitter controversies that we shall have occasion to touch upon hereafter. This was the admission, on the part of France, that "the five nations or cantons of Indians" were "subject to Great Britain."

King George's War, 1744-48, is the American phase of the war of the Austrian succession. The single incident that need be mentioned is the capture, by the English colonists, aided by a British fleet, of Louisburg and the whole island of Cape Breton, an heroic exploit that was rendered abortive by the treaty of Aix-la-Chapelle, which restored all conquests made in the war, on either side, to the original owners. For many years there had been angry disputes between the two powers concerning their American boundaries. In particular had there been a dispute as to the boundaries of Acadia, surrendered by France to England in 1713, His Britannic Majesty claiming the vast region bounded by the Gulf and River St. Lawrence, the ocean, and New England, His most Christian Majesty denying that his royal brother was entitled, by the Treaty of Utrecht, to more than a part of the peninsula of Nova Scotia. The treaty of Aix-la-Chapelle left all these questions open, and provided for a commission empowered to settle them. This commission was appointed, but it never accomplished more in its three years' discussions than to accumulate some volumes of arguments that convinced nobody. The fact is, the question at issue had got beyond the power of diplomatists in the year 1748. All they could do was to leave it for soldiers to settle.

Matters were left in such condition, both in Europe and America, by the treaty of Aix-la-Chapelle, that the peace could not last long on either continent. We are not concerned with the situation on the other side of the ocean, but on this side we must give it a rapid survey.

The close of King George's War was marked by an extraordinary development of interest in the Western country. The Pennsylvanians and Virginians had worked their way well up to the eastern foot-hills of the last range of mountains separating them from the interior. Even the Connecticut men were ready to overleap the province of New York and take possession of the Susquehanna. The time for the English colonists to attempt the Great Mountains in force had been long in coming, but it had plainly arrived.

In 1748 the Ingles-Draper settlement, the first regular settlement of English-speaking men on the Western waters, was made at "Draper's Meadow," on the New River, a branch of the Kanawha. The same year Dr. Thomas Walker, accompanied by a number of Virginia gentlemen and a party of hunters, made their way by Southwestern Virginia into Kentucky and Tennessee. The names of Cumberland River, Cumberland Mountains, Cumberland Gap, and Louisa River are mementos of this excursion. The Cumberlands all take their name from the Duke of Cumberland, the hero of Culloden, celebrated in Campbell's line—

"Proud Cumberland prances, insulting the slain,"

and the Louisa River was named for the royal duke's wife.

The same year the Ohio company, consisting of thirteen prominent Virginians and Marylanders, and one London merchant, was formed. Its avowed objects were to speculate in Western lands, and to carry on trade on an extensive scale with the Indians. It does not appear to have contemplated the settlement of a new colony. The company obtained from the crown a conditional grant of five hundred thousand acres of land in the Ohio Valley, to be located mainly between the Monongahela and Kanawha Rivers, and it ordered large shipments of goods for the Indian trade from London. These goods were to be carried to the Upper Potomac, and then, by a road that the company proposed to build for transportation and travel, to the waters of the Ohio. In 1750 the company sent Christopher Gist, a veteran woodsman and trader living on the Yadkin, down the northern side of the Ohio, with instructions, as Mr. Bancroft summarizes them, "to examine the Western country as far as the Falls of the Ohio; to look for a large tract of good level land; to mark the passes in the mountains; to trace the courses of the rivers; to count the falls; to observe the strength of the Indian nations."[1] Under these instructions, Gist made the first English exploration of Southern Ohio of which we have any report. The next year he made a similar exploration of the country south of the Ohio, as far as the Great Kanawha. The determination of the company is shown by its declaration that it would go to the Mississippi, if nècessary, in order to find good lands. Gist's reports of his explorations added to the growing interest in the over-mountain country. At that time the Ohio Valley was waste and unoccupied, save by the savages, but adventurous traders, mostly Scotch-Irish, and commonly men of reckless character and loose morals, made trading excursions as far as the River Miami. The Indian town of Pickawillany, on the upper waters of that stream, became a great centre of English trade and influence.

Another evidence of the growing interest in the West is the fact that the colonial authorities, in every direction, were seeking to obtain Indian titles to the Western lands, and to bind the Indians to the English by treaties. The Iroquois had long claimed, by right of conquest, the country from the Cumberland Mountains to the Lower Lakes and the Mississippi, and for many years the authorities of New York had been steadily seeking to gain a firm treaty-hold of that country. In 1684, the Iroquois, at Albany, placed themselves under the protection of King Charles and the Duke of York; in 1726, they conveyed all their lands in trust to England, to be protected and defended by his Majesty to and for the use of the grantors and their heirs, which was an acknowledgment by the Indians of what the French had acknowledged thirteen years before at Utrecht. In 1744, the very year that King George's War began, the deputies of the Iroquois, at Lancaster, Pa., confirmed to Maryland the lands within that province, and made to Virginia a deed that covered the whole

---

[1] History, ii., 362, 363.

West as effectually as the Virginian interpretation of the charter of 1609, soon to be noticed. This treaty is of the greatest importance in subsequent history; it is the starting-point of later negotiations with the Indians concerning Western lands. It gave the English their first real treaty-hold upon the West; and it stands in all the statements of the English claim to the Western country, side by side with the Cabot voyages. Again at Albany, in 1748, the bonds binding the Six Nations and the English together were strengthened, and at the same time the Miamis were brought within the covenant chain. In 1750-54 negotiators were busy with attempts to draw to the English interest the Western tribes. Council fires burned at Logstown, at Shawneetown, and at Pickawillany, and generally with results favorable to the English.

There was, indeed, no small amount of dissension among the colonies, and it must not be supposed that they were all working together to effect a common purpose. The royal governors could not agree. There were bitter dissensions between governors and assemblies. Colony was jealous of colony. Mercenary traders appealed to the fears of the Indians, telling them, what was true enough, that the English wanted their lands. Every argument pointed to the necessity of fortifying the Forks of the Ohio; but the dispute as to jurisdiction between Virginia and Pennsylvania which broke out in 1752 not only left the increasing population to its own natural turbulence, because neither colony ventured to appoint magistrates, but made both wary of spending money that might prove to be for the greater advantage of the other. It is to be feared that English interests in the West would have been wrecked at last had they been abandoned wholly to governors and assemblies. There were men among them of statesman-like forecast, but these could not give direction to affairs. Fortunately, the cause of England and the colonies was not abandoned to politicians. The time had come for the Anglo-Saxon column, that had been so long in reaching them, to pass the Endless Mountains; and the logic of events swept everything into the Westward current.

In the years following the treaty of Aix-la-Chapelle the French were not idle. Galissonière, the governor of Canada, thoroughly comprehended what was at stake. In 1749 he sent Cèloron de Bienville into the Ohio Valley, with a suitable escort of whites and savages, to take formal possession of the valley in the name of the King of France, to propitiate the Indians, and in all ways short of actual warfare to thwart the English plans. Bienville crossed the portage from Lake Erie to Lake Chautauqua, the easternmost of the portages from the Lakes to the southern streams ever used by the French, and made his way by the Alleghany River and the Ohio as far as the Miami, and returned by the Maumee and Lake Erie to Montreal. His report to the governor was anything but reassuring. He found the English traders swarming in the valley, and the Indians generally well disposed to the English. Nor did French interests improve the two or three succeeding years.

The Marquis Duquesne, who succeeded Galissonière, soon discovered the drift of events. He saw the necessity of action; he was clothed with power to act, and he was a man of action. And so, early in the year 1753, while the English governors and assemblies were still hesitating and disputing, he sent a strong force by Lake Ontario and Niagara to seize and hold the northeastern branches of the Ohio. This was a masterstroke: unless recalled, it would lead to war; and Duquesne was not the man to recall it. This force, passing over the portage between Presque Isle and French Creek, constructed Forts Le Bœuf and Venango, the second at the confluence of French Creek and the Alleghany River.

George Washington now makes his first historical appearance. He comes with a commission from Lieutenant-Governor Dinwiddie, of Virginia, to inquire of the officer commanding the French force by whose authority and instructions he has invaded the territories of the King of Great Britain, and to demand his peaceable departure. He returns to Williamsburg with the answer that the French commander will refer the matter to the governor, at Quebec, and that in the meantime he shall continue to hold his ground. It was now winter, and nothing more could be done that season, but early the next year a small force of Virginians was sent to seize and fortify the Forks of the Ohio. Before the works that should have been built two or three years before could be completed, or the men building them could be reinforced, the French descended the Alleghany in stronger numbers and captured both fort and garrison. They demolished the English fortification, and built a much stronger one, that they called Fort Duquesne. As usual, they had been too prompt for their rivals. They had seized the door to the West. This was an unmistakable act of war, and it precipitated at once the inevitable contest.

"Inevitable contest!" The words sound like a decree of fate. But when two hostile armies, moving on converging roads, reach the point of convergence, a battle follows. The French column, with the St. Lawrence as a base, has been long moving in the direction of the Ohio; the English column, with the seaboard as a base, has also been moving toward the same destination; they enter the valley at practically the same time, the French asserting their right to the country on the ground of discovery and occupation, the English asserting their right by virtue of the Cabot voyages, the Iroquois protectorate, and the Indian purchases. Given the character of Englishmen and Frenchmen—given the geographical relations of the Atlantic Plain to the St. Lawrence-Lake Basin, and the relations of both these to the Mississippi Valley, a contest for the West was inevitable from the time that the foundations of Jamestown and Quebec were laid down, unless, indeed, one of the two powers should overwhelm the other at an earlier day.

" French America had two heads—one among the snows of Canada, and one among the cane-brakes of Louisiana; one

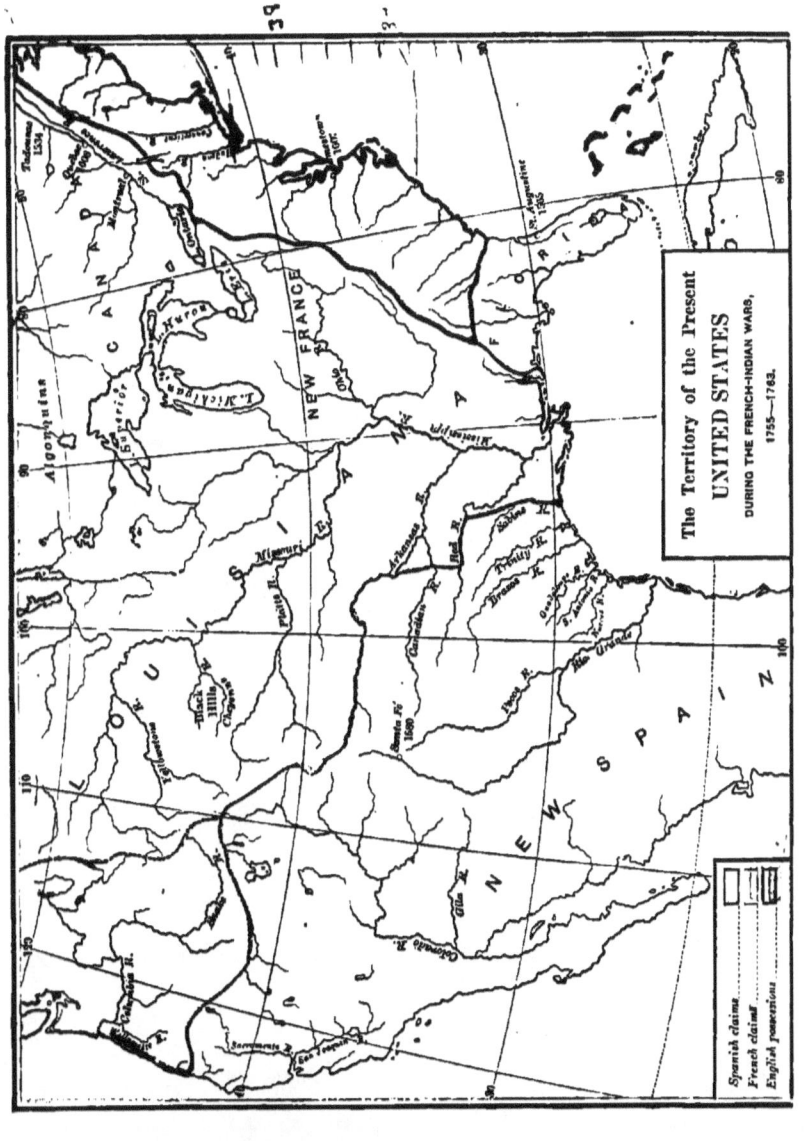

communicating with the world through the Gulf of St. Lawrence, and the other through the Gulf of Mexico. These vital points were feebly connected by a chain of military posts—slender and often interrupted—circling through the wilderness nearly three thousand miles. Midway between Canada and Louisiana lay the Valley of the Ohio. If the English should seize it, they would sever the chain of posts and cut French America asunder. If the French held it, and intrenched themselves well along its eastern limits, they would shut their rivals between the Alleghanies and the sea, control all the tribes of the West, and turn them, in case of war, against the English borders—a frightful and insupportable scourge."[1]

Braddock's army was the wedge intended to split French America asunder, but it was shattered to pieces at the battle of the Monongahela.

The shifting scenes of the French and Indian war will not here be painted even in outline. But it is essential to bring out in bold relief several of its larger features.

Mr. Bancroft says the question at the opening of the struggle was, which of the two languages should be the mother tongue of the future millions of the West—whether the Romanic or the Teutonic race should form the seed of its people. But the question soon became wider than the West. From the moment that William Pitt became, in 1757, the genius of the English Cabinet, England contemplated nothing less than the reduction of all Canada. Pitt's policy was to crush the French colonial empire in both worlds, and he distinctively grasped the American issue. Mr. John Richard Green says of Pitt: "He felt that the stake he was playing for was something vaster than Britain's standing among the powers of Europe. Even while he backed Frederick in Germany, his eye was not on the Weser, but on the Hudson and the St. Lawrence." Pitt himself said in the House of Commons: "If I

---

[1] Parkman: Montcalm and Wolfe, i., 39–40.

send an army to Germany, it is because in Germany I can conquer America."[1]

From the moment that the war became one of conquest it was more than ever a war of geography. The French strongholds were Louisburg in Cape Breton, Quebec and Montreal on the St. Lawrence, Ticonderoga at the head of Lake Champlain, Fort Frontenac at the foot of Lake Ontario, Fort Niagara on the river of that name, Detroit, that held the connection between the lower and upper Lakes, and Fort Duquesne, at the Forks of the Ohio. Niagara and Duquesne were the two keys to the West. Duquesne's military relation to the Ohio Valley was more important then than its commercial relation is now. To Canada there were three lines of approach: one by Lake Ontario, one by Lake Champlain and the Richelieu, and one by the Lower St. Lawrence. The almost insurmountable obstacles offered by every one of these were overcome, and in 1760 the conquest of Canada was effected by three armies that converged at Montreal from the three directions, on the same day. However, when the war became one of invasion and conquest the advantages of the two parties were reversed—the French moved on the exterior and longer, and the English on the interior and shorter, line.

"'Geography,' says Von Moltke, 'is three-fourths of military science;' and never was the truth of his words more fully exemplified. Canada was fortified with vast outworks of defence in the savage forests, marshes, and mountains that encompassed her, where the thoroughfares were streams choked with fallen trees and obstructed by cataracts. Never was the problem of moving troops encumbered with baggage and artillery a more difficult one. The question was less how to fight the enemy than how to get at him. If a few practicable roads had crossed the broad tract of wilderness the war would have been shortened and its character changed."[2]

---

[1] History of the English People, iv., 195.
[2] Parkman; Montcalm and Wolfe, ii., 380.

At the outset both of the powers had much to say of boundaries and rights. The French claimed, by right of discovery and occupation, all lands draining to the St. Lawrence, the Lakes, and the Mississippi, a plain geographical principle of demarcation that would have given them much of New York and Pennsylvania, as well as all the West, and have confined the English to the Atlantic Plain. It is true that French occupation, while perhaps fulfilling the demands of international law, did not answer the purposes of civilization; but when we contrast the heroic ardor of the French *voyageurs*, soldiers, and priests who opened up the Great West to the vision of men with the apathy of the English colonists, although our judgment approve the final issue, we can but agree with Mr. Parkman when he says France's "pretensions were moderate and reasonable compared with those of England."[1] England having nothing to show in the fields of Western discovery and exploration, rested on the Cabot voyages and the Iroquois title. The Cabot title was never allowed in the Court of Nations, and was abandoned in 1763 by England herself, while the acknowledgment of 1713 that the dominion of the Iroquois was in the English Government gave but the flimsiest claim to the lands south of the Lakes.

"The Treaty of Utrecht declared the Iroquois, or Five Nations, to be British subjects; therefore it was insisted that all countries conquered by them belonged to the British Crown. But what was an Iroquois conquest? The Iroquois rarely occupied the countries they overran. Their military expeditions were mere raids, great or small. Sometimes, as in the case of the Hurons, they made a solitude and called it peace; again, as in the case of the Illinois, they drove off the occupants of the soil, who returned after the invaders were gone. But the range of their war-parties was prodigious, and the English laid claim to every mountain, forest, or prairie where an Iroquois had taken a scalp."[2]

---

[1] Montcalm and Wolfe, i., 124, 125.
[2] Parkman: Montcalm and Wolfe, i., 125.

This point is noted with particularity because important political issues turned upon it at a later day.

But the discussion of "rights" was little better than boys' play then, as it is now. The contest was one of force, and the weight of the English sword decided the issue.

Two years after the first skirmishing in the backwoods of Pennsylvania, there broke out in Europe the Seven Years' War, which swept all the great powers into its vortex, which extended to every continent and reached every sea. In Macaulay's sweeping phrase, "Black men fought on the coast of Coromandel, and red men scalped each other by the Great Lakes of North America." It was the first and only European war that began on this side of the Ocean. Its close saw France discomfited and humiliated in both worlds. She had lost greater dominions than, perhaps, ever changed hands at the close of any other war in history. But there is no more glorious moment in the history of England. It was the time when every Englishman could feel, with just pride—

> "That Chatham's language was his mother-tongue,
> And Wolfe's great heart compatriot with his own." [1]

On this continent, the long conflict culminated September 13, 1759, when the armies of Montcalm and Wolfe stood face to face on the Heights of Abraham. The next year saw the capitulation of Canada. When the time came to treat for a general peace in 1763, the King of France bowed to the fortunes of war in the manner following:

"His most Christian Majesty renounces all pretensions which he has heretofore formed, or might form, to Nova Scotia, or Acadia, in all its parts, and guarantees the whole of it, and with all its dependencies, to the King of Great Britain; moreover, his most Christian Majesty cedes and guarantees to his said Britannic Majesty, in full right, Canada, with all its dependencies, as well as the island of Cape Breton, and all other islands and coasts in the Gulf and River St. Lawrence, and, in

---

[1] Seeley: The Expansion of England, 22.

general, everything that depends on the said countries, lands, islands, and coasts, with the sovereignty, property, possession, and all rights acquired by treaty or otherwise, which the most Christian King, and the Crown of France, have had till now over the said countries, islands, lands, places, coasts, and their inhabitants, so that the most Christian King cedes and makes over the whole to the said king, and to the Crown of Great Britain, and that in the most ample manner and form, without restriction, and without any liberty to depart from the said cession and guarantee, under any pretence, or to disturb Great Britain in the possessions above-mentioned.

. . . .

"In order to re-establish peace on solid and durable foundations, and to remove forever all subject of dispute with regard to the limits of the British and French territories on the continent of America, it is agreed that for the future the confines between the dominions of his Britannic Majesty and those of his most Christian Majesty in that part of the world shall be fixed irrevocably by a line drawn along the middle of the River Mississippi from its source to the River Iberville, and from thence by a line drawn along the middle of this river and the Lakes Maurepas and Pontchartrain to the sea; and for this purpose the most Christian King cedes in full right, and guarantees to his Britannic Majesty, the river and port of the Mobile, and everything which he possesses, or ought to possess, on the left side of the River Mississippi, except the town of New Orleans and the island on which it is situated, which shall remain to France, provided that the navigation of the River Mississippi shall be equally free, as well to the subjects of Great Britain as to those of France, in its whole breadth and length, from its source to the sea; and expressly that part which is between the said island of New Orleans and the right bank of that river, as well as the passage both in and out of its mouth."[1]

These are some of the provisions of that treaty, which always caused Count De Vergennes to shudder whenever he

---

[1] Chalmers: A Collection of Treaties, i., 471, 473.

thought of it, and that called out explosions of volcanic wrath from the first Napoleon.

Other territorial changes deeply affecting the course of history were made at the close of the Seven Years' War. Spain had taken part in the contest as an ally of France. England had captured Havana, in the island of Cuba, the very key to the Gulf of Mexico. To regain that, Spain surrendered Florida to England, and then received as a compensation from France all of her possessions on the continent of North America that did not pass to England. The grand result of these changes was that England and Spain now divided North America, the Mississippi River being the only definite boundary between them.

We must not allow our admiration of what the French had done in the West to blind us to the fact that the British cause was the cause of the Northwest and of America. Put in the broadest way, the question was, whether French or English ideas and tendencies should have sway in North America. Montcalm and Wolfe were both gallant soldiers and able commanders; both true patriots and chivalrous gentlemen; but they stood on the Heights of Abraham that September day for very different things: Montcalm for the *old régime*, Wolfe for the House of Commons; Montcalm for the alliance of king and priest, Wolfe for *habeas corpus* and free inquiry; Montcalm for the past, Wolfe for the future; Montcalm for Louis XV. and Madame de Pompadour, Wolfe for George Washington and Abraham Lincoln. It was his clear perception of this point that led Mr. John Fiske to say: "The triumph of Wolfe marks the greatest turning-point as yet discoverable in modern history."[1]

That the war was a war of civilizations becomes perfectly clear when we consider the temper, culture, and aims of the two classes of colonists. The history of French America is far more picturesque and brilliant than the history of British America in the period 1608–1754. But the English were doing work far more solid, valuable, and permanent than

---

[1] American Political Ideas, 56.

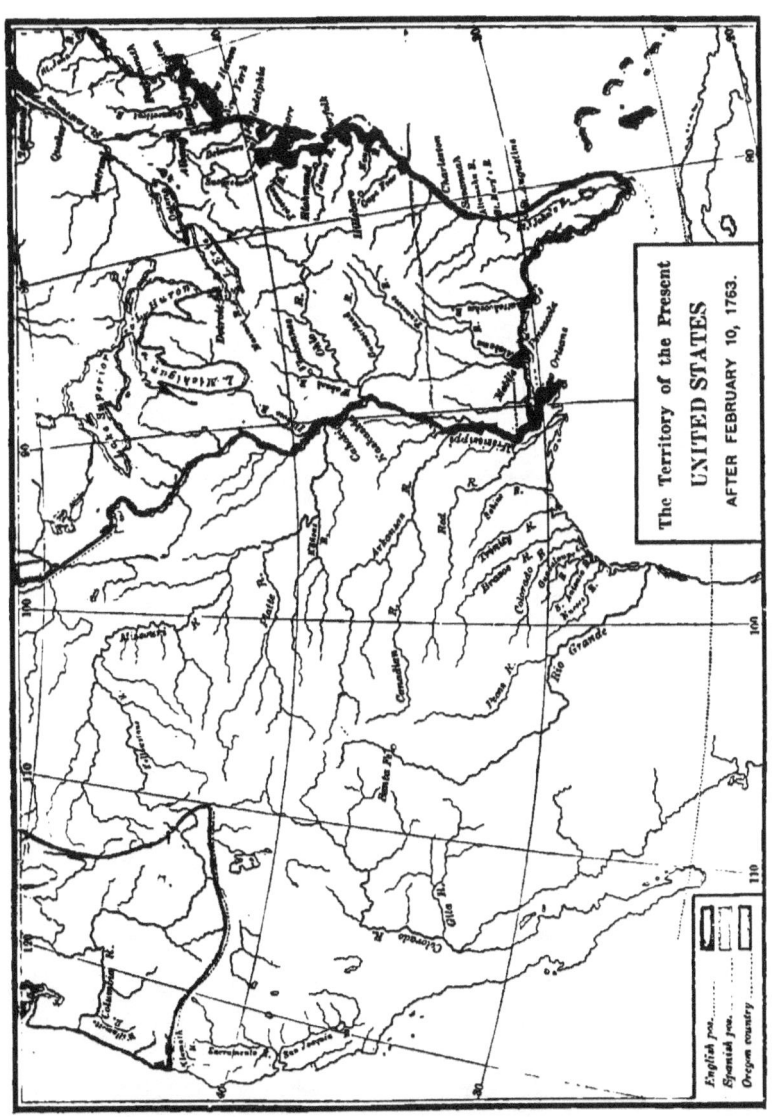

their northern neighbors. The French took to the lakes, rivers, and forests; they cultivated the Indians; their explorers were intent on discovery, their traders on furs, their missionaries on souls. The English did not either take to the woods or cultivate the Indians; they loved agriculture and trade, State and Church, and so clung to their fields, shops, politics, and churches. As a result, while Canada languished, thirteen English states grew up on the Atlantic Plain modelled on the Saxon pattern, and became populous, rich, and strong. At the beginning of the war there were eighty thousand white inhabitants in New France, one million one hundred and sixty thousand in the British colonies. The disparity of wealth was equally striking. In 1754 there was more real civilization—more seeds of things—in the town of Boston than in all New France. In time, these compact and vigorous British colonies offered effective resistance to Great Britain. It is plain that, had they spread themselves out over half a continent, hunted beaver, and trafficked with the Indians, after the manner of the French, Independence would have been postponed many years, and possibly forever. We owe a vast debt to the inherited character of those Englishmen who came to America in the first half of the seventeenth century, and no small debt to the Appalachian mountain-wall that confined them to the narrow Atlantic slope until, by reason of compression and growth, they were gotten ready, first to enter the West in force, and then to extort their independence from England.

But the French and Indian War borrows its great significance from another struggle. It was but the prelude to a grander contest. "With the triumph of Wolfe on the Heights of Abraham," writes Mr. Green, "began the history of the United States."[1] James Wolfe's Highlanders and grenadiers at Quebec, and not the embattled farmers at Lexington, won the first victory of the American Revolution.

---

[1] History of the English People, iv., 193, 194.

VI.

THE THIRTEEN COLONIES AS CONSTITUTED BY THE ROYAL CHARTERS.—(I.)

To encourage American plantations, the British Crown granted from time to time those charters that constitute the first chapter of American Jurisprudence. In bounding the grants of land that those charters conveyed, the Crown was governed neither by a knowledge of American geography nor by a legal principle. The most imaginative man alive could not bound his estates in Spain with greater disregard of Spanish geography and Spanish law. The grants overlapped and conflicted with one another in a way that was then most troublesome to colonists and proprietors, and that is now most exasperating to students of history. Five causes will explain these conflictions: (1) Gross ignorance of American geography; (2) the great size of the early grants; (3) the surrender or vacation of charters; (4) the influence of favorites praying for grants to themselves or their friends; (5) the royal prerogative. I shall transcribe the boundary descriptions found in the principal charters, and show how the Thirteen Colonies took shape under them.[1]

The charter given to Sir Walter Raleigh in 1584 granted

---

[1] The texts found in Poore's Charters and Constitutions of the United States will be followed. In preparing this chapter and the next one the author has received great assistance from " Bulletin of the United States Geological Survey, No. 13: Boundaries of the United States and of the Several States and Territories, with an Historical Sketch of the Territorial Changes," by Henry Gannett, Chief Geographer.

to that "trusty and well-beloved servant" of Queen Elizabeth, his heirs and assigns forever—

"free libertie and licence from time to time, and at all times foreuer hereafter, to discouer, search, finde out, and view such remote heathen and barbarous lands, counteries, and territories, not actually possessed of any Christian Prince nor inhabited by Christian People, as to him, his heires and assignes, and to euery or any of them, shall seeme good, and the same to haue, holde, occupie, and enjoy to him, his heires and assignes, foreuer, with all prerogatiues, commodities, jurisdictions, royalties, priuileges, franchises, and preheminences, thereto or thereabouts both by sea and land, whatsoeuer we by our letters patents may graunt, and as we or any of our noble progenitors haue heretofore graunted to any person or persons, bodies politique or corporate."

The charter further forbade any person or persons whatsoever inhabiting or attempting to inhabit the same countries coming within two hundred leagues of the place or places where Raleigh, his heirs and assigns, or his or their associates in any company, should, within six years ensuing, make their dwellings or abidings, without his or their consent; and it authorized and instructed him or them to encounter and expulse, to repel and resist, as well by sea as by land, all who should attempt to do so. Raleigh's unsuccessful attempts to plant under this charter are among the chivalrous and pathetic stories of early American adventure.

While it was well understood that Raleigh was to plant in the queen's American possessions, the name America does not occur in the document. He was not to go into lands actually possessed by any Christian prince nor inhabited by Christian people, but that was the only limitation. It is plain that her dominions on this continent lay before Elizabeth's eyes an undifferentiated mass without assigned metes and bounds, and that other grants or colonies were not then contemplated. As those dominions then had no distinctive name, Raleigh proposed Virginia, and Elizabeth, who was fond of being called "the Virgin Queen," approved the suggestion.

In 1606 James I. "vouchsafed" to Sir Thomas Gates, Sir George Somers, and divers others of his loving subjects who had been suitors unto him—

"Licence to make Habitation, Plantation, and to deduce a colony of sundry of our People into that part of *America* commonly called Virginia, and other parts and Territories in *America*, either appertaining unto us, or which are not now actually possessed by any *Christian* Prince or People, situate, lying, and being all along the Sea-Coasts between four-and-thirty degrees of Northerly latitude from the Equinoctial Line and five-and-forty Degrees of the same Latitude, and in the main Land between the same four-and-thirty and five-and-forty Degrees, and the Islands thereunto adjacent, or within one hundred Miles of the Coast thereof."

The charter then provided for two companies, the first called the London Company and the second the Plymouth Company. The London Company should make their first plantation at any place upon the said coast of Virginia or America where they should think fit and convenient, between the said four-and-thirty and one-and-forty degrees of the said latitude, and the Plymouth Company should begin their plantation at any place on the said coast of Virginia and America where they should think fit and convenient, between eight-and-thirty degrees and five-and-forty degrees of the same latitude. Each colony should have all lands, soils, etc., from its first seat of plantation, by the space of fifty English statute miles, all along the coast toward the west and southwest as the coast lies; also all the lands, etc., along the coast to the north, northeast, or east for the space of fifty miles; all the islands within one hundred miles directly over and against the sea-coast, and also all the lands from the same fifty miles every way on the sea-coast, directly into the mainland one hundred miles. The charter further provided that no other of the king's subjects should be permitted to plant or inhabit behind them toward the mainland without the express license or consent of the council of the colony affected or interested first obtained in writing. It will be seen that the two zones within which the two companies might plant their colonies overlapped three degrees of latitude. Collisions were, however, guarded against by a provision that neither company should make a settlement within one hundred miles of one already made by the other.

The charter of 1606 marks a decided step toward geographical precision and definiteness. The settlements are to be made on the coasts of Virginia and America, within parallels 34° and 45° north latitude, which lines, falling as far apart as the mouth of the Cape Fear River and the mouth of the St. Croix, comprehended the larger part of King James's American possessions. Two colonies were provided for. Evidently that process of evolution had begun which led to the northern and southern groups of colonies.

The settlement at Jamestown was made under this charter. But as it did not prove satisfactory, the king, in 1609, granted the London Company a second charter, in which he bounded the colony that henceforth monopolized the name Virginia as follows:

" . . . Situate, lying, and being in that Part of *America* called *Virginia*, from the Point of Land called *Cape or Point Comfort*, all along the Sea-Coast to the Northward two hundred miles, and from the said Point of *Cape Comfort* all along the Sea-Coast to the Southward two hundred Miles, and all that Space and Circuit of Land lying from the Sea-Coast of the Precinct aforesaid up into the Land throughout from Sea to Sea, West and Northwest, And also all the Islands lying within one hundred Miles along the Coast of both Seas of the Precinct aforesaid. . . . "

This was the first of the "from sea to sea" boundaries that play so important a part in history. The description "up into the land throughout from sea to sea, west and northwest," led to important results, the least of which is the interminable discussion of what it meant. It has been suggested that it meant a compound boundary line running from the Atlantic Ocean around to the Atlantic Ocean again; but the islands within one hundred miles along the coast of "both seas" are given to Virginia, and this fact is fatal to such a construction. Historians commonly assume that the northern and southern lines of the colony were intended to be due east and west lines, and much can be said in support of this view. The lines drawn by the charter of 1606 were east and west lines. The royal intent in 1606-09 and 1620 was two colonies; Virginia and New England were evidently to embrace all the king's possessions from latitude 34° north to the French territories. The ocean front now given to Virginia carries the colony to the fortieth degree. And, finally, the charter of 1620 bounded New England on the south by that parallel. But the king's language describes one west and one northwest line. If this view be assumed, the description is still open to two constructions that assign to Virginia very different limits. If the construction represented in the following diagram be taken, the colony would be a triangle of very moderate size.

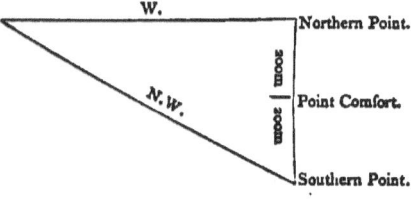

But if the following be the true construction, the colony would be a vast trapezoid, six degrees of latitude in width on the Atlantic Ocean, and from twenty to thirty degrees on the Pacific.

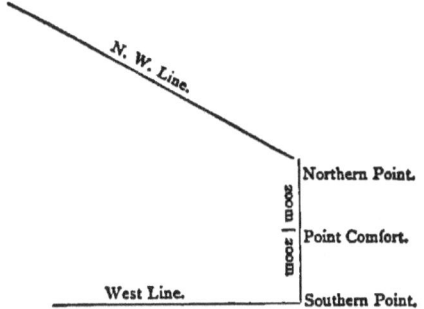

If the theory of one west and one northwest line be adopted, only the second of these constructions will fill the condition "from sea to sea." As this was the construction adopted by Virginia, and as it materially influenced Western history, I shall assume that such is the meaning of the language.

The Plymouth Company was overshadowed by its richer and stronger rival. Only one attempt at colonization was made by its authority under the charter of 1606, and that ended in failure. But a new charter was obtained in 1620, under which the company became more active. This was the second of the two charters into which that of 1606 was merged. It absolutely gave, granted, and confirmed unto the council established at Plymouth, in the County of Devon, England, for the planting, ruling, and governing of the northern parts of Virginia in America, a territory that is thus bounded:

"That aforesaid Part of America lying and being in Breadth from fforty Degrees of Northerly Latitude from the Equinoctiall Line to fforty-eight Degrees of the said Northerly Latitude inclusively, and in Length of, and within all the Breadth aforesaid, throughout all the Maine Lands from Sea to Sea . . . and also within the said Islands and Seas adjoining, Provided always, that the said Islands, or any of the Premises hereinbefore mentioned, and by these Presents intended and meant to be granted, be not actually possessed or inhabited by any other Christian Prince or Estate, nor to be within the Bounds, Limitts, or Territoryes of that Southern Collony heretofore by us granted to be planted by divers of our loving Subjects in the South Part, etc."

The king also declared it to be his will and pleasure, to the end that the said territory should be more certainly known and distinguished, that the same should henceforth be called by the name of New England in America. This grant covered eight degrees of latitude. Fully one-half of the territory that it embraced on the coast was at the time claimed by the French; in fact, the whole of it was covered by the Acadia charter of 1603, and much of it remained in French hands until they retired from the continent in 1763.

Why James I. bounded the grants of 1609 and 1620 on the west by the South Sea, is a question asked early and often. The common answer is found in the mistaken ideas of American geography then current. "How natural the 'from sea to sea' lines," it is said, "to those who thought that at most they would be but a few hundred miles in length! How preposterous if the width of the continent had been known!" But it is not certain that this is the true explanation. England claimed not only the coast that the Cabots had discovered, but all the lands lying beyond that coast. Virtually she strove to incorporate into the public law of Europe a rule in conformity with this claim. She ultimately failed in both these efforts, owing to the resistance of France and Spain; but at the time when these charters were given she was upholding both stoutly, and was ready to do anything that would strengthen her position. To include the whole breadth of the continent within colonial boundary lines might give a faint color of occupancy to her claim; moreover, the charters of 1606, 1609, and 1620 all prove that, to the royal mind, as well as to the companies that proposed to plant, great territorial limits were essential to colonies. Professor Alexander Johnston denies in toto "that the Crown made the Connecticut grant under ignorance, supposing that North America was far narrower than it proved to be." "The Plymouth Council, when it gave up its charter in 1635, notified the king," he says, "that this grant was through all the main-land from sea to sea, *being near about three thousand miles in length;*" and he adds that every geographer in England knew such to be the length of the Connecticut grant.[1] It is easy to make too much of the geographical information imparted to the royal mind by the Plymouth Council. No doubt some men in England had correct views on this point in 1662; but the Virginia and Maryland maps of 1651 and 1670, described in a former chapter, and similar contemporary facts, discredit the strong language used by Mr. Johnston. The fact is, the early erroneous views of North American geography gave place very slowly to correct views. The magnificent distances of the New World were not grasped by James I. and his contemporaries as realities; and there is no reason to suppose that the king or his counsellors really understood that the New England of 1620 embraced as many degrees of longitude as lie between the mouth of the Tagus and the mouth of the Euphrates.

Sandys and Southampton did not administer the London Company in a manner to please the mean and narrow mind of James I. The king caused legal proceedings against the company to be instituted, and in 1624 the Court of King's Bench, by a writ of *quo warranto*, vacated the charter. Thereafter, as long as Virginia continued a British colony, her governors held their commissions from the Crown. The question as to the effect of this *quo warranto* on the territorial limits of the colony has often been asked and never satisfactorily answered. The king had granted the northern half of his American claim, from sea to sea, to the Plymouth Com-

---

[1] Connecticut, in Commonwealth Series, 281.

pany, and there is no reason to think that the writ was intended to affect the limits of the colony, or to derange the king's dual plan of colonization.

Passing the grant to Sir Robert Heath, which did not lead to permanent plantations, the first invasion of Virginia, as bounded in 1609, was on the north.

In 1632 Charles I. granted to Lord Baltimore the province that the king, in honor of his queen, Henrietta Maria, called Maryland. These are the boundaries:

"All that part of the Peninsula or Chersonese, lying in parts of America, between the ocean on the east and the Bay of Chesapeake on the west; divided from the residue thereof by a right line drawn from the promontory or headland called Watkins's Point, situate upon the bay aforesaid, near the River Wighco on the west unto the main ocean on the east, and between that boundary on the south unto that part of the Bay of Delaware on the north, which lieth under the fortieth degree of north latitude from the equinoctial, where New England is terminated; and all the tract of that land within the metes underwritten (that is to say), passing from the said bay, called Delaware Bay, in a right line, by the degree aforesaid, unto the true meridian of the first fountain of the River Potomac; thence verging toward the south unto the farther bank of the said river, and following the same on the west and south unto a certain place called Cinquack, situate near the mouth of said river, where it disembogues into the aforesaid Bay of Chesapeake, and thence by the shortest line unto the aforesaid promontory or place called Watkins's Point, so that the whole tract of land divided by the line aforesaid, between the main ocean and Watkins Point unto the promontory called Cape Charles, may entirely remain forever excepted to us. . . ."

Virginia bitterly resisted this grant as an invasion of her jurisdiction, and she finally acknowledged Maryland as a sister colony, only because she had no alternative. Virginia's composure does not seem to have been ruffled by the grant to

Sir Robert Heath three years before; but the Virginia of 1632, like the Virginia of 1887, was comparatively isolated from the coast to the south, while the multitude of waters that mingle in the mouth of the great bay and flow out together through the Capes invited her to follow them to their northern and northwestern sources. Moreover, the Virginians called Maryland a "papist" settlement; and they coveted the commercial privileges that the Marylanders enjoyed and they did not. But Virginia finally gave up further resistance, and entered on a discussion of boundary lines. Successively there arose two main points of dispute with Maryland, only one of which need be noticed here.

In 1649 Charles II. granted to Lord Hopton the tract bounded by and within the heads of the Rappahannock and Potomac Rivers; in 1689 James II. confirmed this grant to Lord Culpepper, to whom it had passed by sale and purchase, and on Culpepper's death it descended to his son-in-law, Lord Fairfax. The grant was of the soil merely, and left the jurisdiction in Virginia, as before. Nothing in the whole history of royal patents and charters is more absurd and tyrannical than this grant, for at the time it was originally made Charles I. had just been executed, and Charles II. was a fugitive. But in time the question arose whether the southern or the northern branch of the Potomac was the proper boundary between Virginia and Maryland. The answer to that question depended upon the answer to another one, viz., whether the first fountain or westernmost source of the Potomac was on the one branch or the other, which was at the time unknown. It suited Lord Fairfax to claim the northern branch, since that would give the greater extent to the Hopton grant; but Maryland contended for the southern branch, on which the first fountain is really found. Virginia had an obvious motive for taking the same view of the matter as Fairfax. In 1736 a commission appointed by the Crown and Fairfax surveyed a line from the Rappahannock to the Potomac; in 1745 the king confirmed this line; and in 1746 a second commission planted the "Fairfax stone" in conformity with the Virginia view. Maryland was not consulted in the matter; but the "Fairfax stone," although Virginia, in 1776, relinquished to the adjacent States all the territories covered by their charters that had once belonged to her, has remained the southern extreme of the boundary line between Virginia and Maryland, from the Potomac to Mason and Dixon's line.

The boundary descriptions of the three more southern States will be given without particular discussion.

In 1663 Charles II. thus bounded the grant to the Carolina proprietors:

. . . "All that territory or tract of ground situate, lying, and being within our dominions of America, extending from the north end of the island called Lucke Island, which lieth in the Southern Virginia seas, and within six-and-thirty degrees of the northern latitude, and to the west as far as the south seas, and so southerly as far as the River Saint Matthias, which bordereth upon the coast of Florida, and within one-and-thirty degrees of northern latitude, and so west in a direct line as far as the south seas aforesaid." . . .

Two years later this grant was enlarged as follows:

. . . "All that province, territory, or tract of land situate, lying or being in our dominions of America, aforesaid, extending north and eastward as far as the north end of Currituck river or inlet, upon a strait westerly line to Wyonoak Creek, which lies within or about the degrees of thirty-six and thirty minutes, northern latitude, and so west in a direct line as far as the South Seas; and south and westward as far as the degree of twenty-nine, inclusive of northern latitude; and so west in a direct line as far as the south sea." . . .

The Carolina charter of 1665 gave to history a memorable line. The parallel of 36° 30′ is the boundary of six States, but its historical consequence arises more from the fact that the compromise of 1820 made it the boundary between slavery and freedom beyond the western boundary of Missouri. Out of the Carolina grant two colonies were eventually made. The Revised Statutes of North Carolina define the boundary between them as a line running northwest from Goat Island on the west, in latitude 33° 56', to parallel 35°, and thence along that parallel to Tennessee.

An independent plantation in South Carolina had been mooted as early as 1717, and in 1732 James Oglethorpe renewed the proposition, and proposed to make the new colony a home and refuge for debtors in England who were unable to discharge their indebtedness, and for Protestants on the Continent who were persecuted for religion's sake. The plan pleased the king, and he granted to a corporation consisting of Oglethorpe and others a tract of country "in trust for the poor" that he thus bounded:

"All those lands, countries, and territories situate, lying, and being in that part of South Carolina, in America, which lies from the most northern part of a stream or river there, commonly called the Savannah, all along the sea-coast to the southward, unto the most southern stream of a certain other great water or river called the Altamaha, and westerly from the heads of the said rivers, respectively, in direct lines to the south seas."

The royal proclamation of 1763, which will be fully noticed in a future chapter, made some new territorial arrangements in the Gulf region. The lands lying between the rivers Altamaha and St. Marys were annexed to Georgia. The southern boundary of that province now became the St. Marys and a straight line drawn from the source of that river to the confluence of the Flint and Chattahoochee; and such has been its southern boundary until the present time. The grant made to the Georgia trustees in 1732 had bounded South Carolina on the southwest by the Savannah.

The charter of 1620 imparted some new life to the Plymouth Company, but it was never a vigorous corporation. However, both the company and the Crown at once began to exploit the New England soil. No other part of the Atlantic coast is geographically so complex and intricate, and for this or some other reason its territorial history is more difficult than any other to trace out. The course of the company and king alike has been described as but a course of confusion. Minutely to follow their work would require the skill of a trained lawyer in addition to the learning of an accomplished geographer and historian. Nothing beyond the outlines will here be attempted.

In 1621 the Council for New England, by direction of James I., issued a patent to Sir William Alexander, Earl of Stirling, conveying to him the region bounded by the St. Lawrence, the Ocean, and the St. Croix, styled "the Lordship and Barony of New Scotland." This grant was confirmed to the Earl by a royal charter of September 10th, the same year. The Earl was still further favored, for by a patent dated April 22, 1635, the council, this time by the direction of Charles I., gave him a "tract of the main land of New England, beginning at St. Croix, and from thence extending along the seacoast to Pemaquid and the River Kennebeck," together with Long Island and all the islands thereto adjacent.[1] In 1663 the heirs of the Earl sold this grant between the Kennebec and the St. Croix to the Earl of Clarendon, from whom it immediately passed to the Duke of York.

The Pilgrims landed at Plymouth late in the year 1620, without any authority whatever; but June 1, 1621, the Council for New England granted them a "roving patent," which assigned them no boundaries or settled place of habitation, but allowed one hundred acres of land to be taken up for every emigrant, with fifteen hundred acres for public buildings, and also empowered the grantees to make laws and to set up a government. This patent was issued in the name of John Pierce and certain other London merchants who had given the Pilgrims some financial assistance. In 1628 the council

---

[1] Vindication, etc., of Alexander, Earl of Stirling, 34.

gave Plymouth a tract of land on the Kennebec River, and the year following it gave them a new patent, much more favorable than the one given in Pierce's name in 1621. The colony was now bounded west by a line drawn northerly from the mouth of Narragansett River, and on the north by a line drawn westerly from Cohasset Rivulet. The grant on the Kennebec made the previous year was included. The Plymouth people made repeated attempts to obtain a charter from the Crown, which alone could confer prerogatives of government, but these attempts were never successful.

In 1628 the Council at Plymouth made to Sir Henry Roswell and others his associates in the Massachusetts Bay Colony an important grant, which was confirmed by Charles I., with powers of government, March 4, 1629. These are the boundaries of Massachusetts as defined by the Crown:

. . . "All that Parte of Newe England in Amirica which lyes and extendes betweene a great River there, comonlie called Monomack River, alias Merrimack River, and a certen other River there called Charles River, being in the Bottome of a certen Bay there, comonlie called Massachusetts, alias Mattachusetts, alias Massatusetts Bay, and also all and singuler those Landes and Hereditaments whatsoever, lying within the Space of Three Englishe Myles on the South Parte of the said River called Charles River, or of any or every Parte thereof. And also all and singuler the Landes and Hereditaments whatsoever, lying and being within the space of Three Englishe Miles to the southward of the southermost Parte of the said Baye, called Massachusetts, alias Mattachusetts, alias Massatusetts Bay: And also all those Landes and Hereditaments whatsoever, which lye and be within the space of Three English Myles to the Northward of the saide River, called Monomack, alias Merrymack, or to the Norward of any and every Parte thereof and all Landes and Hereditaments whatsoever, lyeing within the Lymitts aforesaide, North and South, in Latitude and Bredth, and in Length and Longitude, of and within all the Bredth aforesaide, throughout the Mayne Landes there from the Atlantick and Westerne Sea and Ocean on the East Parte, to the South Sea on the West Parte.

. . . " Provided alwayes, That yf the said Landes . . . were [on November 3, 1620] actuallie possessed or inhabited by any other Christian Prince or State, or were within the Boundes, Lymytts or Territories of that Southerne Colony, then before graunted by our saide late Father . . . then this present Graunt shall not extend to any such partes or parcells thereof."

The attempt to unify and harmonize the Northern New England patents and charters, real and pretended, is next door to a hopeless undertaking. I shall content myself with stating the facts material to the present purpose. On November 7, 1629, the Plymouth Council made to Captain John Mason, one of the principal adventurers in the company, a grant that, as reaffirmed in 1635, was thus bounded:

"All that part of the Mayn Land of New England aforesaid, beginning from the middle part of Naumkeck River, and from thence to proceed eastwards along the Sea Coast to Cape Anne, and round about the same to Pischataway Harbour, and soe forwards vp within the river Newgewanacke, and to the furthest head of the said River and from thence northwestwards till sixty miles bee finished, from the first entrance of Pischataqay Harbor, and alsoe from Naumkecke through the River thereof vp into the land west sixty miles, from which period to cross over land to the sixty miles end, accompted from Pischataway, through Newgewanacke River to the land northwest aforesaid; and alsoe all that the South Halfe of the Ysles of Sholes, all which lands, with the Consent of the Counsell, shall from henceforth be called New-hampshyre. And alsoe ten thousand acres more of land . . . on the southeast part of Sagadihoc, at the mouth or entrance thereof, from henceforth to bee called by the name of Massonia, etc." . . .

There were earlier grants within the present limits of New Hampshire, but this one may be considered the origin of that commonwealth. It never had a royal charter, but the commission of 1680 to the governor had much the same effect. The feeble settlements within the limits of Mason's grant were annexed to Massachusetts in 1641; they became a royal colony in 1680; they became a second time a part of Massachusetts in 1690, but were again separated in 1692, from which time New Hampshire has had an independent existence.

In 1635 the Council at Plymouth renounced to the Crown their charter, first, however, dividing into eight shares, which they distributed among themselves, the territory of New England. It was ordered when this partition was made that all persons having lawful grants of land, or having made lawfully settled plantations, should enjoy the same on their surrendering their rights of jurisdiction (*jura regalia*) to the proprietor to whom the division fell. The grant of 1620 was from sea to sea, but this partition extended inland only sixty miles, save in one or two cases that reached twice that distance. It was intended to procure confirmations of these grants under the great seal, but this appears to have been done only in the case of Sir Ferdinando Gorges's portion, lying between the Piscataqua and Kennebec rivers, confirmed to him by royal charter in 1639. This was "the province or county of Maine." The grant led to serious disputes with holders under earlier grants. Massachusetts claimed the whole district because it lies south of a due east and west line drawn three miles north of the lake in which the Merrimac has its rise, and she finally bought the Gorges title for £1,250.

The Massachusetts charter of 1629 was cancelled by the High Court of Chancery in 1684. Four years later the Stuarts were expelled the throne, and were succeeded by William and Mary. The new sovereigns favored a policy of colonial consolidation. Accordingly, November 7, 1691, they granted to Massachusetts Bay a new charter which brought together under its jurisdiction all the colonies of Central and Northern New England, viz.: Plymouth, Massachusetts, Maine, including the grant between the St. Croix and the Kennebec made to Earl Stirling, and Nova Scotia. Maine, henceforth consisting of the original grants to Alexander west of the St. Croix, to Gorges, and to Plymouth, remained a part of Massachusetts until admitted to the Union as a State in 1820. Plymouth remained permanently connected with the younger and stronger colony at the north, and thus brought Massachusetts down to the sea in the southeast.

When New Hampshire's dependence upon Massachusetts came to an end in 1692, the territorial strifes of the two colonies began. New Hampshire cut Massachusetts, as bounded on the east by the St. Croix, in two; so there were boundaries to be drawn on the east and on the south. Commissioners appointed by the two colonies failing to agree, these boundaries were referred, by the king's order, to commissioners appointed by the neighboring colonies. The report of this board, confirmed by the king in 1740, and acquiesced in by Massachusetts, drew the eastern line practically where it is to-day. On the south, the report was less favorable to Massachusetts. The charter of 1629 gave her all the lands lying within the space of three English miles to the northward of the River Merrimac and of every part thereof; the charter of 1635 made the southern boundary of New Hampshire on the coast, the Naumkeck River, at Salem. The charter of 1691 reaffirmed the boundary of 1629. Massachusetts insisted, therefore, that her proper northern bonndary was a due east and west line running through a point three miles north of the inflow of Lake Winnipiseogee, which would have blotted New Hampshire from the map. New Hampshire contended that her southern boundary was a latitudinal line running through a point three miles north of the mouth of the Merrimac. The report that the king confirmed gave New Hampshire more than she asked for. It provided, " that the northern boundary of the province of Massachusetts be a similar curve line pursuing the course of the Merrimac River, at three miles distance, on the north side thereof, beginning at the Atlantic Ocean and ending at a point due north of Pautucket

Falls, and a straight line drawn from thence, due west, till it meets with His Majesty's other governments." Massachusetts refused to take part in surveying and marking this line, and it was done by New Hampshire alone in 1741 and 1742. It is the line of our map.

The three towns that constituted the original Connecticut were settled by emigration from Massachusetts in 1636 and 1637. It was then supposed that the ground on which Windsor, Hartford, and Weathersfield were planted belonged to that colony, and the three settlements remained for a year or two under its protection. The old story is that, afterward, the emigrants obtained a title or claim under a patent which proceeded from the Council of New England by the way of the Earl of Warwick to Lord Say and Sele and his associates; but the existence of the grant to Warwick, and so the sufficiency of the old patent of Connecticut, is denied.[1] The New Haven colony, planted in 1638, had no other title than the one obtained from the Indians by purchase. Both the settlers on the river and at New Haven had much trouble with the Dutch, who claimed all the coast from the Hudson to the Connecticut. It is, therefore, hard to see that either the Connecticut or the New Haven colonists had any title to the lands that they occupied, proceeding from the Crown, previous to the charter that constituted the Connecticut Company, granted by Charles II., April 23, 1662, which gave the colony the following limits:

"We . . . do give, grant and confirm unto the said Governor and Company, and their successors, all that part of our Dominions in *New England* in America bounded on the east by *Narraganset River*, commonly called *Narraganset Bay*, where the said River falleth into the Sea, and on the North by the Line of the *Massachusetts Plantation*; and on the South by the sea; and in Longitude as the Line of the *Massachusetts Col-*

---

[1] Johnston: Connecticut, 8-10.

ony, running from *East to West, that is to say*, from the said *Narragansett Bay* on the *East*, to *the South* sea on the *West* Part, with the *Islands* thereunto adjoining."

This charter consolidated Connecticut and New Haven; it cut into the grant made to Roger Williams and his associates in 1643; and it did not recognize the presence of the Dutch on the Hudson even to the extent of making the familiar reservation in favor of a Christian prince holding or Christian people inhabiting.

In 1636 Roger Williams began the Providence plantation on a tract of land that he held either by gift or purchase from the Indians. Settlements were made on Rhode Island in 1638 and 1639, and a beginning was also made on the western coast of Narragansett Bay in 1643. An attempt of Massachusetts to extend her jurisdiction over these settlements was resisted as a usurpation. In 1643 Williams obtained from the Parliamentary Commissioners, the Earl of Warwick, President, a charter of incorporation for the two plantations. In 1663 Charles II. granted a new charter, creating "the Governor and Company of the English Colony of Rhode Island and Providence Plantations in New England in America," that unified all the Bay colonies, and restored to Rhode Island her original limits, which had been invaded by the Connecticut charter of the year before; an overlapping of grants that led to a long and bitter controversy. Boundary disputes between Massachusetts and the colonies on the south began in 1742, and they came to an end, if indeed the end be reached, only a few years ago. These disputes are among the most remarkable of their kind in our history. To follow them through the colonial and State legislatures, the commissions colonial and State, the appeals to the Court of England and to the Supreme Court of the United States, would be a task as tedious as lengthy. Of course the first thing to be done was to fix a latitudinal line that should fall three miles south of the most southern point of Charles River.

"The northern boundary of the colony was not fully settled for more than a century. When Connecticut was settled, the Massachusetts southern line was in the air; and in 1642 that colony sent two men, Woodward and Saffary, to run the line according to the charter. The surveyors are said to have been ignorant men; and Connecticut authorities call them, *lucus a non lucendo,* 'the mathematicians.' They began operations by finding what seemed to them a point 'three English miles, on the south part of the Charles River, or of any or every part thereof:' thence the southern Massachusetts line was to run west to the Pacific Ocean. The two mathematicians, however, either hesitating to undertake a foot journey to the Pacific, or doubting the sympathy of casual Indians with the advancement of science, and being sufficiently learned to know that two points are enough to determine the direction of a line, did not run the line directly west. Instead, they took ship, sailed around Cape Cod and up the Connecticut River, and found what they asserted to be a point in the same latitude as the first. In fact, they had got some eight miles too far to the south, thus giving their employers far too much territory; but they had fulfilled their principal duty, which was to show that Springfield was in Massachusetts. An *ex parte* survey, and of such a nature, could not, of course, be recognized by Connecticut. The oblong indentation in Connecticut's northern boundary is a remnant of the ignorance of Woodward and Saffary; for Massachusetts claimed a line running just north of Windsor, and Connecticut finally reclaimed all but this oblong. She made *ex parte* surveys of her own in 1695 and 1702, and then both colonies appealed to the Crown. This was evidently a dangerous tribunal for both, and in 1714 they agreed on a compromise line, much as it is at present."[1]

This line conforms in general to the parallel of 42° 2'; it marks the southern limit of the Massachusetts claim and the northern limit of the Connecticut claim west of the Delaware. The disputes among the New England colonies

---

[1] Johnston: Connecticut, 207, 208.

will not be further followed, except to quote Rufus Choate's celebrated description of a phase of one of them. "The commissioners might as well have decided that the line between the States was bounded on the north by a bramble-bush, on the south by a bluejay, on the west by a hive of bees in swarming time, and on the east by five hundred foxes with firebrands tied to their tails"[1]—a description that would apply to a good deal of other boundary work done in colonial times.

The cutting up of the territories assigned to the London and Plymouth Companies into two groups of colonies was materially modified by the intrusion, within the dates of the Jamestown and Plymouth settlements, of a foreign body that thus far has not been mentioned. In 1609 Henry Hudson, who, with a Dutch commission, was then searching for a western passage to Cathay, found his way into New York Bay, and into the noble river that bears his name. The Dutch sent ships to the Hudson every year for several years, one motive being discovery and another trade with the Indians. At that time, it will be remembered, the French claimed the coast from the St. Lawrence to the Delaware; moreover, the very year that Hudson ascended the river, Champlain ascended Lake Champlain almost to its source, when, fortunately, he turned back to Quebec. Then there was the Cabot title of the English, disregarding the claims of the Dutch and the French alike. The Dutch proceeded to fasten themselves firmly upon the mouth and valley of the river, which they called North River; and afterward less firmly upon the country east to Fresh River, as they called the Connecticut, and south to South River, as they called the Delaware. The whole country claimed by them they named New Netherlands. The English never acknowledged, but always denied, the validity of the Dutch title; and it is now plain that, in view of the Cabot title, the geographical relations of the Hudson to the regions east and south, and to the interior of the continent, and the later supe-

---

[1] Johnston: Connecticut, 209.

riority of the English, the ultimate ejection of Holland, if not of the Dutch, and the incorporation of New Netherlands into the English system, was only a question of time. The Dutch were in possession only fifty years; but in that time they materially influenced American history, as well territorial as political and social.

In some of the northern "from sea to sea" charters the King of England made the customary exemption of lands possessed by a Christian prince, or inhabited by Christian people; but the fact that the presence of the Dutch was well known, and that they were regarded as intruders, would seem to show that the exemption did not apply to them, or at least was not meant to apply to them. Further, the Connecticut charter bounded that colony " on the south by the sea;" that is, Long Island Sound.

We must also remember that the southern boundary of the New England of 1620 was parallel 40° north, a full degree south of the southernmost point of the New England of 1887. Save the futile Plowden Palatinate, neither the Council nor the Crown had attempted to assign this belt of territory to any grantee. This, no doubt, would have been done had not the Dutch been present in New Netherlands. We may be reasonably certain, at least, that, had it not been for the Dutch, the Hudson Valley would have become the seat of an English colony before the Connecticut lines were drawn in 1662. Perhaps Massachusetts and Connecticut would have protested against a colony at their backs, cutting them off from the west; but the noble river, the picturesque valley, the interior trade, the broad and fertile lands of the Mohawk, would have been attractions too strong for their opposition. The floods of the Hudson would have swept away their "from sea to sea" lines, if they had ever been really carried across that river. But while New York geographically is no part of New England, but has a distinct character of its own, it might have been, historically, a part of New England, and it is fair to presume that such would have been the case, had not the Dutch given another direction to history.

The long-sleeping English title to the Hudson was revived in 1664. On March 12th of that year, "divers good causes and considerations him thereto moving," Charles II., "of his especial grace, certain knowledge, and mere motion," gave and granted to his dearest brother, James Duke of York, his heirs and assigns—

"All that part of the maine land of New England beginning at a certaine place called or knowne by the name of St. Croix next adjoyning to New Scotland in America and from thence extending along the sea coast unto a certain place called Petuaquine or Pemaquid and so up the River thereof to the further head of ye same as it tendeth northwards and extending from thence to the River Kinebequi and so upwards by the shortest course to the River Canada northward and also all that Island or Islands commonly called by the severall name or names of Matowacks or Long Island scituate lying and being towards the west of Cape Codd and ye narrow Higansetts abutting upon the maine land between the two Rivers there called or knowne by the severall names of Conecticutt and Hudsons River togather also with the said river called Hudsons River and all the land from the west side of Conecticutt to ye east side of Delaware Bay and also all those severall Islands called or knowne by the names of Martin's Vinyard and Nantukes otherwise Nantuckett together with all ye lands islands soyles rivers harbours mines minerals quarryes woods marshes waters lakes, etc."

The next year a fleet sent out by the Royal Duke took possession of New Netherlands. A few years later the Dutch recovered the province for a single year; but that article of the Treaty of Westminster, 1674, which required the surrender by both parties of all conquests made in the course of the preceding war, remaining in the hands of the conqueror, gave the English a secure title as against the Dutch. A second charter, dated 1674, confirmed the Duke in possession of the province, the boundary descriptions remaining much as before. The Duke gave the province the name by which it has since been known.

That part of Maine included in the Duke of York's charter, Long Island, and some smaller islands to the east, had been bought by him the year before of the heirs of Earl Stirling, to whom they had fallen on the dissolution of the Plymouth Company, in 1635. Pemaquid, as the Maine tract was called, was annexed to Massachusetts in 1686, and it was confirmed to that colony by the charter of 1691. Martha's Vineyard, Nantucket, and other islands in the neighborhood were also included within the same charter. Long Island, which Nature plainly intended to go with the country on the north side of the Sound, and the possession of which had been disputed by the Connecticut people and the Dutch, was henceforth attached to New York. At the date of the English conquest of New Netherlands, the English colonies east and southwest had become measurably adjusted to the Dutch; but now matters were thrown into greater confusion than ever, and a new series of adjustments became necessary. Before attempting a general account of these arrangements, we should take a closer look of some work that Charles II. did in the years 1662 to 1664.

In the first of those years, he bounded Connecticut on the east by Narragansett Bay, and on the west by the Pacific Ocean; thus jumping half the claim of Rhode Island, and wholly ignoring the Dutch on the Hudson. In the second year, he bounded Rhode Island on the west by the Pawcatuck, thus jumping the eastern part of the grant made the year before to Connecticut. In the third year, he not only gave the Hudson to his brother, but he made the eastern boundary of the Duke's province the Connecticut River, thus sanctioning the widest claim that the Dutch had ever made in that direction, and cutting away from one-third to one-half of the present limits of Massachusetts and Connecticut.

The establishment of the Dutch on the Hudson, if not the geography of the country, had probably convinced Massachusetts and Connecticut that their "from sea to sea" limits never would exist save on parchment. At all events, they never dreamed, now that the Hudson had passed into English hands, of resisting the royal will. New York must be recognized, as a matter of course, and the only thing now to do was to make the best terms as to boundaries that they could.

The issue with Connecticut raised by the Duke's grant was referred to the Royal Commissioners for the Colonies, who promptly fixed a line twenty miles east of the Hudson; but the second charter to York, 1674, reaffirmed the boundaries of 1664, and reopened the whole question. In 1683 Connecticut agreed with Governor Dongan, of New York, upon a line that, with some rectifications, is the basis of the present boundary between the two States. In 1725 and 1737 the line was run practically where it is to-day; but we have a curious example of how the boundary disputes of the seventeenth century project themselves forward in the fact that the line was resurveyed by New York in 1860, agreed upon by the two States in 1878 and 1879, and ratified by Congress in 1881. The western boundary of Connecticut happens to fall, at the sea shore, on the forty-first degree of north latitude; and that fact determines the latitude of a western line that we shall have occasion to consider hereafter.

In the case of Massachusetts, as in the case of Connecticut, New York claimed eastward to Connecticut River. The contest was so bitter that the two colonies never came to an agreement until 1773, and then the Revolution, coming on immediately after, prevented the running of the line until 1787. With a modification or two of no consequence for our purpose, the line of 1773-1787 stands to-day.

Whether Massachusetts and Connecticut, or either of them, considered at the time what the effect of the lines of 1733 and 1773 would be upon their claims in the interior, I have no means of knowing; but it is certain that the Governor of Connecticut, in 1720, had spoken of New York as cutting that colony "asunder," and that a few years later Connecticut men were making their way into the wilderness west of the Delaware. When the two States were afterward told that by consenting to the lines east of the Hudson they had barred their own charter-rights to extend farther west, they replied that the Duke of York's grant was bounded on the west by the Delaware, that he had jumped them, therefore, only to that limit, and that their consenting to the fact in no sense barred them west of his boundary.

No part of the whole coast was more sought after, or was the scene of more experiments in colonization, than the Delaware country and the region east of it to the ocean. The Swedes, the Fins, the Dutch, and men from New Haven, all mingled in the opening scenes in that region; and it was in New Jersey that Sir Edmund Plowden sought to set up the palatinate of "New Albion." In 1655 the country passed into the hands of the Dutch, who, however, received it only as trustees for the nation whose navigators had discovered the continent. The Duke of York laid claim, when the time came, to the western side as well as the eastern side of the river, although it was not included in his grant, basing the claim on the Dutch capitulation. In 1664, two months before the expedition sent to the Hudson sailed, the Duke sold to Lord John Berkeley and Sir George Carteret a territory that he thus described:

"All that tract of land adjacent to New England, and lying and being to the westward of Long Island and Manhitas Island, and bounded on the east part by the main sea and part by Hudson's River, and hath upon the west Delaware Bay or river, and extendeth southward to the main ocean as far as Cape May, at the mouth of Delaware Bay, and to the northward as far as the northernmost branch of the said bay or river of Delaware, which is forty-one degrees and forty minutes of latitude, and crosseth over thence in a strait line to Hudson's River in forty-one degrees of latitude; which said tract of land is hereafter to be called by the name or names of New Ceaserea or New Jersey."

New Jersey had a changeful history until 1702, when the proprietors surrendered the province to the Crown. Royal Commissioners fixed the boundary line between the colony and New York substantially where it is to-day, in 1769.

In the Massachusetts, New Hampshire, and New York grants, we find the key to another memorable territorial contest. The Massachusetts of 1629 included all lands lying within the space of three English miles to the northward of any and every part of Merrimac River. The New Hampshire of 1635 reached on the south to the Naumkeck, and on the west sixty miles inland. The commissioners of 1740, to whom the dispute between the two colonies was referred, laid down a line three miles north of the Merrimac, following its course to a point north of Pawtucket Falls, and then proceeding due west "till it meets with His Majesty's other governments." Under this decision New Hampshire claimed that she extended as far west as Massachusetts, but Massachusetts continued to assert her right to the country west of Connecticut River extending north to the possessions of France. New York said the region between Lake Champlain and Connecticut River belonged to her, under the grant of 1664, 1674. New Hampshire and Massachusetts claimed that New York was barred by the twenty-mile line drawn by the Royal Commissioners between Connecticut and New York in 1664; but New York denied that this line held north of Massachusetts, and in 1764 the King in Council decided the issue in her favor. Both before and after the decision of 1740 was rendered, Massachusetts and New Hampshire made grants of land in the disputed district. Settlers from all the New England colonies flowed into the territory, and especially from Connecticut. After the king's decision of 1764 New York strove to extend her jurisdiction over the "New Hampshire Grants," as the district came to be called. She repudiated the New England titles of land-holders, and sought to compel the settlers to purchase anew of her. This was the beginning of the long and bitter quarrel between the "Green Mountain Boys" and the "Yorkers." The settlers made common cause against New York's selfish policy. Their determination to maintain their titles and to repel aggression ripened into a desire for independence. In 1777 a convention declared the Grants a separate and independent State, with the name of "New Connecticut." The next year a constitution was adopted and the name Vermont selected. It is hardly too much to say that Vermont was before Congress asking for admission to the circle of States for fifteen years. For much of that time the people hardly considered themselves a part of the United States at all; they denied allegiance to all other States, and were not a State themselves. Through the Revolution they waged a separate war against Great Britain, and even entered into negotiations for a separate peace. Their condition is an anomaly in the history of our system. Not to touch on intermediate points, Vermont was finally admitted to the Union in 1791.

VII.

THE THIRTEEN COLONIES AS CONSTITUTED BY THE ROYAL CHARTERS.—(II.)

WE come now to a charter that is the source of more boundary disputes than any other in our whole history. This is the charter given to William Penn, in 1681, by Charles II., in discharge of a debt that the king owed to Penn's father.

" . . . all that Tract or Parte of Land in *America*, with all the Islands therein conteyned, as the same is bounded on the East by *Delaware* River, from twelve miles distance Northwards of *New Castle* Towne unto the three and fortieth degree of Northerne Latitude, if the said River doeth extende so farre Northwards ; But if the said River shall not extend soe farre Northward, then by the said River soe farr as it doth extend ; and from the head of the said River the Easterne Bounds are to bee determined by a Meridian Line, to bee drawne from the head of the said River, unto the said three and fortieth Degree. The said Lands to extend westwards five degrees in longitude, to bee computed from the said Easterne Bounds ; and the said Lands to bee bounded on the North by the beginning of the three and fortieth degree of Northern Latitude, and on the South by a Circle drawne at twelve miles distance from *New Castle* Northward and Westward unto the beginning of the fortieth degree of Northern Latitude, and then by a streight Line Westward to the Limitt of Longitude above mentioned."

Penn proceeded at once to extend his province and to perfect his title. He bought Delaware of the Duke of York, and also obtained from him the relinquishment of all his claim to the western shore of the river above the twelve-mile circle, which had been drawn to leave the town of New Castle and neighborhood in the Duke's hands. The Duke's deeds to Penn, which bear the date 1682, completed the limitation of his province of New York on the sea-coast.

The grant to Penn confused the old controversy between Virginia and Lord Baltimore as to their boundary, and led to fresh controversies. The question soon arose: "What do the descriptions 'the beginning of the fortieth,' and 'the beginning of the three and fortieth degree of northern latitude' mean?" If they meant the fortieth and forty-third parallels of north latitude, as most historians have held, Penn's province was the zone, three degrees of latitude in width, that leaves Philadelphia a little to the south and Syracuse a little to the north; but if those descriptions meant the belts lying between 39° and 40°, and 42° and 43°, as some authors have held, then Penn's southern and northern boundaries were 39° and 42° north. A glance at the map of Pennsylvania will show the reader how different the territorial dispositions would have been if either one of these constructions had been carried out. The first construction would avoid disputes on the south, unless with Virginia west of the mountains; on the north it would not conflict with New York, but would most seriously conflict with Connecticut and Massachusetts west of the Delaware. The second construction involved disputes with the two southern colonies concerning the degree 39–40 to the farthest limit of Pennsylvania, and it also overlapped Connecticut's claim to the degree 41–42. Perhaps we cannot certainly say what was the intention of the king, or Penn's first understanding; but the Quaker proprietary and his successors adopted substantially the second construction, and thus involved their province in the most bitter disputes.

The first quarrel was with Lord Baltimore. It has been well said that this "notable quarrel" "continued more than eighty years; was the cause of endless trouble between individuals; occupied the attention not only of the proprietors of the respective provinces, but of the Lords of Trade and Plantations, of the High Court of Chancery, and of the Privy Councils of at least three monarchs; it greatly retarded the settlement and development of a beautiful and fertile country, and brought about numerous tumults, which sometimes ended in bloodshed."[1] The eastern boundary of Maryland was Delaware Bay and River, from the intersection of the line drawn across the peninsula from Watkins's Point to the main ocean, on the south, "into that part of the Bay of Delaware on the north which lieth under the fortieth degree of north latitude from the equinoctial where New England is terminated," on the north; the northern boundary was "the fortieth parallel from the bay to the true meridian of the first fountain of the River Potomac." But Baltimore's charter described the country granted to him as "not yet cultivated," *hactenus inculta;* and at once, on his taking possession in 1634, the question arose whether this was a mere description of the land, or a condition of the grant equivalent to the familiar "not actually possessed by any Christian prince nor inhabited by Christian people" of the seventeenth-century charters. Some Virginians were already within the limits marked out for Baltimore when the Ark and the Dove entered the St. Marys. Notably, Claiborne had set up his trading-post on Kent Island in 1632; and, not unnaturally, *hactenus inculta* was at once invoked in the Virginia interest. After much strife and some bloodshed, this controversy was finally settled in Baltimore's favor. In 1659, when Baltimore attempted to expel them from his limits, the Dutch said *hactenus inculta* applied to them as the first possessors of the country; and historians of our day have invoked the phrase in the Dutch

---

[1] Scaife: Pennsylvania Magazine of History, 1885, 241.

interest. Considering that the Kings of England never acknowledged the Dutch claims on the Delaware more than on the Hudson, it would not be necessary to notice this point but for one fact. Such title as the Dutch had, passed by conquest to the Duke of York, in 1664, who sold it to Penn; and he did not fail to make the most of it in maintaining his cause against his Southern neighbor.

But the principal contention between Penn and Baltimore grew out of the inconsistent and conflicting boundaries that the Crown had given them. First, Baltimore's northeast corner should be "in the Bay of Delaware" as well as on the fortieth parallel, while the fortieth parallel crosses the Delaware many miles north of the head of the bay. We are forced to the conclusion that Charles I. intended to bound Baltimore on the north by the fortieth parallel, for we cannot suppose that he intended, in 1632, to leave either for Virginia or the Crown a narrow strip of territory south of the New England line; but it was very unfortunate for Baltimore that the reference to the bay left open a door for Penn to enter with his equally impossible boundary, when the day came to deal with him. Penn's southern boundary was "a circle drawn at twelve miles distance from New Castle northward and westward unto the beginning of the fortieth degree of northern latitude, and thence by a straight line westward" to the limit of longitude fixed by the charter. There was a dispute whether this circle should be drawn "horizontally" or "superficially;" but no matter which way it was drawn, it would not touch either the thirty-ninth or the fortieth degree of latitude.

Definite and precise as the boundaries of 1632 and 1681 apparently were, it is clear that they were drawn in ignorance of the geography of the Delaware region. Nor was this ignorance soon removed; maps of the next century are extant on which the heads of both Delaware and Chesapeake Bays are laid down north of the fortieth parallel.[1] Moreover, the

---

[1] Scaife: Pennsylvania Magazine of History, 1885, 248.

mistake consisted in carrying the parallel too far south, rather than in bringing the heads of the bays too far north; at least both Penn and Baltimore were surprised to find, when they came to make surveys, that parallel falling so far north.

The proofs that the king intended to bound Penn on the south by the fortieth parallel are the fact that said parallel was the southern boundary of New England, established in 1620, and the Maryland charter. Baltimore stood stoutly for that construction of his charter, relying on the literal force of the language. Penn claimed to the thirty-ninth parallel, but he could hardly have expected at any time to maintain that line. His determination was to gain a frontage on both Delaware and Chesapeake Bay, and to push his southern boundary as far south as possible. Fortunately for Penn and unfortunately for Baltimore, Penn's line must touch the twelve-mile circle, as well as be "the beginning of the fortieth degree," while Baltimore's northern line must touch Delaware Bay as well as be the fortieth degree. It will be seen that each one of the descriptions contains a major and a minor point; and also that the two major points supported Baltimore's, and the two minor points Penn's pretensions. Hence Penn urged that the particular and the definite should control the general and the indefinite. This was holding that the Delaware Bay and the twelve-mile-circle limitations should override those in regard to the fortieth degree. Penn had a further advantage in the fact that he had obtained his title to the three counties of Delaware, which were also within Baltimore's grant, by purchase from the Duke of York. First and last, Baltimore stood for his charter-line, while Penn was disposed to compromise, but not in such a way as to give the Delaware counties to his rival or to surrender Philadelphia.

After conferences, arguments, propositions, litigations in the courts and hearings before the Privy Council, the proprietors compromised the case in 1760. This compromise, which practically carried out an older one, as well as a decision by Lord Chancellor Hardwicke, was to this effect: (1) To run a due east and west line across the peninsula through Cape Henlopen (but not the Henlopen of our maps); (2) to run a line from the middle of this Henlopen line tangent to the twelve-mile circle drawn horizontally; (3) to run a line from the point where the tangent touches the circle due north to the parallel of latitude fifteen miles south of the southern limit of Philadelphia; (4) to run the said parallel of latitude— the lands north and east of this series of lines to belong to Pennsylvania, the lands south and west to Maryland. The proprietors sent over two distinguished mathematicians, Jeremiah Mason and Charles Dixon, who established the various lines in the years 1763-67. The east and west line, which they ran and marked two hundred and forty-four miles west of the Delaware, is the Mason and Dixon's line of history, so long the boundary between the free and the slave States. Its precise latitude is $39° 43' 26.3''$ north. The Penns did not, therefore, gain the degree 39-40, but they did gain a zone one-fourth of a degree in width, south of the fortieth degree, to their western limit, because the decision of 1760 controlled that of 1779, made with Virginia. Had the heads of the two bays really extended north of the fortieth degree, we should no doubt have seen the Penns struggling to limit Baltimore by that line, rather than by a point in Delaware Bay, and to carry their grant north to latitude $43°$. As it is, Pennsylvania is narrower by nearly three-fourths of a degree than the charter of 1681 contemplated. No doubt, however, the Penns considered the narrow strip gained at the south more valuable than the broad one lost at the north. With the Revolution, Delaware ceased to be a dependency of Pennsylvania, and became an independent state with the boundaries of 1760.

But the grant to Penn conflicted with the Virginia boundaries of 1609. No matter whether the beginning of the fortieth degree meant the thirty-ninth or the fortieth parallel, it would cut that northwest line running "throughout from sea to sea" which that province claimed as her northern boundary. The issue was not raised as soon as the issues between Maryland and the other two States, for an obvious reason; but that great awakening to Western interests that followed the close of King George's war in 1748 brought it at once to the fore. Virginians and Pennsylvanians alike now began to find their way over the mountains, not furtively, as hunters, but openly, as traders and tillers of the soil, and their meeting in the valley of the Upper Ohio was alone sufficient to force the issue. Besides, building works of defence against the Indians and the French, that the renewed mutterings of war made necessary, hastened it. The controversy began formally in 1752, eight years before Penn and Baltimore reached their agreement and fifteen years before Mason and Dixon planted their two hundred and forty-fourth mile-post from the Delaware.

Mention has already been made of Governor Spotswood's famous ride over the Blue Ridge in 1716. The Virginians had been one hundred and ten years in reaching the Valley of Virginia, and even then the glowing reports that the governor's company made of its fertility and beauty did not lead to its immediate settlement. But in 1738 the General Assembly created Augusta County, bounding it on the east by the Blue Ridge and on the west and northwest by "the utmost limits of Virginia." Whether these limits were the Pacific Ocean or the Mississippi River, they included all Western Pennsylvania. Accordingly, when the Pennsylvanians began to settle west of the mountains they were within the limits of a Virginia county already organized. When Washington led the Virginia Blues into that region to dispute the progress of the French, he went not only to defend the territory of His Britannic Majesty, but also to defend the territory of the Old Dominion. Moreover, the Pennsylvania Assembly declined Lieutenant-Governor Dinwiddie's proposal to assist in fortifying the Forks of the Ohio, on grounds that gave Lord Dunmore some advantage in the correspondence with Governor Penn, soon to be mentioned. To stimulate volunteering in 1754, Governor Dinwiddie issued a proclamation offering 200,000 acres of land in bounties, 100,000 near the Forks of the Ohio, to be called the "garrison lands," and the remainder down the river, and this was in part the stimulus that brought into the field the force that Washington commanded that year. While the Pennsylvanians were too apathetic to assist the Virginia governor in building the proposed fortifications, they would not brook this invasion of their rights. Governor Hamilton expostulated, and Dinwiddie defended himself on the ground that the issue was doubtful and the case urgent. The grant was approved by the king, 1763, but it was not until the very eve of the Revolution that the patents were issued to the claimants.[1]

Braddock's defeat gave the French commander on the Ohio the opportunity that he so well improved, and also so well described, of "ruining the three adjacent provinces, Pennsylvania, Maryland, and Virginia, driving off the inhabitants, and totally destroying the settlements from a tract of country thirty leagues wide reckoning from the line of Fort Cumberland;"[2] and of course adjourned the boundary-war until the war of arms should cease. With the fall of Fort Duquesne into the hands of the English in 1758, settlers began again to find their way to the valleys of the streams flowing to the Mississippi. For some years Virginia allowed her claim to the part of Pennsylvania west of the mountains to sleep; she did not even remonstrate when Mason and Dixon carried their line west of the meridian of the "Fairfax stone;" but Virginians, as well as Pennsylvanians, continued to make their way into the disputed region. In 1769 the lands about Pittsburg

---

[1] In some cases, at least, patents for land in Pennsylvania issued by the Governor of Virginia were affirmed by Pennsylvania courts. Thus, in 1775, Lord Dunmore gave Washington a patent for 2,813 acres, described as being in Augusta County, Virginia, on the waters of Miller's run, etc., that are within Washington County, Pennsylvania. The lands were occupied by squatters, who denied the validity of the title, but the Pennsylvania court sustained the patent and ejected the intruders in 1784. Butterfield: Washington and Crawford Letters, 73.

[2] Parkman: Montcalm and Wolfe, I., 329.

were surveyed for the Pennsylvania proprietors, and settlements under the government of this province now became more rapid. Bedford County, embracing all Western Pennsylvania as claimed by the Penns, was organized in 1771, and Westmoreland County, embracing the part of Bedford west of Laurel Hill, in 1773. This region was also included in Augusta County, Virginia, as already related. The result was, that some of the inhabitants sided with one State, some with the other, and some with neither. As early as 1771 the more turbulent entered into an agreement, which they proclaimed openly, to keep off all officers of the law whatever, under a penalty of £50, to be forfeited by the party who should refuse to keep the contract.[1] Arthur St. Clair, of whom we shall soon hear more on a greater theatre of action, made his home in the disputed district in 1770, where he became first a surveyor, and then a magistrate, with a Pennsylvania commission. In January, 1774, Dr. John Connolly, who figures in the history of those times as a land-jobber and political tool of Lord Dunmore, the Governor of Virginia, appeared at the Forks of the Ohio with a commission from his Lordship, with the high-sounding title of "Captain-Commandant of the Militia of Pittsburg and its dependencies." Connolly seized Fort Pitt, dismantled two years before, named it Fort Dunmore, and issued a proclamation declaring that the Governor of Virginia was about to take steps to redress the grievances of the people of the region, and calling them to meet as a militia the twenty-fifth of that month. St. Clair caused him to be arrested for the act, but he was soon released on his own recognizance. Afterward Pennsylvania magistrates were arrested and hurried off to Staunton in the Virginia Valley.

The arrest of Connolly led to a correspondence between Governors Penn and Dunmore, to only one feature of which attention will be paid. Penn stated that, according to the Pennsylvania calculations, Fort Pitt was " near six miles east-

---

[1] St. Clair Papers, I., 258.

ward of the Western extent of the province." Dunmore rejected this view, and asserted the Virginia claim. He also said that the Pennsylvania Assembly, at the time when Dinwiddie was proposing to fortify the Upper Ohio, had admitted that Pittsburg was not within the limits of that government; but Penn replied denying that the assembly had made such an admission, and affirming that the act would not conclude anything if the assembly had done so.

In May, Messrs. Tilghman and Allen, appointed commissioners on the part of Pennsylvania, visited Williamsburg to arrange matters, if possible. Propositions were made on both sides, and all were rejected.

Meantime the strife went on. St. Clair wrote, in 1774: "As much the greatest part of the inhabitants near the line have removed from Virginia, they are inexpressibly fond of everything that comes from that quarter, and their minds are never suffered to be at rest."[1] He also describes the panic as so great that it threatened to depopulate the country. He charged Dunmore with desiring to bring on an Indian war, which charge proved to be true. His Lordship was more than suspected of having an interest in lands over which he proposed to extend the jurisdiction of Virginia. Governor Penn told the Westmoreland magistrates that, as he could not raise a militia like the Governor of Virginia, it was vain to contend with the Virginians "in the way of force," and warned them not to enter into such contests with Dunmore's officers, or even to proceed against them by way of criminal prosecution for exercising the powers of government. Dunmore himself visited Pittsburg; and in 1775 the Augusta County Court sat for two terms at Pittsburg, at which terms Pennsylvanians were arraigned for defying Virginia authority. Finally, the Pennsylvanians carried Connolly off to Philadelphia, and then the Virginians retaliated by sending some Pennsylvanians to Wheeling as hostages.

---

[1] St. Clair Papers, I., 284.

It is but fair to say that this unhappy controversy was forced by Lord Dunmore rather than by Virginia. He continued to carry things with a strong hand, despite the steady resistance of the Pennsylvania authorities, down to the Indian war that takes its name from him, which was another part of his arbitrary Western policy, and even to the time that he went on board the man-of-war that saved him from the vengeance of the Virginians.

Perhaps there is no better illustration of the confused state of affairs in those Pennsylvania wilds than the conduct of Colonel William Crawford, the mention of whose name always suggests the terrible tragedy that closed his life. Crawford was a Virginian by birth, and marched to Fort Duquesne with the Virginia troops in 1758. In 1765 he made his home on the Youghiogheny River, in the disputed district. He was Washington's Western land-agent for many years, and his letters to him and to St. Clair throw much light on the events in the midst of which he moved. He accepted a commission as a Pennsylvania magistrate in 1770, and sided with this State in the boundary-controversy until 1774; then, accepting a commission from Dunmore, he took an active part in the Indian war, calling out from St. Clair the remark: "I don't know how gentlemen account for these things to themselves;" and afterward he became a Virginia magistrate for the County of Augusta.

At the opening of the Revolution the dispute between the two States threatened danger to the patriot cause. The subject did not come before Congress as a body, but, July 25, 1775, the members of Congress united in the following recommendation to the people living in the disputed territory: "We recommend it to you that all bodies of armed men, kept up by either party, be dismissed; and that all those on either side who are in confinement, or on bail, for taking part in the contest, be discharged."[1] And this was the end of active strife.

---

[1] St. Clair Papers, I., 361.

In 1779 commissioners appointed by the two States met at Baltimore to agree upon the common boundaries of Pennsylvania and Virginia. In the ensuing correspondence the Pennsylvania commissioners had much to say of "the beginning of the fortieth degree," the Virginia commissioners much of the twelve-mile circle. On both sides there was an evident desire to end the dispute. Various lines were proposed and rejected. On August 31 the commissioners signed this agreement: "To extend Mason and Dixon's line due west five degrees of longitude, to be computed from the River Delaware, for the southern boundary of Pennsylvania, and that a meridian line drawn from the western extremity thereof to the northern limit of the said State be the western boundary of Pennsylvania forever."[1] This contract was duly ratified by the legislatures of the two States. In 1785 Mason and Dixon's line was extended, and the southwestern corner of Pennsylvania established. The "Pan-handle" is what was left of Virginia east of the Ohio River and north of Mason and Dixon's line, after the boundary was run from this point to Lake Erie in 1786.[2]

Ere this Virginia had acknowledged, in her constitution of 1776, the validity of the grants made at her expense so far as the shore States are concerned:

"The territories, contained within the charters, erecting the colonies of Maryland, Pennsylvania, North and South Carolina, are hereby ceded, released, and forever confirmed to the people of these Colonies respectively, with all the rights of property, jurisdiction, and government, and all other rights whatsoever, which might, at any time heretofore, have been claimed by Virginia, except the free navigation and use of the rivers Pato-

---

[1] The correspondence is found in X. Hening's Statutes of Virginia.
[2] "When the State of Ohio was formed, in 1802, the Pan-handle first showed its beautiful proportions on the map of the United States. It received its name in legislative debate from Hon. John McMillan, delegate from Brooke County, to match the Accomac projection, which he dubbed the Spoon-handle."—Cregh. Hist. Wash. Co., Pa., quoted by Butterfield. Crawford's Expedition, 14, note.

maque and Pokomoke, with the property of the Virginia shores and strands, bordering on either of the said rivers, and all improvements, which have been, or shall be made thereon."

The most serious of all the disputes that originated in the grant to William Penn was that with Connecticut; a dispute that, in the words of a Pennsylvania writer, "was over the political jurisdiction and right of soil in a tract of country containing more than 5,000,000 acres of lands;" that "involved the lives of hundreds, was the ruin of thousands, and cost the State millions;" that "wore out one entire generation;" that "evoked strong partisanship," was "urged, on both sides, by the highest skill of statesmen and lawyers," and was "righteously settled in the end."[1]

The grant made to Penn, carried to latitude 43° north, jumped half a dozen New England charters; carried to 42° north, it jumped all those in which Connecticut was interested, and notably the one given by Charles II. to the Governor and Company of Connecticut in 1662. West of the Delaware, south of the forty-second parallel, north of the forty-first, and east of the western limit of Pennsylvania, was the tract of 5,000,000 acres that the two colonies claimed; a tract full of coal, iron, and oil, and of great fertility. Apparently the earliest intimation that anybody in Connecticut was thinking of these Western lands is found in a letter written to the Lords of Trade in 1720, by Governor Saltonstall: "On the west the province of New York have carried their claim and government through this colony from north to south, and *cut us asunder* twenty miles east of the Hudson."

New Haven had taken an early interest in the Delaware region. At one time there was a considerable probability that the major part of the town would go there in a body; and Mr.

---

[1] Hoyt: Brief of a Title in the Seventeen Townships in the County of Luzerne, 5.

Levermore says that after 1666 the New Haven of Davenport and Eaton must be sought upon the banks of the Passaic.[1]

Following the Peace of Aix-la-Chapelle there was a great outburst of interest in the West, and particularly in Virginia and Connecticut; the first finding her "West" in the Ohio Valley, and the second hers in the Susquehanna country. Connecticut was now well filled up with people, according to the ideas of those days, and a scheme to settle the colony's lands west of New York was thrown before the public in 1753. One hundred petitioners, many of them of high standing in the colony, asked the General Court for a grant of land. The Susquehanna Company was organized to promote the scheme; and in 1755 the General Court recommended it to the favor of the king.

The company sent its agents to Albany in 1754, when the Albany Congress was in session, where they purchased from certain Iroquois chiefs, for £2,000, a tract of land lying within the Connecticut parallels, one hundred and twenty miles in length, from ten miles east of the Susquehanna westward.

Another important thing was done at Albany in 1754. The Congress itself, by a unanimous vote, not even the Pennsylvania Commissioners objecting, adopted a series of resolutions declaring the validity of the Connecticut and Massachusetts claims west of the Delaware, and also of the western claims of Virginia. Besides, the "Plan of Union" recommended by the Congress provided a machinery for carrying on Western colonization; and Franklin, in his notes on the "plan," remarked that "the from 'sea to sea' colonies, having boundaries three thousand or four thousand miles in length to one or two hundred in breadth, must in time be reduced to domains more convenient for the common purposes of government."[2]

In 1755 the Susquehanna Company sent out surveyors to

---

[1] The Republic of New Haven, 113-120.
[2] Sparks: Writings of Franklin, III., 32-55.

survey the lands on the Lackawaxen and in the Wyoming Valley. The colonization-fever rose so high that a second company, called the Delaware Company, was organized, and this also made a purchase of lands from the Indians. Notwithstanding the French and Indian war, a settlement was made on the Delaware in 1757, and another on the Susquehanna in 1762. In 1768 the elder company directed the survey of five townships in the heart of the Wyoming Valley, and in the same year Captain Zebulon Butler, with forty men, took possession of one of them, taking the precaution to build a fort as a protection against the Indians, and possibly the Pennsylvanians also.

Thus far the Penns had done nothing but object to the Susquehanna Company and its aims. Up to 1769 not a single Pennsylvania settler was anywhere in the neighborhood of the plantings that the Connecticut men had made. But now the proprietors began to bestir themselves. They improved the opportunity furnished by the Congress at Fort Stanwix, in 1768, to buy " of the Indians all that part of the province of Pennsylvania not heretofore purchased of the Indians," and this included the whole Connecticut claim. They also began to lease lands in the Connecticut district on the condition that the lessees should defend them against the Connecticut claimants; and the attempt of these lessees to oust the settlers already in possession, backed by the Pennsylvania authorities, brought on a skirmish of writs and arrests that soon led to the first " Pennamite and Yankee War," in which the lessees literally, and the settlers figuratively, spread out as their respective banners the Penn leases and the charter of 1662.

Connecticut men pressed into the territory in increasing numbers. The accomplished historian of Windham County says : " The fertility of the soil, the mildness of the climate, the beauty of the country, and the abundance of its resources far excelled expectations; and such glowing reports came back to the rocky farms of Windham County, that emigration raged for a time like an epidemic and seemed likely to sweep away a great part of the population."[1] Hitherto the Connecticut government had done nothing to promote the Susquehanna and Delaware schemes, but commended the first to the good graces of the king. Even in 1771 Governor Trumbull, on being interrogated by the authorities at Philadelphia, wrote that the persons engaged therein had no order or direction from him, or from the General Assembly for their proceedings, and that the Assembly, he was confident, would "never countenance any violent, much less hostile, measures in vindicating the rights which the Susquehanna Company supposed they had to lands in that part of the country within the limits of the charter of their colony." As the State did not recognize them, and as they could not get on without government, the colonists proceeded to organize a government of their own after the purest democratic model. Townships, settlements, fortifications, taxes, civil and criminal legal processes, and a militia, were provided for. But the colony had taken too strong a hold of Connecticut for the government to disown it, even if the charter-claim to the country had been much weaker than it was. So the General Court resolved, in 1773, "That this Assembly, at this time, will assist, and in some proper way support their claim to those lands contained within the limits and boundaries of their charter which are westward of the province of New York." Commissioners were sent to Philadelphia to arrange matters with the Penns, if possible, but they returned empty-handed. So the Assembly, in 1774, erected the territory from the Delaware to a line fifteen miles west of the Susquehanna, into the town of Westmoreland, attaching it to Litchfield County, Connecticut; and two years later it organized the same territory into the County of Westmoreland. The extemporized government of the settlers now gave place to the government set up by the mother colony. Thus the colonists and Connecticut carried things with a strong hand down to

---

[1] Miss Larned: History of Windham County, IL, 49-51.

8

the Revolution, when the population numbered three thousand. How great the promise was for a new Connecticut in Northern Pennsylvania, a Connecticut writer shall tell.

"Connecticut laws and taxes were enforced regularly; Connecticut courts alone were in session; and the levies from the district formed the Twenty-fourth Connecticut Regiment in the Continental armies. The sordid, grasping, long-leasing policy of the Penns had never been able to stand a moment before the oncoming wave of Connecticut democracy, with its individual land ownership, its liberal local government, and the personal incentive offered to individuals by its town system. So far as the Penns were concerned, the Connecticut town system simply swept over them, and hardly thought of them as it went. But for the Revolution, the check occasioned by the massacre, and the appearance of a popular government in place of the Penns, nothing could have prevented the establishment of Connecticut's authority over all the regions embraced in her Western claims."[1]

But the Penns were not idle. In 1761 they obtained from Attorney-General Pratt, afterward Lord Camden, an opinion that firmly supported their cause. Connecticut, too, sought unto men learned in the law. She obtained from Lord Thurlow, Wedderburn, afterward Lord Loughborough, Chancellor Dunning, and Mr. Jackson the counsel that she wanted. The Penns determined at last to resort to that argument which their great ancestor had so much deprecated. In 1772 one Colonel Plunkett, under orders from the government, destroyed some Connecticut settlements on the west bank of the Susquehanna; and late in 1775, with a strong force, he attempted to drive the settlers out of the Wyoming Valley, but was repulsed. At this point the Continental Congress broke in upon the dispute, in the name of the common cause against the mother country, with a "whereas" that the quar-

---

[1] Johnston: Connecticut, 278.

rel, if continued, would be productive of consequences very prejudicial to the common interest of the colonies, and with an urgent recommendation "that the contending parties immediately cease all hostilities, and avoid every appearance of force, until the dispute can be legally decided."[1] This remonstrance produced the desired effect.

The Westmorelanders stood as an outpost in the war against Great Britain, and in 1778, when nearly all the able-bodied men were absent in the army, two savages, Butler the Tory and Brandt the Indian, wrought at Wyoming a deed of blood that, wherever told during a hundred years, has never failed to move horror and pity. The men, women, and children who then fell at the hands of the enemy, or perished miserably in the wilderness from hunger, disease, or fatigue, were not Pennsylvanians. The Gertrudes of Wyoming were all Connecticut girls. The massacre materially strengthened Pennsylvania's case: a Westmoreland containing thousands of thriving people was one thing; a Westmoreland that was waste and desolate, quite another.

The parties had submitted the dispute to the King in Council, but the war rendered the appeal to that fountain of justice nugatory. Article IX. of the Confederation vested jurisdiction over such disputes between States in Congress. So, as the war was now drawing to a close, Pennsylvania called upon that arbiter to decide between the contestants. A Federal court was accordingly organized to try the issue; and this court, at Trenton, December 30, 1782, after a full hearing, rendered the following decision:

"We are unanimously of opinion that the State of Connecticut has no right to the lands in controversy.

"We are also unanimously of opinion that the jurisdiction and pre-emption of all the territory lying within the charter-boundary of Pennsylvania, and now claimed by the State of Connecticut, do of right belong to the State of Pennsylvania."[2]

---

[1] Journals of Congress, I., 211.   [2] Ibid., IV., 140.

Ten or more years after the trial, it became known that the court agreed beforehand "that the reasons for the determination should never be given," and "that the minority should concede the determination as the unanimous opinion of the court." The first of the two rules suggests at once, what, indeed, has always been understood to be true, that the court did not consider the points of law involved at all, but that the case, as lawyers say, " went off on State reasons."

The Trenton decision, while final and conclusive as to the public corporate rights of Connecticut, in no way touched the land-owners, who, the war over, began to find their way back to their old homes. These were left to the justice or mercy of Pennsylvania; and it is to be feared that the treatment they received sometimes made them think more kindly of Butler and of Brandt. The Trenton judges all commended the unfortunate holders to the favorable consideration of the victor State, urging that they should be quieted in all their claims by an act of the Assembly, and that the right of soil, as derived from Connecticut, should be held sacred. There now ensued that generation of legislation and litigation, " Yankee claims," and "accommodation" and " intrusion " acts, of Ethan Allen and his Vermont methods, of plans to organize a new State and to force its recognition upon Pennsylvania and Congress, and reckless agitation which together make up the second " Pennamite and Yankee War." The " Accommodation Act," once repealed and then re-enacted, put an end to the strife.

Had the court of 1782 decided this issue the other way, Connecticut could not permanently have retained the country; a State of Westmoreland would have been the almost certain result. The conviction that one State within the present limits of Pennsylvania would be better than two was probably one of the State reasons that led the court to its conclusion. However, when the second " Pennamite and Yankee War" was in progress, and still more when it was over, Connecticut men flowed into the Northern belt of Pennsylvania, where their presence is seen to-day in New England names, towns, and manners.

The decision of 1782 was wider than the case submitted, applying as it did to the whole Connecticut claim within the charter-limits of Pennsylvania; but Connecticut made no objection on that score. Fortunately for her, Pennsylvania had a definite boundary on the west. Carrying her stake westward, she resolutely drove it into the ground five degrees west of the Delaware; that is, she asserted her right to the strip of land lying between 41° and 42° 2' west of Pennsylvania to the Mississippi River, which, by the treaties of 1763 and 1783, had taken the place of the South Sea as the western boundary. In 1783 Governor Trumbull issued a proclamation forbidding all persons to settle on those lands without permission first obtained of the General Assembly.

The good grace with which Connecticut submitted to the Trenton decision has excited the surprise of historians, who have cast about for the cause. Governor Hoyt supposes "that Connecticut had prearranged the case with Pennsylvania and Congress, and that out of the arrangement she was to get the Western Reserve," and refers for proof to a congressional report on finance, made a month after the decision, which says: "Virginia and Connecticut have also made cessions, the acceptance of which, for particular reasons, have been delayed."[1] Mr. Johnston also supposes "that Connecticut had reasons apart from the justice of the decision," and he finds them in the relation of the Western lands to the question of American nationality.[2] The suggestion is ventured that if Connecticut was actuated by any reason other than deference to the authority of the Trenton tribunal, it was a desire to strengthen her position west of the Pennsylvania line. She would evidently be better able to deal with the new dispute if the old one was off her hands.

The Pennsylvania construction of the charter of 1681 was

---

[1] Brief of Title, etc., 46, 47.   [2] Connecticut, 280, 281.

wholly satisfactory to New York, when the time came for her to look after the country west of the Delaware. That construction saved her a dispute, and, possibly, a large extent of her present territory as well.[1] Commissioners appointed by the two colonies fixed the northeastern boundary of Pennsylvania on an island in the Delaware in 1774; the line west of that point was surveyed in 1786-87, and ratified in 1789.

The northern boundary of Connecticut is 42° 2', the southern boundary of New York 42°; and the overlapping tract, called at the time "the Gore," led to a controversy between the two States. In 1795 Connecticut, for the consideration of $40,000, quit-claimed to Ward and Halsey all her right and title to the said strip of land. Those to whom they sold the lands found settlers with New York titles already in possession. In 1796 suits were brought in the United States Circuit Court to eject the New York claimants. Before the cases were heard, Connecticut wholly renounced her right and title to land or jurisdiction west of the line of 1733, which threw the suitors out of court. This act of renunciation led to long and bitter murmuring on the part of those holding the Ward and Halsey titles, which was finally quieted, partly by time and partly by a compensation voted from the State treasury.

Massachusetts fared much better than Connecticut in maintaining her Western title. Her cession of 1785 to the nation will be treated in another place; but here it is important to remark that that cession did not touch her contest with New York for the lands within her charter-limits west of the Delaware and east of the north and south cession-line. That issue was compromised in 1786. Massachusetts surrendered to New York all her claim to the jurisdiction over said tract; and New York surrendered to Massachusetts all claim to the lands within the Massachusetts limits lying west of a line

---

[1] Maps of the middle of the last century often bound Pennsylvania north by parallel 43°.

running from the eighty-second mile-post west of the northeast corner of Pennsylvania north to Sodus Bay in Lake Ontario. This tract, the southeast corner of which is a little southwest of Elmira, embraced several million acres of land, including the famous Genesee Valley.

In June, 1788, Congress instructed the Geographer to run the meridian by which New York and Massachusetts had limited themselves on the west, and to ascertain the quantity of land in the triangular tract lying west of said meridian and north of parallel 42° north. This tract was sold to the State of Pennsylvania the same year. The act of Congress authorizing the President to issue the letters patent bears date, January 3, 1792.

Mr. H. G. Stevens writes: "Dear fussy old Richard Hakluyt, the most learned geographer of his age, but with certain crude and warped notions of the South Sea 'down the back of Florida,' which became worked into many of King James's and King Charles's charters, and the many grants that grew out of them, was the unconscious parent of many geographical puzzles."[1] Puzzles there are in abundance, whether Hakluyt was the parent of them or not. The principal of these puzzles on the Atlantic slope we have sought to solve. In future chapters we shall consider the similar ones found in the Northwest.

---

[1] Narrative and Critical History, V., 180.

VIII.

THE WESTERN LAND POLICY OF THE BRITISH GOVERNMENT FROM 1763 TO 1775.

THE ink with which the Treaty of Paris was written was hardly dry when Great Britain took a very important step in the line of a new land-policy. Just how much this step meant at the time is a matter of dispute, but the consequences flowing from it were such as to mark it a distinct new departure.

Previous to the war, England had virtually affirmed the principle that the discoverer and occupant of a coast was entitled to all the country back of it; she had carried her colonial boundaries through the continent from sea to sea; and, as against France, had maintained the original chartered limits of her colonies. Moreover, the grant to the Ohio Company in 1748 proves that she then had no thought of preventing over-mountain settlements, or of limiting the expansion of the colonies in that direction. But now that France had retired from the field vanquished, England began to see things in new relations. In fact, the situation was materially changed. She was left in undisputed possession of the eastern half of the Mississippi Valley. Canada and Florida were British dependencies, and governments must be provided for them. The Indians of the West were discontented and angry; and, strange to say, at the very moment that they lost the support of France, they formed, under Pontiac, a widespread combination against the British power. Then the strength and resource that the colonies had shown in the war had both pleased and disturbed the mother country;

pleased her because they contributed materially to the defeat of France, and disturbed her because they portended a still larger growth of that spirit of independence which had already become somewhat embarrassing. The eagerness with which the Virginians and Pennsylvanians were preparing to enter the Ohio Valley in the years 1748–1754 told England what might be expected now that the whole country lay open to the Mississippi. The home government undertook to meet the occasion with the royal proclamation of October 7, 1763.

After congratulating his subjects upon the great advantages that must accrue to their trade, manufactures, and navigation from the new acquisitions of territory, His Majesty proceeded to constitute four new governments, three of them on the continent and one in the West Indies. His new territories on the Gulf he divided into East Florida and West Florida, by the Appalachicola River; separating them from his possessions to the north by the thirty-first parallel from the Mississippi River to the Chattahoochee, by that stream to its confluence with the Flint, by a straight line drawn from this point to the source of the St. Marys, and then by the St. Marys to the Atlantic Ocean. The next year, in consequence of representations made to him that there were considerable settlements north of the thirty-first parallel which should be included in West Florida, he drew the northern boundary of that province through the mouth of the Yazoo. The territory lying between the Altamaha and St. Marys Rivers, so long the subject of dispute between Spain and England, as well as between South Carolina and Georgia, was given to Georgia. It was the proclamation of 1763 that first defined what afterward became the first southern boundary of the United States. As I shall have occasion to refer to them again, it will be well to give the boundaries of Quebec in the words of the royal proclamation.

"The Government of Quebec, bounded on the Labrador coast by the River St. John [Saguenay], and from thence to a line drawn from the head of that river, through the Lake St. John, to the south end of the Lake Nipissim; from whence the said line crossing the River St. Lawrence and the Lake Champlain, in forty-five degrees of north latitude, passes along the highlands which divide the rivers that empty themselves into the said River St. Lawrence, from those which fall into the sea; and also along the north coast of the Baie des Chaleurs, and the coast of the Gulf of St. Lawrence to Cape Rosieres, and from thence crossing the mouth of the River St. Lawrence by the west end of the Island of Anticosti, terminates at the aforesaid River St. John."[1]

The king gives directions for constituting the governments of the new provinces on the principle of representation. He also instructs the royal governors to grant lands to the officers and men who have served in the army and navy in the war, according to a prescribed schedule.

It will be seen that the country west of the mountains, from parallel 31° to the lakes, was not embraced within the new governments. But this was not due to a sensitive regard for the chartered rights of the old colonies, as the following paragraph defining the new departure shows:

"We do, therefore, with the advice of our privy council, declare it to be our royal will and pleasure, that no governor or commander-in-chief, in any of our Colonies of Quebec, East Florida, or West Florida, do presume, upon any pretense whatever, to grant warrants of survey, or pass any patents for lands beyond the bounds of their respective governments, as described in their commissions; as also that no governor or commander-in-chief of our other colonies or plantations in America, do presume, for the present, and until our further pleasure be known, to grant warrants of survey or pass patents for any lands beyond the heads or sources of any of the rivers which fall into the Atlantic Ocean from the west or northwest; or upon any lands whatever, which not having been ceded or purchased by us," etc.

---

[1] The Annual Register, 1763.

Just what was the meaning of this prohibition has been a matter of dispute from that day to this; the opinions of the disputants depending, often at least, upon the relation of those opinions to other matters of interest. Solicitude for the Indians, and anxiety for the peace and safety of the colonies, are the reasons alleged in the proclamation itself. The "whereas" introducing the proclamation says it is essential to the royal interest and the security of the colonies that the tribes of Indians living under the king's protection shall not be molested or disturbed in the possession of such parts of his dominions and territories as, not having been ceded to or purchased by him, are reserved to them as their hunting grounds; and a declaration follows the prohibition that it is his royal will and pleasure, for the present, to reserve under his sovereign protection and dominion, for the use of the said Indians, all the lands within the new governments, within the limits of the Hudson Bay Company and beyond the sources of the rivers falling into the sea from the west and northwest. The king strictly forbids his loving subjects making any purchases or settlements whatever, or taking possession of any of the lands described, without his special leave and license; and he further enjoins all persons who have seated themselves upon any of the lands so reserved to the Indians, forthwith to abandon them. If at any time the Indians are inclined to dispose of their lands, they shall be purchased only in the king's name, by the governor or commander-in-chief of the colony within which the lands lie. The proclamation winds up with some wholesome regulations respecting the Indian trade.

No doubt a desire to conciliate the Indians was one of the motives that led to the prohibition of 1763. But was it the only motive? Was it also the royal intention permanently to sever the lands beyond the sources of the rivers flowing into the Atlantic from the old colonies within whose charter-limits they lay? and, when the time should come, to cut them up into new and independent governments?

"The Annual Register" for 1763 says many reasons may be assigned for the prohibition. It states the necessity of quieting the Indians, and then presents the desirability of limiting the "from sea to sea" boundaries.

"Another reason, we suppose, why no disposition has been made of the inland country, was, that the charters of many of our old colonies give them, with very few exceptions, no other bounds to the westward but the South Sea; and consequently these grants comprehended almost everything we have conquered. These charters were given when this continent was little known and little valued. They were then scarce acquainted with any other limits than the limits of America itself; and they were prodigal of what they considered as of no great importance. The colonies settled under royal government have, generally, been laid out much in the same manner; and though the difficulties which arise on this quarter are not so great as in the former, they are yet sufficiently embarrassing. Nothing can be more inconvenient, or can be attended with more absurd consequences, than to admit the execution of the powers in those grants and distributions of territory in all their extent. But where the western boundary of each colony ought to be settled, is a matter which must admit of great dispute, and can, to all appearance, only be finally adjusted by the interposition of Parliament."[1]

Obviously, Edmund Burke, or whoever wrote the "Register's" review for that year, thought the prohibition meant something more than simply to guard the rights of the Indians. Washington, on the other hand, wrote his Western land-agent, Colonel Crawford, in 1767: "I can never look upon that proclamation in any other light (but this I say between ourselves) than a temporary expedient to quiet the minds of the Indians. It must fall, of course, in a few years, especially when those Indians consent to our occupying the

---

[1] The Annual Register, 1763, 20, 21.

lands."[1] The authors of the Report on the Territorial Limits of the United States, made to Congress, January 8, 1782, examined the proclamation very thoroughly, and came to the same conclusion that Washington had arrived at fifteen years before. They declare the king's object to have been "to keep the Indians in peace, not to relinquish the rights accruing under the charters, and especially that of pre-emption."[2] Dr. Franklin held the same view, as we shall soon see. Mr. Bancroft says the West " was shut against the emigrant from fear that colonies in so remote a region could not be held in dependence. England, by war, had conquered the West, and a ministry had come which dared not make use of the conquest."[3] No matter what the proclamation meant, it was a great disappointment to the colonies. "Wherein are we better off, as respects the Western country," they said in substance, "than we were before the war?"

No man of his time more thoroughly comprehended the Western question than Dr. Franklin. Notices of his principal writings on the subject will more clearly define that question, and throw much light on its shifting phases.

Reference has already been made to the Plan of Union adopted by the Albany Congress in 1754, and to Franklin's exposition of the same. This "plan" placed the regulation of the Indian trade, the purchasing of Indian lands, and the planting of new colonies under the control of the Union. Franklin supported this part of the scheme with the obvious arguments. A single colony could not be expected to extend itself into the West; but the Union might establish a new colony or two, greatly to the security of the frontiers, to increase of population and trade, and to breaking the French connections between Canada and Louisiana.[4] The "from sea to sea" colonies must be suitably limited on the west.

Soon after the Albany Congress, Franklin wrote his

---

[1] Butterfield: Washington-Crawford Letters, 3.
[2] Secret Journals of Congress, III., 154.   [3] History, III., 32.
[4] Sparks: Writings of Franklin, III., 32-55.

"Plan for Settling two Western Colonies in North America, with Reasons for the Plan." He says the country back of the Appalachian Mountains must become, perhaps in another century, a populous and powerful dominion, and a great accession of power to either England or France. If the English delay to settle that country, great inconveniences and mischiefs will arise. Confined to the region between the sea and the mountains, they cannot much more increase in numbers owing to lack of room and subsistence. The French will increase much more, and become a great people in the rear of the English. He therefore recommends that the English take immediate possession of the country, and proceed at once to plant two strong colonies, one on the Ohio and one on Lake Erie. The new colonies will soon be full of people; they will prevent the disasters sure to follow if the French are allowed to have their way in the West; the Ohio country will be a good base for operations against Canada and Louisiana in case of war; and the colonies will promote the increase of Englishmen, of English trade, and of English power. Franklin again assumes that the "from sea to sea" charters are still in force, and argues that they must be limited by the Western mountains. The tract closes with a plea for urgency.[1] War with the French had now begun, and new colonies were necessarily postponed until the sword should decide the destiny of the West; but Franklin still kept the subject in mind. In 1756 he wrote to Rev. George Whitfield:

"I sometimes wish that you and I were jointly employed by the Crown to settle a colony on the Ohio. I imagine that we could do it effectually, and without putting the nation to much expense; but I fear we shall never be called upon for such a service. What a glorious thing it would be to settle in that fine country a large, strong body of religious and industrious people! What a security to the other colonies and advantage to Britain, by increasing her people, territory, strength, and com-

---
[1] Sparks: III., 69-77.

merce! Might it not greatly facilitate the introduction of pure religion among the heathen, if we could, by such a colony, show them a better sample of Christians than they commonly see in our Indian traders?—the most vicious and abandoned wretches of our nation."[1]

Immediately after Wolfe's victory in 1759, men on both sides of the ocean began to speculate upon the terms of the peace that they saw must soon come. It seemed inevitable that England would be able to dictate her own terms to her old enemy; and the question arose, what territorial indemnities and securities she should exact. More specifically, the question arose whether Canada should be retained or returned to France in exchange for Guadaloupe. Two or three pamphlets discussing this question appeared in London. To one of them, that advocated the surrender of Canada, published without a name, but sometimes ascribed to Edmund Burke, Franklin wrote a reply that he entitled "The Interest of Great Britain Considered with Regard to the Colonies and the Acquisition of Canada and Guadaloupe," but that is commonly called "The Canada Pamphlet." A rapid review of this vigorous production will throw much light upon the state of opinion touching the West both in America and in Europe.

Franklin holds, in opposition to his antagonist, that England might properly demand Canada as an indemnification, although she had not, in the outset, put forward such an acquisition as one of the objects of the war. He argues that the relations of England and France in America are such as to prevent a lasting peace, declaring that such a peace can come only when the whole country is subject to the English government. Disputes arising in America will be the occasion of European wars. Wars between the two powers originating in Europe will extend to America, and give oppor-

---

[1] Bigelow: Works of Franklin, II., 467.

tunities for other powers to interfere. The boundaries between the English and French in North America cannot be so drawn as to prevent quarrels. The frontier must necessarily be more than fifteen hundred miles in length. Happy was it for both Holland and England that the Dutch, in 1674, ceded New Netherlands to the English; since that time peace between them has continued unbroken, which would have been impossible if the Dutch had continued to hold that province, separating, as it does, the eastern and middle British colonies.

Franklin next contends that erecting forts in the back settlements will not prove a sufficient security against the French and Indians, but that the retention of Canada implies every security. The possession of that province, and that alone, can give the English colonies in America peace.

He then devotes several pages to the proposition that the blood and treasure spent in the war were not spent in the cause of the colonies alone. This is in reply to the argument that the interests at stake in America were rather colonial than British or imperial. The retention of Canada will widen the landed opportunities of the colonists, and will tend to keep them agricultural and to prevent manufactures. Franklin then enunciates a proposition that would make Pennsylvania economists of to-day stare and gasp. "Manufactures are founded in poverty. It is the multitude of poor without land in a country, and who must work for others at low wages or starve, that enables undertakers to carry on a manufacture, and afford it cheap enough to prevent the importation of the same kind from abroad, and to bear the expense of its own exportation." He contends that the North American colonies are the western frontier of the British Empire; that they must be defended by the empire for that reason, and that Canada will be a conquest for the whole, the advantage of which will come in increase of trade and ease of taxes.

To the argument that the colonies are large and numerous enough, and that the French ought to be left in North

LAND POLICY OF THE BRITISH GOVERNMENT.

America to keep them in check, Franklin replies that, in time of peace, the colonists double by natural generation once in twenty-five years, and that they will probably continue to do so for a century to come; but that the colonies will not cease to be useful to the Mother Country for that reason. On this point he accumulates a variety of information relating to the industrial and commercial possibilities of the country east of the Mississippi River that is as interesting as curious. One hundred millions of people can subsist in the agricultural condition east of that river and south of the Lakes and the St. Lawrence. The facilities for inland navigation are dwelt upon with admiration. Franklin dwells at much length upon the improbability of the colonists taking up manufactures, and upon the vast quantities of British goods that they will be sure to buy and consume.

Having striven at such length to prove that the colonies will not be useless to the Mother Country, he takes up the proposition that they will not be dangerous to her. This is the most delicate subject handled in the whole pamphlet, and one that attracted attention before the war began. Kalm, the Swedish naturalist who visited the colonies in 1748, and who saw so much more than natural objects in the course of his travels, reports that in New York he found much doubt whether the King of England, if he had the power, would wish to drive the French out of Canada. Kalm thus expresses his own opinion: "As this whole country is toward the sea unguarded, and on the frontier is kept uneasy by the French, these dangerous neighbors are the reason why the love of these colonies for their metropolis does not utterly decline. The English Government has, therefore, reason to regard the French in North America as the chief power that urges their colonies to submission."[1] It is well known that Choiseul warned Stanley when the two ministers were discussing the treaty of 1763, that the English colonies in America " would

---

[1] Bancroft: History, II., 310-311.

not fail to shake off their dependence the moment Canada should be ceded."[1] This feeling was shared by many people in England, and it probably influenced those who said "Guadaloupe not Canada" quite as much as the superiority of the Guadaloupe sugar to the Canada furs. Such is a fair statement of the argument that Franklin sets himself to answer.

His reply is "that the colonies cannot be dangerous to England without union, and that union is impossible." To prove that union is impossible, he sets forth the jealousies of the colonies and the failure of all attempts hitherto made to bring them to act together. There are now fourteen separate governments on the sea-coast, and there will probably be as many more behind them on the inland side. These have different governors, different laws, different forms of government, different interests, different religious persuasions, and different manners. "If they could not agree to unite for their defence against the French and Indians, who were perpetually harassing their settlements, burning their villages, and murdering their people, can it reasonably be supposed there is any danger of their uniting against their own nation, which protects and encourages them, with which they have so many connections and ties of blood, interest, and affection, and which, it is well known, they all love much more than they love one another?" And yet Franklin was careful to leave an open door through which he could have escaped the charge of inconsistency if such charge had been preferred a dozen years later. "When I say such a union is impossible, I mean without the most grievous tyranny and oppression." "The waves do not rise," he says, "but when the winds blow." What such an administration as the Duke of Alva's might bring about he does not know; but he has a right to deem that impossible. Under this head he answers the argument "that the remoteness of the Western territories will bring about their separation from the Mother Country." "While our

---

[1] Parkman: Montcalm and Wolfe, II., 403.

strength at sea continues, the banks of the Ohio, in point of easy and expeditious conveyance of troops, are nearer to London than the remote parts of France and Spain to their respective capitals, and much nearer than Connaught and Ulster were in the days of Queen Elizabeth." Of the two, the presence of the French in Canada will engender disaffection in the colonies rather than prevent it. The only check on their growth that the French can possibly be, is that of blood and carnage.

Franklin then argues that Canada can·be easily peopled from the colonies without draining Great Britain of her inhabitants. Last of all comes the proposition that the value of Guadaloupe is much overestimated by those who prefer that island to Canada.

Many of the arguments contained in this famous pamphlet would now be set aside by an economist as fallacious; but, fallacious as they may be, they have that plain directness which, along with other qualities, rendered Franklin's political tracts so conclusive to the common mind. The pamphlet attracted great attention at the time, and "was believed," according to Dr. Sparks, " to have had great weight in the ministerial councils, and to have been mainly instrumental in causing Canada to be held at the peace."[1]

In 1765, Sir William Johnson, Governor Franklin, and other influential persons formed a project for establishing a new colony in the Illinois country. They applied to Dr. Franklin, then in London, acting as agent for Pennsylvania, for assistance, and he entered warmly into the enterprise, in which he also had an interest. For a time the application for a grant of lands was regarded with much favor, but was finally rejected. The Doctor's letters to his son, in the years 1766–1768, report the progress of the negotiation, and help us to understand English opinion touching Western settlements. He found the following objections urged against

---

[1] Sparks: IV., 1-53.

the plan: (1) The distance would render such a colony of little use to England, as the expense of the carriage of goods would urge the people to manufacture for themselves; (2) the distance would also render it difficult to defend and govern the colony; (3) such a colony might, in time, become troublesome and prejudicial to the British Government; (4) there were no people to spare, either in England or the other colonies, to settle a new colony. Lord Hillsborough was terribly afraid of "dispeopling Ireland." To overturn these objections, Franklin brought forward the arguments with which we are now familiar. Some London merchants, who were called upon for testimony, gave the unanimous opinion that colonies in the Illinois country and at Detroit would enlarge British commerce. Franklin "reckoned" that there would be 63,000,000 acres of land in the proposed colony. He also reported an inclination on the part of ministers to abandon the Western posts as more expensive than useful, unless the colonies should see fit to keep them up at their own expense. Fort Pitt was actually abandoned soon after.

Here I must interrupt the narrative concerning Franklin, to state some other facts material to the purpose. In 1768 Stuart, the Southern Indian agent, following the proclamation of 1763, and the instructions of Lord Hillsborough, negotiated with the Cherokees, who had no claim whatever to lands on the south side of the Ohio, a treaty that was very obnoxious to Virginia, since it limited her on the west by the Kanawha River. A few days later Sir William Johnson, the Northern agent, negotiated with the Six Nations, who claimed the country to the Cumberland Mountains, a treaty that was much more to her liking. This treaty established the following boundary-line between the lands that the Nations claimed in the West and the lands of the whites on the East: The Ohio and Alleghany Rivers from the mouth of the Cherokee, as the Tennessee was then called, to Kittan-

---

[1] Sparks: IV., 233-241.

ning, above Fort Pitt; thence by a direct line east to the west branch of the Susquehanna; thence through the mountains to the east branch, and on to the Delaware; and finally by the Delaware, the Tianaderher, and Canada Creek to Wood Creek, above Fort Stanwix. While this line left nearly one-half of the State of New York in the hands of the Six Nations, it gave to the colonies the whole southeastern half of the Ohio Valley to the Tennessee. This line itself shows that the Nations regarded their Western possessions but lightly. It should be observed, also, that the alienation of their claim still left the English to deal with the Indians actually on the Western soil. In the end, this boundary came very near giving Virginia a still closer limitation on the west than the one drawn by Stuart, as will soon appear. The opening up of the country south of the Ohio to settlement was followed by great land-speculations, and by quickened emigration to that region.

In 1769 the proposition to establish a Western colony was revived, but in a new form. Thomas Walpole, Samuel Wharton, Benjamin Franklin, Thomas Pownal, and others petitioned the king for the right to purchase 2,400,000 acres of land on the south side of the Ohio River, on which to found a new government. After the delays incident to such business, this petition was granted by the King in Council in 1772. Slow progress was made in perfecting the details; but the price of the land was finally fixed, the plan of government agreed upon, and the patent actually made ready for the seals, when the Revolution broke out, and dashed the new colony forever. Walpole, the leading promoter of the scheme, was an eminent London banker, and the company and grant were commonly called by his name. The company called itself the Grand Company, and proposed to name the colony Vandalia. Although the project finally failed, its history presents some exceedingly interesting features. It should be observed that the Ohio Company of 1748, which had been kept alive thus far, although thwarted in its original purposes by the war, was absorbed in this new scheme.

In May, 1770, the Privy Council referred the Walpole petition to the Lords Commissioners for Trade and Plantations; and two years later their Lordships made an elaborate report, drawn by their president, Lord Hillsborough. This report objected to the petition, that the tract of land prayed for lay partly within the dominion of Virginia south of the Ohio; that it extended several degrees of longitude westward from the mountains; and that a considerable part of it was beyond the line that had been drawn between His Majesty's territories and the hunting grounds of the Six Nations and the Cherokees. Besides, to grant the petition would be to abandon the principle adopted by the Board of Trade, and approved by His Majesty at the close of the war. "Confining the Western extent of settlements to such a distance from the sea-coast as that those settlements should lie within the reach of the trade and commerce of this Kingdom, upon which the strength and riches of it depend," and also within the exercise of that authority and jurisdiction which were conceived to be necessary for the preservation of the colonies in due subordination to, and dependence upon, the Mother Country—are declared the "two capital objects" of the proclamation of 1763. Lord Hillsborough, indeed, admits that the line agreed upon at Fort Stanwix in 1768 is, in the southwest, far beyond the sources of the rivers that flow into the Atlantic; but since this Stanwix line still further restricts the Indians' hunting grounds, he sees in this fact a new reason for adhering closely to the restrictive policy. His Lordship declares the proposition to form inland colonies in America "entirely new;" he says the great object of the North American colonies is to improve and extend the commerce, navigation, and manufactures of England; shore colonies he approves because they fulfil this condition, and inland colonies he condemns because they will not fulfil it. To the argument that settlers are flowing westward, and that Western settlements are inevitable, Lord Hillsborough replies that His Majesty should take every method to check the progress of such settlements, and should not make grants of land that would have an immediate tendency to encourage them. The report closes with a recommendation that the Crown immediately issue a new proclamation forbidding all persons taking up or settling on lands west of the line of 1763.

It would be hard to say whether this report won for its author the wider fame by reason of its odious application of the doctrines of the colonial system to the question of Western settlements, or by reason of the crushing reply that it called out from Dr. Franklin. Before taking up that reply, however, the remark is pertinent that Lord Hillsborough's notion that royal proclamations were going to keep the adventurous people of Pennsylvania, Virginia, and the Carolinas out of the Western country, is one of a multitude of proofs of the incapacity of the British mind, at that time, to understand American questions. It was only less absurd than Dean Tucker's famous plan for guarding the frontier against the incursions of the Indians, viz., that the trees and bushes be cut away from a strip of land a mile in breadth along the back of the colonies from Maine to Georgia.[1]

Franklin begins his reply with correcting the noble Lord's ideas of American geography. The land asked for lies between the Alleghany Mountains and the Ohio River, which are separated, "on a medium," by not more than a degree and a half. The grant will not be an invasion of the dominion of Virginia, because that colony is bounded on the west by the mountains. The country west of the Alleghanies was in the possession of the Indians previous to the Stanwix treaty, and since that time the king has not given it to Virginia. To support the proposition that Virginia does not extend beyond the mountains, which is absolutely essential to his argument, he draws up a territorial history of the region within which the grant will fall, entirely ignoring the Virginia charter.

---

[1] Sparks: Writings of Franklin, III., 48, 49.

1. The country southward of the Great Kanawha, as far as the Tennessee River, originally belonged to the Shawanese Indians.

2. The Six Nations, beginning about the year 1664, carried their victorious arms over the whole country, from the Great Lakes to the latitude of Carolina, and from the Alleghanies to the Mississippi. They, therefore, became possessed of the lands in question by right of conquest.

3. Much stress is then laid on the English protectorate over the Six Nations, acknowledged by the French in 1713, and by the Nations in 1726. When the French came into Western Pennsylvania, in 1754, the English held them invaders on the express ground that the country belonged to their allies and dependents. This was the view held by the British court in discussing the subject with Paris in 1755. In the French and Indian war the English had simply maintained their old rights; they expelled the French from the West as intruders, and held the country not by conquest, but by the Iroquois title. At Fort Stanwix the Iroquois sold to the Crown all their lands south of the Ohio, as far down as the Tennessee. The Crown is, therefore, vested with the undoubted right and property of those lands, and can do what it pleases with them.

4. The Cherokees never resided or hunted in the country between the Kanawha and the Tennessee, and had no right to it. The claim that this region ever belonged to the Cherokees is a fiction altogether new and indefensible, invented in the interest of Virginia. When that government saw that it was likely to be confined on the west by the mountains in consequence of the Stanwix purchase, it set up the Cherokee title in opposition to the Northern Indians.

5. Nor do the Six Nations, the Shawanese, or the Delawares now reside or hunt in the region where the grant will fall.

Franklin's object is to find room for the new colony between the Alleghanies and the Ohio. He follows closely the facts of history touching the matter immediately in hand. The Iroquois had pretended to own the whole West north of the Cumberland Mountains, and the British government and New York had humored them in that pretension. But Franklin's reasoning on this point recalls forcibly what Mr. Parkman says in a passage already quoted concerning Iroquois conquests and titles. What is more, the Iroquois never occupied the Ohio Valley, while the Indians who were occupying it did not acknowledge the Iroquois title. The signers to the Stanwix treaty were all Iroquois, the Delaware and Shawanese delegates present at the council refusing, or at least neglecting, to sign. But granting that the British-Iroquois title was perfectly good as against the French and Western Indians, it had no force as against Virginia. The right that priority of discovery gave the discoverer was the right of pre-emption, and the fact that the Indian title to the Ohio Valley was acquired long after the Virginia charters in no way affected the rights of Virginia, if she ever had any. If the English had waited to acquire Indian titles before sending over colonies, America would be a wilderness at this day. Even the humane Penn first sent over his colony, two thousand strong, and then treated with the Indians. Franklin had himself, in 1754, expressly acknowledged the binding force of the "from sea-to-sea" charters until they should be duly limited. It is hard to see, therefore, that the Fort Stanwix purchase affected Virginia's rights, unless it be claimed that the purchase was made by a royal officer at the expense of the Crown, and not by the colony at her own expense; but it must be remembered that the Crown had taken Indian affairs out of the hands of the colonies, and that New York, Massachusetts, and Connecticut never regarded the purchase as at all easing their rights in the West. At the same time, Franklin's reasoning was admirably adapted to his immediate purpose. It would appear, from Franklin's account of things, that Virginia had concluded that after all she had more to fear from Johnson's line than from Stuart's.

Franklin restates the old arguments in favor of interior settlements, and, after a thorough examination of the whole subject, comes to the conclusion that the proclamation of 1763 was intended solely to pacify the Indians at a critical time, and that the Stanwix treaty has set the proclamation-line effectually aside. Looking into the West, he reports that in the years 1765–1768 great numbers of the king's subjects from Virginia, Maryland, and Pennsylvania were settling over the mountains; that this emigration led to great irritation among the Indians; that the emigrants refused to obey the proclamations issued ordering them to return to the other side of the king's line; that attempts to remove them by force ended only in failure; that the frontier troubles were among the causes that led to the treaty of 1768; that the said treaty, negotiated by Sir William Johnson under express orders from the home government, proves that the permanent exclusion of settlers from the Western country could not have been intended in 1763. The Doctor states that Pennsylvania had made it felony to occupy Indian lands within the limits of that colony; that the Governor of Virginia had commanded settlers to vacate all Indian lands within the limits of his government; and that General Gage had twice sent soldiers to remove the settlers from the Monongahela region, but all these efforts to enforce the restrictive policy had proved unavailing. He asserts that the object of the Stanwix purchase was to avert "an Indian rupture, and give an opportunity to the king's subjects quietly and lawfully to settle thereon."

Franklin does not fail to convict the Board of Trade of inconsistency. In 1748 it was anxious to promote settlements in the Ohio Valley; in 1768 it was of the opinion that the inhabitants of the middle colonies should be permitted gradually to extend themselves backward; in 1770 Lord Hillsborough recommended a new colony there, and two years later he made to the council the adverse report to which Franklin is now replying. The promoters of the new colony have no idea, he says, of draining Great Britain or the old colonies of their population. That will be wholly unnecessary. If the colony is planted the colonists will not become lawless or rebellious, because they will be subjected to government; but if the present restriction be continued the country will become the resort of desperate characters. Moreover, there is already a considerable population in the very district that the petitioners pray for; and if these lawless people are not soon made subject to some authority, an Indian war will be the consequence. They are beyond the jurisdiction of Virginia, which cannot be extended over them without great difficulty, if at all. Hence, the only way to prevent the back country becoming the home of violence and disorder is to establish a new government there.

Many pages of Franklin's paper are devoted to the economical bearings of the proposed colony. He does not deny the doctrines of the colonial system; he rather assumes them; but he contradicts Hillsborough's applications of those doctrines to the matter in hand. On these points he collects a mass of information concerning the Ohio country and its capabilities, its relations to the commercial world, methods of reaching it, etc., that makes the report exceedingly readable.

Franklin's reply to Hillsborough, read in Council, July 1, 1772, immediately led to granting the Walpole petition. His Lordship, who had considered his report overwhelming, at once resigned his office in disgust and mortification. Hillsborough, it is said, " had conceived an idea, and was forming the plan of a boundary-line to be drawn from the Hudson River to the Mississippi, and thereby confining the British colonists between that line and the ocean, similar to the scheme of the French after the peace of Aix-la-Chapelle which brought on the war of 1756." The fact is, the British government had borrowed of the French their restrictive scheme.[1]

It appears from Franklin's pamphlet that the Virginia gov-

---

[1] The Hillsborough Report, Franklin's reply, and the proclamation of 1763 are in Sparks, IV., 302-380.

ernment had been disturbed by the proceedings at Fort Stanwix. It was still more seriously disturbed by the proceedings of Walpole and his associates in London. On April 15, 1770, George Washington wrote a letter to Lord Botetourt, the governor, explaining how the Walpole grant would affect that colony. He says the boundary would run from the mouth of the Scioto River south through the pass of the Ouasioto Mountains near to the latitude of North Carolina; thence northeast to the Kanawha at the junction of the New River and the Greenbrier; thence by the Greenbrier and a due-east line drawn from the head of that river to the Alleghany Mountains; after which the boundaries will be Lord Fairfax's line, the lines of Maryland and Pennsylvania, and the Ohio River to the place of beginning—a large surface, surely, over which to spread 2,400,000 acres of land. Washington says that many Virginians are already settled on New River and the Greenbrier upon lands that Virginia has patented. He declares that the grant will give a fatal blow to the interests of Virginia. Having thus delivered his "sentiments as a member of the community at large," he begs leave to address his Excellency from "a more interested point of view," alleging that the 200,000 acres of land promised the Virginia troops called out in 1754 lie within these very limits. He protests earnestly against any interference with the rights of these men, and prays his Lordship's interposition with His Majesty to have these lands confirmed to the claimants and rightful owners. Washington continued to watch the new colony with a lively interest. In a letter to Lord Dunmore, written June 15, 1771, he says the report gains ground that the grant will be made and the colony established, and declares again that the plan will essentially interfere with the interests and expectations of Virginia. He also renews his plea in behalf of the officers and soldiers of 1754.[1]

---

[1] The two letters are found side by side in Sparks: Writings of Washington, II., 355-361.

The facts presented show conclusively that in the years following the French war the Western policy of the British was not steady or consistent, but fitful and capricious; prompted by a solicitude for the Indians that was partly feigned, and partly by a growing jealousy of the shore colonies. Vandalia was the more welcome to the Council because it would limit Virginia on the west, and so weaken her influence. It is perfectly plain that George III. did not excel James I. in regard for the charter of 1609.

The policy of restriction culminated in 1774 in the Quebec Act. This act guaranteed to the Catholic Church in the Province of Quebec the possession of its vast property, said to equal one-fourth of the old French grants; it confirmed the Catholic clergy in the rights and privileges that they had enjoyed under the old *régime;* it set aside the provisions of the proclamation of 1763, creating representative government, and restored the French system of laws; it committed taxation to a council appointed by the Crown; it abolished trial by jury in civil cases; and, finally, it extended the province on the north to Hudson's Bay, and on the southwest and west to the Ohio and the Mississippi. Some features of this enactment can no doubt be successfully defended. As a whole it had two great ends. One was to propitiate the French population of Canada, to attach them by interest and sympathy to England, and so to prevent their making common cause with the colonies in case worse should come to worst; the other was permanently to sever the West from the shore colonies, and put it in train for being cut up, when the time should come, into independent governments that should have their affiliations with the St. Lawrence basin rather than with the Atlantic slope. Here it may be observed that twice the old Northwest was subject to a jurisdiction whose capital was on the St. Lawrence; once in the old French days, and once in the last year of the British control of the colonies—a fact that shows how thoroughly the home government had adopted French ideas concerning the West.

The year 1774 is remarkable for odious colonial measures; it was the year of the Boston Port Bill and the Massachusetts Bay Bill; but no one of these measures was more odious to the colonists than the Quebec Act. They regarded the changes made in the government of Canada as a stroke at their own governments, while they looked upon the new boundaries as a final effort to wrest the West from them forever. The act provoked a general outcry of denunciation. The youthful Hamilton made it the subject of one of his first political papers. The Continental Congress, enumerating "the acts of pretended legislation" to which the king had given his assent, included in the formidable list the act "for abolishing the free system of English laws in a neighboring province, establishing therein an arbitrary government, and enlarging its boundaries so as to render it at once an example and fit instrument for introducing the same absolute rule in these colonies." The Declaration of Independence arraigned the king on another charge. "He has endeavored to prevent the population of these States; for that purpose obstructing the laws for the naturalization of foreigners; refusing to pass others to encourage emigration hither, and raising the conditions of new appropriations of lands." The presence of these counts in the indictment of 1776 shows the power with which the royal policy had taken hold of the colonial mind. Those colonies that had definite Western boundaries joined in the indictment, as well as those that claimed to the Mississippi River. There was a universal feeling that "lands which had been rescued from the French by the united efforts of Great Britain and America were now severed from their natural connections with the settlements of the seaboard, and formed into a vast inland province like the ancient Louisiana."[1]

The enlargement of the province was defended in Parliament, according to the "Annual Register," on the ground that

---

[1] Adams: Maryland's Influence on Western Land Cessions to the United States, 19.

there were French inhabitants beyond the proclamation-limits of 1763 "who ought to have provision made for them; and that there was one entire colony at the Illinois." The "Register" thus sums up the objections of the opposition:

"Further they asked, why the proclamation limits were enlarged, as if it were thought that this arbitrary government could not have too extensive an object. If there be, which they doubted, any spots on which some Canadians are settled, provide, said they, for them; but do not annex to Canada immense territories now desert, but which are the best part of that continent, and which run on the back of all your ancient colonies. That this measure cannot fail to add to their other discontents and apprehensions, as they can attribute the extension given to an arbitrary military government, and to a people alien in origin, laws, and religion, to nothing else but that design, of which they see but too many proofs already, of utterly extinguishing their liberties, and bringing them, by the arms of those very people, whom they had helped to conquer, into a state of the most abject vassalage."[1]

The restoration of the French system of laws was defended on the ground that the Canadians were indifferent to English institutions, and were incapable of carrying on representative government.

But the Quebec Act did not accomplish its expected purpose. It was nullified by the Revolution. By and by, when the limits of the Thirteen Colonies, as they were after 1763, were set up as the criterion to determine the boundaries of the United States, England, France, and Spain, all took the position that the Royal Proclamation and the Quebec Act limited the States on the west. To this claim the replies, "The king's line of 1763 was a temporary expedient to quiet the Indians," and "The Quebec Act was one of the causes that brought on the war, and that we are fighting to resist,"

---

[1] Annual Register, 1774, 76, 77.

are pressed once and again in the American state papers of the period.

Even Lord Dunmore, that bitter enemy of the colonies and steadfast upholder of the British cause, ignored the Western policy of the home government. His personal characteristics, love of money and of power, contributed to this end. "His passion for land and fees," says Bancroft, "outweighing the proclamation of the king and reiterated most positive instructions from the Secretary of State, he supported the claims of the colony to the West, and was a partner in two immense purchases of land from the Indians in Southern Illinois. In 1773 his agents, the Bullets, made surveys at the Falls of the Ohio; and parts of Louisville and parts of the towns opposite Cincinnati are now held under his warrant." The Indian war that takes its name from his Lordship, which was brought on by his own Western policy, was in contravention of the policy of the home government; and the historian just quoted goes so far as to say: "The royal Governor of Virginia, and the Virginian Army in the Valley of the Scioto, nullified the Act of Parliament which extended the Province of Quebec to the Ohio, and in the name of the King of Great Britain triumphantly maintained for Virginia the Western and Northwestern jurisdiction which she claimed as her chartered right." Virginia "applauded Dunmore when he set at naught the Quebec Act, and kept possession of the government and right to grant lands on the Scioto, the Wabash, and the Illinois."[1] Dunmore's invasion of the Northwest, in 1774, added another link to the Virginia chain of titles to those regions. "From its second charter, the discoveries of its people, the authorized grants of its governors since 1746, the encouragement of its legislature to settlers in 1752–53, the promise of lands as bounties to officers and soldiers who served in the French war, and the continued emigration of its inhabitants, the Ancient Dominion derived its title to occupy the Great West."[2]

---

[1] History, IV., 82, 83, 88.   [2] Bancroft: History, III., 320.

LAND POLICY OF THE BRITISH GOVERNMENT. 145

Strangely enough, the British Government strove to keep the Northwest a waste, years after having lost all control of it. The British commissioners at Ghent, in 1814, proposed as one of the first conditions of peace, "that the United States should conclude a peace with the Indian allies of Great Britain, and that a species of neutral belt of Indian territory should be established between the dominions of the United States and Great Britain, so that these dominions should be nowhere conterminous, upon which belt or barrier neither power should be permitted to encroach even by purchase, and the boundaries of which should be settled in this treaty" [about to be negotiated]; and Dr. Adams, one of those commissioners, answering the question what should be done with the one hundred thousand citizens of the United States already settled in Ohio, Michigan, and Illinois, replied that they must shift for themselves.[1]

There was one English statesman, at least, at the period of the Revolution who saw the futility of all attempts to carry out the restrictive policy. In his famous "Speech on Conciliation of America," delivered in the House of Commons, March 22, 1775, Edmund Burke replied to the suggestion that, as a means of checking the too rapidly growing population, the Crown should make no further grants of land, thus working an "avarice of desolation" and a "hoarding of a royal wilderness." If the grants are stopped, the people will occupy without grants, as they have already done in many places; if driven from one locality, they will remove to another, for in the back settlements they are little attached to particular situations. And then, launching out into one of those glowing descriptive passages for which his eloquence is so celebrated, the orator proceeds:

"Already they have topped the Appalachian Mountains. From thence they behold before them an immense plain, one vast, rich level meadow: a square of five hundred miles.

Morse: John Quincy Adams, in Statesmen Series, 78, 80.

10

Over this they would wander without a possibility of restraint; they would change their manners with the habits of their life; would hence soon forget a government by which they were disowned; would become hordes of English Tartars, and, pouring down upon your unfortified frontiers a fierce and irresistible cavalry, become masters of your governors and your counsellors, your collectors and comptrollers, and of all the slaves that adhered to them. Such would, and in no long time must be, the effect of attempting to forbid as a crime, and to suppress as an evil, the command and blessing of Providence, 'Increase and multiply.' Such would be the happy result of an endeavor to keep as a lair of wild beasts that earth which God by an express charter has given to the children of men."

Signally as England failed in the attempt to exclude civilization from the Great West, she did not abandon the attempt to apply the principles of the Royal Proclamation to the American wilderness. In discussing the Oregon Question with the United States in 1818–1846, she stubbornly strove to prevent settlements on the waters of the Columbia, and to devote the shores of the distant Pacific to the purposes of the Hudson Bay Company. Fortunately she was again foiled by the power that had foiled her before—the enterprise and hardihood of the American pioneer.[1]

---

[1] See Barrows: Oregon, in Commonwealth Series.

IX.

THE NORTHWEST IN THE REVOLUTION.

MR. BANCROFT says the French and Indian war was begun by England "for the acquisition of the Ohio Valley. She achieved this conquest, but not for herself. . . . England became not so much the possessor of the valley of the West as the trustee, commissioned to transfer it from the France of the Middle Ages to the free people who were making for humanity a new life in America."[1] How unfit England was, in the days of George III., to be the possessor of the valley is shown by the policy that she pursued from the close of the French war to the beginning of the Revolution. She was first anxious to secure possession of the Ohio, and then reluctant to see it put to any civilized use. Her restrictive Western policy, as we have seen, was one of the causes leading to the War of Independence, and so leading to the loss of the whole West.

Although a solitude, and because a solitude, the overmountain country had more at stake in the Revolution than the Atlantic slope. On the slope, whatever the issue of the war, an Anglo-Saxon civilization, although it might be greatly stunted and impoverished, was assured; but in the Western valleys such few seeds of civilization as had been planted were Gallican and not Saxon. Moreover, there were uncertainties and perils growing out of the relation of that country to the Franco-Spanish civilization of Louisiana. Between 1748 and 1783 the Western question presented three

---

[1] History, IL., 565.

distinct phases. In 1748-1763 it was the supremacy of England or France in the West; in 1763-1775 it was whether the country should belong to the red man or the white man; and in 1775-1783 it was whether it should form a part of the United States or of some foreign power. In general, this last question was settled by the "skirmishes of sentinels and outposts" east of the mountains, as Lafayette called the Revolution. Still the Northwest appears in the Revolution in two or three aspects that must be presented.

For a few years before the beginning of the French war the Western Indians had been disposed to listen to the English envoys who visited them rather than to the French; but the defeat of Braddock brought upon the English frontier-settlements all the scalping knives of the Western hordes. The Indians were really a part of the soil, like the trees and the buffalo, but France could not transfer them in 1763 with the same facility to their new masters. The savages understood perfectly that the English were far more dangerous to them than the French had been. The posting of garrisons in the Western forts would be likely to bring to their best hunting grounds swarms of colonists greedy for lands. The officers of the garrisons sent to the West reported the Indians sullen and angry. Pontiac was at that very time organizing his formidable conspiracy, the aim of which was to roll back the tide of English invasion. In the summer of 1763 the storm of war burst upon the wilderness-garrisons: Mackinaw, St. Joseph, Sandusky, Ouiatenon, Fort Miami, Presque Isle, Le Bœuf, and Venango fell into the hands of the savages; and Fort Pitt and Detroit were beleaguered. But Boquet's brave march to the heart of Ohio and Gladwin's heroic defence of Detroit broke the power of the Ottawa chieftain, and the Indians were compelled to come to terms. And now began a process of mutual reconciliation. The royal proclamation of 1763, the subsequent restriction of the Western population, the measurable adoption of French methods by the British officers, the growing conviction of the savage that the British Government and the colonies were not the same, and that his danger came from the latter—these causes, with the widening breach between the Mother Country and the colonies, gradually won the Indians over to the British side, and made them ready to accept the war-belt whenever the British commandant at Detroit should send it to them. It is a fact, and perhaps a curious one, that whenever the St. Lawrence Valley and the Atlantic Slope have been arrayed against each other in deadly strife, the Western Indians have sided with the former—in 1755, in 1775, and in 1812.

In 1763 Sir William Johnson estimated the Western Indians, exclusive of the Illinois, at 9,000 warriors,[1] and we may accept that as the number at the beginning of the Revolution. Of these the large majority were already enemies of the Americans, fully prepared to do their part to wrap the long frontier from the Susquehanna to the Tennessee in flames and blood. Left to themselves, these savages would have been a formidable foe; but with a base of supplies on the Detroit, with rallying points in the wilderness-forts, and with the constant stimulation and frequent leadership of British officers, they were simply portentous. The American Revolution in its Northwestern aspect was a continuation of the French and Indian war, the old conflict renewed with some change of parties. The States find the savage power of the Northwest arrayed against them as before. France has dropped out and England has taken her place, succeeding to all her ideas—even that of employing the savage's tomahawk against her revolted colonies—and to all the advantages of the old French position.

The proposition to employ the scalping knife called out from Lord Chatham one of his immortal bursts of eloquence. It was repugnant to the feelings of General Howe and Sir Guy Carleton; but it was heartily approved by Governor Hamilton, at Detroit, who at once made ready to use all the re-

---

[1] Walker: Michigan Pioneer Collections, III, 16.

sources that his position gave him, to bring upon the rear and flank of the States the only form of warfare known in those regions. He employed Elliot, McGee, and the Girty brothers. He subsidized the Indians. Time and again he sent to the tribes the war-belt, summoning them to bloody forays that he himself had planned. His acts will not be here recounted, nor will the history of this phase of the Revolution be written; but it is due to Hamilton to say that his hand was seen at Wheeling, at Harrodsburg, at Boonsborough, at the Blue Licks, where the flower of Kentucky fell, as well as in a hundred attacks upon outlying stations and defenceless farms.

The only other force that the British commander at Detroit could wield was that of the *habitants*. Before we can describe the part that they played in the struggle, we must sketch their history from the close of the previous war.

The moment the French settlements in the West passed into English hands, they began to decline in both the number and the quality of their population. The causes of this decline are easily found.

The sources of such strength as they had had were now sapped. The proclamation of 1763 left them outside the pale of any civil jurisdiction, subject only to military authority. Nor did the Quebec Act work any real change. All through the Revolution, the commander of the Detroit garrison was the civil as well as the military head of the whole Northwest, and most of his subordinates were military officers. There were magistrates, but their commissions came from the commandant, and they dealt out a very arbitrary and capricious justice. For example, Governor Hamilton adjudged a defendant, who pleaded that he could not pay a debt, to give the plaintiff an old negro wench; and Dejean, a magistrate who cuts a great figure in Detroit in those days, condemned men to the gallows whom a jury had found guilty of theft. The orderly was a more conspicuous officer of the law than the constable. Military officers sometimes solemnized marriages, and even administered the rite of baptism. The Canadian officers of the time knew almost nothing of the country beyond the Lakes. Sir Guy Carleton, Governor of Canada, told the House of Commons in 1774 that Michigan was a part of Canada, but that Detroit was not; and that he did not know where Canada ended and Illinois began. At that time, it must be remembered, English statesmen had less knowledge of the boundaries of great provinces in North America than they have now of narrow valleys or small oases in the deserts of Turkistan. Between the Western *habitants* and the British officers there was a strong mutual dislike. They had been trained for generations to believe the British their implacable enemies, and they could not suddenly consent to be governed by them. To be sure, the capitulation of 1760 and the treaty of 1763 both guaranteed them fullest protection, with the full enjoyment of their religion; but these pledges did not overcome their repugnance to the change of governors. Then most of them had sympathized with Pontiac, and this made them shy of the British authorities. The authorities of Louisiana offered the French in Illinois and Michigan special inducements to remove to that province. The mild climate, productive soil, a congenial population, and the French laws, religion, and customs, together with the more direct inducements, made the invitation very attractive. The Illinois people had only to cross the Mississippi to find another Illinois. Then just at that time La Clede founded St. Louis. Very naturally, therefore, the Northwestern settlements began to diminish in numbers and to deteriorate in quality. In a few years Kaskaskia and Detroit dwindled to one-third their former population. Nor did a British population come in to take their places. No doubt men from New York and other colonies would have flocked to Detroit, had it not been for the adoption by the British Government of the French policy of restriction. Judge Walker says that in 1778 there were at Detroit thirty Scotchmen, fifteen Irishmen, and two Englishmen; and he estimates the total permanent population of the territory between the two rivers and the lakes as five thousand at the beginning of the Revolution.[1]

Evidently this was not an inviting field in which to find recruits for the British service.

In the fall of 1775 Lord Dunmore despatched his creature Dr. Connolly, who had just figured so prominently in the Western Pennsylvania troubles, to Detroit, with orders to raise a regiment of Canadians and a force of Indians with which to join his Lordship; but Connolly's arrest and imprisonment in Maryland, and Dunmore's precipitate flight, nipped this enterprise in the bud. The next year Captain de Langlade, of Green Bay, who had seen service in the French war, recruited a motley force of whites and Indians, mainly upon the upper waters, with which he descended to Montreal and joined the British army.

It must not be supposed that the men of the frontier sat nerveless while the Indians were making their raids and the British officers were seeking to array the French against them. Mention will not here be made of the minor invasions of the Indian country; but one heroic movement, that was fraught with large consequences, must be treated somewhat at length.

In the middle of the last century Virginia, owing to her position, her vast land-claims, and the stage of civilization which she had attained, had more Western enterprise than any other colony. In 1774 Dunmore's war gave her the "back-lands," into which her frontiersmen had been for some time pressing. Boone was a Carolinian, but Kentucky was a distinctively Virginia colony. In 1776 the Virginia legislature erected the County of Kentucky, and the next year a Virginia judge dispensed justice at Harrodsburg. Soon the colony was represented in the legislature of the parent state. While thus extending her jurisdiction over the region southwest of the Ohio, the Old Dominion did not forget the lan-

---

[1] Michigan Pioneer Collections, III., 12 et seq.

guage of 1609, "up into the land throughout from sea to sea, west and northwest."

George Rogers Clark, a Virginian who had made Kentucky his home, was endowed with something of the general's and statesman's grasp. While floating down the Ohio in 1776, being then twenty-four years of age, he conceived the conquest of the country beyond the river. It does not appear that he saw the remote bearings of such an achievement; at least, in his own account of it he says he was "elivated with the thoughts of the great service we should do our country in some measure puting an end to the Indian war on our fronteers."[1] But this was a great object. The savages scattered through the Northwestern wilderness were constantly attacking at one point or another the long thin line of frontier settlements; and they drew their supplies of powder and lead and other necessaries, and often received leaders as well as direction, from the fortified forts, Detroit, Vincennes, and the rest. Accordingly, if the posts could be captured, the Indians would lose their rallying points and supplies, they would be overawed and restrained in a degree, and the war on the frontier would be put an end to "in some measure," if not altogether. Probably this was as far as Clark saw. But Thomas Jefferson saw much further. In a letter to Clark, the date of which is lost but that was written before the issue of the campaign was known in Virginia, that great statesman wrote: "Much solicitude will be felt for the result of your expedition to the Wabash; it will at least delay their expedition to the frontier-settlement, and if successful have an important bearing ultimately in establishing our northwestern boundary."[2]

Clark says he had since the beginning of the war taken pains to make himself acquainted with the true situation of the Northwestern posts; and in 1777 he sent two young hunters to spy out the country more thoroughly, and especially to ascertain the sentiments of the *habitants*. On the return of these

---

[1] Clark's Campaign in the Illinois, 24. [2] Ibid., 2, note.

hunters with an encouraging report, he went to Williamsburg, then the capital of Virginia, where he enlisted Governor Patrick Henry and other leading minds in a secret expedition to the Illinois. Acting under a vaguely worded law, authorizing him to aid "any expedition against their Western enemies," Governor Henry gave Clark some vague public instructions, directing him to enlist, in any county of the commonwealth, seven companies of men who should act under his command as a militia, and also private instructions that were much more full and definite. He is to attack the post of Kaskaskia, but this he is to confide to as few as possible. If the white inhabitants of the post "will give undoubted evidence of their attachment to this State (for it is certain they live within its limits)," says the governor, they shall be treated as fellow-citizens; but if not, they must feel the miseries of war. He remarks that it is in contemplation to establish a post near the mouth of the Ohio. Boats, provisions, powder and lead, will be provided at Fort Pitt. Both the public and private instructions are dated January 2, 1778.[1] The governor also gave the young captain a small supply of money.

Clark immediately recrossed the mountains, and began to recruit his command. The secrecy that he was obliged to maintain made his undertaking difficult in the extreme. He complains bitterly of the obstructions thrown in his way by "many leading men in the frontier," which prevented the enlistment of as many men as had been contemplated, and also led to frequent desertions. Overcoming as best he could the difficulties that environed him, he collected his feeble command at the Falls of the Ohio. On June 26, 1778, he began the descent of the river. Leaving the Ohio at Fort Massac, forty miles above its mouth, he began the march to Kaskaskia. This fell into his hands, July 5th, and Cahokia soon after, both without the loss of a single life. Clark found few Englishmen in these villages, and the French, who were weary

---

[1] Appendix to Clark's Campaign in the Illinois.

of British rule, he had little difficulty in attaching to the American interest. Vincennes, soon after, surrendered to a mere proclamation, when there was not an American soldier within one hundred miles of the place. The ease with which this conquest was accomplished was largely due to the Kaskaskia priest, Father Pierre Gibault, who entered into Clark's plans with the greatest warmth and energy.[1]

"I now found myself," says Clark, "in possession of the whole, in a country where I found I could do more real service than I expected, which occasioned my situation to be the more disagreeable as I wanted men."[2] At no time had he had two hundred men in his command; and now, the time for which they had enlisted having expired, and the immediate object of the expedition having been gained, they were anxious to return home. Although the Illinois and the Wabash had fallen almost without a blow, it was necessary that they should be held or all would be lost, no matter whether the situation was viewed with the eyes of George Rogers Clark or the eyes of Thomas Jefferson. Clark prevailed upon one hundred men to re-enlist for eight months; he then filled up his companies with recruits from the villages, and sent an urgent call to Virginia for re-enforcements.

---

[1] The editor of Clark's Campaign in the Illinois quotes from Judge Law, Colonial History of Vincennes, the remark that to Gibault, "next to Clark and Vigo, the United States are indebted for the accession of the States comprised in what was the original Northwest Territory [more] than to any other man "— 33, 34, note.

In 1778, St. Louis was a young town fourteen years of age, and the Spanish as well as the French population were very friendly to the Americans. Colonel Francis Vigo was a St. Louis merchant who rendered Clark and the American cause most valuable services. Among others, he cashed Clark's drafts for $12,000 on New Orleans, a large sum in the Mississippi Valley one hundred years ago, and thus enabled him to keep the field. Clark's drafts were protested; and the debt due Vigo was not paid until 1876, and then after many hearings by congressional committees and protracted litigation in the United States courts. See Tract 35 of the Western Reserve and Northern Ohio Historical Society, "A Centennial Lawsuit," by Judge C. C. Baldwin.

[2] Clark's Campaign, 36.

The salutary influence of the invasion upon the Indians was felt at once; it "began to spread among the nations even to the border of the lakes;" and in five weeks Clark settled a peace with ten or twelve different tribes. With great ability Clark outwitted the English, counteracted their influence upon the savages, and kept "spies continually in and about Detroit for a considerable time." He even captured Ouiatenon, which stroke, he says, "completed our interest on the Wabash."

And now Clark began really to feel the difficulties of his situation. Destitute of money, poorly supplied, commanding a small and widely scattered force, he had to meet and circumvent an active enemy who was determined to regain what he had lost. Governor Hamilton projected a grand campaign against the French towns that had been captured and the small force that held them. The feeble issue was the capture, in December, 1778, of Vincennes, which was occupied by but two Americans. Clark, who was in the Illinois at the time of this disaster, at once put his little force in motion for the Wabash, knowing, he says, that if he did not take Hamilton, Hamilton would take him; and, February 25, 1779, at the end of a march of two hundred and fifty miles, that ranks in peril and hardship with Arnold's winter march to Canada, he again captured the town, the fort, the governor, and his whole command. Hamilton was sent to Virginia a prisoner of war, where he was found guilty of treating American prisoners with cruelty, and of offering the Indians premiums for scalps, but none for prisoners.

American statesmen and soldiers perfectly understood the importance of Detroit. Congress considered the feasibility of capturing it as early as April, 1776, and often returned to the subject thereafter. But nothing was done, or really attempted, in the early years of the war, for want of men, munitions, and money. Washington gave the subject his earnest attention. In December, 1778, he considered it in connection with a grand invasion of Canada, then projected. In January,

1779, when a Northwestern expedition, under General McIntosh, was proposed, he said the best way to deal with the Indians was to carry the war into their own country. In April of the same year he inquired of Colonel Broadhead the best time to attempt a march to Detroit, and suggested the winter, because the British would not then be able to use their naval force on Lake Erie.[1] Naturally, Clark's achievement, since it made the reduction of the post seem more feasible, led to more serious consideration of the subject. Clark himself considered his work only half done, and was very ambitious to lead an army through the wilderness to the gateway of the Northwest. More than once a force seemed almost on the point of starting. A joint Virginia and continental expedition was at one time contemplated. But the same causes that operated to defeat the earlier attempts continued to operate. Clark, who probably did not appreciate the difference between seizing Detroit and seizing Kaskaskia, was compelled to abandon the enterprise, and Detroit remained in British hands at the end of the war, and, in fact, until 1796. "Detroit lost for a few hundred men," was his pathetic lament as he surrendered an enterprise that lay near his heart. Had he been able to achieve it, he would have won and held the whole Northwest. As it was he won and held the Illinois and the Wabash in the name of Virginia and of the United States. The bearing of this conquest on the question of western boundaries will be considered in another place, but here it is pertinent to remark that the American Commissioners, in 1782, at Paris, could plead *uti possidetis* in reference to much of the country beyond the Ohio, for the flag of the Republic, raised over it by George Rogers Clark, had never been lowered. It would not be easy to find in our history a case of an officer accomplishing results that were so great and far-reaching with so small a force. Clark's later life is little to his credit, but it should not be forgotten that he

---

[1] Sparks: Writings of Washington, VI, 120, 156, 225.

rendered the American cause and civilization a very great service.

All this time the British were not idle. War-party after war-party was sent against the American border. In 1780 a grand expedition was organized at Detroit and sent to Kentucky, under the command of Captain Bird. But it accomplished nothing commensurate with its magnitude and cost. Great efforts were made to raise a white contingent, but they brought together only some eighty men. Judge Walker finds, among the bills for supplies furnished the British Indian Department, items that plainly reveal the character of Bird's command; viz., 476 dozen scalping-knives, 1,206 pounds of vermilion, 21,663 yards tinsel roll, 301 dozen looking-glasses, 8,200 ear-bobs, etc.

The Northwest had been won by a Virginia army, commanded by a Virginia officer, put in the field at Virginia's expense. Governor Henry had promptly announced the conquest to the Virginia delegates in Congress. He spoke of Detroit as being "at present defended by so inconsiderable a garrison, and so scantily furnished with provisions, for which they must be still more distressed by the loss of supplies from the Illinois, that it might be reduced by any number of men above five hundred," and closed his interesting communication with the words: "Were it possible to secure the St. Lawrence and prevent the English attempts up that river by seizing some post on it, peace with the Indians would seem to be secured."[1] In the same letter he also expressed much gratification at the spirit in which Clark's command had been received by the French settlers. But before Patrick Henry wrote this letter Virginia had welded the last link in her chain of title to the country beyond the Ohio. In October, 1778, her Legislature declared: "All the citizens of the commonwealth of Virginia, who are actually settlers there, or who shall hereafter be settled on the west side of the Ohio,

---

[1] Tyler: Patrick Henry, 230, 231.

shall be included in the district of Kentucky, which shall be called Illinois County." Nor was this all. Soon after, Governor Henry appointed a lieutenant-commandant for the new county, with full instructions for carrying on the government.[1] The French settlements remained under Virginia jurisdiction until March, 1784.

Attention should more particularly be drawn to the spirit in which the French settlers beyond the Ohio received the Americans. It is perfectly clear that had they actively taken the side of the British, Clark could never have done his work. The ancient antipathy to the British; a desire to see the work of 1763 apparently undone, although it was only being perfected; the French alliance of 1778, which made them think they were again opposing the old enemy—these, with the intelligent and spirited conduct of the Kaskaskia priest, decided the *habitants* of the Illinois and the Wabash. In the far North, where the straggling white men were more reckless, and at Detroit, the centre of British influence, the French were more favorably disposed to the British. But even at Detroit the British officers complained of the apathy of the Canadians, and the small number of volunteers enrolled in the expeditions there organized confirms the complaints. It is not too much to say that, in the end, the settlements upon which the British so much relied proved a means of their destruction.

In future chapters we shall have occasion to refer to these French settlements again. But this is the place to say that the welcome which they gave the Americans did not arrest their fate or retard their decline. The breath of Anglo-American civilization seemed almost as fatal to them as to the Indians themselves. Louisiana and the fur lands continued to draw away their strength; and scarcely a trace of them can be found in Northwestern life to-day. Champlain laid the foundation of the British Province of Quebec; the State of

---

[1] Edwards: History of Illinois, and Life of Ninian Edwards, 5, 7.

Louisiana is the child of the French colony; but the *habitants* of the Northwest seem as effectually lost in the past as the Mound Builders.

Although the French settlements did not become an element in the civilization of the Northwest, they will always remain an attractive and, in many respects, a pleasing chapter of American history. The story of Northwestern discovery and exploration will long be drawn upon for examples of heroic endurance, high courage, and unyielding devotion. It will long point the moral that sound ideas and practical purposes are as essential to success as zeal and enthusiasm. The French colonies as much surpass the English in poetic elements as the English surpass them in strength and permanence; and the long procession of discoverers, explorers, priests, *coureurs des bois*, traders, *voyageurs*, soldiers, and *habitants*, with its retinue of bedizened savages, will stir the hearts of those who respond to high qualities, and catch the attention of those who have an eye for the picturesque. French life was marked by a good humor, contentment, simplicity, freedom from cankering care and desire for acquisition, hospitality, childlike faith, and sociability that make it very attractive. Cable has touched some of its phases in his Creole pictures. Longfellow idealizes some of its traits, as well as much of its scenery, in "Evangeline." The descriptions written by tourists and United States officers at the time of the Louisiana purchase are more prosaic, but still have many elements of charm. Detroit stood the shock of the American emigration better than any other of the Western posts; and many of the striking features of the old French town remained until they were fixed in enduring colors. Mr. Bela Hubbard's chapters, entitled "French Habitants of the Detroit," are a series of delightful pictures of the "pipe-stem farms," the uncouth ploughs and carryalls, the pony-carts, the races, the apple-orchards, the cider-mills, and ancient pear-trees whose origin no one can explain, the quaint houses, the windmills, the jaunty costumes, the fishing, the language, religion, manners, and recreations, and the *voyageurs*, with a few specimens of their songs.[1]

But while the French life has so thoroughly disappeared from the old Northwest, some of its wilder aspects may still be seen far north in the Great Fur Land. The *voyageur*, for example, has disappeared from the streams of Michigan and Wisconsin; but he still paddles his canoe on the rivers falling into Hudson's Bay and on the affluents of the Mackenzie. His blood is more mixed, his language more corrupt, and he is more a savage than one hundred years ago; but he still preserves the main features of the type. A traveller who has visited those haunts describes him as merry, light-hearted, obliging, hospitable, and extravagant; when idle, devoted to singing, dancing, gossip, and drinking to intoxication; having vanity as his besetting sin; intensely superstitious; completely under the influence of his priest; devoted to the forms of religion, grossly immoral, often dishonest, and generally untrustworthy; with no sense of duty in his daily life; controlled by passion and caprice, and having little aptitude for continuous labor. "No man will labor more cheerfully and gallantly at the severe toil pertinent to his calling; but those efforts are of short duration, and when they are ended, his chief desire is to do nothing but eat, drink, smoke, and be merry—all of them acts in which he greatly excels."[2]

---

[1] "The labor of the oar," says Mr. Hubbard, "was relieved by songs, to which each stroke kept time, with added vigor. The poet Moore has well caught the spirit of the *voyageurs'* melodious chant, in his 'Boat-song upon the St. Lawrence.' But to appreciate its wild sweetness, one should listen to the melody as it wings its way over the waters, softened by distance, yet every measured cadence falling distinct upon the ear."—Memorials of a Half Century, 107-154.

[2] Robinson: The Great Fur Land, 108, 109.

X.

THE UNITED STATES WREST THE NORTH-WEST FROM ENGLAND.

The Second Treaty of Paris.

ON the Fourth of July, 1776, the thirteen British colonies in North America, by their chosen representatives in general congress assembled, solemnly published and declared that they were, and of a right ought to be, free and independent States. By this act they assumed a separate and equal place among the powers of the earth as the United States of America. Less than two years thereafter—that is, on February 6, 1778—the King of France entered into two treaties with the new nation: one of alliance, and one of amity and commerce; the essential and direct end of the first being, as declared in the second article, "to maintain effectually the liberty, sovereignty, and independence absolute and unlimited of the said United States, as well in matters of government as of commerce." Article 5 stipulated that, if the United States should conquer the British in the Northern parts of America, or the Bermuda Islands, those countries or islands should be confederated with, or be made dependent upon, the said United States. Article 7 stipulated that if His Majesty the King of France should attack any of the islands in the Gulf of Mexico, belonging to Great Britain, or islands near that gulf, such islands should, in case of success, appertain to the Crown of France. In Article 6 the king renounced the possession of the Bermudas, as well as those parts of North

America that, by the treaty of 1763, were acknowledged to belong to Great Britain, or to the United States, before called British colonies, or which then were, or had lately been, under the power of the Crown of Great Britain. By Article 11 the United States guaranteed to His Majesty his present possessions in America, as well as those he might acquire by the future treaty of peace; while His Majesty guaranteed to the United States not only their liberty, sovereignty, and independence in both matters of government and commerce, but also their possessions, and the conquests that they might make from Great Britain during the war, as provided in the previous article. The Declaration of Independence bore the caption: "The unanimous Declaration of the United States of America;" the names of the States were given, with the signers at the end. One of the French treaties was made with "the thirteen United States of North America," the other with "the United States of North America;" the names of the States being added in both cases. Beyond these general terms neither the Declaration nor the treaties contained one word describing the new nation. Were the terms clothed with such definite meaning that all the world knew just what the new nation was?

In a social and political sense "the thirteen British colonies in North America," previous to 1776, stood for clear and definite ideas. They were the thirteen communities planted by England, at least by Englishmen, in the seventeenth and eighteenth centuries on the eastern shore of North America, between the St. Croix and Altamaha Rivers; communities that had an individual history and a collective history which plainly marked them off, to the minds of Europeans, from the French settlements to the north and the Spanish settlements to the south. Nor did they lose their individuality even when these French and Spanish settlements, after 1763, took rank with them as American colonies of the British Crown. Who were the people that put forth the Declaration of Independence was therefore well underderstood wherever that Declaration was read ; as it was, likewise, who entered into the treaties with France in 1778.

But what the names found in the Declaration and French treaties stood for in a geographical and territorial sense was not equally plain. " Massachusetts," " Virginia," " Carolina," for example, had meant very different things at different times. Nor did they represent definitely ascertained units in 1776. Probably, too, there were no two States lying side by side between which there were not pending boundary-disputes. The chapters on the "Thirteen Colonies as Constituted by the Royal Charters" make that sufficiently plain. Then there arose sharp controversies as to the division and proprietorship of the country beyond the Alleghany Mountains. But above these internal territorial questions towered one that may be called external, viz.: " What is the extent of the thirteen States of America considered as a whole ? " Neither the Declaration nor the treaties contained any answer; so far from it, the name used in these documents might mean, and soon came to mean, very different things to different people. For instance, although the King of France entered into the defensive alliance of 1778 solely to make sure and effectual the liberty, sovereignty, and absolute independence of the United States, in less than two years he used his influence to induce his allies to consent to the Alleghany Mountains as a western boundary, which would have cut off fully one half of the territory that the United States claimed, and that Great Britain ultimately conceded. Again, the United States described in 1779 in the instructions to John Adams, commissioner to negotiate a peace, are not geographically the same United States whose independence was acknowledged at Paris in 1782. Hence it is plain that England might, the day after the French treaties were signed, or even the day after the Declaration was published, have conceded the independence of the States in the very terms used in those documents, and still have left unsettled a territorial question larger than the one which brought on the French and Indian war in 1754. It is quite clear, therefore, that in 1776 the United States were not as definitely marked off from other nations territorially as they were from other peoples politically and socially.

At the beginning the United States were a purely federal [1] nation and government. They could not touch directly a single citizen, a single dollar, or a single foot of land. They were dependent upon the States individually for a Congress, a treasury, an army, and a capital. The States made up the United States. At different times, in the course of the war, Congress offered land-bounties for volunteers in the continental line, but when the offers were made Congress had no lands, and, had it not been for the Northwestern cessions, it would have been compelled to ask the States for special grants with which to satisfy them. When the time came to instruct the national representatives abroad in regard to the national limits, the federal principle was strictly followed. Hence Mr. Jay, who went to Spain in 1779, was instructed, October 4, 1780, to insist upon the Mississippi River because it was "the boundary of several States in the Union." On January 8, 1782, a committee of which Mr. Madison was a member, to which had been referred certain papers in regard to the prospective negotiations for peace with His Britannic Majesty, thus stated the rule by which the national boundaries should be ascertained :

" Under his authority the limits of these States, while in the character of colonies, were established ; to these limits the

---

[1] As Mr. G. T. Curtis points out, the term "federal" or "federalist" has been used in our politics in three distinct senses : First, in its philosophical sense, in that of federal in distinction from national ; second, in that of a supporter of the Constitution, when it was before the people for their adoption ; third, in that of a member of the political party at the head of which stood Washington. The three meanings all appeared within the limits of a few years. In 1787 Hamilton was not a Federalist, because opposed to the continuance of the Confederation, and desirous of a National Government ; in 1788 he was a Federalist, because he desired the adoption of the Constitution, and he continued a Federalist, because he favored a particular political policy. History of the Constitution, II., 497. The word is used above in its proper philosophical sense.

United States, considered as independent sovereignties, have succeeded. Whatsoever territorial rights, therefore, belonged to them before the Revolution were necessarily devolved upon them àt the era of independence."

Then follows a long argument to show that this principle would give the United States the territories that they claimed in the instructions soon to be mentioned.[1] This report was referred to a second committee, which reported it back, August 16th following, with a mass of "facts and observations" sustaining its positions. This document covers forty pages of the printed journal, and is the best statement extant of the territorial rights of the States. It makes very prominent the fact that Massachusetts, Connecticut, New York, Virginia, and the two Carolinas and Georgia claimed to the Mississippi River. This was pleading the royal charters as modified by the treaty of 1763. But if His Majesty should reply that at the beginning of the war he, and not the colonies, was seized of the Western country, the American Commissioners could meet the claim with the argument that—

"The character in which he was so seized was that of king of the thirteen colonies collectively taken. Being stripped of this character, its [his] rights descended to the United States for the following reasons : (1) The United States are to be considered in many respects as one undivided independent nation, inheriting those rights which the King of Great Britain enjoyed as not appertaining to any one particular State, while he was what they are now, the superintending governor of the whole. (2) The King of Great Britain has been dethroned as King of the United States by the joint efforts of the whole. (3) The very country in question hath been conquered through the means of the common labors of the United States."[2]

Under the third specification the reference is, of course, to the conquest of George Rogers Clark.

---

[1] The Secret Journals, III., 151 et seq.
[2] Ibid., 198, 199.

In these reports the charge that the from sea-to-sea charters were due to geographical ignorance is rebutted; the view that they sprang from a desire to hold the West against Spain is advanced;[1] and the theory that the proclamation of 1763 had worked a limitation of the colonies on the west is expressly set aside in favor of the theory held by Washington in 1767, viz., a temporary device for quieting the Indians. The stress laid on the chartered extension of certain States to the West becomes all the more significant when we remember that for several years some of the States, and particularly Maryland, had been denying that the West belonged to the claimant States at all. At the same time, the American commissioners were to plead *uti possidetis*, growing out of the Clark conquest of the country beyond the Ohio, if the appeal to the charters did not prove effectual.

The events that at last compelled England to treat for peace are not pertinent to the present inquiry. The year 1782 found her ready to treat; the final commission given to Mr. Oswald, her principal representative in the Paris discussions with the Americans, owing to the insistance of Mr. Jay, formally acknowledged the independence of the United States; and this acknowledgment became the point of departure for the later negotiation. But all this left many very difficult questions to be adjusted, such as the fisheries, compensation to Loyalists, and especially the boundaries.

The instructions given to John Adams by Congress, bearing date August 14, 1779, are the earliest authoritative statement of the territorial claims of the United States with which I am acquainted. Only disappointment came from Mr. Adams's mission to Europe at that time; but these instructions were

---

[1] "Had the interval between those seas been precisely ascertained, it is not probable that the King of England would have divided the chartered boundaries now in question into more governments. For perhaps his principal object at that time was to acquire by that of occupancy which originated in this Western World, to wit, by charters, a title of the lands comprehended therein against foreign powers."—The Secret Journals, III., 177.

substantially those under which the commissioners acted in 1782. They claimed on the northeast the St. Johns River; on the north, the proclamation line of 1763 as far as the foot of Lake Nipissing, and beyond that point a straight line drawn to the source of the Mississippi; on the west, the Mississippi to parallel 31° north; on the south, the northern boundary of Florida as established in 1763; and on the east, the ocean. Mr. Adams was instructed "strongly to contend that the whole of the said countries and islands lying within the boundaries aforesaid . . . be yielded to the powers of the States to which they respectively belong," a clear outcropping of the federal idea; "but, notwithstanding the clear right of these States, and the importance of the object, yet they are so much influenced by the dictates of religion and humanity, and so desirous of complying with the earnest request of their allies, that if the line to be drawn from the mouth of the Lake Nipissing to the head of the Mississippi cannot be obtained without continuing the war for that purpose, you are hereby empowered to agree to some other line between that point and the River Mississippi; provided the same shall in no part thereof be to the southward of latitude 45° north." Similarly, Mr. Adams was authorized to consent that the northeastern boundary be afterward adjusted by commissioners duly appointed for that purpose, if the St. Johns could not be obtained. The cession of Canada and Nova Scotia was declared "of the utmost importance to the peace and commerce of the United States, but it should not be made an ultimatum."[1]

Save the ocean and the St. Johns, these were the lines established by the French treaty and the royal proclamation of 1763. The line northwest of the St. Lawrence could be defended on the ground that the grant to the Plymouth Company was bounded north by the forty-fifth parallel in 1606, and by the forty-eighth parallel in 1620. The source of the

---

[1] The Secret Journals, II., 225-228.

Mississippi had not been discovered in 1779, but it was supposed to be at least as far north as the Lake of the Woods. Had this supposition been correct, the Nipissing line would have excluded Great Britain from all the great lakes but Lake Superior; the real Nipissing line, however, would have left nearly the whole of that lake, with large parts of Michigan, Wisconsin, and Minnesota to that power. At the close of the Revolution the Mississippi was the natural, and, we may say, indispensable western boundary of the United States; next to independence, which was, in fact, already conceded, our extension to that river was the most important question involved in the negotiation, far transcending the St. Johns, compensation to the Loyalists, and even the fisheries. This was the question, whether the trustee commissioned twenty years before to transfer the West from the France of the Middle Ages to the free people who were making for humanity a new life in North America, should execute the commission.

On the British side the negotiation was opened by Mr. Oswald, under the direction of the Rockingham ministry; on the American side, by Dr. Franklin. The promptness with which the British Commissioner consented to all the boundaries of the Adams instructions appeared to show that the trustee was ready to transfer the West without objection. In fact, those boundaries were incorporated in the treaty draft sent to London as late as the early days of October. Nor is it probable that these lines would have been seriously objected to if the courts of Paris and Madrid had not meddled with the question. Before taking up that topic, however, attention must be drawn to another fact that strikingly illustrates the pliable temper of Mr. Oswald, as well as the yielding spirit of the Court of London in the first stage of the negotiations. Dr. Franklin actually proposed that the British Crown should cede the whole of Canada to the United States.[1]

---

[1] "The territory of the United States and that of Canada, by long extended frontiers, touch each other. The settlers on the frontiers of the American prov-

This proposition was finally rejected on the one side, and dropped on the other, but for a time there seemed to be a probability that the cession would actually be made. Mr. Oswald certainly listened to it with favor, and he reported the British ministers, to whom he communicated the proposition, as not offering particular objection.

In previous chapters we have seen that in the sixteenth century Spain despised her grand opportunity to take possession of the Mississippi River, and that in the seventeenth she allowed it to pass quietly into the hands of France. At the close of the French and Indian war, the western half of the great valley, with the exclusive possession of the mouth of the river, passed into her hands; but this was only a partial recovery of what she had before lost, and was a compensation for Florida, that she was obliged to cede to England in exchange for Havana.

Responding to the pressing intercessions of France, and to the promptings of her own ambition, Spain declared war against England in June, 1779. In America she hoped to recover Florida and to strengthen her position on the Missis-

---

inces are generally the most disorderly of the people, who, being far removed from the eye and control of their respective governments, are more bold in committing offences against neighbors and are forever occasioning complaints and furnishing matter for fresh differences between their States. . . . .

"Britain possesses Canada. Her chief advantage from that possession consists in the trade for peltry. Her expenses in governing and defending that settlement must be considerable. It might be humiliating to her to give it up on the demand of America. Perhaps America will not demand it. Some of her political rulers may consider the fear of such a neighbor as a means of keeping the thirteen States more united among themselves and more attentive to military discipline. But, on the mind of the people in general, would it not have an excellent effect if Britain should voluntarily offer to give up this province; though on these conditions: That she shall in all times coming have and enjoy the right of free trade thither, unencumbered with any duties whatsoever; that so much of the vacant lands there shall be sold as will raise a sum sufficient to pay for the houses burnt by the British troops and their Indians, and also to indemnify the Royalists for the confiscation of their estates."—Diplomatic Correspondence, III., 388 et seq.

sippi. How thoroughly these projects had been thought out at that time may be questionable; but Spain was careful to demand in her engagement with France a stipulation that left her free to exact from the United States, " as the price of her friendship, a renunciation of every part of the basin of the St. Lawrence and the lakes, of the navigation of the Mississippi, and of all the land between that river and the Alleghanies."[1] Hoping to effect treaties with the Court of Madrid similar to those already effected with the Court of Paris, Congress despatched John Jay as an envoy at the end of the year 1779, authorizing him to guarantee to His Catholic Majesty, Florida, East and West, if he should conquer it and the fortunes of war should leave it in his hands at the peace : " Provided always, that the United States shall enjoy the free navigation of the River Mississippi into and from the sea." He was also particularly to endeavor to obtain some convenient port or ports below the thirty-first degree of north latitude on the Mississippi for all merchant-vessels, goods, wares, and merchandises belonging to the inhabitants of the United States.[2] The free navigation of the Mississippi was already a practical question. In 1779 both Pennsylvania and Virginia had considerable populations west of the mountains; settlements were springing up in the valleys of the Holston and the Kentucky, while Louisville dates from the George Rogers Clark expedition; and there were the old French settlements on the Wabash and in the Illinois that had always enjoyed the free use of the great river. By that time, too, there were several American merchants in New Orleans—men from Boston, New York, and Philadelphia; and these merchants, in the years 1776–78, with the consent of the Spanish governor, shipped arms and munitions up the Mississippi and Ohio to Pittsburg. Plainly, therefore, Congress was simply doing its duty in looking out for the interests of the scattered settle-

---

[1] Bancroft: History, VI., 183. Boston, 1879.
[2] The Secret Journals, II., 261 et seq.

ments beyond the mountains. But the Spanish Court would not listen to the overture, nor receive Mr. Jay as an accredited envoy. The reasons that controlled its conduct are a material part of this chapter of Western history.

First, the war was proving to be much more protracted and more costly than France and Spain had anticipated; and at the opening of 1780 they desired nothing so much as a speedy peace, provided measurably satisfactory terms could be made. This desire led France to wish a full alliance between the United States and Spain, since such an alliance would lead to a more vigorous prosecution of the war while it lasted; and it would no doubt have had the same effect upon Spain, but for her dread of everything that touched, or seemed to touch, her own interests on the Mississippi. France therefore began to exert a steady pressure upon Congress, to induce that body to recede from its demand for the free navigation of the river, and Congress, yielding to the pressure and to the depression of feeling produced by the wasting continuance of the war, withdrew, February 15, 1781, the offensive ultimatum. Moreover, the French representatives at Philadelphia, first Gerard and afterward Luzerne, told Congress repeatedly that the United States had no valid claim to the country west of the king's line of 1763. One object of the French ministers in insisting upon this boundary was, as we shall soon see, to keep the United States out of the way of Spain in the Western country, and another object was to keep the conditions of peace on the part of the United States within narrow limits.

But this modification of Mr. Jay's instructions, made contrary to his advice, wholly failed to accomplish its object. At first Count Florida Blanca, the Spanish Prime Minister, had tacitly consented to the Mississippi as our western boundary; but, now that the other obstacle to a treaty was out of the way, he held that such a westward extension was altogether inadmissible. The fact is, the Clark conquest of the Northwest, the spread of Western settlements, and the staying power that the States were showing in the war, were revealing to the Spanish Court the fact that an Anglo-American republic, stretching down the Atlantic slope from Nova Scotia to Florida and spreading over the Alleghanies to the great lakes and the great river, meant a future menace to His Catholic Majesty's North American dominions; and the annexation of Louisiana, Florida, Texas, and portions of Mexico to the United States show how well grounded these fears were. Spain had always striven to exclude all rival powers from the Gulf of Mexico; she expected to regain Florida and the practical control of the Gulf at the peace; and to allow the United States to extend westward to the river and southward to parallel 31° seemed little less than abandoning her dearest American interests. At that time, too, Spain was the greatest colonial empire of the world; and it was no more the business of her king to offer a premium on colonial revolutions than it was the business of Francis of Austria to foster rebellion.

In the third place, Galvez, the gallant young Governor of Louisiana, had captured and was holding possession of the British posts on the Gulf and the Mississippi: Pensacola, Mobile, Baton Rouge, and Natchez. These conquests had dazzled the Spanish imagination, opening up new possibilities of territorial expansion in the vast region west of the Appalachian Mountains, including, perhaps, a complete retrieval of the great blunder of one hundred years before. Now that West Florida was in her hands, she remembered its ancient extension northward. Her ambition growing with what it fed on, Spain now conceived the thought of laying claim to the whole West, as far as the lakes. To lay the foundation for such claim, the Spanish commandant at St. Louis, in the dead of the winter of 1780–81, sent an expedition into the very heart of the Northwest, to seize the post of St. Joseph, established by La Salle in 1679, just after he had sent back the Griffin from Green Bay. This expedition was completely successful; Don Eugenio Purre, the commander, seized the post, capturing the garrison, and took formal possession of the region commanded by it, and of the Illinois River, displaying the Spanish standard in token of conquest and carrying off the English colors as a Spanish title-deed. News of this exploit reached Philadelphia by way of Madrid and Paris in the Spring of 1782, accompanied by this message from Mr. Jay to Mr. Livingston: "When you consider the ostensible object of this expedition, the distance of it, the formalities with which the place, the country, and the river were taken possession of in the name of His Catholic Majesty, I am persuaded it will not be necessary for me to swell this letter with remarks that would occur to a reader of far less penetration than yourself."[1] Dr. Franklin also saw in the expedition a purpose to "coop up" the United States between the Alleghanies and the sea, and he demanded that Congress should insist upon the Mississippi as a western boundary, and upon its free navigation from its source to the ocean. Nor can there be any doubt that the Illinois towns would have been seized and held by the Spaniards, if they had not already passed into the custody of the Virginia troops. While this Northwestern expedition did not occur in time to influence the discussions with Mr. Jay at Madrid, it is still a material part of the history as a whole, and it strikingly illustrates the Spanish policy.

Mr. Jay wholly failed to accomplish the object for which he was sent to Madrid; but he acquired a knowledge of Spanish purposes, and had an experience of Spanish character, that enabled him to render his country invaluable service at Paris as one of the commissioners who negotiated the treaty of peace with Great Britain.

As Mr. Jay was leaving Madrid for Paris, in the early summer of 1782, Count Florida Blanca told him that the Count de Aranda, the Spanish ambassador at the French Court, was authorized to continue the discussion of a treaty

---

[1] Diplomatic Correspondence, VIII., 78.

between Spain and the United States. In due time, Jay put himself in communication with the Count; but as the Spaniard would never show his full powers, and the American would not treat without seeing them, their frequent conferences were all informal and non-official. However, in these conferences the Spanish diplomatist fully disclosed the ideas of his government touching the Western country.

Having drawn from Mr. Jay the statement that the United States claimed on the south to the proclamation line of 1763, and on the west to the middle of the Mississippi, the Count replied: That the Western country had never belonged to the ancient English colonies, or been claimed by them; that, previous to the Treaty of Paris, the West had belonged to France, and that it continued, after that treaty, a distinct part of the British dominions; that, in consequence of Spanish conquests in West Florida and on the Mississippi and Illinois Rivers, the title had become vested in Spain; and that, supposing the Spanish right did not cover *all* the country, it was possessed by nations of Indians, free and independent, whom the States had no right to disturb. He therefore proposed a longitudinal line on the east side of the river as a boundary between Spain and the United States, adding that he did not mean to dispute about a few acres or miles. What De Aranda's "longitudinal line" was he afterward made plain, by drawing a red line on a copy of Mitchell's map "from a lake near the confines of Georgia, but east of the Flint River, to the confluence of the Kanawha with the Ohio; thence round the western shores of Lake Erie and Huron; and thence round Lake Michigan to Lake Superior."[1] West and south of this line Spain should hold; east, the United States; while north of the lakes the United States might make such terms with Great Britain as she could. Here we may drop the so-called negotiation with Spain, with the remark that until the year 1795 the Missis-

---

[1] Diplomatic Correspondence, VIII., 150–152.

sippi River remained an insuperable obstacle in the way of an American treaty with that power.

The Spanish claim to the West was dangerous mainly because, in a modified form, it was supported by France. When Dr. Franklin and Mr. Jay pointed out to the Count de Vergennes, the French Minister for Foreign Affairs, the extravagance of De Aranda's claim, the Count was "very cautious and reserved;" but M. Rayneval, his principal secretary, who was present, was talkative, and expressed the opinion that the Americans claimed more than they had a right to. Soon after, Rayneval suggested to Mr. Jay a "conciliatory line;" and in a memoir dated September 6th he explained at length what he meant by it. In this paper the secretary stated the conflicting United States and Spanish claims, and then urged that the one had no support in colonial history, and that the other was not justified by the Spanish conquests. His conciliatory line he drew from a point on the Gulf midway between the Chattahoochee and the Mobile, nearly due north to the Cumberland River, and then down the Cumberland to the Ohio. The savages west of this limit should be free, under the protection of Spain; those east should be free, under the protection of the United States. Spain would lose almost the whole course of the Ohio; America would retain her settlements on that river, and have a large space in which to plant new ones. Spain had no claim to the lands north of the Ohio; "their fate must be regulated with the Court of London." The navigation of the Mississippi would be controlled by the power owning its banks.[1]

Mr. Jay very naturally concluded that the Count de Vergennes was the real author of this scheme. He concluded, also, that in case the American Commissioners would not consent to it, then France would aid Spain in a negotiation to divide the West with England. It is now well known that such was, in substance, the programme of the two counts.

---

[1] Diplomatic Correspondence, VIII., 156 et seq.

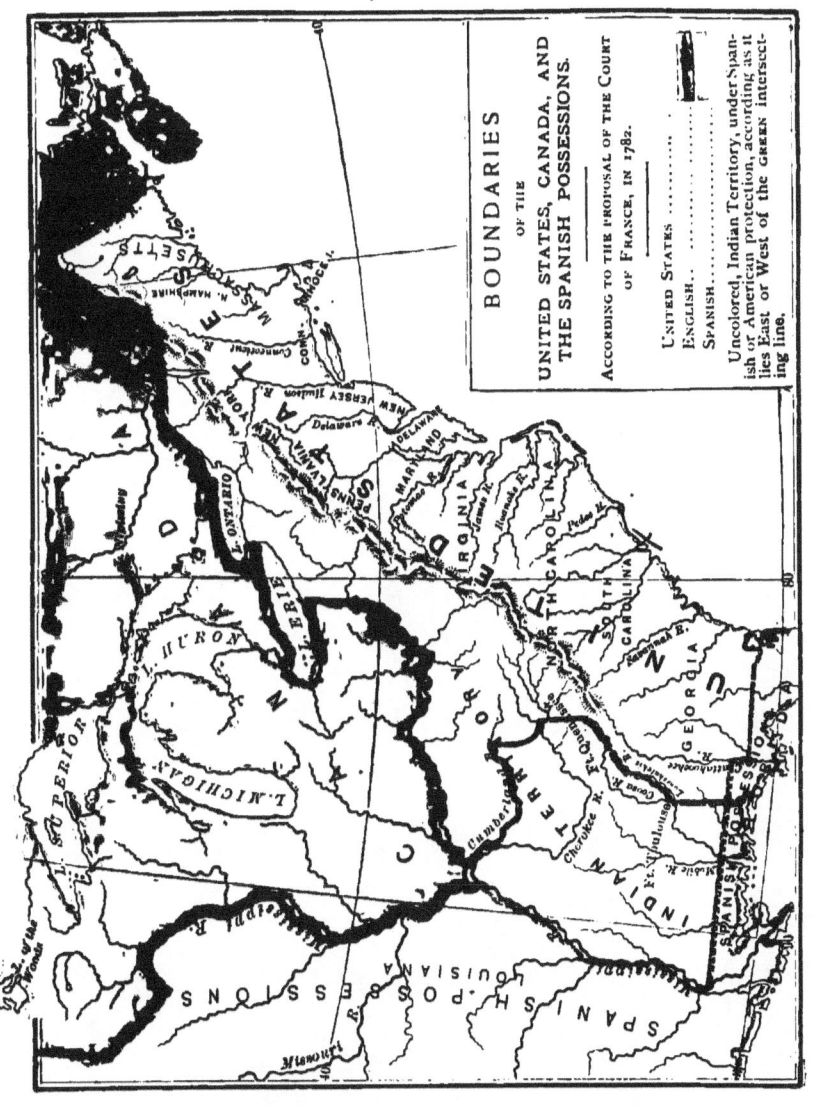

As a first step toward carrying it out, M. Rayneval was sent on a secret mission to England, where he informed Lord Shelburne that his chief would not support the Americans in several of their claims, as the fisheries and the Mississippi.

The destiny of the West had thus become a European question involving the three powers, all of which had interests of their own to look after in both worlds. England would naturally make the best terms that she could with her enemies, one and all; more specifically, she would obtain whatever advantage she could in the negotiations with the Americans from the jealousies of the two other powers. Spain was resolved on the recovery of Gibraltar as well as of Florida, and France was committed to her support. France had not entered into alliance with America from love of the American cause, but from hatred of England; and now that a rival power to England had been raised up on the shores of the New World, Vergennes was apprehensive that power would become so strong as to feel wholly independent of France. He was, indeed, committed irrevocably to the independence of the United States so far as England was concerned; but he was also determined that their independence should not be finally settled until a general peace had been arrived at. Possibly the country beyond the Alleghany Mountains could be traded off for Gibraltar, or be balanced against some other make-weight in the diplomatic scale. Fortunately, for his purpose, the treaty of 1778 bound the United States not to conclude a peace with England until France should also conclude one; and, as early as June, 1781, he had induced Congress to instruct the commissioners who were to negotiate with England "to make the most candid and confidential communications upon all subjects to the ministers of our generous ally the King of France; to undertake nothing in the negotiations for peace or truce without their knowledge and concurrence, and to make them sensible how much we rely upon His Majesty's influence for effectual support in everything that may be necessary to the present security or future prosperity of the United States."[1]

Such, in brief, was the diplomatic situation in Paris when the American negotiation entered on its second stage. In this tremendous game of politics, the fate of the West seemed to hang on issues wholly beyond the control of the American Commissioners. No more critical or anxious moment can be found in the whole history of our diplomacy. Determined, if possible, to keep their country from becoming the football of the three powers, the commissioners resolved, in disregard of their instructions,[2] to propose to the British Cabinet a negotiation to be conducted without the knowledge of the French ministers. Lord Shelburne, now Prime Minister, for reasons of state that are here immaterial, promptly accepted this overture, and the negotiation took a new departure.

Owing to important successes of the British arms in the West Indies and at Gibraltar, and to the discovery of a want of good understanding between America and France, the British ministers now held a firmer tone than in the first negotiation. The determination of the ministers to obtain a compensation for the British refugees whose property had been confiscated by the States became the occasion for reopening the question of boundaries in the Northeast, the West, and the Northwest. Mr. Strachey was sent over the Channel to assist Mr. Oswald in retreating from some of his concessions; and Lord Fitzmaurice tells us that his instructions were:

"To urge the claims of England, under the proclamation of 1763, to the lands between the Mississippi and the Western boundary of the States, and to bring forward the French boun-

---

[1] The Secret Journals, II., 435.

[2] Mr. Lyman, Diplomacy of the United States, I., 121, note, relates the following anecdote, which he says he has from a direct source. Dr. Franklin, one day sitting, during the discussion of the question of instructions, in Mr. Jay's room at Paris, said to that gentleman, "Will you break your instructions?" "Yes," replied Mr. Jay, who was smoking a pipe, "as I break this pipe;" and immediately threw it into the fire.

dary of Canada, which was more extensive at some points than that of the proclamation of 1763. He was to urge these claims, and the right of the King to the ungranted domain, not indeed for their own sake, but in order to gain some compensation for the refugees, either by a direct cession of territory in their favor, or by engaging the half, or some proportion of what the back lands might produce when sold, or a sum mortgaged on those lands ; or by the grant of a favorable boundary of Nova Scotia, extending, if possible, so as to include the province of Maine ; or, if that could not be obtained, the province of Sagadahock, or, at the very least, Penobscot."[1]

Lord Shelburne urged the same view, in a strong despatch to Oswald.

"As a resource to meet the demands of the refugees the matter of the boundaries and back lands presents itself. Independent of all the nonsense of charters, I mean, when they talk of extending as far as the sun sets, the soil is, and has always been acknowledged to be the King's. For the good of America, whatever the government may be, new provinces must be erected on those back lands and down the Mississippi ; and supposing them to be sold, what can be so reasonable as that part of the province, where the King's property alone is in question, should be applied to furnish subsistence to those, whom for the sake of peace he can never consistently with his honor entirely abandon."[2]

This was a very different view from the one that Oswald had held when he declined "any attempt at asserting the claims of the English Crown over the ungranted domains, deeming that no real distinction could be drawn between them and other sovereign rights which were necessarily to be ceded."

It is impossible to say much about the Western boundary discussions, because we know next to nothing about them.

---

[1] Life of Earl Shelburne, III., 281, 282.   [2] Ibid., III., 284.

Other controversies at Paris, far less important, were reported much more fully; but here the information that we possess only piques our curiosity. The right to fish on the banks of Newfoundland was thought more valuable in 1782 than the ownership of the valleys of Ohio, the prairies of Illinois, and the forests of Michigan. What would we not give for a full review of the whole subject from the pen that wrote the "Canada Pamphlet," and the "Reply to Hillsborough?"

The Mississippi was finally conceded by the British Cabinet. Still, this concession left unanswered the question where the northern boundary should strike the Mississippi. Writing to Minister Townsend, November 8th, Mr. Strachey says: "I despatch the boundary line originally sent to you by Mr. Oswald, and two other lines proposed by the American Commissioners after my arrival at Paris. Either of these you are to choose. They are both better than the original line, as well in respect to Canada as to Nova Scotia."[1] Mr. Adams tells us that one of these lines was the forty-fifth parallel, northwest of the St. Lawrence, and the other the line of the middle of the lakes. Most fortunately for us, the British ministers, owing, no doubt, to their desire to give Canada frontage on the four lakes, and to a preference for a water boundary, chose that line which left the Northwest intact. Had the forty-fifth parallel become the boundary, nearly one-half of Lakes Huron and Michigan, and of the States of Michigan and Wisconsin, and part of Minnesota, would have fallen to Great Britain. Writing to Robert R. Livingston, the American Secretary for Foreign Affairs, the commissioners say: "Congress will observe, that although our northern line is in a certain part below the latitude of forty-five, yet in others it extends above it, divides the Lake Superior, and gives us access to its western and southern waters, from which a line in that latitude would have excluded us."[2] If the com-

---
[1] Fitzmaurice: Life of Earl Shelburne, III., 295.
[2] Diplomatic Correspondence, X., 118.

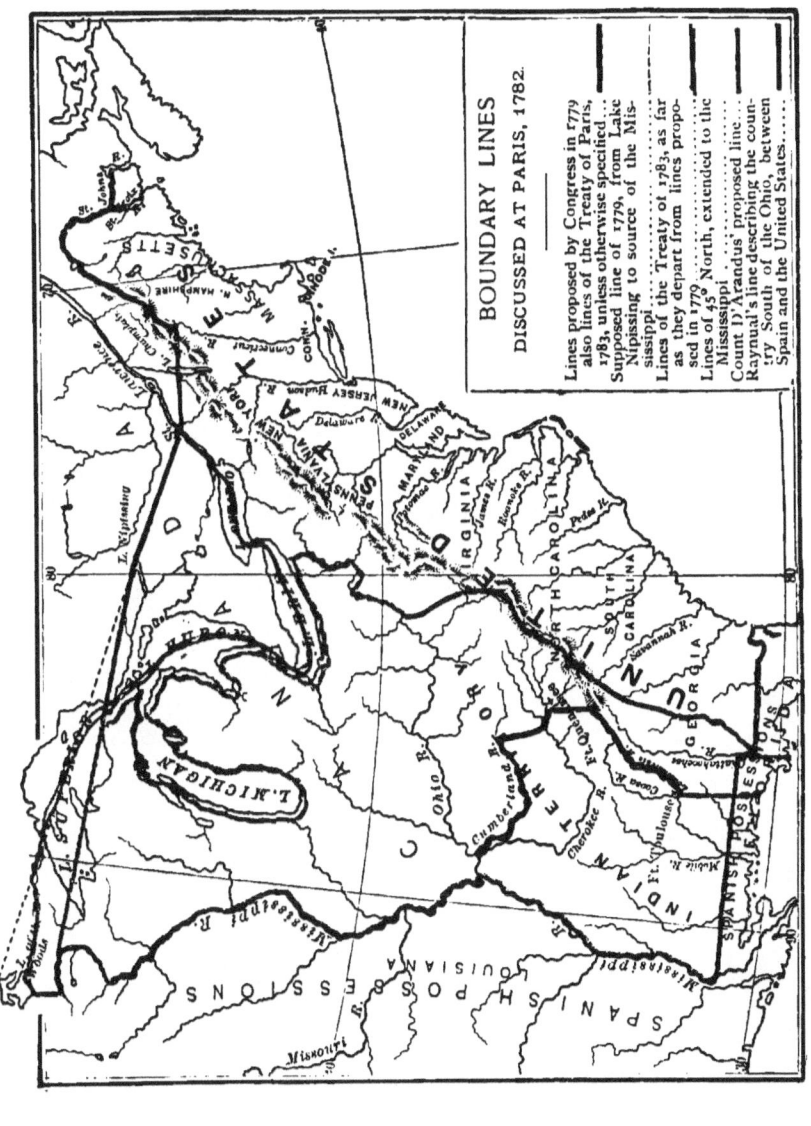

missioners had understood Northwestern geography better, to say nothing of the then unknown resources of Lake Superior, they would have stated the argument with even greater strength.

To close the war that began on Lexington Green, April 19, 1775, three separate treaties were necessary. France and the United States conducted simultaneous negotiations with different English commissioners, the understanding being that the preliminaries should be signed the same day. On November 29th Dr. Franklin wrote to M. de Vergennes that the American articles were already agreed upon, and that he hoped to lay a copy of them before his Excellency the next day. Except a single secret article, they were duly communicated; but, to the astonishment and mortification of the Count, they were already signed, and therefore binding, as far as the commissioners could make them so. The game for despoiling the young Republic of one-half her territorial heritage was effectually blocked. Vergennes bitterly reproached Franklin for the course that he and his associates had followed, and Franklin replied, making such defence as he could, admitting no more than that a point of *bienséance* had been neglected. The American Congress and Secretary for Foreign Affairs at first were also disposed to blame the commissioners; but so anxious was the country for peace and so much more favorable were the terms obtained than had been expected, that murmurs of dissatisfaction soon gave place to acclaims of gratification and delight. The preamble to the treaty contained the saving clause that it should not go into effect until France and England came to an understanding, a fact that the astute Franklin did not fail to press upon the attention of the irate Vergennes. However, that condition was soon fulfilled, and a general peace assured.

The definitive treaty of peace between the United States and England, which is merely the preliminary treaty over again, with the exception of the secret article to be noticed in the note at the end of this chapter, was signed September 3,

1783. His Britannic Majesty acknowledged the United States to be free, sovereign, and independent States, and relinquished for himself, his heirs, and successors "all claim to the government, propriety, and territorial right of the same and every part thereof;" assigning them boundaries that have proved to be more satisfactory than those proposed by Congress in 1779 could have been. It was a treaty of partition of the British Empire, and of the English-speaking world. At the time, British statesmen generally dreaded its effect on the Mother Country, but time has proved it a godsend to her as well as to America.

The happy issue of this negotiation was very largely due to William, Earl of Shelburne, afterward first Marquis of Lansdowne. Both as Secretary for the Colonies in the Rockingham Cabinet, and as Prime Minister, he was governed by the sentiment that he thus expressed: "Reconciliation with America on the noblest terms by the noblest means." Had the negotiation remained open at the downfall of his ministry, which was largely the result of the liberal terms that he gave the Americans, and so passed into the hands of the Fox-North coalition, no one can tell what the fate of the West would have been.

It is impossible nicely to divide among Dr. Franklin, Mr. Adams, and Mr. Jay, the honor of saving the West to their country. On that issue, Mr. Adams was unquestionably firm. A tradition has floated down the stream of diplomacy to the effect that Dr. Franklin was indifferent, or at least disposed to yield; but we have Mr. Jay's express testimony to the contrary,[1] to say nothing of the improbability of the Doctor's taking such a course, in view of his Western record as set forth in a previous chapter. However, the man who goes through the original documents, including the discussions at Madrid as well as those at Paris, will be pretty certain to conclude that the old Northwest has greater reason for gratitude to John Jay than to either of his colleagues.

---

[1] Sparks: Works of Franklin, X., 8.

It is not easy to tell what were the decisive arguments in this Western controversy. It is often said, and particularly by Western writers, that the issue turned mainly on the George Rogers Clark conquest. This view rests on tradition rather than on historical evidence, and I venture the opinion that it is largely erroneous. No man, at least, can read the reports on the national boundaries submitted to Congress without seeing that far more reliance was laid, by the committees that prepared them, on the colonial charters than on Clark's great achievement. The report of August 16, 1782, urges the argument: "The very country in question hath been conquered through the means of the common labors of the United States;" "for a considerable distance beyond the Alleghany Mountains, and particularly on the Ohio, American citizens are actually settled at this day"—"fencible men," not "behind any of their fellow-citizens in the struggle for liberty," who will be thrown back within the power of Great Britain if the Western territory is surrendered to her; but the same report contains page after page of arguments based on the charters and on colonial history. It was indeed most fortunate that the Virginia troops were in possession of the Illinois and the Wabash at the close of the war, but there is no reason to think that the Clark conquest, separate and apart from the colonial titles, ever would have given the United States the Great West. Writing to Secretary Livingston, the American Commissioners give color to the idea that the decision turned on the charters and not on the conquest. They say the Court of Great Britain "claimed not only all the lands in the Western country and on the Mississippi, which were not expressly included in our charters and governments, but also all such lands within them as remained ungranted by the King of Great Britain." "It would be endless," they add, "to enumerate all the discussions and arguments on the subject."[1] It is highly probable that the British ministry, see-

---

[1] Diplomatic Correspondence, X., 117.

ing that the West would go to Spain if not to the United States, preferred to give it the latter direction. Moreover, the Clark conquest was much more potent in keeping the West from falling into the hands of Spain than in wresting it from the hands of England.

The refusal of England to surrender so much of the Northwest as remained in her hands at the close of the war is a very striking proof of the reluctance with which she consented to the Northwestern boundaries. In July, 1783, Washington sent Baron Steuben to General Haldiman, British commander in Canada, with a commission to receive possession of Oswego, Niagara, Detroit, Mackinaw, and the minor posts; but Haldiman made reply that he had not received instructions for their surrender, and that he could not even discuss the subject with him. At the time there was no reason for retaining the posts consistent with national good faith; afterward the British Government alleged as a reason the non-fulfilment by this country of certain stipulations of the treaty of peace. For thirteen years the Northwestern posts were sharp thorns in the sides of the United States. The Revolution was followed by a harassing Indian war that, in reality, never ceased until Wayne's victory of the Fallen Timbers, in 1794; and from its first day to its last the savages found always sympathy, and often active support, at the British garrisons. British officers, audaciously invading territory which they did not hold at the end of the war, built Fort Miami at the rapids of the Maumee, where Perrysburg, O., now stands. General Wayne pursued the Indians under the very muzzles of the cannon of this fortification, and laid waste the surrounding country to its gates. The Indian war and the British occupation, that had been so closely connected, virtually ceased at the same time. In 1795, Wayne negotiated with the Indians the Treaty of Greenville, and, the year before, Jay negotiated with the British Government the treaty that bears his name, by which England bound herself to yield possession of the posts that she should have yielded in

1783. On July 11, 1796, a detachment from Wayne's army raised the stars and stripes above the stockade and village of Detroit, where the French and British colors had successively waved, and this act completed the tardy transfer of the old Northwest to the United States. No doubt England had some reason to complain of the United States for the imperfect fulfilment of the treaty of 1783; but her retention of the posts, so calamitous in results to the growing Western settlements, was largely due to a lingering hope that the young republic would prove a failure, and to a determination to share the expected spoil. The fact is, neither England nor Spain regarded the Treaty of Paris as finally settling the destiny of the country west of the mountains.

It is not improbable that the War of 1812, for a time, revived English hopes of again recovering the Northwest. Tecumseh strove to erect his "dam" to resist "the mighty water ready to overflow his people." Hull's surrender placed all Michigan in British hands. General Proctor sought to compel the citizens of Detroit to take the oath of allegiance to the King of England; and although Harrison's successes on the Maumee and Perry's victory on Lake Erie forced Proctor to evacuate Detroit, a British garrison continued to hold Mackinaw to the close of the war. Only three of the thirty-two years lying between 1783 and 1815 were years of war; but for one-half of the whole time the British flag was flying on the American side of the boundary-line. In the largest sense, therefore, the destiny of the Northwest was not assured until the Treaty of Ghent.

The Iroquois called themselves the owners of the lands northwest of the Ohio; the Indians living on those lands they considered simply as occupants or tenants. It is obvious that the tenants valued them much more highly than the owners. The long wars that the Western Indians waged for Ohio tell the story of their affection for their homes. The same wars also tell at what fearful cost the American frontier was extended west of the Alleghany Mountains. From the defeat of Braddock, in 1755, onward to Wayne's Treaty, in 1795, with a few short intermissions, that frontier was undergoing a constant baptism of fire and blood.

The original United States were bounded on the north by Great Britain, on the west and south by Spain, and on the east by the Ocean—the last named being the only neighbor with whom we never had any trouble. One of the most striking evidences of the value of this domain, and of its admirable position, is the remarkable growth of the United States. An area of eight hundred and twenty-seven thousand square miles has become an area of three million six hundred thousand. Parallel thirty-one degrees north and the Mississippi have given place, as boundaries, to the Gulf of Mexico, the Rio Grande, and the Pacific Ocean. Our marvellous territorial expansion and material development westward discourage prophecy; but, at this time, it does not seem probable that the territory wrested from England will soon, if ever, cease to be the most valuable part of our whole national domain, described by Mr. Gladstone as "a natural base for the greatest continuous empire ever established by man."

The man curious about "what might have been" cannot help speculating on the course of history provided any one of the limitation-schemes proposed at Paris had prevailed. As he reflects on the facts of geography, on the strength and audacity of American civilization, on the weakness of Spanish America and of Spain herself, and on the feeble Canadian settlements in 1783, he may conclude that the eastern half of the Mississippi Valley and the Atlantic Plain would have been reunited even if once separated; that the idea of separation, supported in some form by the three powers, was against Nature; that Spain, in particular, lost her only opportunity to control the Father of Waters in the sixteenth and seventeenth centuries, and that the great valley of the West was the predestined field of Anglo-Saxon institutions and life. There is undeniable force in this reasoning; perhaps it is altogether conclusive. At the same time, the proposed limitation might have turned American events into wholly different channels. What if the Confederacy had fallen to pieces? What if the Constitution of 1787 had never been framed or ratified? What if the United States had become dependent upon one of the European powers? In any one of these events, the world would never have seen that magnificent growth which has absorbed territories four times as great as that bounded by the treaty of 1783, and which furnishes the main argument for the conclusion, "It would have made little difference." The longer one considers the subject, the less will he be disposed to think that the delivery of the West by the trustee appointed in 1763 was a foregone conclusion; the more will he think the retention of the Northwest by Great Britain would have been a much more serious mischance than the gaining of the Southwest by Spain; and the more reason will he discover for congratulation that the logic of events gave us our proper boundaries at the close of the War of Independence, and did not leave us to succumb to untoward fate or to renew the struggle with two European powers instead of one in after years.

NOTE.—Article 2 of the Treaty of Paris reads thus : "And that all disputes which might arise in future on the subject of the boundaries of the United States may be prevented, it is hereby agreed and declared that the following are and shall be their boundaries, namely : From the northwest angle of Nova Scotia, namely, that angle which is formed by a line drawn due north from the source of St. Croix River to the Highlands; along the said Highlands, which divide those rivers that empty themselves into the River St. Lawrence from those which fall into the Atlantic Ocean, to the northwesternmost head of Connecticut River ; thence down along the middle of that river to the forty-fifth degree of north latitude ; from thence, by a line due west on the said latitude, until it strikes the River Iroquois or Cataraquy [that is, the St. Lawrence] ; thence along the middle of said river into Lake Ontario, through the middle of said lake until it strikes the communication by water between that lake and Lake Erie; thence along the middle of said communication into Lake Erie, through the middle of said lake until it arrives at the water communication between that lake and Lake Huron; thence along the middle of said water communication into the Lake Huron; thence through the middle of said lake to the water communication between that lake and Lake Superior; thence through Lake Superior northward of the isles Royal and Philipeaux to the Long Lake; thence through the middle of said Long Lake and the water communication between it and the Lake of the Woods to the said Lake of the Woods; thence through the said lake to the most northwestern point thereof, and from thence on a due west course to the River Mississippi; thence by a line to be drawn along the middle of the said River Mississippi until it shall intersect the northernmost part of the thirty-first degree of north latitude. South, by a line to be drawn due east from the determination of the line last mentioned, in the latitude of thirty-one degrees north of the equator, to the middle of the River Appalachicola or Catahouche; thence along the middle thereof to its junction with the Flint River; thence straight to the head of St. Mary's River, and thence down along the middle of St. Mary's River to the Atlantic Ocean. East, by a line to be drawn along the middle of the River St. Croix, from its mouth in the Bay of Fundy to its source, and from its source directly north to the aforesaid Highlands, which divide the rivers that fall into the Atlantic Ocean from those which fall into the River St. Lawrence; comprehending all islands within twenty leagues of any part of the shores of the United States, and lying between lines to be drawn due east from the points where the aforesaid boundaries between Nova Scotia, on the one part, and East Florida, on the other, shall respectively touch the Bay of Fundy and the Atlantic Ocean, excepting such islands as now are or heretofore have been within the limits of the said province of Nova Scotia."

The fullest report of the discussion of the Western question, at Paris, found in any contemporary State paper, is in the letter that the Commissioners wrote to Mr. Livingston, July 18, 1783,

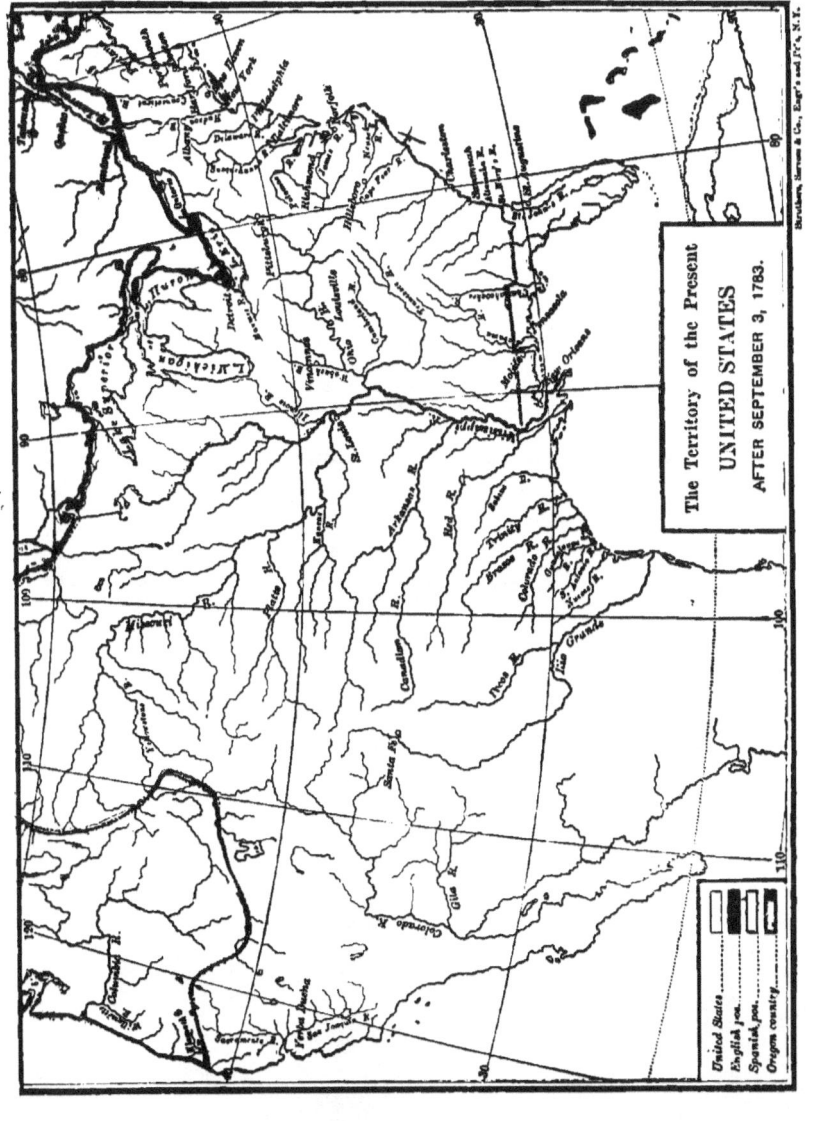

in reply to his censure "for signing the treaty without communicating it to the Court of Versailles till after the signature, and in concealing the separate article from it even when signed." The preceding narrative is sufficiently full touching the reasons for secrecy, but a few remarks may properly be added concerning the secret article, which was in these words: "It is hereby understood and agreed that in case Great Britain, at the conclusion of the present war, shall recover or be put in possession of West Florida, the line of north boundary between the said province and the United States shall be a line drawn from the mouth of the River Yazoo where it unites with the Mississippi due east to the River Appalachicola." This line was the northern boundary of West Florida as established in 1764. At the time of the negotiation this province was in the possession of the Spanish troops, and it was a question what disposition would be made of it at the general peace. The Commissioners show very plainly that this question materially affected the whole Western negotiation. Mr. Oswald, wishing to cover as much of the eastern shores of the Mississippi with British claims as possible, had much to say of "the ancient boundaries" of Canada and Louisiana; and the British Court, expecting to regain the Floridas, "seemed desirous of annexing as much territory to them as possible, even up to the mouth of the Ohio."

Oswald avowed the desire to render the British countries on the gulf large enough "to be worth keeping and protecting," and also to gain a convenient retreat for the Tories; but he finally consented to yield to the United States the country north of the Yazoo line, if the Commissioners would yield to England south of that line. Hence it will be seen that the secret article was a bargain between the parties. At the same time the Commissioners say: "We were of opinion that the country in conquest was of great value, both on account of its natural fertility and of its position, it being, in our opinion, the interest of America to extend as far down toward the mouth of the Mississippi as we possibly could."[1]

---

[1] Diplomatic Correspondence, X., 187 et seq.

This boundary-description flows smooth, but it is doubtful if the same number of words in a treaty ever concealed more seeds of controversy. To draw boundary-lines on paper is one thing; to go upon the ground where they are supposed to fall, with instruments to run and mark them, is quite another, as the high contracting parties in this case found to their cost the moment an attempt was made to transfer the treaty-lines to the surface of the earth. No doubt the diplomatists at Paris used the language in good faith; but their lines had to be drawn, not only on paper, but also through vast wildernesses uninhabited and unexplored, and some of the lines, naturally, were found impracticable. In part, however, the disputes that arose had other sources than ignorance of geography. Serious doubts having arisen as to the practicability of reaching the Mississippi by a due west line from the northwesternmost point of the Lake of the Woods, Jay's Treaty provided that measures should be taken in concert to survey the Upper Mississippi, and that, in case the due-west line was found impracticable, the "two powers would thereupon proceed by amicable negotiation to regulate the boundary in that quarter," etc. I have found no trace of such a survey being made, and the boundary was not fixed for more than twenty years thereafter.[1]

A convention was signed, May 12, 1803, by the representatives of the two powers, which contained arrangements for determining the boundary from the Lake of the Woods to the Mississippi. But at the same time that Rufus King was negotiating this treaty in London with Lord Hawkesbury, Messrs. Livingston and Monroe were negotiating a much more familiar one in Paris with the ministers of the First Consul. This was the treaty for the cession of Louisiana to the United States, signed April 30, 1803. When the London treaty came before the Senate, the argument was made that the Louisiana cession would affect the line from the Lake of the Woods to the Mississippi River; the Senate accordingly struck out the article, which the

---

[1] The best maps of the period put down the course of the river above the forty-fifth parallel as "the Mississippi by conjecture." McMaster: History of the People of the United States, II., 153.

British Government resented, and so the whole treaty fell. By the purchase of 1803 we succeeded to all the rights, as respects Louisiana, that had belonged to Spain or France, and this carried us, west of the Mississippi, north to the British possessions. By a convention dated October 20, 1818, the United States and England settled the Lake of the Woods controversy, and established the boundary between them to the Rocky Mountains.

"It is agreed that a line drawn from the most northwestern point of the Lake of the Woods, along the forty-ninth parallel of north latitude, or if the said point shall not be in the forty-ninth parallel of north latitude, then that a line drawn from the said point due north or south, as the case may be, until the said line shall intersect the said parallel of north latitude, and from the point of such intersection due west along and with the said parallel, shall be the line of demarcation between the territories of the United States and those of His Britannic Majesty, and that the said line shall form the northern boundary of the said territories of the United States, and the southern boundary of the territories of His Britannic Majesty, from the Lake of the Woods to the Stony Mountains."

This extract, together with the facts of geography, explains the singular projection of our northern boundary on the west side of the Lake of the Woods, which first appeared on ordinary maps some ten years ago.

The line from the intersection of the St. Lawrence and parallel 45° north to the foot of the St. Marys was established in 1823, by joint commission under the Treaty of Ghent; the line from the foot of the St. Marys to the northwesternmost point of Lake of the Woods, by the Webster-Ashburton Treaty in 1842.

XI.

THE NORTHWESTERN LAND-CLAIMS.

THE second part of the chapter devoted to the territorial questions growing out of the royal patents and charters closed with a promise to consider, in the proper place, the similar question affecting the old Northwest. In fact, the only reason for introducing the charters at all is their bearing on Western questions. Accordingly, this chapter will be given to a statement of the Western land-claims; the two following chapters, to their settlement. Unfortunately, the discussion of the whole subject is often colored by State feeling or by patriotism. Connecticut writers are apt to stand for the Connecticut claim, New York writers for the New York claim, while Virginians pride themselves on Virginia's being the mother of States as well as of statesmen. Again, Western men, little disposed to admit that the Northwestern States were the children of the Atlantic commonwealths, and fond of looking at the subject from a national point of view, tend either to belittle or to deny the titles of the claimant States to the Western lands.

In her constitution of 1776, Virginia ceded, released, and forever confirmed to the people of Maryland, Pennsylvania, and North and South Carolina, the territories contained within their charters, so far as they were embraced in her charter of 1609, with all the rights of property, jurisdiction, and government, and all other rights that had ever been claimed by Virginia, except the navigation of certain rivers; after which she said:

THE NORTHWESTERN LAND-CLAIMS. 193

"The western and northern extent of Virginia shall, in all other respects, stand as fixed by the charter of King James I., in the year one thousand six hundred and nine, and the public treaty of peace between the Courts of Britain and France, in the year one thousand seven hundred and sixty-three; unless, by act of this Legislature, one or more governments be established westward of the Alleghany Mountains. And no purchases of lands shall be made of the Indian natives, but on behalf of the public, by authority of the General Assembly."

This declaration meant, that Virginia claimed the whole Northwest as falling within her west and northwest lines. The claim has been often denied by historians, statesmen, lawyers, and pamphleteers, on grounds that will be stated as concisely as is consistent with clearness.

Probably no bolder or stronger denial was ever made than that of Hon. Samuel F. Vinton, of counsel for the defendants in the case of Virginia *vs.* Peter M. Garner and others,[1] before the General Court of Virginia, in December, 1845. The legal question involved was that of the boundary between the States of Virginia and Ohio. In the course of his argument to the court Mr. Vinton affirmed the following historical propositions:

(1) "That Virginia, during the War of the Revolution, set up a claim to the country beyond the Ohio;" (2) "that she never had a valid title to it;" (3) "that her title, not only to it, but to both sides of the Ohio, was disputed by the Con-

---

[1] Garner and the other defendants, citizens of Ohio, were seized by a party of Virginians, between low-water and high-water mark, on the north side of the Ohio River, in the act of assisting some slaves belonging to one Harwood, a Virginian, to escape from slavery. The case went up from Wood County to the General Court on a special verdict, the question being whether the defendants were, at the time of meeting and assisting the slaves, within the jurisdiction of Virginia or of Ohio. The case is reported at length in Grattan, Reports of Cases decided in the Supreme Court of Appeals and in the General Court of Virginia, III., 655. Mr. Vinton's argument was published in pamphlet, Marietta, O., 1846; and it is also found in the Second Annual Report of the Ohio State Fish Commission, 1877.

federacy, and by other States;" (4) "that they claimed all that she asserted a right to;" (5) "that, in the end, she adjusted her claim by compromise;" (6) "that she relinquished her claim beyond the Ohio with the express understanding that the acceptance of her act of cession was not to be taken as an admission by the Confederacy (who was the grantee) that Virginia had a title to the country ceded by her;" (7) "that the separate and acknowledged right of Virginia to the country on the lower, and of the Confederacy to that on the upper, bank of the Ohio, began with this compromise."

From these propositions Mr. Vinton deduced others of a legal nature that do not here concern us.

These seven propositions may all be reduced to two, for convenience. The first of these, the absolute denial of the charter-title, is supported by this chain of reasoning: (1) The Virginia grant of 1609 was made in total ignorance of the extent of the continent and of the grant sought to be conveyed; (2) the English king at that time had no right or title to the lands included within the limits beyond the Atlantic slope; (3) the charter was annulled by a writ of *quo warranto* issued by the Court of King's Bench in 1624, and was never renewed; (4) the English Crown's later title to the country between the Alleghanies and the Mississippi was the treaty with France in 1763; (5) the Crown plainly signified by numerous acts, as the proclamation of 1763 and the Walpole grant of 1772, that colonial Virginia did not extend beyond the mountains, and that the over-mountain lands were Crown lands; and (6) later grants than that of 1609, as those to the Carolina proprietors, to Baltimore and Penn, and to the New England colonies, show that the Crown did not regard those limits as conclusive, either on the sea-shore or in the West. Mr. Vinton rested his second cardinal proposition, that Virginia's title to the country southeast of the Ohio is a compromise with other States and with Congress, made in 1784, on the history of the cessions. The cessions will be treated in the next chapters, and need not be anticipated here. Nearly all the judges who gave opinions in Garner's case waived the historical issue that Mr. Vinton had raised, on the ground that a Virginia court could not question the fundamental law of the State; but the temptation proved so strong that some of them discussed the subject more or less at length. McComas, Judge, thus touched some of the points involved:

"It will not be necessary to inquire into the rights of the British king, because no civilized nations had claim to the country except England and France; and, by treaty between those two nations, the boundaries were ascertained and fixed between them; and the territory in controversy was acknowledged to be in the English Crown, and of course by that treaty the title of Virginia to the lands contained in her charter, and comprehended in the limits of the British possessions, was confirmed, and thereby made good. The British king by several acts, and particularly by grants of large tracts of land, acknowledged that the Northwestern territory was within the jurisdiction and limits of Virginia. . . . But it is stated that the charter of Virginia was annulled, and that she has no right to claim under said charter. It has been decided, and I think rightly, 'that the charter was annulled so far as the rights of the company were concerned, but not in respect to the rights of the Colony. The powers of government, the same powers which the charter had vested in the company as proprietor, were vested in the Crown: the same title to the lands within its chartered limits, which the charter had vested in the company, was revested in the Crown.' . . .

"In relation to the territory northwest of the Ohio River, it ought to be recollected that during the Revolutionary War, and before the cession, Virginia conquered the territory by her own troops, unaided by the other States of the Union; and formed the whole territory into the county of Illinois. It therefore seems to me, as the territory was not within the chartered limits of any other State, and as it undoubtedly belonged to the British Crown, this conquest would give Virginia an undoubted right to it."

Lomax, Judge, held that:

"The charter of 1609 was the commencement of the colonial or political existence of Virginia ; and it was that charter which separated and designated the country called Virginia, and the community which was settled upon it. That charter became the primal and perpetual law of this Commonwealth. The Crown of England, when by the judgment of *quo warranto* against the company in London it took the charter out of their hands, did not cancel the charter. The government of the Colony, when it thereby became a Royal Colony, was still administered according to the scheme of government established by the previous charters. The rights guaranteed to the people of Virginia by that charter, were frequently and strenuously appealed to, down to the time of the Revolutionary contest, as the chartered rights of Virginians. In March, 1651, the treaty between Virginia and the commonwealth of England, stipulated that Virginia should have, and enjoy the ancient bounds and limits granted by the charters of the former Kings. This was a recognition in the most solemn form, notwithstanding the judgment above referred to in 1624, of the boundaries of Virginia and of her ancient charters. The subsequent grants by the King to Penn, Baltimore, and Carteret could not disturb those limits, but to the extent that those grants conveyed ; and even to that extent were remonstrated against by the colony. . . . There are many public acts of the Colonial government of Virginia, in which her title was asserted, and dominion exercised by her over the territories she claimed, as her western territories, extending to the River Ohio, and beyond it, including the present State of Ohio ; nor was any question ever raised as to that title or dominion by any civilized people, except for a time by the French. These acts show that she had extended her jurisdiction over the Northwestern territory which was ceded, and that she had made grants of lands and settlements on the Ohio. In all these acts the consent of the King, the proprietor of the colony, must necessarily have been given by himself or those who were authorized by him to give it. For in all the laws and public acts of the Colony, the approbation of the sovereign, or of a substitute, fully representing him as to that matter, was indispensable."

The learned judge then recounts a long series of public acts in which Virginia exercised sovereignty west of the mountains. Among the most prominent of these are the creation of counties: Orange, in 1734; Augusta, in 1738; Botetourt, in 1769, " bounded west by the utmost limits of Virginia." The act creating one of these counties speaks of " the people situated on the waters of the Mississippi " as living " very remote from their court-house." Other counties erected before the Revolution extended to the Ohio, and embraced Kentucky. The Dinwiddie proclamation of 1754, offering lands to volunteers to serve against the French—one hundred thousand acres contiguous to the fort at the Forks of the Ohio, and one hundred thousand on or near the Ohio —was recognized by the Virginia land-law of 1779. In 1752 and 1753 Virginia passed acts for encouraging persons to settle on the Mississippi (" meaning, doubtless, the waters of Ohio "); and in 1754 and 1755 acts for their protection. Grants of land on the southeastern side of the Ohio, made in the colonial period, were numerous. Marshall's " Life of Washington " is quoted as authority for the statement that the grant made to the Ohio Company in 1748 was made as a part of Virginia. The proclamation of 1763 was obviously designed for the preservation of peace with the Indians, and their enjoyment of the hunting-grounds. The Treaty of Paris, 1763, limited the colony on the west; but Virginia continued to fill up and occupy, both geographically and politically, the territory to the Mississippi, " until that signal act of her sovereignty over the Western territories was exercised by her in the cession she made of them in March, 1784, and which was consummated by the acceptance of it by the United States in Congress assembled upon the same day."

These facts certainly demolish Mr. Vinton's proposition that the Virginia claim was " set up " during the Revolution.

The grant made to the Duke of York in 1664 was bounded on the west by the Delaware River. But at the beginning of the Revolution, as well as before that time, New York claimed a far greater western extension, on these grounds : (1) That the grant to the Duke of York and the boundary east of the Hudson barred the New England colonies on the west ; (2) that the *quo warranto* of 1624 and the grant to Penn limited Virginia and Pennsylvania on the west, the first by the Alleghanies, the second by the five-degree line west of the Delaware; (3) that the country west of these lines belonged to the Iroquois, in the north from times immemorial, in the south after the Iroquois conquest of 1664 ; (4) that after 1624, 1664, and 1681, the pre-emption of the West was vested in the Crown, not in particular colonies ; (5) that the accession of the Duke of York, the proprietary of the province, to the throne, in 1685, affiliated the territory on the two sides of the Delaware north of Penn's line ; and (6) that the later Iroquois treaties made the whole Western country, from the Lower Lakes to the Cumberland Mountains, and from Virginia and Pennsylvania to the Mississippi River, a part of New York. A report on the Western land-claims, made in Congress, November 3, 1781, preferred the New York claims to all those with which it conflicted, and thus justified the preference :

" 1. It clearly appeared to your committee, that all the lands belonging to the Six Nations of Indians, and their tributaries, have been in due form put under the protection of the crown of England by the said Six Nations, as appendant to the late government of New York, so far as respects jurisdiction only.

" 2. That the citizens of the said colony of New York have borne the burthen both as to blood and treasure, of protecting and supporting the said Six Nations of Indians, and their tributaries, for upwards of one hundred years last past, as the dependents and allies of the said government.

" 3. That the crown of England has always considered and treated the country of the said Six Nations, and their tributa-

THE NORTHWESTERN LAND-CLAIMS. 199

ries, inhabiting as far as the 45th degree of north latitude, as appendant to the government of New York.

"4. That the neighboring colonies of Massachusetts, Connecticut, Pennsylvania, Maryland, and Virginia, have also, from time to time, by their public acts, recognized and admitted the said Six Nations and their tributaries, to be appendant to the government of New York.

"5. That by Congress accepting this cession, the jurisdiction of the whole western territory belonging to the Six Nations, and their tributaries, will be vested in the United States greatly to the advantage of the Union."[1]

At this distance it is difficult, notwithstanding the particularity of this report, to repel Mr. Hildreth's characterization of the New York claim as the "vaguest and most shadowy of all."[2] Furthermore, there is reason to think the report part of a political scheme that will be duly noticed hereafter. But here it is pertinent to point out that this claim was virtually the claim to the Northwest which England made just before the French War, characterized by Mr. Parkman as including every mountain, forest, or prairie where an Iroquois had taken a scalp.[3]

The two New England States rested their claims on the charters with which the reader is already familiar. Connecticut's claim, at the beginning of the Revolution, was the zone lying between parallels 41° and 42° 2' north latitude, and Massachusetts's, the zone north of this to the parallel of three miles beyond the inflow of Lake Winnipiseogee in New Hampshire; both claims extending from the Delaware and the line thereof to the Mississippi. Connecticut's claim was largely reduced by the Trenton decision of 1782; but this in no way affected her rights west of Pennsylvania. It was urged that these claims were barred west of the present west-

---

[1] Journals of Congress, IV., 21, 22. [2] History, III., 399.
[3] Montcalm and Wolfe, I., 125.

ern limits of these States: (1) By the words, "actually possessed and occupied by a Christian people or prince," found in the Plymouth charter of 1620, because they related to the lands west of the Dutch settlements; (2) by the presence of the Dutch on the Hudson in 1620, 1629, and 1662; (3) by the grant to the Duke of York; (4) by the boundary-settlement of 1733; (5) by the grant to Penn in 1681; and (6) by New York's Iroquois title. Stress was also laid on the old argument against the from sea-to-sea grants; viz., they were made in ignorance of geography, and included vast tracts of land that did not, at the time, belong to the English Crown. The most important of these points were sustained by Attorney-General Pratt in 1761, who also held that there were State reasons for deciding the Wyoming controversy in favor of Pennsylvania; but Thurlow, and the other Crown lawyers consulted by Connecticut, held that the reservation made in the charter of 1620 did "not extend to lands on the west side of the Dutch settlements;" that the Plymouth grant did not mean to except in favor of anyone anything to the westward of such plantations; that the agreement of 1733 between Connecticut and New York extended "no further than to settle the boundaries between the respective parties," and " had no effect upon other claims that either of them had in other parts;" and that as the charter to Connecticut was granted but eighteen years before that to Penn, there was "no ground to contend that the Crown could, at that period, make an effective grant to him of that country which had been so recently granted to others."[1]

The two New England claims rested on substantially the same foundation; but it is curious to note how differently they were treated east of the western limits of Pennsylvania and New York. A Federal court threw the one claim aside as invalid, while the State of New York virtually conceded

---

[1] Hoyt gives the substance of the two opinions: Title in the Seventeen Townships in the County of Luzerne, 32, 33.

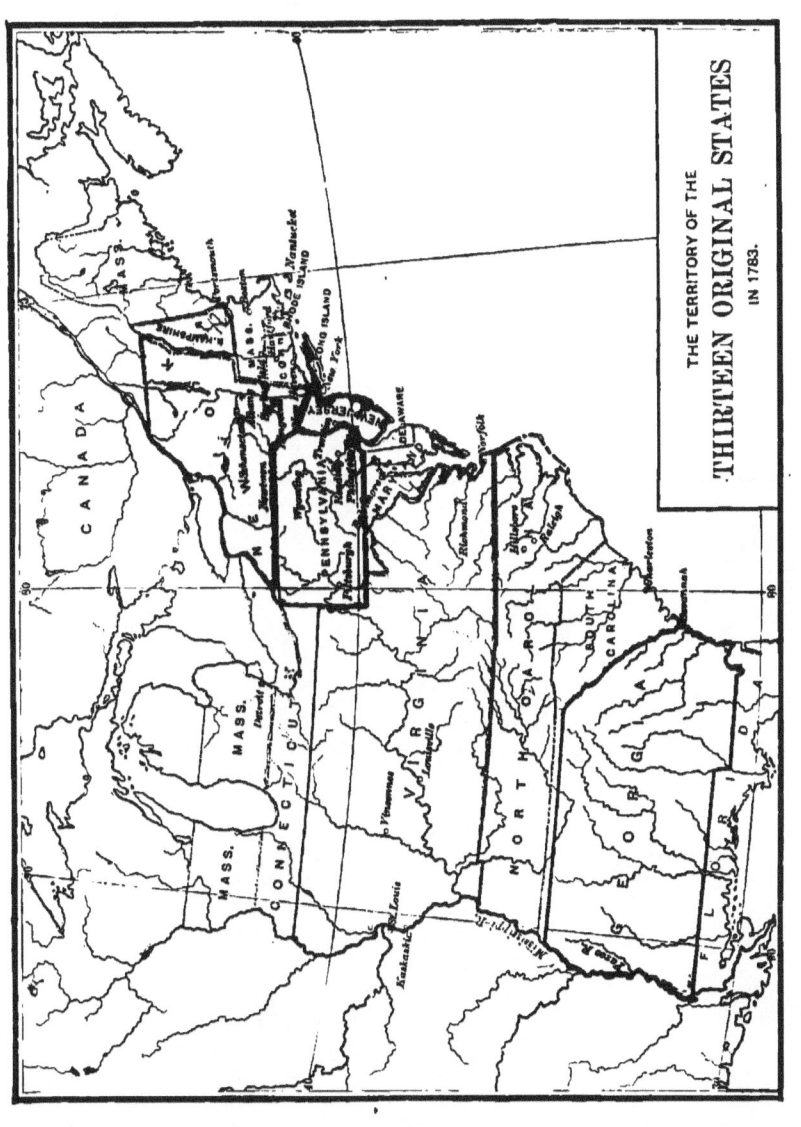

the validity of the other in her compromise with Massachusetts in 1786.

The report of the committee on the national limits made August 16, 1782, assigns the treaties of 1684, 1701, 1726, 1744, and 1754, with the Six Nations, as the sources of New York's title to the West.[1] The report of January 8th on the same subject speaks of the royal geographer, in a map describing and distinguishing the British, Spanish, and French dominions in America according to the treaty of 1763, as carrying the States of Georgia, North Carolina, South Carolina, and Virginia as far as the Mississippi.[2] Some maps of that period, it may be added, do carry the east and west lines of these States as far as the great river; others carry them no farther than the mountains; but all maps making any pretentions to thoroughness lay down the lines of the royal proclamation.

Such were the Northwestern land-claims that, for many years, were a foremost question of domestic polity. Practically they were not heard of until the time came for the American column to pass the Endless Mountains and take possession of the Great West. And, strange to say considering the vehemence with which they were afterward disputed, the first time they were brought before a Congress of the Colonies they met with a unanimous approval.

NOTE.—These are the resolutions in which the Albany Congress set its seal to the claims in 1754.

"That His Majesty's title to the northern continent of America appears to be founded on the discovery thereof first made, and the possession thereof first taken in 1497, under a commission from Henry the Seventh of England to Sebastian Cabot : That the French have possessed themselves of several parts of this continent, which by treaties have been ceded and confirmed to them.

"That the right of the English to the whole sea-coast from Georgia on the south, to the river St. Lawrence on the north,

---

[1] Secret Journals, III., 168.   [2] Ibid., III., 154.

excepting the Island of Cape Breton, and the Islands in the bay of St. Lawrence remains indisputable :

"That all the lands or countries westward from the Atlantic Ocean to the South Sea, between 48 and 34 degrees north latitude, was expressly included in the grant of King Charles the First to divers of his subjects, so long since as the year 1606, and afterwards confirmed in 1620, and under this grant the colony of Virginia claims extent as far west as the South Sea, and the ancient colonies of the Massachusetts Bay and Connecticut, were by their respective charters made to extend to the said South Sea ; so that not only the right to the sea-coast, but all the inland countries from sea to sea, has at all times been asserted by the crown of England :

"That the bounds of those colonies, which extend to the South Seas, be contracted and limited by the Alleghany or Appalachian mountains; and that measures be taken for settling from time to time, colonies of his Majesty's Protestant subjects west of said mountains, in convenient cantons to be assigned for that purpose ; and finally, that there be a union of his Majesty's several governments on the continent, that so their councils, treasures, and strength, may be employed in due proportion against their common enemy."

XII.
THE NORTHWESTERN CESSIONS.—(I.)

THE United States and the States taken together might possibly have continued conterminous until the Louisiana annexation in 1803, provided all the States had been bounded on the west by the Mississippi River. But such was not the case. New Hampshire, Rhode Island, New Jersey, Delaware, and Maryland were all confined to the Atlantic Plain, and Pennsylvania did not extend far beyond the Forks of the Ohio; while the seven remaining States claimed the whole West, from the Florida line to the Lakes, and some of it two and even three times over. The division of the States into the two classes, in connection with the nature of the war, made the Western lands an inevitable issue. The claimant States were more numerous, more populous, and more wealthy than the non-claimant States, not to speak of their territorial superiority; they also stood on the plain federal principle that the Confederation was the States confederated; but they could not prevent the issue being raised or prevent its going against them in the end. Before the boundaries of 1783 were agreed upon, Congress had adopted a policy that ultimately gave the jurisdiction of the West, and a large part of the lands, to the nation; and we are now to follow the development of this policy so far as it relates to our subject.

On October 14, 1777, Congress adopted the following rule for supplying the treasury of the United States:

"All charges of war and all other expenses that shall be incurred for the common defence or general welfare, and allowed by the United States in Congress assembled, shall be defrayed out of a common treasury which shall be supplied by the several states, in proportion to the value of all land within each state granted to, or surveyed for, any person, as such land and the buildings and improvements thereon shall be estimated according to such mode as the United States in Congress assembled shall from time to time direct and appoint."[1]

This rule, which left the States wholly free to raise the supplies for the treasury in their own way, was made a part of Article VIII. of the Articles of Confederation. The vote on this rule does not appear to have been influenced by the land-issue. That issue was first raised the following day, when this proposition, submitted no doubt by one of the delegates from that State, received the single vote of Maryland:

"That the United States in Congress assembled shall have the sole and exclusive right and power to ascertain and fix the western boundary of such states as claim to the Mississippi or the South Sea, *and lay out the land beyond the boundary so ascertained into separate and independent states, from time to time, as the numbers and circumstances of the people thereof may require.*"

Because this was the first proposition " that Congress should exercise sovereign jurisdiction over the Western country," Prof. H. B. Adams calls it a "pioneer thought.[2]" In one respect it is a very different thought from that which finally prevailed. The proposition was really double—an end to be gained and a means of gaining it. The end was national jurisdiction over the Western lands; the means, the assertion of this jurisdiction by Congress, no more attention being paid to the claimant than to the non-claimant States. It was a

---

[1] The history of the Confederation in Congress is found in the Secret Journals of Congress, I., 283 et seq. The citations will be found under the appropriate dates.

[2] Maryland's Influence upon Land Cessions to the United States, 23.

plain proposition to nationalize the lands. The end was the highest statesmanship; but if Congress had adopted the means of reaching it proposed by Maryland, it is reasonably certain that the Confederation and the patriot cause would have been hopelessly wrecked.

Scenting danger, the claimant States, October 27th, caused a declaration to be incorporated in the Articles that the United States in Congress assembled should be the last resort, on appeal, in all disputes and differences between two or more States concerning boundaries, jurisdiction, or any other cause whatever, with an elaborate machinery for the exercise of such jurisdiction. The amendment closed with this bulwark against "pioneer thoughts," or other encroachments, on the Western preserves: "No State shall be deprived of territory for the benefit of the United States." Massachusetts, Rhode Island, New York, Pennsylvania, Virginia, and North Carolina voted for the amendment; New Hampshire voted against it; New Jersey and South Carolina were divided; Maryland and Georgia were not present or voting; and Connecticut was not counted, as but one member was present.

Within a month of the time that Maryland brought forward her "pioneer thought," the Congress had perfected the Articles of Confederation; and November 17, 1777, they were sent out to the States, with a circular letter recommending that they empower their delegates in Congress to ratify them in their name and behalf.

Some of the legislatures promptly gave their delegates such instructions, and some hesitated. A number of amendments to the Articles were proposed, and of these several related to the land-question.[1] One of those that came from Maryland was a virtual renewal of the proposition of the year before, but in a somewhat less emphatic form. Rhode Island,

---

[1] All the amendments proposed may be found in the Secret Journals, I., under June 22, 23, 1778.

New Jersey, Pennsylvania, Delaware, and Maryland, all non-claimant States, voted for this amendment; New Hampshire, Massachusetts, Connecticut, Virginia, and South Carolina, all claimant States but the first, voted against it; New York was divided; North Carolina and Georgia were not present or voting. Rhode Island submitted the following amendment, which was also lost, nine votes to one:

"That all lands within these States, the property of which, before the present war, was vested in the Crown of Great Britain, or out of which revenues from quit rents arise payable to the said Crown, shall be deemed, taken, and considered as the property of these United States, and be disposed of and appropriated by Congress for the benefit of the whole Confederacy, reserving, however, to the States, within whose limits such Crown lands may be, the entire and complete jurisdiction thereof."

New Jersey laid before Congress a lengthy "representation," in which she stated, though not in the form of amendments, her views on various provisions of the Articles. This document touched the land-issue at two points: (1) "The boundaries and limits of each State ought to be fully and finally fixed and made known;" and if circumstances did not admit of this being done before the Articles were ratified and went into effect, then it should be done afterward, not exceeding five years from the final ratification of the Confederation. (2) It was urged that the war was undertaken for the general defence of the confederating States; that the benefits derived from a successful contest should be general and proportionate; that the property of the common enemy, acquired during the war, should belong to the United States and be appropriated to their use; that the Articles of Confederation should empower Congress to dispose of such property, and especially the vacant and unpatented lands, commonly called the "Crown Lands," for defraying the expenses of the war, and for other general purposes; but that the jurisdiction ought, in every instance, to belong to the respective States within the charter or determined limits of which such lands may be seated. These recommendations were voted down, receiving but three votes to six against them.

None of the amendments proposed by the States received much consideration; they were voted down one and all, in the apparent belief that the surest and quickest way to complete the Confederation was to adhere to the Articles as originally adopted. It is clear, however, that the opposition to the land-claims of the claimant States was broadening and deepening. At the same time, we must not overlook the difference between the "pioneer thought" brought forward by Maryland in 1777 and the propositions now submitted by Rhode Island and New Jersey. The first was that the United States in Congress assembled should assert jurisdiction over the Western lands; the others were, that the lands, or parts of them, should be disposed of for the benefit of all the States, or of the nation as a unit, not disturbing the jurisdiction.

The Confederation had now been fully ratified by eight States, and of the five others, North Carolina had empowered her delegates to do so. The four that had not ratified were Maryland, Delaware, New Jersey, and Georgia. To these Congress, on July 10, 1778, sent a circular letter, urging them to instruct their delegates to ratify "with all convenient despatch," putting forward as the one conclusive argument that Congress had "never ceased to consider a confederacy as the great principle of union, which can alone establish the liberty of America, and elude forever the hopes of its enemies." Future deliberations should be trusted to make such alterations and amendments as experience might show to be expedient and just. Georgia responded to this appeal at once, and New Jersey soon followed.

In the act empowering her delegates to ratify the Articles, the legislature of New Jersey reaffirmed that they would, in diverse particulars, be unequal and disadvantageous to that State, but that she was willing, in reliance on the justice and candor of the several States, to surrender her State interest to the general good of the Union.[1] On February 22, 1779, the Delaware delegates ratified the Articles in behalf of that State, and the day following laid before Congress some resolutions which the Delaware Council had adopted, asserting that moderate limits should be assigned to the States claiming to the Mississippi; that Congress should have the power of fixing those limits; also that Delaware was justly entitled to a right, in common with the other members of the Union, to the lands westward of the frontiers, the property of which was vested in individual States at the beginning of the war, but that ought now "to be a common estate to be granted out on terms beneficial to the United States," since they have been or must be gained by the blood and treasure of all. Congress received and filed this paper, but declared "that it should never be considered as admitting any claim by the same set up or intended to be set up."

The ratification of Delaware left Maryland standing solitary and alone; but she still refused her ratification as stoutly as ever. Moreover, she refused it on the sole ground that she defined in the amendment Article proposed October 15, 1777. As her assent alone was wanting to complete the Confederation, Maryland felt compelled to justify herself to Congress and to her sister States. In fact, she had already taken the first steps in that direction before Delaware's final assent to the Articles was given.

On December 15, 1778, the Maryland Legislature adopted a "declaration," stating her objections to the policy touching the Western lands thus far pursued. It was declared fundamentally wrong and repugnant to every principle of equity and good policy that Maryland, or any other State entering into the Confederation, should be burdened with heavy expenses for the subduing and guaranteeing of immense tracts of country, if she is not in any way to be benefited thereby.

---

[1] The Secret Journals, IV., 422.

Maryland will ratify the Confederation when it is so amended as to give full power to Congress to ascertain and fix the western limits of the States claiming to extend to the Mississippi, and expressly to reserve to the United States a right in common in and to all the lands lying to the westward of the frontiers as thus fixed, not granted to, or surveyed for, or purchased by individuals at the commencement of the war. Further, the exclusive claim set up by some States to the whole Western country is declared to be without any solid foundation; and it will, if submitted to, prove ruinous to Maryland and to other States similarly circumstanced, and, in process of time, be the means of subverting the Confederacy.[1] This document, which was intended to influence public opinion as well as Congress, was brought forward in Congress, January 6, 1779; but a longer and more earnest one, adopted by the General Assembly on the same day, entitled "Instructions to the Maryland Delegates," was not presented until May 21st.[2] The two documents are the defence of her position that Maryland made to the country.

The "instructions" assume that some of the States have acceded to the Confederation from dread of immediate calamities growing out of the war and other peculiar circumstances, and that, when these causes cease to operate, said States will consider it no longer binding, but will improve the first favorable opportunity to assert their just rights and secure their independence. The Western lands, if the course marked out is persisted in, will present such an opportunity. The same grasping spirit that leads the claimant States "to insist on a claim so extravagant, so repugnant to every principle of justice, so incompatible with the general welfare of the States, will urge them on to add oppression to injustice." The depopulation and impoverishment of the non-claimant States,

---

[1] This declaration, with other important papers relating to the same subject, is found in Hening's Statutes of Virginia, X., 546 et seq.
[2] Found in the Secret Journals, under this date.

if not their oppression by open force, will follow. The probable consequences to Maryland of the undisputed possession by Virginia of the Western country that she claimed are thus vigorously described:

"Virginia, by selling on the most moderate terms a small proportion of the lands in question, would draw into her treasury vast sums of money; and in proportion to the sums arising from such sales, would be enabled to lessen her taxes. Lands comparatively cheap, and taxes comparatively low, with the lands and taxes of an adjacent state, would quickly drain the State thus disadvantageously circumstanced of its most useful inhabitants; its wealth and its consequence in the scale of the confederated States would sink of course. A claim so injurious to more than one-half, if not to the whole of the United States, ought to be supported by the clearest evidence of the right. Yet what evidences of that right have been produced? What arguments alleged in support either of the evidence or the right? None that we have heard of deserving a serious refutation."

To the argument that some of the States were too large for one practicable government, and that it would be found necessary to divide them into two States even if the Articles stood as they were, it was replied that, for a State to divide its territory to erect under its auspices and direction a new State, upon which it would impose its own form of government, binding the new State to itself by some alliance or confederacy, and influencing its councils, thus forming a sub-confederacy, *imperium in imperio*, would certainly be opposed by the other States as inconsistent with the letter and spirit of the proposed Confederation. Moreover, if these States contemplate such a policy, why insist now upon the territories that they intend to surrender? But two motives can be assigned. Either the suggestion is made to lull suspicion and to cover the designs of the secret coalition, or the purpose is to reap an immediate profit from the sale of the lands.

THE NORTHWESTERN CESSIONS.

The Maryland proposition as presented in 1777 is then reaffirmed, and the Maryland delegates are instructed not to ratify the Confederation unless an amendment be added in conformity with that view; but should the delegates succeed in obtaining such an amendment, then they are fully empowered to ratify it. The document closes with a fervent hope that Congress may be led by these arguments to amend the Articles in such a manner as to bring about a permanent union.

The fallacy that there is value in wild lands appears to have been universally accepted in Congress and the States one hundred years ago. It was constantly assumed that the Western lands, when sold, would enormously enrich the claimant States or the Nation, as the case might be; while experience has proved, in this case as in many others, that the man who subdues such land "can," as Professor W. G. Sumner puts it, "only afford to give a remuneration for the survey which secures him a definite description and identification of the land which he has appropriated, and for the authority of a civil government which protects his title."[1] In the long run, the national Government has not found the public domain a source of revenue.

The economical arguments so warmly urged by the non-claimant States were, therefore, next to worthless. Besides, the most weighty political arguments in favor of nationalizing the lands were practically overlooked, or at least not carried out to their results.

As the Articles were Articles of Confederation and Perpetual Union among thirteen States, the ratifications of the twelve did not give them force and effect even over the twelve. Maryland refused to close the circle, and her refusal was followed by very serious results. The machinery that

---

[1] Andrew Jackson as a Public Man.—Professor Sumner says (p. 185): "Down to September 30, 1832, the lands had cost $49.7 million and the total revenue received from them had amounted to $38.2 million."

the Articles furnished for filling the treasury and recruiting the army could not be set in motion; the domestic and foreign enemies of the national cause were elated at the appearance of serious dissensions among the States; and the friends of the cause were correspondingly depressed.

Virginia now prepared practically to assert her claim to the lands west of the Alleghany Mountains. In May, 1779, the very month that the Maryland instructions were read to Congress, her legislature passed an act directing the opening of a land-office the ensuing October, and fixing the terms on which lands should be sold; and, about the same time, a second act, regulating the land-patents issued by royal authority to the Virginia officers and troops in the French and Indian War. The meaning of the two acts was unmistakable: Virginia proposed to disregard the growing sentiment in favor of endowing the United States with the Western lands. To her surprise she immediately called into activity a power that had been sleeping since the beginning of the war; the range of controversy was at once widened, and the way to agreement prepared by increasing the confusion.

On September 14, 1779, a memorial signed by George Morgan in behalf of certain land claimants, was read in Congress. This memorial recited: That at the Indian Congress held at Fort Stanwix in 1768, in consideration of the loss of some £85,000 sustained by certain traders, the Six Nations granted a tract of land, lying on the southern side of the Ohio between the southern limit of Pennsylvania and the Little Kanawha River, called Indiana; that afterward, but before the war began, this tract of land, as included within the bounds of a larger tract called Vandalia, was by the King in Council separated from the dominion which, in right of the Crown, Virginia claimed over it; that, as the memorialists are advised, the said tract is not subject to the jurisdiction of Virginia or any particular State, but of the United States; and that the action of Virginia directing the sale of the lands in question seems intended to defeat the interposition of Congress. Hence, the memorialists pray Congress to take such speedy action as shall arrest the sale of the lands until Virginia and the memorialists can be heard by Congress, and the rights of the owners of the tract called Vandalia, of which Indiana is a part, shall be ascertained, in such a manner as may tend to support the sovereignty of the United States and the just rights of individuals. A memorial signed by William Trent, in behalf of Thomas Walpole and his associates in the Grand Company, was presented at the same time.[1] New Hampshire, Massachusetts, Virginia, and both the Carolinas voted against the motion to refer the Morgan memorial to a committee, but the motion prevailed. Messrs. Witherspoon, Jenifer, Atlee, Sherman, and Peabody, on October 8th, were appointed said committee. The Trent memorial had the same reference. It should be observed that, when the memorials were introduced, the Virginia delegates objected that Congress had no jurisdiction over their subject-matter. The committee was also instructed to inquire into the foundation of this objection, and first to report the facts relating to that point. This action is evidence that Congress was prepared at least to inquire whether the Nation had any title to lands in the West.

On October 29, 1779, the committee reported that they had considered the facts presented to them by the Virginia delegates; and that they "could not find any such distinction between the question of the jurisdiction of Congress and the merits of the cause as to recommend any decision upon the first separately from the last." The next day a preamble and resolution offered by the Maryland delegates, but somewhat amended, was adopted as follows:

"Whereas, the appropriation of vacant lands by the several states during the continuance of the war will, in the opinion of Congress, be attended with great mischiefs; therefore,

---

[1] The Morgan memorial is found in the Journals of Congress, III., 359. The Trent memorial is not found in the Journals at all.

"*Resolved*, That it be earnestly recommended to the State of Virginia to reconsider their late act of assembly for opening their land office ; and that it be recommended to the said State, and all other States, similarly circumstanced, to forbear settling or issuing warrants for unappropriated lands, or granting the same during the continuance of the present war."[1]

Virginia and North Carolina are the only States that voted in the negative, but New York was divided. This action at once shifted the *onus* from Maryland to Virginia. The Old Dominion was now compelled to speak. On December 14, 1779, her legislature addressed to the delegates of the United States in Congress assembled a "remonstrance" of which these are the leading points: (1) That Virginia has already enacted a law to prevent further settlements on the northwest banks of the Ohio River; (2) That Virginia learns with surprise and concern that Congress has received and countenanced petitions from the Indiana and Vandalia Companies asserting claims to lands within her limits as claimed ; and that for Congress to assume a jurisdiction and right of adjudication such as granting these petitions would imply, would be contrary to the fundamental principles of the Confederation, would introduce a most dangerous precedent which might be urged to deprive one or more of the States of territory, or subvert its sovereignty and government, and establish in Congress a power which would degenerate into an intolerable despotism ; (3) that there are many other land-companies than those that have already petitioned Congress, claiming lands in the West, repugnant to Virginia's laws; and that listening with consideration to the Indiana and Vandalia Companies will encourage these to bring forward their claims ; (4) Congress have stated their ultimatum as to boundaries in their terms of peace (in the instructions to Mr. Adams, mentioned in a previous chapter). "The United States hold no terri-

---

[1] Journals of Congress, III., 385.

tory but in right of some one individual State in the Union; the territory of each State from time immemorial hath been fixed and determined by their respective charters, there being no other rule or criterion to judge by." The setting aside of this rule will end in bloodshed among the States. "Nor can any argument be fairly urged to prove that any particular tract of country within the limits claimed by Congress on behalf of the United States, not part of the chartered territory of some one of them, but must militate with equal force against the right of the United States in general; and tend to prove that tract of country (if northwest of the Ohio River) part of the British Province of Canada;" (5) the limits of Virginia are defined in her constitution of 1776; (6) Virginia is ready to listen to any just and reasonable proposition for removing the *ostensible* causes of delay to the complete ratification of the Confederation—referring, of course, to Maryland. Virginia is now ready, as she has before declared herself ready, to furnish lands northwest of the Ohio to the troops on the continental establishment of such of the States as have not unappropriated lands for that purpose; but she solemnly "protests against any jurisdiction or right of adjudication in Congress upon the petitions of the Vandalia or Indiana Companies, or any other matter or thing subversive of the internal policy, civil government, or sovereignty of this or any other of the United American States, as unwarranted by the Articles of Confederation.[1]

Firm as is the tone of the remonstrance, it is plain that Virginia is becoming more yielding and pliable.

Particular attention should be drawn to the bearing of the question with which we are dealing on the national boundaries. Virginia states the point with great force in her remonstrance; and it is perfectly clear, in the light of the facts already presented, that a denial of the Western titles on the ground that the Western lands belonged to the Crown,

---

[1] Hening's Statutes of Virginia, X.

tended to subvert the very foundation on which Congress instructed its foreign representatives to stand while contending with England, France, and Spain for a westward extension to the Mississippi. Accordingly, the Maryland doctrine was a dangerous one; it left no standing ground on which to contend for the Western country but that of conquest and occupancy. But Congress wisely kept wide of the Maryland path leading to the Maryland goal, and eventually worked out a solution of the Western question on the principle of compromise and concession.

The first practical step toward a solution of the question was taken by the State of New York. On January 17, 1780, her legislature passed an "Act for facilitating the completion of the Articles of Confederation and perpetual Union among the United States of America." After reciting the desirability of a more perfect Union, the dissatisfaction of some States with the Articles, growing out of the waste lands, and the desire of New York to accelerate the Union by removing, as far as possible, this impediment, the legislature provides: (1) That the delegates of the State in Congress, or the majority of them, are authorized and empowered, in behalf of the State, to limit and restrict its boundaries in the western parts by such line or lines, and in such manner and form, as they shall judge to be expedient, with respect either to the jurisdiction or the right of soil, or both; (2) that the territory so ceded shall be and inure for the use and benefit of such of the United States as shall become members of the federal alliance of the said States, and for no other use or purpose whatever; (3) that such of the lands, so ceded, as shall remain within the jurisdiction of the State, shall be surveyed, laid out, and disposed of only as Congress may direct.

Virtually this act was the first of the cessions. It immediately changed the whole situation. Henceforth, the claimant states were compelled to justify themselves to Congress and the country for not following New York's example. Moreover, the act is remarkable for the large powers with which it clothed the New York delegates in Congress, making them the sole judges whether the boundaries of the State should be restricted, and, if so, what should be the manner and the extent of the restriction. This act was the result of a growing conviction that the Western country ought not to belong solely to the seven claimant States, and of the growth of national ideas. Professor Adams seeks to prove that it was the distinct result of Maryland's influence, and his argument, whether wholly conclusive or not, contains some valuable information, chiefly drawn from a letter written by General Philip Schuyler, then a delegate in Congress, to the New York Legislature, that immediately preceded the Facilitating Act.[1]

On September 6, 1780, a committee to whom all the documents in relation to the subject, accumulated on the table, had been referred, submitted a report on which the final issue turned.

"That having duly considered the several matters to them submitted, they conceive it unnecessary to examine into the merits or policy of the instructions or declaration of the general assembly of Maryland, or of the remonstrance of the general assembly of Virginia, as they involve questions, a discussion of which was declined, on mature consideration, when the articles of confederation were debated; nor, in the opinion of the committee, can such questions be now revived with any prospect of conciliation: That it appears more advisable, to press upon those states which can remove the embarrassments respecting the western country, a liberal surrender of a portion of their territorial claims, since they cannot be preserved entire without endangering the stability of the general confederacy; to remind them how indispensably necessary it is to establish the federal union on a fixed and permanent basis, and on principles acceptable to all its respective members; how essential to public credit and confidence, to the support of the army, to

---

[1] Maryland's Influence upon Land Cessions to the United States, 30 et seq.

the vigor of our councils, and success of our measures, to our tranquillity at home, our reputation abroad, to our very existence as a free, sovereign, and independent people; that they are fully persuaded the wisdom of the respective legislatures will lead them to a full and impartial consideration of a subject so interesting to the United States, and so necessary to the happy establishment of the federal union; that they are confirmed in these expectations by a review of the before-mentioned act of the legislature of New York, submitted to their consideration; that this act is expressly calculated to accelerate the federal alliance by removing, as far as depends on that state, the impediment arising from the western country, and for that purpose to yield up a portion of territorial claim for the general benefit;

"*Resolved*, That copies of the several papers referred to the committee be transmitted, with a copy of the report, to the legislatures of the several states; and that it be earnestly recommended to these states who have claims to the western country to pass such laws, and give their delegates in Congress such powers, as may effectually remove the only obstacle to a final ratification of the articles of confederation: and that the legislature of Maryland be earnestly requested to authorize their delegates in Congress to subscribe the articles."[1]

This report was agreed to without call of the roll. Its adoption marks a memorable day in the history of the land-controversy. No other document extant shows so clearly the wise policy that Congress adopted. That policy was neither to affirm nor to deny, nor even to discuss, whether Congress had jurisdiction over the wild lands, but to ask for cessions and to trust the logic of events to work out the issue. The appeal made to Maryland was one that she could not well refuse to heed. And then, that nothing but selfish interest might stand in the way of the other claimant States following the example of New York, Congress adopted, October 10th, this further resolution:

---

[1] Journals of Congress, III., 516, 517.

"*Resolved*, That the unappropriated lands that may be ceded or relinquished to the United States, by any particular state, pursuant to the recommendation of Congress of the sixth day of September last, shall be disposed of for the common benefit of the United States, and be settled and formed into distinct republican states, which shall become members of the federal union, and have the same rights of sovereignty, freedom and independence as the other states: That each state which shall be so formed shall have a suitable extent of territory, not less than one hundred nor more than one hundred and fifty miles square, as near thereto as circumstances will admit: That the necessary and reasonable expenses which any particular state shall have incurred since the commencement of the present war, in subduing any British posts, or in maintaining forts or garrisons within and for the defence, or in acquiring any part of the territory that may be ceded or relinquished to the United States, shall be reimbursed;

That the said lands shall be granted or settled at such times and under such regulations as shall hereafter be agreed on by the United States in Congress assembled, or any nine or more of them."[1]

The offer to reimburse the reasonable expenses that any State had incurred in subduing any British posts, etc., was, in substance, a proposition to reimburse Virginia for the cost of the George Rogers Clark expedition.

The papers sent to the claimant States under the resolution of September 6th called out immediate responses. Connecticut replied by a legislative act, October 10th, offering a cession of lands within her charter-limits, west of the Susquehanna purchase and east of the Mississippi, on condition that the State retain the jurisdiction, the quantity of land so ceded to be " in just proportion of what shall be ceded and relinquished by the other States claiming and holding vacant lands as aforesaid with the quantity of such their claim un-

---

[1] The Journals of Congress, III., 585.

appropriated at the time when the Congress of the United States was first convened and held at Philadelphia." The preamble of this act explains that its enactment was due to the anxiety of the State to promote the liberty and independence of " this rising empire."

Virginia was the next State to respond. On January 2, 1781, her legislature resolved to yield to Congress, for the benefit of the United States, all the right, title, and claim which Virginia had to the lands northwest of the River Ohio, upon eight conditions. The seventh of these conditions was, that all purchases and deeds from any Indian or Indians, for any lands within the cession made for the use of any private person or persons, as well as grants inconsistent with the chartered rights of Virginia, should be deemed and declared absolutely void, in the same manner as if the said territory had still remained part of the commonwealth of Virginia. The last condition was that all the remaining territory of Virginia, enclosed between the Atlantic Ocean and the southeast side of the River Ohio, and the Maryland, Pennsylvania, and North Carolina boundaries, should be guaranteed to Virginia by the United States. Plainly, these two conditions, if agreed to, would involve a declaration of the validity of Virginia's claim to the Northwest, and a ruling out of the claims of New York, if not of Connecticut and Massachusetts, and so be a departure from the policy that Congress had thus far pursued.[1] In the year or more that elapsed before Congress replied to this overture, some very important things were done.

On February 2, 1781, the Maryland Legislature empowered the Maryland delegates in Congress to subscribe and ratify the Articles of Confederation. The preamble of the act recites the reasons why the circle of the Confederation should be closed, and declares the devotion of Maryland to the common cause. The act also declares that the State

---

[1] Journals of Congress, IV., 265, 266.

does not, by acceding to the Confederation, relinquish any right or interest that she had, with the other States, in the back country. She still stands on the declaration of 1778; but she relies on the justice of the States hereafter as to the said claim. Further, she says no Article in the Confederation can bind Maryland, or any other State, to guarantee any exclusive claim of any particular State to the soil of the back lands. This act was read in Congress on the 12th of the same month,[1] and preparations were made for the immediate consummation of the Confederation.

Messrs. Duane, Floyd, and McDougal, the New York delegates, now prepared a deed of limitation, in the name of the State, ceding to the United States all her right, title, interest, jurisdiction, and claim to all lands and territories northward of the forty-fifth parallel of north latitude and westward of a meridian line drawn through the western bent or inclination of Lake Ontario, or westward of a meridian line twenty miles west of the most westerly bent of the Niagara River, provided the former meridian should not be found to fall that distance beyond said river. At the same time, the New York delegates prepared another paper, that they named an "act or declaration," calling attention to the guarantee that Virginia demanded for the territory that she did not cede; asserting that it was unjust to ask New York to guarantee the territories that other States making cessions reserved, at the same time that she was herself making large cessions of lands and receiving no guarantee for those she did not cede; and declaring, therefore, that the deed of cession was not absolute, but, on the contrary, should be subject to ratification or disavowal by the people of the State, represented in the legislature, at their pleasure, unless the territories reserved for the future jurisdiction of New York should be guaranteed by the United States in the same manner as the territories of other States making cessions of lands were guaranteed.

---

[1] See Journals of Congress, under that date.

On March 1, 1781, two important transactions were consummated. Messrs. Duane, Floyd, and McDougal executed, in the name of New York, the deed of limitation and the "act or declaration;" and John Hanson and Daniel Carroll, delegates in behalf of the State of Maryland, signed and ratified the Articles of Confederation, "by which act [so runs the "Journal"] the Confederation of the United States of America was completed, each and every of the Thirteen United States, from New Hampshire to Georgia, both included, having adopted and confirmed, and by their delegates in Congress ratified the same." Congress had anticipated this auspicious event by providing that the completion of the Confederation should be announced to the public at noon of that day; that the Boards of War and of Admiralty should take order accordingly; that information be communicated to the executives of the several States; that the American ministers abroad be informed, and that they be instructed to notify the respective courts at which they resided; that information be given to the honorable the minister plenipotentiary of France; that information be transmitted to the commander-in-chief, and that he announce the same to the army under his command. We now note a change in the style of the "Journals of Congress." On and after March 2, 1781, the style is, "The United States in Congress Assembled."

That Maryland had not theoretically abandoned her old ground is proved by the Act of February 2, 1781; that she had not abandoned it practically, is proved by the history thus far recited. The Connecticut and Virginia cessions were far from satisfactory either to Maryland or to Congress, but they were an earnest of what might, in time, be looked for. The resolutions of September and October, 1780, proved conclusively the drift of national sentiment. The New York cession arrayed that great State on the side of the small States, and was an example that the other claimant States could not long refuse to follow. So much had been gained that Maryland could well afford to close the circle of the Confederation, "relying on the justice of the several States hereafter" to dedicate the Western lands to the Nation. The completion of the Confederation took away the great argument hitherto relied upon in favor of the limitation-policy; and henceforth, the strong appeal addressed to the claimant States is the needs of the treasury.

In a recent article, Professor Alexander Johnston says the provision of the national Constitution "for the admission of new States was the result of State experience only. All the States had experienced the British system of treating colonies as mere creatures of an omnipotent Parliament; and they had been determined that their territories should be treated in a different way, as inchoate States. The Constitution's provision had its origin in the Congress of the Confederation. It is to the Ordinance of 1787, not to the Convention of that year, that we must look for the conception of this powerful factor in our peculiar national development; and the Congress of the Confederation took it, not from creative genius, but from the natural growth of State feeling."[1] There is, indeed, a wide difference between dependent colonies and independent States. Mr. Bancroft's felicitous chapter, "The Colonial System of the United States," does not bear a felicitous name. Professor Johnston's praise of this feature of the Constitution is well deserved; but its ultimate source is the "pioneer thought" of Maryland, which antedates the ordinance of 1787 by ten years. However, nothing is said of new States in either the New York Facilitating Act or the New York Deed of Limitation; the only arguments upon which those documents rest are the desirability of closing the Confederation and the justice of distributing the lands among the States.

---

[1] The New Princeton Review, September, 1887, 184.

XIII.
THE NORTHWESTERN CESSIONS.—(II.)

ON January 31, 1781, the resolution of October 10, 1780, together with the accumulated acts and resolutions of the States of Connecticut, New York, and Virginia, had been referred to a committee consisting of Messrs. Witherspoon, Duane, Root, Adams, Sullivan, Burke, and Walton. The petitions of the Indiana and Vandalia Land Companies, as well as of two other companies that had memorialized Congress concerning their claims, were also referred to the same committee. Ultimately this committee, and another one that came in its room, became a sort of clearing house to which all troublesome questions that in any way touched the land-issue were sent. One of the first questions that it had to deal with, as well as one of the most difficult, was the guarantee demanded by Virginia as the condition of ceding the country beyond the Ohio. We must see what such a guarantee really involved.

First, the lands claimed by the Indiana and Vandalia Companies lay on the southeastern side of the Ohio. Secondly, the State of New York, before her deed of cession, claimed the whole country west of the Alleghanies, from the Lakes to the Cumberland Mountains. Thirdly, it was held by some, irrespective of the claims of the company and of New York, that the Crown had limited Virginia on the west by the Alleghanies, and that her claim to what is now West Virginia and Kentucky was spurious. Hence the committee was compelled to inquire into the merits of the case as between the companies and New York on the one part and Virginia on the other, unless, indeed, Congress should either give or rufuse the guarantee without any inquiry whatever. It will be remembered that the question had been touched by the report of October 29, 1779, when it declared that, in the matter of the Indiana and Vandalia claims, it could "not find any such distinction between the question of the jurisdiction of Congress and the merits of the cause as to recommend any decision upon the first separately from the last." In the light of these facts, the motive of Virginia in asking a guarantee of her whole territorial claim east and south of the Ohio River is obvious. Evidently, Congress must waive the Virginia cession altogether, or it must inquire whether part of the territories to be guaranteed did not belong to the land-companies, as also whether a still larger part of them had not already been ceded to the United States by New York.

Accordingly, the committee of seven called on the Connecticut, New York, and Virginia delegates in Congress, as well as the agents of the four land-companies, to present their respective claims, with the proofs on which they rested them. On October 16, 1781, the Virginia delegates submitted to Congress a representation urging that such an inquiry as was contemplated into the claims of companies claiming lands within the limits of particular States was beyond its jurisdiction, and asking whether Congress had intended that the committee should hear evidence, in behalf of the companies, that was adverse to the claims or cessions of Virginia, New York, or Connecticut. The paper declared it derogatory to the sovereignty of a State, thus to be drawn into contest with a land-company.[1] On the 26th of the same month the Virginia delegates brought up the question again, this time seeking to carry a motion denying to the committee the right "to admit counsel, or to hear documents, proofs, or evidence not among the records, nor on the files of Congress, which have not been specially referred to them." This was all in har-

---

[1] The citations to proceedings in Congress are now found in the Journals of Congress, under the respective dates, unless otherwise indicated.

mony with the Virginia remonstrance of two years before. But Congress persisted, voting down the motion of October 26th, five votes to three; and on November 3, 1781, the committee submitted an elaborate report covering the whole ground. In the first paragraph of this very important document, the committee state that the New York and Connecticut delegates had submitted the claims of their States, with vouchers to support the same, but that the Virginia delegates, "declining any elucidation of their claim, either to the lands ceded in the act referred to your [the] committee, or the lands requested to be guaranteed to the said State by Congress, delivered to your [the] committee the written paper hereto annexed and numbered 20."[1] This paper is not printed in the "Journals," but the original is found among the unpublished papers of Congress. It is signed by the Virginia delegates, including Mr. Madison, and is a statement of the reasons why they refused to present the grounds of the Virginia claim to the committee. This is the most important:

"The acts of Congress in compliance with which the above mentioned cessions [viz., those of New York, Connecticut, and Virginia] were made, are founded on the supposed inexpediency of discussing the question of right, and recommended to the several states having territorial claims in the western country, a liberal surrender of a portion of these claims for the benefit of the United States, as the most advisable means of removing the embarrassments which such questions created. To make these acts of surrender, then, the basis of a discussion of territorial rights, is a direct contravention of the acts of Congress, and tends to diminish the weight and efficacy of future recommendations from them to their constituents."[2]

---

[1] This report is found in the Journals under the date of May 1, 1782. Messrs. Boudinot, Varnum, Jenifer, Smith, and Livermore are here given as constituting the committee. I have not found any mention, in the Journals, of a second committee being appointed.

[2] See argument of Samuel F. Vinton in case of Virginia *vs.* Garner and others, Marietta, O., 1846.

It cannot be denied, that for Congress to conduct an inquiry into the grounds of title by which any State held, or claimed to hold, her territories was a departure from the policy hitherto pursued; nor that Virginia, in asking for the guarantee, had presented sufficient occasion for the departure to be made. In view of the outcome, it is plain that Virginia made a false step when she asked for the guarantee. But the conclusions reached by the committee were still more distasteful to Virginia than the inquiry itself, as we shall now see.

The report made, November 3, 1781, came up for action, May 1, 1782. First, it recommended the acceptance of the New York cession as contained in the deed executed by Messrs. Duane, Floyd, and McDougal, March 1, 1781. The reasons that induced the committee to recommend the acceptance of this cession are an important part of the literature relating to the ownership of the Western lands. These were fully presented, with remarks, in the statement of the Northwestern claims made in the last chapter. The additional observation is called for that, at this distance, the New York claim appears the most flimsy of all the Western claims; and it is hard to resist the conclusion that it was preferred by the committee from a desire to get a leverage on the other States, and particularly on Virginia. This view is supported by the general history of the subject, by the composition of the committee, and by the testimony of Mr. Madison, soon to be adduced. The five men who composed the committee were Boudinot of New Jersey, Varnum of Rhode Island, Jenifer of Maryland, Smith of Pennsylvania, and Livermore of New Hampshire.

The report strongly urged Massachusetts and Connecticut to make an immediate release of all their claims and pretensions to the Western territories, without condition or reservation. Not a word was said about the conditional cession that Connecticut had already made.

Coming to the cession proffered by Virginia, the committee reported that it was not consistent with the interest of the United States, the duty that Congress owed to their constituents, or the rights necessarily vested in Congress as the sovereign power of the United States, to accept the said cession, or to guarantee the tract of country claimed by Virginia southeast of the Ohio; assigning the following reasons for this conclusion:

"1. It appeared to your committee from the vouchers laid before them, that all the lands ceded, or pretended to be ceded, to the United States by the state of Virginia, are within the claims of the states of Massachusetts, Connecticut, and New York, being part of the lands belonging to the said Six Nations of Indians and their tributaries.

"2. It appeared that great part of the lands claimed by the state of Virginia, and requested to be guaranteed to them by Congress, is also within the claim of the state of New York, being also a part of the country of the said Six Nations and their tributaries.

"3. It also appeared that a large part of the lands last aforesaid are to the westward of the west boundary line of the late colony of Virginia, as established by the King of Great Britain, in Council, previous to the present revolution.

"4. It appeared that a large tract of said lands hath been legally and equitably sold and conveyed away under the government of Great Britain before the declaration of independence by persons claiming the absolute property thereof.

"5. It appeared that in the year 1763, a very large part thereof was separated and appointed for a distinct government and colony by the King of Great Britain, with the knowledge and approbation of the government of Virginia.

"6. The conditions annexed to the said cession are incompatible with the honor, interests, and peace of the United States, and therefore, in the opinion of your committee, altogether inadmissible."

These reasons, together with those given for adopting the resolution accepting the New York cession, totally deny the validity of Virginia's claim to territory west of the mountains, and fully affirm the sufficiency of New York's title. Still, to put an end to all questions, the committee recommended the following resolution:

"That it be earnestly recommended to the state of Virginia, as they value the peace, welfare and increase of the United States, that they re-consider their said act of cession, and by a proper act for that purpose, cede to the United States all claims and pretensions of claim to the lands and country beyond a reasonable western boundary, consistent with their former acts while a colony under the power of Great Britain, and agreeable to their just rights of soil and jurisdiction at the commencement of the present war, and that free from any conditions and restrictions whatever."

The committee further reported that the Indiana claim was a *bona fide* claim, made in the usual way; and it therefore recommended that, in case the said lands were finally ceded to the United States by Great Britain, Congress should confirm to such of the purchasers as were citizens of the United States their respective shares and proportions of such lands.

After reciting the facts relating to the Vandalia grant, the committee declared it wholly incompatible with the interests of the United States to permit such inordinate grants of lands to be vested in individual citizens of the States; nevertheless, in order to do strictest justice to such of the said company as should remain citizens of the United States, it recommended that, in case the tract should finally be adjudged to the United States, Congress should make reasonable provision for them out of the lands.

The committee recommended, further, that the claims of the Illinois and Wabash Companies be dismissed, on the ground that they were originally illegal.

Finally, the committee declared that many inconveniences would arise unless the jurisdiction of Congress in regard to Indian affairs was more clearly defined, and so submitted a number of resolutions intended to accomplish that end.

This report was never acted upon as a whole; and to follow it through the "Journals" is a wearisome undertaking, especially as the land-issue soon becomes complicated with other subjects, as the national finances.

As early as 1776, attention was drawn to the Northwestern lands "as a resource amply adequate, under proper regulations, for defraying the whole expense of the war."[1] Now that the Confederation had been completed, and the financial embarrassments of the country were becoming greater and greater, the eyes of the people and of Congress were more and more turning to the Northwest to find the means of relief. On July 31, 1782, a grand committee of one from each State, appointed to consider and report the most effective means of supporting the credit of the United States, recommended Congress to decide upon the cessions made by Connecticut, New York, and Virginia. "It is their opinion," say the committee, "that the Western lands, if ceded to the United States, might contribute toward a fund for paying the debt of these States." As a substitute for this part of the report, Mr. Witherspoon offered a series of resolutions asserting that such cessions, if made agreeably to the resolutions of 1780, "would be an important fund for the discharge of the national debt," and strongly urging them upon the claimant States. For some reason these resolutions, as well as the foregoing item of the report, were lost; but the phrase "national debt"[2] shows that the national idea was growing.

Replying, January 30, 1783, to the complaints of Pennsylvania that she could not procure payments of money due her from the Federal Government, Congress called attention to the steps taken to secure the Western cessions, begging Pennsylvania to consider the subject "as of importance, not only as may affect the public credit, but as it will contribute to

---

[1] Silas Deane: See Adams's Maryland's Influence upon Land Cessions to the United States, 22.

[2] Journals of Congress, IV., 68, 69; 82, 83.

THE NORTHWESTERN CESSIONS. 231

give general satisfaction to the members of the Union." On April 18th the subject came up again as a part of the well-known financial scheme of that year, as will soon be pointed out more at length.

Next to the "Journals of Congress," the "Madison Papers" and Mr. Madison's reports of the debates in Congress, found in "Eliot's Debates," are the principal sources of information concerning the land-cessions. Mr. Madison was in Congress in 1780, 1781, 1782; and his letters to his Virginia correspondents in those years throw a flood of light on the whole subject, making clear the motives that governed the Virginia delegates, revealing hidden springs of action, and showing conclusively that politics played a large part in those transactions.

Writing to Edmund Pendleton, September 12, 1780, of the resolution of Congress adopted six days before, he expresses the sanguine belief that the States to which that appeal is made "will see the necessity of closing the union in too strong a light to oppose the only expedient that can accomplish it."[1] To Joseph Jones, September 19th, October 19th, and November 21st of the same year, he suggests that the States making cessions can shut off the land-companies, called by him "land-mongers," by expressly excluding them from all participation in the lands ceded; he does not believe there is any design in Congress to gratify the avidity of land-mongers, but the best security for their virtue in this respect will be to keep it out of their power; and declares a proposition to arbitrate the issue between the Indiana Company and Virginia, submitted by Morgan, irreconcilable with the honor and sovereignty of the State. Writing to Jones, November 28th, he thus touches the Connecticut cession: "They reserve the jurisdiction to themselves, and clog the cession with some other conditions which greatly depreciate it, and

---

[1] Unless otherwise designated, the citations from Madison are from the Madison Papers. See the respective dates.

are the more extraordinary as their title to the land is so controvertible a one." December 19th, he expresses to Jones regret that the Virginia Assembly has not acted on the congressional recommendation, because the delay will tend to postpone Maryland's ratification of the Confederation. To Edmund Randolph he writes, May 1, 1781, that the attempt to secure the acceptance of the Virginia cession "has produced all the perplexing and dilatory objections which its adversaries could devise." He declares to Randolph, October 30th of the same year, that "an agrarian law is as much coveted by the little members of the Union as ever it was by the indigent citizens of Rome;" he cherishes "little hope of arresting any aggression upon Virginia which depends solely on the inclination of Congress;" he thinks the rule requiring seven States to carry a vote will be a check on the "agrarians," but in another letter he speaks of the same rule as retarding business. November 13th, he tells Pendleton that the Virginia cession will not "be adopted with the conditions annexed to it;" and then states the programme of the opposition as follows:

"The opinion seems to be, that an acceptance of the cession of New York will give Congress a title which will be maintainable against all the other claimants. In this, however, they will certainly be deceived; and even if it were otherwise, it would be their true interest, as well as conformable to the plan on which the cessions were recommended, to bury all further contentions by covering the territory with the titles of as many of the claimants as possible."

In a letter to Thomas Jefferson, November 18, 1781, Madison writes of the "hostile machinations of some of the States against our territorial claims;" says the report of the committee, made November 3, 1781, "is not founded on the obnoxious doctrine of an inherent right in the United States to the territory in question, but on the expediency of clothing them with the title of New York, which is supposed to be maintainable against all others;" utters the opinion that the principles of the report will not be ratified by Congress; and adds that the committee was composed of a member each from Maryland, Pennsylvania, New Jersey, Rhode Island, and New Hampshire, "all of which States, except the last, are systematically and notoriously adverse to the claims of Western territory, and particularly those of Virginia." In this, as in others of his letters, Mr. Madison expresses the fear that the Virginia Assembly will become offended at the unreasonable course pursued by Congress, and so refuse further help to end the controversy. He says, also, that the investigation made by the committee of the rights of States and companies was vindicated on the ground that the conditions annexed by Virginia to the cession made it necessary. In a second letter to Jefferson, bearing date, January 15, 1782, he reviews the history of the cessions to date. He speaks again of the "machinations" against Virginia, and of the perseverance with which her territorial rights are "persecuted;" he says an accurate and full collection of the documents bearing on Virginia's title would be of great service to the Virginia delegation, and calls upon Mr. Jefferson to investigate the whole subject from the original charter down. Writing to Mr. Jefferson again, April 16th, he describes the line of attack on the Virginia title. The adversaries of the State will be either the United States or New York, or both. "The former will either claim on the principle that the vacant country is not included in any particular State, and consequently falls to the whole, or will clothe themselves with the title of the latter by accepting its cession." He again calls on his distinguished correspondent to trace the title of Virginia to the disputed lands.

In a letter to Randolph, of August 13, 1782, he says "several of the Middle States seem to be facing about." Maryland, however, "preserves its wonted jealousy and obstinacy." In another letter to Randolph he discusses the financial bearings of the land-question in reference to a recent debate in Congress, and states the circumstances leading to the Witherspoon resolutions already cited.

"After the usual discussion of the question of right, and a proposal of opposite amendments to make the report favor the opposite sides, a turn was given to the debate to the question of expediency, in which it became pretty evident to all parties, that unless a compromise took place no advantage would ever be derived to the United States, even if their right were ever so valid. The number of States interested in the opposite doctrines rendered it impossible for the title of the United States ever to obtain a vote of Congress in its favor, much less any coercive measure to render the title of any fiscal importance; whilst the individual States, having both the will and the means to avail themselves of their pretensions, might open their land offices, issue their patents, and, if necessary, protect the execution of their grants, without any other molestation than the clamors of individuals within and without the doors of Congress. This view of the case had a manifest effect on the temperate advocates of the Federal title. . . .

"Every review I take of the western territory produces fresh conviction that it is the true policy of Virginia, as well as of the United States, to bring the dispute to a friendly compromise. A separate government cannot be distant, and will be an insuperable barrier to subsequent profits. If, therefore, the decision of the state on the claims of companies can be saved, I hope her other conditions will be relaxed."

He means, no doubt, that Virginia shall drop her demand for a guarantee.

Replying, March 24, 1782, to Madison's loud calls for help, Mr. Jefferson expresses surprise at the plan to set up New York's claim against Virginia's. Previous to the receipt of Madison's letter, he had never been able to comprehend a ground on which Virginia's right could be denied that "would not at the same time subvert the right of all the States to the whole of their territory." He confesses his inability to add anything to the argument on the Virginia side, and ventures the opinion that, if the decision of Congress is unfavorable to Virginia, it will not close the question; and supposes that men on the Western waters who are ambitious of office will urge a separation of the West by authority of Congress. Neither Mr. Madison's correspondents nor Mr. Madison himself ever suggested any standing ground for Virginia other than the charter of the colony.

We are indebted to Mr. Madison's correspondence for the information that the Western issue hinged on another famous question of those days. This is the question of the admission of Vermont to the Union, that has already been treated in another place. This issue became involved with the land-question as early as 1781. On August 14th of that year, Mr. Madison predicted the speedy triumph of Vermont, assigning this as one of his reasons: "The jealous policy of some of the little states which hope that such a precedent may engender a division of some of the large ones." Under date of May 1, 1782—the very day that the report of 1781 was taken up—Mr. Madison committed to writing some noteworthy "observations relating to the influence of Vermont and the Territorial Claims on the politics of Congress."

The New England States, with the exception of New Hampshire, patronize the independence of Vermont from ancient hostility to New York, from the interest of their citizens in Vermont lands, but principally from the accession of weight this will give that section in Congress. Pennsylvania and Maryland also patronize the pretensions of Vermont, as do New Jersey and Delaware; the first two, "with the sole view of reinforcing the opposition to claims of Western territory, particularly those of Virginia;" the other two, "with the additional view of strengthening the interests of the little states." Rhode Island is also influenced by these considerations, as well as by those that influence the other New England States. New York opposes Vermont for obvious reasons. Virginia, the Carolinas, and Georgia oppose Vermont on four grounds: A habitual jealousy of Eastern predominance; the opposition that it is expected Vermont, if admitted, will oppose to Western claims; the inexpediency of admitting so small a State on an equal footing with the first members of the Union; the tendency of the example to bring about a premature dismemberment of the other States.

It is plain that the admission of Vermont under the circumstances would be a sort of premium on rebellion, and might encourage the Virginians west of the mountains to revolution. Mr. Madison then defines the motives from which the States act on the other question. Of those that oppose the Western claims, Rhode Island is influenced by a desire to share the lands as a revenue-fund, and by the envy excited by superior resources and importance; New Jersey, Pennsylvania, Delaware, and Maryland are influenced by these considerations, but more by the intrigues of their citizens who are interested in the land-companies. The peculiar hostility of these States to Virginia is due to the fact that the claims of the companies lie within the limits of Virginia. Pennsylvania and Maryland would oppose Vermont, only their allies in the Western combination require them to favor her; Massachusetts and Connecticut thwart the settlement of the Western question until the admission of Vermont is made sure. With these States, Vermont is first and the lands second; with Pennsylvania and Maryland, the lands are first and Vermont second. No direct interest in the lands is accorded to Massachusetts, and but a slight one to Connecticut. New York, Virginia, the Carolinas, and Georgia all have Western claims in which they take an interest; South Carolina least of all. New York's claim is very extensive, but her title is very flimsy. She urges it, expecting to obtain some advantage or credit by its cession rather than hoping to maintain it.

It should be observed that the cession-policy was actually attended by some dangers that do not appear on the surface of the subject. On the one hand, the cessions tended to strengthen the Union by conciliating the non-claimant States; on the other, they tended, or at least might tend, to engender dangerous divisive tendencies. Discussing the admission of Vermont, in a letter dated September 19, 1780, Mr. Madison says: " For my own part, if a final decision must take place, I am clearly of opinion that it ought to be made on principles that will effectually discountenance the erection of new governments without the sanction of proper authority, and in a style marking a due firmness and decision in Congress."

Again, November 19, 1782, he writes that he has seen a letter from General Irvine, then at Fort Pitt, " which displays in full colors the avidity of the Western people for the vacant lands and for separate governments." Mr. Jefferson's correspondence bears a similar testimony. The over-mountain people of North Carolina, in defiance both of the parent State and of Congress, actually sought to set up the State of Franklin. And this divisive tendency was no doubt a fact to be considered by cautious statesmen.

Having let in this side-light on the stage, we are ready to follow the movement of the scenes.

On motion of the Maryland delegation, October 29, 1782, Congress accepted the New York cession as defined in the deed executed, March 1, 1781, Virginia alone voting in the negative. November 5th, Mr. Madison explained to Mr. Randolph the reasons that led to this negative vote: " In the first place, such a measure, instead of terminating all controversy—the object proposed by the original plan—introduces new perplexities; and, in the second place, an assent from us might be hereafter pleaded as a voluntary acceptance of the United States in the room of New York as a litigant against Virginia." The acceptance of the New York cession, however, did not include the approval of the reasons given by the committee of 1781 for its recommendations. This was a fortunate circumstance, as it proved, for the way was thus left open for the compromise finally made. At the same time, the acceptance of the New York cession was understood to be a decisive defeat of Virginia. Some members of Congress expected never again to hear of Virginia's land-claims. Such was the consummation of the long and determined effort made by Virginia to secure the acceptance by Congress of her cession with the guarantee. After this, the final success of the cession-policy was only a question of time.

In the letter to Randolph last cited, Mr. Madison recounts the action of October 29th, and points out its bearings. " The success of the Middle States in obtaining the cession of New York has given great encouragement, and they are pursuing steadily the means of availing themselves of the other titles. That of Connecticut is proposed for the next object. Virginia will be postponed for the last. By enlisting the two preceding into their party, they hope to render their measures more effectual with respect to the last." He says the "coalition" of the Middle States with New York will hurt the pretensions of Vermont. New York, "by ceding a claim which was tenable neither by force nor by right," " has acquired with Congress the merit of liberality, rendered the title to her reservation more respectable, and at least damped the ardor with which Vermont has been abetted."

The lands again came to the front in connection with the national finances.

In a note to his report of the debate of February 26, 1783, on the famous revenue-plan of that year, Mr. Madison defines the position of the States with reference thereto. New Hampshire would approve of a share in the vacant territory. Rhode Island, New Jersey, Pennsylvania, Delaware, and Maryland are deeply interested in the lands. New York, since the acceptance of her cession, is interested in those of other States. Virginia, the Carolinas, and Georgia must make larger or smaller sacrifices of territory. Massachusetts, so far as appears, has no interest in the question. Connecticut may, perhaps, consider herself interested in the acquisition of the vacant lands " since the condemnation of her title to her

Western claims,"[1] the reference being, of course, to the refusal to accept her cession.

On April 9, 1783, a memorial praying Congress to grant a tract of land on Lake Erie to the Canadian refugees who had engaged in the cause of the United States led to a protracted discussion of the land-question. On the 18th of the same month the revenue-plan was adopted, containing the following recommendation:

"That as a further means, as well of hastening the extinguishment of the debts as of establishing the harmony of the United States, it be recommended to the states which have passed no acts towards complying with the resolutions of Congress of the 6th of September and 10th of October, 1780, relative to the cession of territorial claims, to make the liberal cessions therein recommended, and to the states which may have passed acts complying with the said resolutions in part only, to revise and complete such compliance."

Mr. Madison's reports of these discussions contain no arguments with which we are not already familiar.

Many members of Congress supposed that this recommendation was a finality; they thought that, with the acceptance of the New York cession, it sealed the fate of Virginia's Western claims. But the delegates from that State apparently had not given up the hope of obtaining the acceptance of the Virginia cession. At least, Mr. Bland made a motion to accept it, and the motion was referred to a committee. This committee reported, June 9, 1783, that action should be postponed until Congress had proceeded to a determination on the report of November 3, 1781. Accordingly, Congress resumed the consideration of that report, and so much of it as related to the Virginia cession was referred to a committee consisting of Messrs. Rutledge, Ellsworth, Bedford, Gorham, and Madison. This reference alarmed the States that had so

---

[1] Eliot's Debates, V., 59, 60.

unflaggingly opposed the pretensions of Virginia, and that supposed the acceptance of the New York cession and the finance scheme meant the limitation of Virginia's claim on the west by the Alleghany Mountains. They feared that the reference meant a reopening of the whole question, and possibly a backing down from the position taken, April 18th. This view of the case is well put in a vigorous remonstrance that New Jersey sent to Congress, June 20th, expressing surprise at the reopening of the question; applying the recommendation of April 18th expressly to Virginia, whose cession is declared "partial, unjust, and illiberal," and requesting Congress not to accept that cession but to press Virginia " to make a more liberal surrender of that territory of which they claim so boundless a proportion." The same day the report of the Rutledge Committee was considered. This report, after being under discussion for three months, was finally adopted, September 13, 1783. Mr. Madison thinks this report, when first offered, "a fit basis for a compromise," and expresses the hope, when it is finished, that it will meet the ultimatum of Virginia.[1] How well grounded his view was, is shown by an examination of the report itself, and by the subsequent history.

The report states the eight conditions that Virginia annexed to the cession of January 2, 1781, and disposes of them one by one; pointing out that some of them have been met already, that others are reasonable and should be met, and that some are unnecessary because they are covered by others. The last condition, that requiring the guarantee, is thus disposed of:

"As to the last condition, your committee are of opinion, that Congress cannot agree to guarantee to the commonwealth of Virginia, the land described in the said condition, without entering into a discussion of the right of the state of Virginia

---

[1] Madison Papers, 543, 572.

THE NORTHWESTERN CESSIONS. 241

to the said land ; and that by the acts of Congress it appears to have been their intention, which the committee cannot but approve, to avoid all discussion of the territorial rights of individual states, and only to recommend and accept a cession of their claims whatsoever they might be, to vacant territory. Your committee conceive this condition of a guarantee, to be either unnecessary or unreasonable ; inasmuch as, if the land above mentioned is really the property of the State of Virginia, it is sufficiently secured by the Confederation, and if it is not the property of that state, there is no reason or consideration for such guarantee."

The report closes with a recommendation that, if the legislature of Virginia make a cession conformable to these views, Congress shall accept such cession. Maryland and New Jersey alone voted in the negative.

The report adopted, September 18, 1783, is in marked contrast with the one offered November 3, 1781, and for which, in some sense, it was a substitute. Particularly is it impossible to harmonize what is said of the guarantee in 1783 with the arguments adduced two years before to prove the validity of the New York claim and the invalidity of the Virginia claim. The one document gives the results of an inquiry into the question of right ; the other waives such inquiry altogether, on the ground that it is the settled policy of Congress to avoid all such inquiries and discussions, and only to recommend the cession of State claims, whatever they may be. Evidently a change had come over the temper of Congress. In 1781 the policy was to put pressure on Virginia with a view of inducing her to cede the territory between the Alleghanies and the Ohio. Hence the affirmation of New York's claim. The Union was to be clothed with New York's title, as Mr. Madison states in his letters. Such was the plan of the non-claimant States in 1781. Time has told against that plan, and a new one has been agreed upon as a compromise. Nothing is said in the report of 1783 about the lands southeast of the Ohio; the right to inquire into titles

16

is denied; Congress can only recommend cessions and accept them when made. This leaves the way open for Virginia to withdraw her demand for a guarantee, at the same time that she renews the cession of the Northwest. As the reasons of 1781 have never been adopted, Congress can tacitly assent to the southern limitation of the cessions by the Ohio River. This will leave the lands within the present States of West Virginia and Kentucky in Virginia's possession, which is exactly what she has been contending for from the first. The details of this plan were evidently arranged by the Rutledge Committee.

Virginia promptly performed the part assigned her. On October 20, 1783, her legislature passed an act authorizing a cession of the territory northwest of the Ohio. Before stating the terms of this cession, however, we must attend to an attempt that was made to break up the compromise, and to wrest the lands claimed by the Indiana Company from the grasp of Virginia.

Alarmed at the prospect of being abandoned by Congress, Colonel George Morgan, the petitioner of three years before, in behalf of himself and his fellow-proprietors, applied to New Jersey for protection, of which State some of them were citizens. He proposed, virtually, that the State should adopt the Indiana Company's claim as its own, at least to the extent of suing for an investigation of the title by a Federal court. The legislature, probably in the hope of defeating the compromise, accepted the proposal, and appointed Morgan its agent for the purpose of bringing the claim before Congress.

In his petition, dated February 24th, and presented in Congress, March 1, 1784, Morgan recites the fact of his appointment, quotes the finding of the committee of 1781 concerning the Indiana Company, says Virginia still claims the same lands, denies the validity of her claim, and prays for a hearing in the premises agreeably to the Ninth Article of the Confederation. A motion to commit was lost, as was a motion for a committee to prepare an answer to New Jersey.

THE NORTHWESTERN CESSIONS. 243

We have no intimation why Congress refused this application—possibly because it did not consider Article IX. as covering the case. Mr. Madison, in one of his letters, says he does not understand the policy of the land-companies in opposing the Virginia compromise. " They can never hope for specific restitution of their claims; they can never even hope for a cession of the country between the Alleghany and the Ohio by Virginia; as little can they hope for an extension of a jurisdiction of Congress over it by force. I should suppose, therefore, that it would be their truest interest to promote a general cession of the vacant country to Congress; and in case the titles of which they have been stripped should be deemed reasonable, and Congress should be disposed to make any equitable compensation, Virginia would be no more interested in opposing it than the other states."[1] The petition of March 1, 1784, is the last that we hear of the Indiana Company in the Old Congress.

Having thus refused to do anything with Morgan's petition, Congress the same day took up and accepted the deed of cession that Mr. Jefferson and his colleagues had already presented in behalf of Virginia. After reciting the resolutions of Congress of 1780, the Virginia cession of 1781, and the report adopted by Congress, September 13, 1783, the act on which the deed is based stipulates that "the territory so ceded shall be laid out and formed into states, containing a suitable extent of territory, not less than one hundred nor more than one hundred and fifty miles square, or as near thereto as circumstances will admit, and that the states so formed shall be distinct republican states, and admitted members of the Federal Union, having the same rights of sovereignty, freedom, and independence as the other states;" that the reasonable expenses incurred by Virginia in subduing and garrisoning any part of this territory shall be paid; that the inhabitants of the Kaskaskia, Vincennes, and the neighboring French vil-

---

[1] Madison Papers, 543, 544.

lages who have become citizens of Virginia shall have their titles confirmed to them; that one hundred and fifty thousand acres of land promised by Virginia to Clark and the officers and men who served under him in the Northwest shall be granted to them; that in case certain lands reserved for the Virginia troops on the continental establishment, south of the Ohio River between the Cumberland and Tennessee Rivers, should "prove insufficient for their legal bounties, the deficiency shall be made up to the said troops, in good lands, to be laid off between the Rivers Scioto and Little Miami, on the northwest side of the River Ohio;" and that all the lands so ceded, not reserved for any of the enumerated purposes, and not disposed of in bounties to the officers and soldiers of the American army, shall be a common fund for the use, aid, and benefit of the members of the Union, present or future, Virginia included, "according to their usual respective proportions in the general charge and expenditure, and shall be faithfully and *bona fide* disposed of for that purpose, and for no other use or purpose whatsoever." The cession is of "all right, title, and claim, as well of soil as of jurisdiction, which the said commonwealth hath to the territory or tract of country within the limits of the Virginia charter, situate, lying, and being to the northwest of the River Ohio." The act also expresses the hope that Congress, in justice to Virginia for her liberal cession, will earnestly press upon the other States claiming large bodies of waste lands to make cessions equally liberal for the common benefit and support of the Union.

A motion to add to the resolution accepting the deed the proviso that its acceptance should not be considered as implying any opinion or decision of Congress respecting the extent or validity of the claim of Virginia to Western territory, by charter or otherwise, received the votes of only New Jersey and Pennsylvania. New Jersey alone voted against accepting the deed, South Carolina was divided, Maryland was not present.

Such was the end of the long struggle between Congress

THE NORTHWESTERN CESSIONS.   245

and Virginia. The sole question at issue had long been the territory southeast of the Ohio. Virginia demanded a guarantee in 1781 as a reply to the demand that she should be bounded on the west by the mountains. That guarantee was not given, and yet Virginia won a substantial victory. Now that the demand to shut her up between the sea and the mountains was pressed with less vigor, and there was a disposition to recede from the reasons of the report of 1781, she was quite willing to let the guarantee go, and accept in its stead a tacit understanding that she should not be molested in the possession of the back lands. By this time the dispute had become wearisome; the compromise suggested by the report of 1783 offered a practicable settlement, and a large majority of Congress, as the votes show, were very glad to accept that compromise and let the matter drop. The controversy with Virginia was considerably affected by the events of the war. Hildreth says the terror inspired by Arnold's approach to Richmond was a main motive with Virginia in making the cession of 1781.[1] After the peace of 1783 Congress was less disposed to press Virginia to make a more liberal cession, and Virginia was less disposed to yield. Had the war gone on a year or two longer —at least, had Maryland's ratification of the Articles been postponed so long—it is highly probable that Virginia's western boundary would have been drawn where it now is, at the close of the Revolution rather than at the beginning of the Civil War.

In the course of the long discussion about the West, there was a considerable fluctuation of opinion as to the proper number and size of the new States. Virginia was the only State making a cession which stipulated that the territory ceded should be formed into States; and she imposed a rule of division that would have given anywhere from ten to twenty States in the Northwest. But in 1788, in response to a representation made by Congress two years before, that such

---

[1] History, III., 399.

division would "be productive of many and great inconveniences," growing out of geographical conditions, Virginia consented to such a modification of her deed and cession as would admit of "not more than five states nor less than three, as the situation of that country and future circumstances may require." This was simply ratifying Article V. of the compacts of 1787.

The two States making largest land-pretensions had now ceded as much of their lands as they proposed to cede. Connecticut and Massachusetts still retained their claims in the Northwest, and the Carolinas and Georgia theirs in the Southwest. It was confidently expected, however, that the two cessions would bring about the others in time. From this point the subject is less prominent in the national councils, is less interesting, and can be more rapidly despatched.

In April, 1784, Congress again called attention to the Western territory as an important financial resource, and urged those States that had not complied with the recommendation of September 6, 1780, to make immediate and liberal cessions. On November 13, 1784, the General Court of Massachusetts passed an act authorizing her delegates in Congress to execute a deed of cession of such part of the tract of land lying between the Hudson River and the Mississippi, belonging to the State, as they might think proper, in such manner and on such conditions as should appear to them most suitable. On April 19, 1785, Samuel Holton and Rufus King, delegates, executed and Congress accepted, such deed, conveying and releasing to the United States all of Massachusetts's right and title to lands, both soil and jurisdiction, lying within the charter-limits of the State, west of a meridian line drawn through the western bent or inclination of Lake Ontario, provided such line should fall twenty miles or more west of the western limit of the Niagara River; and if not, then west of the meridian falling that distance west of said river. This was adopting the New York line of four years before. It will be remembered that Massachusetts then claimed nearly all Western New York. The New York and Massachusetts cessions did not in any way touch that controversy. It was finally settled by a joint commission of the two States in 1786. The meridian marking the eastern limit of the New York and Massachusetts cession, which is also the western boundary of the former State from latitude 42° to Lake Erie, was surveyed and marked in 1790.

The State of Connecticut, by an act of May 11, 1786, authorized "an ample deed of release and cession of all the right, title, interest, jurisdiction, and claim of Connecticut to certain western lands, beginning at the completion of the 41° of north latitude, 120 miles west of the western boundary line of the commonwealth of Pennsylvania, as now claimed by said commonwealth, and from thence by a line drawn north, parallel to and 120 miles west of the said west line of Pennsylvania, and to continue north until it come to 42° 2' north latitude." The effect of this cession, if adopted, would be to leave in the hands of Connecticut that part of her original claim which is bounded north by the international boundary-line, east by Pennsylvania, south by parallel 41°, and west by a meridian line one hundred and twenty miles west of the western boundary of Pennsylvania—the Western Reserve. It also left the controversy between New York and Connecticut as to the "Gore" unsettled. The extent of one hundred and twenty miles east and west was given to the reservation because that was the extent of the Susquehanna purchase of 1754. The acceptance of this cession was strongly opposed in Congress because it was partial, and because to accept it would be indorsing the charter of 1662. After a severe struggle it was accepted, May 26, 1786, Maryland alone voting in the negative. Messrs. Johnson and Sturgess executed the deed September 14th, following.

Mr. Grayson, of Virginia, writing to Washington, said the result of the Connecticut reservation was a clear loss of about six million acres of land to the United States, which had already been ceded by Virginia and New York. Connecticut, he said, would at once open a land-office and sell the lands. Grayson then states the reasons urged in Congress for accepting the cession:

"That the claim of a powerful State, although unsupported by right, was, under present circumstances, a disagreeable thing; that sacrifices must be made for the public tranquillity, as well as to acquire an indisputable title to the residue; that Connecticut would settle it immediately with emigrants well disposed to the Union, who would form a barrier, not only against the British but the Indian tribes; and that the thick settlement they would immediately form would enhance the value of the adjacent country and facilitate emigration thereto."

Washington ascribed the acceptance of the cession, with the reservation, to "a want of competent knowledge of the Connecticut claim to Western lands."[1] Grayson can be excused for magnifying three million two hundred and fifty thousand acres of land into six million, as the geography of the Lake Erie region was not then carefully known; but what shall we say of Mr. Bancroft, who repeats the blunder in the last edition of his history![2]

It has always been the fashion to berate Connecticut for illiberality in making her cession. No State came through the cession controversy with less credit. This feeling is hard to explain. Connecticut was more tardy than New York, Virginia, and Massachusetts, but she was much more prompt than the Carolinas and Georgia. She reserved some lands, but so did all the other ceding States, and particularly Virginia, whose course at the time provoked much more ill-feeling. Her charter had been jumped by later charters, but so had those of Virginia and Massachusetts. The lands that she retained were separated from her home territory; but so were those that Massachusetts retained in Western New York. Of course she had not the reasonable excuse that

---
[1] Sparks: Writings of Washington, IX., 177, 178. [2] VI., 279, 280.

New York and Virginia had; for the first of these States wished to have a Lake Erie front, and the second desired to be brought out to the Ohio River.

The Connecticut cession completed the national title to the Northwest, except the Connecticut reservation. The next year Congress enacted the Ordinance of 1787, and the civil life of the territory began in 1788. At that time the Southwest attracted less attention than the Northwest; the framing of the Constitution and the organization of the government under it, as well as the foreign embarrassments of the government coming soon after, drew more and more of the public attention; and, very naturally, the subject of cessions fell somewhat into the background. Moreover, the Southwestern cessions were delayed and complicated by domestic disturbances and by foreign troubles. They do not come within the scope of this inquiry.

This history shows that four different ideas as to the Western lands were first and last suggested. The original idea of the claimant States was to retain them for their own exclusive use; and for a time the other States seemed to acquiesce in this policy. Secondly, it was proposed to distribute the lands or their proceeds, in whole or in part, among the States, leaving the jurisdiction in the hands of the claimant States. Connecticut acted on this idea in offering her first cession. The third proposition was the one for which Maryland contended so long and valiantly, viz.: That Congress should assert the sovereign power of the United States over the Western country without waiting for cessions. Lastly the plan of cession. This ultimately reached the same practical end that Maryland proposed, but by a different road. Manifestly, to persuade the claimant States to cede their lands to the Nation was not to assert a national title to them.

But the lands were not, and could not be fully nationalized as long as the Confederation lasted. The Articles gave Congress no resources except those that came from the States; and although the Nation should ultimately receive the proceeds of the cessions, it could receive them only by way of the States. Accordingly, the deeds made to the United States stipulated that the lands, or their proceeds, should be distributed among all the States in the Union, and this was the principle on which the Land-Ordinance of 1785, that will form the subject of the next chapter, was constructed. When the Constitution went into effect, in 1789, it fully nationalized the public domain.

Unfortunately, the history of the cessions has not always been so presented as clearly to define the course that Congress pursued. For example, Chief Justice Chase speaks of the "claim" of the United States, which rested on the ground that the "Western lands had been the property of the Crown, and naturally fell, on the declaration of independence, to the opponent of the former sovereign." He thus balances this "claim" against the claims of the States:

"Of these various claims, that of the United States seems to have been the most rational and just. The charter of Virginia had been vacated by a judicial proceeding; the company to which it was granted had been dissolved, the grant itself had been resumed by the Crown, and large tracts of the country included by its original limits had been patented to various individuals and associations, without remonstrance on the part of the colony of Virginia. The expenses incurred, and the efforts made by Virginia, in the reduction of the British posts, and in the defence and protection of the frontier, created a just claim upon the treasury of the Union, but could not, of themselves, confer a valid title to the Western lands. The western boundary of Connecticut had been so clearly defined in her agreement with New York, that her claims to territory beyond that line could not be entitled to much consideration; the pretentions of New York were liable to easy refutation upon an appeal to western geography, and an investigation into the real extent of the territory of the Six Nations; and the claim of Massachusetts rested upon a charter granted at a period when the territory now claimed under it was actually possessed and occupied by France. In opposition to these various pretentions, the Congress, as the common head of the United States, maintained its title to the Western lands upon the solid ground that a vacant territory wrested from the common enemy, by the united arms, and at the joint expense of all the States, ought of right to belong to Congress, in trust for the common use and benefit of the whole union."[1]

Congress never maintained a national "claim" on this "ground" or on any other ground. The argument here stated as a ground of title was often urged in discussion in and out of Congress, and is found in State resolutions. It no doubt had a material effect in forming the opinion of the time, but it cannot be found in a single act or resolution that ever passed the doors of Congress. The great arguments advanced by Congress in its appeals for cessions were the desirability of perfecting the Union, the need of harmony among the States, and the necessities of the treasury. Effective as the national view was, Congress kept it sedulously in the background, and constantly acted on the federal theory of the national territory. The Western lands came to the Nation by a series of cessions that proceeded upon the assumption that the States making them ceded something, and that Congress received something in accepting them.

The longer one studies the land-question of the Revolution the more he is impressed by its difficulty, by its importance, and by the wisdom and self-restraint that marked its settlement. No one can deny that the young republic had a happy escape from what might easily have been a great disaster. The cessions prevented a series of inevitable controversies growing out of conflicting claims; and we may well question whether the machinery provided for settling such controversies by the Articles of Confederation was adequate to the task that their adjustment would have entailed. The cessions satisfied the non-claimant States, and so removed

---

[1] Statutes of Ohio : Preliminary Sketch of the History of Ohio, I., 12, 13.

jealousy and heart-burning. They tended materially to nationalize the government, by creating the public domain for Congress to control and to prepare for future republics. They prepared the way for "the more perfect union" of the Constitution. Next to independence and union, the Western lands were the most important question that the old Congress dealt with; and no small part of their importance arose from their relation to independence and union.

NOTE.—There has been much discussion as to the value of the claims and titles now described, and therefore as to the value, in a legal point of view, of the cessions growing out of them. Sometimes the cessions are set wholly aside, and the Northwestern titles derived immediately from the treaty with Great Britain in 1783. An example of this procedure may be found in the Report of the Tenth Census, 1880. But such is not the procedure of the Supreme Court of the United States. The case of Handley's Lessee *vs.* Anthony [1] involved the question whether a certain tract of land on the Indiana side of the Ohio River, that was an island at high water and a peninsula at low water, belonged to the jurisdiction of Indiana or of Kentucky, and so a construction of the language found in the Virginia deed of cession, "situate, lying, and being to the northwest of the River Ohio." Chief Justice Marshall, delivering the opinion of the Court, stated the question to be whether the river at low-water mark, or at its middle state, is the boundary between the States of Kentucky and Indiana. He said two cases were to be considered. When a great river forms the boundary between two nations or states, if the original property is in neither, and there is no convention respecting it, each nation holds to the middle of the stream. The second case is that of a state's being the original proprietor, and granting the territory on one side only. Here the rule is that the grantor retains the river within its own domain, and the newly created state extends to the river only. The Chief Justice declared that the case before the Court fell under the second rule; and that

---

[1] Wheaton, V., 691.

the only question to be determined was, What is the river in such a case? "Wherever the river is a boundary between states, it is the main, the permanent river, which constitutes that boundary," he says; "and the mind will find itself embarrassed with insurmountable difficulties in attempting to draw any other line than the low-water mark." "The sole question in the cause respected the boundary of Kentucky and Indiana; and the title depended entirely upon that question." He held that low-water mark on the northwest bank is the boundary between the two States, and closed his opinion with the words, "the shores of a river border on the water's edge."

To the historian the principal interest of this decision arises from the fact that it recognizes the Virginia cession of 1784 as the ground of title on the southern limit of Indiana, and so, by parity of reasoning, throughout the whole Northwest wherever there had been no conflict of claims between Virginia and other States. Marshall's reasoning all proceeds on that assumption, and he expressly says: "The question whether the lands in controversy lie within the State of Kentucky or Indiana depends chiefly on the land-laws of Virginia, and on the cession made by that State to the United States." The distinguished jurist had a good opportunity, if he had desired one, to ignore the Virginia cession altogether; and to base the title on the treaty with Great Britain he had only to apply the rule of international law that makes the middle thread of a river flowing between two states the boundary, when the original property was in neither, and there is no convention respecting it. He quotes this rule, but sets it aside as not applying to the case before the Court. He bases the decision distinctly on the other rule. "When, *as in this case*, one state is the original proprietor, and grants the territory on one side only, it retains the river within its own domain, and the newly-created state extends to the river only."

In Garner's case, Mr. Vinton sought to break the force of this decision on the ground that the Virginia cession was not in the record of the case before the Chief Justice; but the General Court of Virginia followed the precedent that Marshall had set, and directed the defendants to be set at liberty, because the offence with which they were charged was not committed within the jurisdiction of the State.

In 1800, Marshall reviewed the Connecticut title to the Western Reserve in an elaborate report to the House of Representatives.[1] He held that title to be good and sufficient in this report; and there can be no reasonable doubt that he would have done the same thing, if the occasion had arisen, from the Supreme Bench of the United States.

---

[1] State Papers: Public Lands, I., 94 et seq.

XIV.

THE LAND-ORDINANCE OF 1785.

ONE of the great arguments used in urging the claimant States to surrender some portion of their Western lands was the needs of the State and Federal treasuries. In the resolutions of Congress asking for them, the cessions are considered as lands to be sold as well as territory to be made into new States. The idea of revenue is also prominent in the acts of cession. It was almost distinctively a new idea. In colonial days, waste lands had not proved a source of income to either the colonies or the Crown. The Crown had reserved a small quit-rent, but it was rarely paid. Virginia imposed an annual rental of two cents per acre upon her waste lands, and then threw them open to indiscriminate locations. Whole States, as West Virginia, Tennessee, and Kentucky, were disposed of without affording any public revenue whatever. It is, therefore, somewhat difficult to understand how the idea that the over-mountain lands would be a source of large income became current. But so it was. Whatever is the explanation, the new idea could not be realized without a system of surveys such as was unknown to any one of the colonies. This need was met by Congress in "An Ordinance for ascertaining the mode of disposing of lands in the Western territory," enacted May 20, 1785, but applying only to such lands as had already been ceded by individual States to the United States, and also been purchased by the United States of the Indians. Before presenting the salient features of this ordinance, it is necessary to glance at two or three of these Indian treaties.

By the Treaty of Fort Stanwix, 1768, the Six Nations had sold all their right and title to lands lying south and southeast of the treaty-line running from the mouth of the Tennessee to Wood Creek, save those in the Province of Pennsylvania, the pre-emption of which belonged to the Penns. North and west of that line they continued in as full possession as ever. The protectorate of the Iroquois, recognized in 1713 and in 1726, in no way touched the fee of the Indian lands. Braddock marched toward the Forks of the Ohio to defend the allies of England, whose dominions were invaded, and he called upon the Indians to come to his help for that reason. But by a second Treaty of Fort Stanwix, negotiated in 1784 by Oliver Wolcott, Richard Butler, and Arthur Lee, commissioners appointed by Congress, and the representatives of the Six Nations, they yielded to the United States all their claims to the country west of a line drawn from Johnston's Landing Place on Lake Ontario southerly to the mouth of Buffalo Creek on Lake Erie, and always four miles south of the "carrying path" between the two lakes; thence south to the north boundary of Pennsylvania; thence west to the end of the said north boundary; and thence south to the Ohio River. The first practical effect of this line was the alienation by the Iroquois of all their interest in the Northwest.

The United States still had to deal with the Western Indians—those on the soil—for these tribes did not acknowledge that the Six Nations could deed away their lands. A treaty concluded at Fort McIntosh, January 21, 1785, between commissioners of the United States and the sachems and warriors of the Wyandot, Delaware, Chippewa, and Ottawa nations, made the Cuyahoga River, the portage between that stream and the Tuscarawas branch of the Muskingum, and the Tuscarawas as far as the crossing place above Fort Laurens; a line drawn thence westerly to the portage of the Great Miami; the portage between the Miami and the Maumee, and the Maumee; and Lake Erie to the north of the Cuyahoga, the boundaries between the United States and the said tribes. Within these lines the Indians could still live and hunt; but lands east, south, and west were declared to belong to the United States, "so far as the said Indians formerly claimed the same." This treaty, which was reaffirmed at Fort Harmar in 1789, was the first of a long series of treaties that finally put the United States in full possession of all the Northwestern lands. The two treaties now sketched show how matters stood when the old Congress enacted the land-ordinance that we are now to examine.

This ordinance provided for a corps of surveyors, to be appointed by Congress, or a committee of the States, one from each State, to survey the lands already ceded and purchased, under the directions of the Geographer of the United States. These paragraphs describe the main features of the plan of survey:

"The surveyors . . . shall proceed to divide the said territory into townships of 6 miles square, by lines running due north and south, and others crossing these at right angles, as near as may be. . . .

"The first line, running north and south as aforesaid shall begin on the River Ohio, at a point that shall be found to be due north from the western termination of a line, which has been run as the southern boundary of the State of Pennsylvania; and the first line running east and west shall begin at the same point and shall extend throughout the whole territory; provided that nothing herein shall be construed as fixing the western boundary of the State of Pennsylvania. The Geographer shall designate the townships, or fractional parts of townships, by numbers progressively from south to north; always beginning each range with No. 1; and the ranges shall be distinguished by their progressive numbers to the westward. The first range, extending from the Ohio to the Lake Erie being marked No. 1. The Geographer shall personally attend to the running of the first east and west line; and shall take the latitude of the extremes of the first north and south line, and of the mouths of the principal rivers.

"The lines shall be measured with a chain; shall be plainly marked by chaps on the trees, and exactly described on a plat, whereon shall be noted by the surveyor, at their proper distances, all mines, salt-springs, salt-licks, and mill-seats, that shall come to his knowledge; and all water-courses, mountains and other remarkable and permanent things, over and near which such lines shall pass, and also the quality of the lands.

"The plats of the townships respectively, shall be marked by subdivisions into lots of one mile square or 640 acres, in the same direction as the external lines, and numbered from 1 to 36; always beginning the succeeding range of the lots with the number next to that with which the preceding one concluded. And where, from the causes before mentioned, only a fractional part of a township shall be surveyed, the lots, protracted thereon, shall bear the same numbers as if the township had been entire. And the surveyors, in running the external lines of the townships, shall, at the interval of every mile, mark corners for the lots which are adjacent, always designating the same in a different manner from those of the townships.

"The Geographer and surveyors shall pay the utmost attention to the variation of the magnetic needle; and shall run and note all lines by the true meridian, certifying, with every plat, what was the variation at the times of running the lines thereon noted." [1]

As soon as seven ranges were surveyed, the Geographer should transmit the plats to the Board of Treasury, to be carefully recorded; and so for every succeeding series of seven ranges. It was made the duty of the Secretary of War, from time to time, to take by lot from the whole number of townships and fractional townships making up each series of seven ranges, as well those to be sold entire as those to be sold in lots, one-seventh of the whole, for the use of the Continental Army; until enough land should be drawn to satisfy the claims arising under the resolutions of Congress, adopted September 16 and 18, 1776, and August 12 and September 22,

---

[1] Journals of Congress, IV., 520.

THE LAND-ORDINANCE OF 1785. 259

1780. The Board of Treasury should cause the remaining numbers "to be drawn for in the name of the thirteen States respectively, according to the quotas in the last preceding requisition on all the States," and should certify the results of such drawings to the Commissioners of the State Loan offices. The State Commissioners should now proceed to sell the lands at public vendue, after first advertising them, in the following manner: Townships 1, 3, 5, etc., whole or fractional, in the first range, entire; Nos. 2, 4, 6, etc., in the same range, in lots; townships 1, 3, 5, in the second range, in lots; Nos. 2, 4, 6, entire; and so on, alternating throughout, provided that no lands should be sold at a less price than one dollar an acre in specie or its equivalent in certificates of State or United States indebtedness, and the cost of surveying and other charges, which are rated at $36 a township. Lots Nos. 8, 11, 26, 29, in all whole townships, and such of them as were found in the fractional townships, were reserved to the United States for future sale. The ordinance also declared: "There shall be reserved the lot No. 16 of every township for the maintenance of public schools, within the said township; also one third part of all gold, silver, lead, and copper mines to be sold or otherwise disposed of as Congress shall hereafter direct."

The lands between the Scioto and Little Miami Rivers, that Virginia had contingently reserved, were excepted from the operation of the ordinance. Three townships adjacent to Lake Erie were reserved for the use of the Canada and Nova Scotia refugees who had adhered to the cause of the colonies in the war, and lands on the Muskingum were reserved for the Christian Indians of Gnadenhütten, Schönbrunn, and Salem. Deeds should be given for lands by the Loan Commissioners of the States; records of deeds should be kept in the loan offices; and a regular system of accounting between the Federal and State authorities should be observed. All moneys received by the commissioners for the lands sold should be charged to them. Provision was also made for distributing the lands reserved for bounties for service in the Continental Army.

Under this ordinance, the Federal Government made its first land-surveys, the so-called "seven ranges" adjoining Pennsylvania, south of the forty-first parallel, frequently mentioned in histories of Ohio.

The Land-Ordinance of 1785 is eminently characteristic of the time in which it was enacted. It is a curious medley of state and national ideas. In operation it would have been exceedingly complex and cumbersome. But its state features passed away when the Constitution went into operation, while national features are still alive. It contained the germs of our present admirable system of national land-surveys: Base-lines; boundaries carefully run, measured, and marked according to a uniform plan; the six-mile township and the "section;" maps and plats, deeds and records. In no case was the land to be sold or otherwise disposed of before it had been surveyed. The greatest defect of the plan of survey was the lack of subdivisions smaller than a square mile, but this was afterward overcome.

With all its defects, this ordinance was perfection itself compared with the old colonial methods; say, that of Virginia. Here the State made no surveys whatever before disposing of the lands to the settler or speculator. The prospective owner sought out a tract of land that pleased him, and caused a survey to be made and marked, the latter generally by "blazing" the trees with a hatchet. The survey was then recorded in the State land-office, and became the basis for warrants covering the land. Such was the way in which the lands of West Virginia and Kentucky were "taken up." The reader of Washington's correspondence with Crawford finds it well illustrated in practice, and at the same time gets an insight into a phase of Washington's character. This method gave the greatest scope to settlement. The pre-emptor was never obliged to wait for the surveyor. Such a system led to the "running out" of all sorts of tracts of land. Half a dozen patents would sometimes be given for the same tract. Pieces of land, of all shapes and sizes, lay between the patents; and in time, as lands became more valuable, huge "blanket" patents were thrown out to catch these pieces. Such a system naturally begot no end of litigation, and there remain in Kentucky curious vestiges of it, that Professor Shaler thus describes:

"Of all these conflicts the Virginia, and, following it, the Kentucky land-office took no note. To this day one can, if he please to pay the costs, 'patent' any land that lies in Kentucky, and repeat the process on the same area each year. The State only guarantees the entry if the land is unpossessed under previous title of valid kind. In time a vast amount of litigation and no end of trouble came out of this scheme. At this moment, owing to the absence of records, there are hundreds of thousands of acres in Kentucky over which no sort of ownership has ever been exercised. No taxes are collected on them. If they have ever been surveyed, no one knows under what patents they are claimed."[1]

As it was, there was a sufficiency of land-litigation in the Northwest Territory; but the first settlers and their descendants have the greatest reason to be grateful to the old Congress for saving them from such confusion as Virginia suffered to come upon Kentucky.

The system of surveys inaugurated did not extend to the Connecticut and Virginia reservations on the southern shore of Lake Erie and the northern bank of the Ohio. Every Ohioan can join with Dr. Andrews, of Marietta, in this opinion: "It would have been desirable if the system of uniform ranges, townships and sections, which commenced with the seven ranges in the summer of 1786, could have been carried out over the whole surface of the State; avoiding the confusion of the five-mile system of the Western

---

[1] Kentucky, 49, 51.

Reserve and the no system of the Virginia Military District."[1]

The reservation to Congress of one-third of the gold, silver, and copper came to naught; but the dedication to the support of public schools of lot No. 16 in every township was a far-reaching act of statesmanship that is of perpetual interest. It was the first and greatest of the long series of similar dedications made by Congress to education; and the funds derived from the sale of these original "school lands" are the bulk of the public-school endowments of the five great States of the old Northwest.

NOTE.—There has been some controversy as to the author of the plan of survey incorporated in the Ordinance of 1785. The late Colonel Charles Whittlesey accords the honor to Thomas Hutchins, first Geographer of the United States, whose duties were similar to those now performed by the Surveyor-General of the Public Lands. Whittlesey says Hutchins conceived "this simplest of all known modes of survey" in 1764, when he was a captain in the Sixtieth Royal Regiment, and engineer to the expedition to Ohio, under Colonel Henry Bouquet. It formed a part of his plan of military colonies north of the Ohio as a protection against Indians. The seven ranges were surveyed in 1786-87, under the protection of United States troops. The base-line of this survey, known as "the Geographer's line," runs west from the north bank of the Ohio, where the State line crosses it, forty-two miles.

Hutchins died at Pittsburg in 1788, where his remains now lie unnoticed, in the cemetery of the First Presbyterian Church.—Ohio Surveys, Tract No. 59, of Western Reserve and Northern Ohio Historical Society.

---

[1] Ohio Archæological and Historical Quarterly, 4, June, 1887.

XV.

THE ORDINANCE OF 1787.

THE ordinance enacted, July 13, 1787, for the government of the territory of the United States northwest of the River Ohio is one of the memorable documents that passed the doors of the old Congress. It ranks with the great State papers of 1774 and 1775, that won from Lord Chatham the encomium: "For solidity of reason, force of sagacity, and wisdom of conclusion, under a complication of difficult circumstances, no nation or body of men stand in preference to the General Congress at Philadelphia;" with the Declaration of Independence, that should always hang, Lord Brougham said, in the cabinets of kings; with, or rather above, the Articles of Confederation, that, with all their imperfection and weakness, still formed the first constitution of the American people, and contained the elements for the evolution of a more perfect union.

The Ordinance of 1787 stands at the convergence of three series of important events. The first of these entered into many great questions of the time, as Confederation, finance, the national boundaries, foreign relations, Western settlements, the Northwestern and Southwestern territories, the admission to the Union of Vermont as a State, the navigation of the Mississippi, and the fidelity of the Southwest to the Union. These events are the cessions that have already been treated, so far as they relate to the old Northwest. Except the Western Reserve, and the lands that Virginia had retained in Southern Ohio to discharge her obligations to her soldiers, the four cessions gave the United States a clear title to the territory bounded by the Lakes, the Ohio, and the Mississippi. This was the original public domain. It was a territory in which all the States had a common interest; it furnished national subjects of legislation; and it prepared the way for the Constitution. The happy effects of the cessions upon the States, and upon the Nation, cannot be overestimated; one of them being the escape from the difficulties attending any attempt to adjust the conflicting jurisdictions. These Northwestern cessions are the culmination of the first series of events leading up to the Ordinance. Moreover, they put the United States in what was really a very anomalous position. The Articles of Confederation were "articles of confederation and perpetual union" among States; and they no more contemplated a Federal territory to be managed by Congress than the Constitution of 1787 contemplated the acquisition of territory beyond the boundaries of 1783. To some extent, no doubt, this fact explains the remarkable form of government that was devised for the Northwest.

Previous to 1748, the English colonies had taken little interest in the interior of North America. After that all was changed. The Ohio Company, organized in 1748; the "Plan of Union," adopted by the Albany Congress of 1754; Dr. Franklin's comments on the "Plan," and his "Plan for settling two Western Colonies in North America," have all been fully treated in another place. Governor Thomas Pownall, who has been called the only British official in the country who had a statesman-like grasp of colonial questions, favored what he called "barrier colonies," after the fashion of the marks and marches of the Middle Ages. Pownall wrote home: "If the English would advance one step farther, or cover themselves where they are, it must be at once, by one large step over the mountains, with a numerous and military colony."[1] The coming on of the French and Indian war adjourned the

---

[1] Sparks: Works of Franklin, III., 69.

plans of the Ohio Company, of Franklin, and of Pownall, until the sword should decide to whom the West belonged; and even when the sword had rendered a verdict in favor of England, the proclamation of 1763 still further adjourned similar plans. But the paths that the wild deer had made over the mountains could not be blocked up. The hunter followed the deer, and the settler followed the hunter. Adventurous Pennsylvanians and Virginians began to enter the valleys leading to the Ohio; James Robertson was at Watauga in 1769, and John Sevier came soon after; Boone entered the Dark and Bloody Ground the same year; and when the embattled farmers fired the shot heard round the world, a party of hunters in the valley of the Elkhorn heard the echo, and baptized the station that they were building " Lexington." It has been said that the English race has a hunger for the horizon. " Have not all America extended their back settlements in opposition to laws and proclamations?" is a question that Judge David Campbell asked Governor Caswell, when the people of the back counties of North Carolina were trying to set up the State of Franklin. But sporadic settlements under the jurisdiction of the old States did not fill the ambition of the times; and in less than three years from the signing of the royal proclamation the discussion of interior colonies was boldly renewed. Again Franklin bore a prominent part in the discussion. In 1766, 1767, and 1768 he pressed upon the home government a grant for a colony in the Illinois, and was refused. In 1769 he presented another, praying for a grant on the southern side of the Ohio. This time he was successful; the petition was granted in 1772, terms of government were agreed upon, and the charter was made ready for the seals, when the breaking out of the war with England again adjourned Western colonies to more peaceful times.

All through the Revolution the over-mountain settlements were slowly growing; the Maryland amendment of 1777, and the Congressional resolutions of 1780, kept the thought of new and independent States before the country; and with the return of peace, the acknowledgment of independence, and the concession of the Lakes and the Mississippi as our northwestern and western boundaries, together with the land-cessions, the hour of preparation for planting the West with new States struck. There was no time to lose if the West was to remain in our hands; for the Briton and the Spaniard continued to retain considerable portions of our territory, and neither looked upon the boundaries of 1783 as finalities. In his well-known letter to Governor Harrison, Washington wrote in 1784: "The flanks and rear of the United States are possessed by other powers, and formidable ones, too;" it is necessary to "apply the cement of interest to bind all parts of the Union together by indissoluble bonds;" "the Western States stand, as it were, upon a pivot—the touch of a feather would turn them any way."[1]

On the 1st of March, 1784, the very day that Virginia completed her cession, Mr. Jefferson, as chairman of a committee, reported to Congress a temporary plan of government for the Western territory; and this plan, variously amended, became an ordinance of Congress on April 23d following. This ordinance did not organize a territorial government, but left everything inchoate; and, with all its merits, was a nullity, and was repealed by the Ordinance of 1787. Between April 23, 1784, and July 9, 1787, as many as three ordinances for the government of the Western territory were reported to Congress: May 10, 1786, September 19, 1786, and April 26, 1787. These ordinances, one and all, were quite different documents from the one whose history we are now tracing. On May 10, 1787, the last one had reached the third reading, when its further progress was suddenly arrested by a third series of events that we must now follow.

But first, the facts now related in regard to new States and governments are the second series, at the junction of which

---

[1] Sparks: Writings of Washington, IX., 62, 63.

with the two others we find the Ordinance for the Government of the Northwest Territory.

November 2, 1783, Washington took leave of the rank and file of the Continental army, and two days later, of the officers. He left both in a most distressful condition; the majority were poor, many broken in health; they were all unpaid, and Congress could do no more than give them the "final certificates" that were almost worthless; eight years of suffering lay behind, and they knew not how many more of poverty before. In that dark hour some of them looked beyond the Western mountains for a theatre where they might repair their broken fortunes, as they had in darker hours often looked there as a place of retreat from the enemy in case of overwhelming disaster; and Washington, in his final order, had cheered them with these words: "The extensive and fertile regions of the West will yield a most happy asylum to those who, fond of domestic enjoyment, are seeking for personal independence."[1] Even before that order was issued, a plan for forming a new State westward of the Ohio was in contemplation; and on June 16, 1783, two hundred and eighty-five officers of the Continental line of the army had petitioned Congress to assign and mark out the tract of land bounded by Lake Erie on the north, Pennsylvania on the east, the Ohio on the south, a meridian twenty-four miles west of the mouth of the Scioto, and the Miami of the Lakes on the west, as the seat of a distinct colony of the United States, "in time to be admitted one of the confederated States of America."[2] The petitioners also asked that their bounty lands be set off to them in this district. This petition was really the foundation of the Ohio Company of Associates, organized at the

---

[1] Sparks: Writings of Washington, VIII., 493.
[2] Of the two hundred and eighty-five names, two hundred and thirty-five belonged to New England, thirty-six to New Jersey, thirteen to Maryland, and one to New York. The New England names belonged, one hundred and fifty-five to Massachusetts, thirty-four to New Hampshire, and forty-six to Connecticut.
—Ohio Archæological and Historical Quarterly, June, 1887, 46.

"Bunch of Grapes," in Boston, March 3, 1786. This organization meant, as has been well said, "The conversion of those old final certificates into future homes, westward of the Ohio," and "the formation of a new State." The directors sent one of their number, General S. H. Parsons, of Middletown, Conn., to Congress to negotiate the purchase of a tract of land; and it was his arrival in New York, May 10th, that arrested the progress of the ordinance that had been reported the previous month. Parsons presented his memorial, which was referred to a committee, and returned home. His place was shortly taken by Dr. Manasseh Cutler, of Ipswich, Mass. Cutler reached New York on July 5th, the day before the pending ordinance was to be taken up. The few days following his waiting upon Congress are big with the issues of futurity. They are the convergence of the three lines of events that we have been following—the land-cessions, the growing interest in Western colonization, and the objects of the Ohio Company—where we find the immortal Ordinance.

Dr. Cutler's ostensible business in New York was to purchase as much of the land bounded by the petition of 1783 as Congress would exchange for $1,000,000 of the evidences of the public debt. But he was really as much interested in the ordinance that Congress was then considering as in the memorial of General Parsons; for what would homes be worth to New England men without good government? He seems, indeed, to have had almost as much to do with the one as with the other. It is impossible and unnecessary to give in detail the history of those eventful July days, but a rapid summary of events is essential to our purpose.

Only eight States were then present by their delegates in Congress—Massachusetts, New York, New Jersey, Delaware, Virginia, North Carolina, South Carolina, and Georgia. On the 9th of July the ordinance of April preceding was referred to a new committee—Carrington and Lee of Virginia, Dane of Massachusetts, Kean of South Carolina, and Smith of New York—three of them Southern men. On the 10th, Dr. Cutler, in response to an invitation of the committee, submitted in writing his views touching an ordinance; on the 11th, the committee reported; and on the 13th, after receiving some amendments, the report was adopted by the unanimous vote of the States present, and the unanimous vote of the eighteen delegates, with the exception of Yates of New York. Thus, an act of legislation that had been before Congress for more than three years was consummated within a week from the time that Dr. Cutler, who had been twelve days on the way, drove his gig up to the "Plough and the Harrow," in the Bowery.

Admirable in matter and in literary style as the Ordinance is, its provisions are not arranged with that careful method which Gouverneur Morris gave to the Constitution of the United States. I shall make no attempt at classification beyond remarking that the Ordinance created a machinery of government for immediate use, defined the method and spirit of its administration, provided for the creation of the long-promised new States, and established certain principles of civil polity that should be of perpetual obligation.

Section 1 constituted the Territory one district for temporary government, but reserved to Congress the power to divide it into two districts in the future.

Section 2 ordained that landed estates in the Territory, of persons dying intestate, should be divided among the children of the intestate, or if none, among the next of kin, in equal shares. This provision Jefferson had introduced into the ordinance for Western lands that he reported in 1784, and that Congress never acted upon, in the words: "The lands therein shall pass in descent and dower according to the customs known in the common law by the name of gavelkind." It adds interest to the fact to recall that, not long before, entails and primogeniture had been eradicated from the laws of Virginia.

Sections 3 to 12, inclusive, created a Territorial government, and directed how it should be administered. Congress should appoint a governor for a term of three years, a secretary for a term of four years, and three judges for good behavior. Until the election of a general assembly, the governor and judges should adopt and publish in the district such of the laws, civil and criminal, of the original States as they deemed necessary and best suited to the circumstances of the people, subject to the approval of Congress. The governor should be commander-in-chief of the militia, should appoint and commission militia officers below the rank of general officers, and appoint such magistrates and other civil officers in counties and townships as he deemed necessary to the maintenance of peace and good order. The secretary's duties are sufficiently indicated by his title. Any two of the judges should form a court having a common-law jurisdiction. A general assembly was authorized as soon as there should be five thousand free male inhabitants, of full age, in the district. The legislature should consist, when formed, of a governor, a legislative council, and a house of representatives; the representatives to be chosen by the people, but the five members of the council to be chosen by Congress from a list of ten nominated by the house of representatives. The legislature should elect a Territorial delegate to Congress. All the officers must reside in the Territory. The governor must own a freehold of 1,000 acres of land in the district; the secretary, the judges, and the members of the council must have similar freeholds of 500 acres each; representatives must hold, in their own right, 200 acres of land in the district, and no man was a qualified elector of a representative, the only elective office, unless he filled the following requirement: " That a freehold in 50 acres of land in the district, having been a citizen of one of the States, and being resident in the district, or the like freehold and two years' residence in the district, shall be necessary to qualify a man as an elector of a representative."

What havoc these rules would make with the legislatures

and electoral bodies of to-day! They were intended to confine the government of the Territory to those men who had, as the English say, "a stake in the country." Moreover, they were in accord with the temper of the times, and they stand on the statute-book of 1787 a landmark from which we may measure how far the American people have drifted on the tide of democracy in one hundred years. The whole government was centralized to a degree that would not now be endured in the United States outside of Utah.

Then follow the articles of compact between the original States and the people and States in the Territory, forever unalterable, unless by common consent—the six bright jewels in the crown that the Northwest Territory was ever to wear.

Article I. declares that "No person demeaning himself in a peaceable and orderly manner shall ever be molested on account of his mode of worship or religious sentiments, in the said Territory."

Article II. guarantees to the inhabitants the writ of *habeas corpus*, trial by jury, proportional representation in the legislature, and the privileges of the common law. The article concludes with the declaration "That no law ought ever to be made or have force in the said Territory that shall, in any manner whatever, interfere with or affect private contracts, or engagements *bona fide*, and without fraud previously formed." A few weeks later, this provision was copied into the Constitution of the United States, but this is its first appearance in a charter of government. It was an outgrowth of the troublous commercial condition of the country. Lee, who originally brought it forward, intended it as a stroke at paper money.

Article III. contains those words that should be emblazoned on the escutcheon of every American State: "Religion, morality, and knowledge being necessary to good government and the happiness of mankind, schools and the means of education shall forever be encouraged." It also says that good faith shall be observed toward the Indians.

Article IV. ordained "That the said Territory, and the States which may be formed therein, shall forever remain a part of this Confederacy of the United States of America, subject to the Articles of Confederation, and to such alterations therein" as might be made, and to the laws enacted by Congress. It concludes, after some provisions in regard to taxation: "The navigable waters leading into the Mississippi and St. Lawrence, and the carrying places between the same, shall be common highways, and forever free, as well to the inhabitants of the said Territory as to the citizens of the United States, and those of any other States that may be admitted into the Confederacy, without any tax, imposts, or duty therefor."

Article V. provided for the formation in the Territory of States, not less than three nor more than five, and drew their boundary-lines subject to changes that Congress might afterward make. A population of 60,000 free inhabitants should entitle every one of these States to admission—not "into the Union," a phrase that came in with the Constitution, but—"by its delegates into the Congress of the United States, on an equal footing with the original States in all respects whatever," and to "form a permanent constitution of State government," with the proviso that "the constitution and government so to be formed shall be republican, and in conformity to the principles contained in these articles."

Article VI. dedicated the Northwest to freedom forever. "There shall be neither slavery nor involuntary servitude in the said Territory, otherwise than in the punishment of crimes whereof the party shall have been duly convicted." But this prohibition was coupled with a proviso that stamps the whole article as a compromise. "Provided always, that any person escaping into the same, from whom labor or service is lawfully claimed in any one of the original States, such fugitive may be lawfully reclaimed, and conveyed to the person claiming his or her labor or service as aforesaid."

Mr. W. F. Poole says that "in the whole range of topics

in our national history there is none which has been more obscure, or the subject of more conflicting and erroneous statements, than the Ordinance of 1787."[1] Much labor and acuteness have been devoted to the discovery of the authorship of its different parts. I shall neither emulate these labors nor particularize their results, but shall content myself with three or four observations.

We have seen that four different ordinances had been previously reported to Congress, and that one had already been enacted. The fifth and great Ordinance, as Mr. Bancroft says, embodied the best parts of all its predecessors. But it embodied more; and all the evidence points to the conclusion that much of the new material was contained in the paper that Dr. Cutler handed to the committee, July 10th, after he had studied the ordinance then pending. Whoever may have brought them forward, the imperishable principles of polity woven into the Ordinance of 1787 were the ripe fruit of many centuries of Anglo-Saxon civilization; but the best places to search for them are the bills of rights of the Revolutionary constitutions.

The immortal prohibition of slavery has been the subject of many a heated controversy. In the "great debate" of 1830, Mr. Webster claimed it for Nathan Dane, of Massachusetts, and Mr. Hayne and Mr. Benton claimed it for Thomas Jefferson. Mr. Dane claimed it for himself. President King of Columbia College claimed it for his father, Rufus King. William Grayson and Richard Henry Lee have also been nominated for the honor. The facts are these: Mr. Jefferson's draught of the Ordinance of 1784 contained a prohibition of slavery in all Western territory, south as well as north of the Ohio River, to take effect at the beginning of the year 1801, but it was struck out in Congress. In March, 1785, Mr. King moved to commit a proposition to prohibit slavery in the Northwest immediately; the motion prevailed, but Congress

---

[1] North American Review, No. 251.

never acted upon the subject. The first draught of the Ordinance of 1787 did not contain the prohibition; but Mr. Dane, who was a member of the committee of July 9th, and who wrote that draught, brought it forward on the second reading, apparently on a suggestion from Virginia, and it was made the sixth article of compact. Nothing can be finer than Mr. Bancroft's distribution of the honors among those who helped to bring about this grand result:

"Thomas Jefferson first summoned Congress to prohibit slavery in all the territory of the United States; Rufus King lifted up the measure when it lay almost lifeless on the ground, and suggested the immediate instead of the prospective prohibition; a Congress composed of five Southern States to one from New England and two from the Middle States, headed by William Grayson, supported by Richard Henry Lee, and using Nathan Dane as scribe, carried the measure to the goal in the amended form in which King had caused it to be referred to a committee; and as Jefferson had proposed, placed it under the sanction of an irrevocable compact."[1]

The value of Rufus King's suggestion will appear when we come to study, farther on, the efforts afterward made in Ohio, Indiana, and Illinois to break the prohibition down, and when we reflect upon the enormous power that slavery would have had in the Northwest if once it gained a foothold. Any man who believes that it was Article VI. of the compacts of 1787 that decided the great issue brought to a close at Appomattox in 1865 must read the history of those July days with bated breath. Once that prohibition had been voted down, and once it had been set aside; it had been rejected by Southern men when Mr. Jefferson first brought it forward, and now five of the eight States present are Southern States and eleven of the eighteen men Southern men.

We have now traced the main events that led up to July

---

[1] History, VI., 290.

13, 1787; but we should also observe that at last the Ordinance could not have been secured, as it is, had it not been for the happy constitution of Congress at that time, for the address of Dr. Cutler in conducting his mission, and for the blessed influences of peace and wisdom that brooded over America in that year. How admirable the words of Bancroft:

"Before the Federal Convention had referred its resolutions to a committee of detail, an interlude in Congress was shaping the character and destiny of the United States of America. Sublime and humane and eventful in the history of mankind as was the result, it will take not many words to tell how it was brought about. For a time wisdom and peace and justice dwelt among men, and the great Ordinance, which could alone give continuance to the Union, came in serenity and stillness. Every man that had a share in it seemed to be led by an invisible hand to do just what was wanted of him; all that was wrongfully undertaken fell to the ground to wither by the wayside; whatever was needed for the happy completion of the mighty work arrived opportunely, and just at the right moment moved into its place."[1]

But Dr. Cutler came to New York to buy land? Strange to say, the land-purchase was attended by more trouble than the ordinance of government; but on July 27th Congress authorized the sale of 5,000,000 acres lying north of the Ohio, west of the seven ranges, and east of the Scioto River, 1,500,000 for the Ohio Company, and "the remainder," to quote Dr. Cutler's diary, "for a private speculation in which many of the principal characters of America are concerned."[2] The total price agreed upon was three and a half millions of dollars, but as the payments were made in public securities worth only twelve cents on a dollar, the real price was only eight or nine cents per acre.

---

[1] History, VI., 277.
[2] The "private speculation" was the Scioto Company. See note at the end of chapter.

"The Ordinance of 1787 and the Ohio purchase," says Mr. Poole, "were parts of one and the same transaction. The purchase *would* not have been made without the Ordinance, and the Ordinance *could* not have been enacted except as an essential condition of the purchase." The meaning of this is, that the New England men would not buy the land unless a satisfactory government was secured, and that Congress would not have enacted the Ordinance had it not been for the opportunity to make a large sale of lands. This alone makes the sale and purchase memorable, but it is memorable for other reasons. The agent who negotiated it says it was "the greatest private contract ever made in America," up to that time. Besides, the "Powers to the Board of Treasury" authorizing the sale contain some features that rank with those of the Ordinance itself. The Land Ordinance of 1785 reserved lot No. 16 in every township, or a thirty-sixth part of the whole West, for the maintenance of public schools within the township; and the "powers" reaffirmed the reservation. Other kindred provisions were these: The lot No. 29 in each township or fractional part of a township to be given perpetually for the purposes of religion. Not more than two complete townships to be given perpetually for the purposes of a university, to be laid off by the purchaser or purchasers, as near the centre as may be, so that the same shall be of good land, to be applied to the intended object by the legislature of the State. These two townships of land are the endowment of the Ohio University at Athens. Once more, it was in consequence of the Ordinance and the purchase that Marietta, the first colony in the Northwest Territory, was planted at the mouth of the Muskingum, April 7, 1788.

No act of American legislation has called out more eloquent applause than the Ordinance of 1787. Statesmen, historians, and jurists have vied with one another in celebrating its praises. In one respect it has a proud pre-eminence over all other acts of legislation on the American statute-books. It alone is known by the date of its enactment, and not by its subject-matter. It was more than a law or statute. It was a constitution for the Territory Northwest of the River Ohio. More than this, it was a model for later legislation relating to the national territories; and some of its provisions, particularly the prohibition of slavery, stand among the greatest precedents of our history. The sixth compact was the old-time platform of the Republican Party previous to 1861.

The record of the vote on the Ordinance shows eighteen delegates present in Congress. As we look over the list, we are surprised to see how few of them have any place in history.

Massachusetts, Holten and Dane; New York, Smith, Harring, and Yates; New Jersey, Clark and Scheurman; Delaware, Kearny and Mitchell; Virginia, Grayson, Lee, and Carrington; North Carolina, Blount and Hawkins; South Carolina, Kean and Huger; Georgia, Few and Pierce. We must remember, however, that the Old Congress was not now what once it had been; also that the Federal Convention was sitting at Philadelphia, and that Franklin, Sherman, King, Hamilton, the Morrises, Madison, Rutledge, the Pinckneys, Randolph, Wilson, and Washington were in attendance there. The ease with which the Ohio Company carried its proposition through Congress has been the subject of surprise for a hundred years. No doubt the explanation consists largely in the fact that the new colony was proposed by a body of men fully able to make it successful. Contrasting it with earlier propositions, Mr. Bancroft says:

"For vague hopes of colonization, here stood a body of hardy pioneers, ready to lead the way to the rapid absorption of the domestic debt of the United States; selected from the choicest regiments of the army; capable of self-defence; the protectors of all who should follow them; men skilled in the labors of the field and of artisans; enterprising and laborious; trained in the severe morality and strict orthodoxy of the New England villages of that day. All was changed. There was the same difference as between sending out recruiting officers and giving marching orders to a regular corps present with music and arms and banners."[1]

But, after all, one cannot help thinking that the silence and celerity with which the Ordinance was enacted was partly due to the fact that the Federal Convention was in session. Men's eyes were fixed upon the statesmen who were discussing in secret the National Constitution; and Grayson and Lee and Carrington and Dane, assisted by Manasseh Cutler, were left with fourteen men, all but one of whom were willing to follow them, to enact in serenity and stillness an ordinance of government that might not have been secured if New York and not Philadelphia had been the focus of public attention. The year 1787 is thus doubly memorable; it gave us the Ordinance for the Territory Northwest of the River Ohio, and the Constitution of the United States.

> "Peace hath her victories
> No less renowned than war;"

and History may yet adjudge that year the greatest in our annals.

NOTE.—Hitherto Mr. W. F. Poole's article, "Dr. Cutler and the Ordinance of 1787," in the *North American Review*, No. 251, has been the best single account of the origin of the Ordinance of 1787, and particularly of the part that Dr. Cutler played in its enactment. But now a much fuller account may be found in the " Life, Journals, and Correspondence of Rev. Manasseh Cutler, LL.D." This work will immediately take rank with the "St. Clair Papers," as a contribution to Northwestern history. The circumstances leading up to the organization of the Ohio Company and the planting of Marietta, are narrated with great fulness and particularity. Much the best account extant of the Scioto purchase will also be found in this work. This purchase was "the private speculation in which many of

---

[1] History, VL, 285.

the principal characters of America are concerned," that Cutler was compelled to include in his proposition to Congress before he could buy the lands that he wanted for the Ohio Associates. The Scioto purchase was purely a speculation, projected by Colonel William Duer, and proved to be very disastrous to all concerned.

XVI.

THE TERRITORY OF THE UNITED STATES NORTHWEST OF THE RIVER OHIO.

THE region beyond the Ohio that the Virginia troops and the American Commissioners at Paris wrested from England, that the four States ceded to the Nation, and that Congress constituted a district for the purposes of government in 1787, of itself is a noble physical base for an empire. It contains 265,878[1] square miles of land to Austria-Hungary's 240,943, Germany's 212,091, France's 209,091, Great Britain and Ireland's 120,874, and Italy's 114,296. Triangular in form, its sides are washed by about three thousand miles of navigable waters. The Great Lakes, one of which reaches its very centre, contain nearly one-half the fresh water of the globe. The volume of the waters of the Mississippi is equal to that of three Ganges, of nine Rhones, of twenty-seven Seines, or eighty Tibers, or of all the rivers of Europe, exclusive of the Volga.[2] The Ohio, one thousand miles in length, is one of

---

[1] The territory northwest of the River Ohio contained an area of 265,878 square miles, and from it were formed and now lie in its original territory—

		Square Miles.
The State of Ohio		39,964
" " " Indiana		33,809
" " " Illinois		55,414
" " " Michigan		56,451
" " " Wisconsin		53,924
" " " Minnesota, east of the Mississippi River and international boundary of 1783, estimated to contain		26,000
" Erie Purchase (in Pennsylvania) about		316

Grand Total, 170,161,867 acres.—Donaldson: The Public Domain, 161.

[2] Carnegie: Triumphant Democracy, 301.

the largest affluents of the Mississippi. The rivers flowing to these three water-ways render every part of the interior of the Northwest easily accessible; and some of them, as the Wabash, the Illinois, and the Wisconsin, are small streams only because they appear in such noble company. The surface is exceedingly favorable to the construction of canals and railroads; and such are the geographical relations of the region to the remaining parts of the country that it gathers in its grasp nearly all the great lines of transportation and travel uniting the Mississippi River and the Atlantic Ocean. With a very large proportion of arable land unsurpassed in fertility and adapted to a wide range of productions; rich in forests of hard and soft woods; the waters abounding in fish; abundant in coal, iron, and lead, copper, oil, gas, and salt, it is the fit home of the great people who are making its history.

On July 13, 1787, this great domain was an unbroken wilderness. By far the larger number of the few inhabitants were savages, who were resolved that the wilderness should remain unbroken. Passing by the roving hunters and traders, the few Americans then making a small beginning at New Design on the Mississippi, and the occasional Moravian missionaries, the French colonists, not five thousand in number, were the only civilized population. As Michigan was in the hands of the British, the *habitants* of the Illinois and the Wabash, who had practically been without government since 1784, were the only people on the ground calling for a government. However, the Territory was not established for the resident population. A new colonial period was opening, promising grander results than the old one. The Ordinance of 1787 and the Powers to the Board of Treasury take rank with the colonial charters of one hundred and fifty years before. The magnificent territory that the Indian had for centuries put to uses but little superior to those of the buffalo, the bear, and the wolf; that the Frenchman had used for purposes but little higher than those of the Indian; and that the Englishman had refused to use at all, was now to be devoted to the greatest of human objects—was now to become the homes of a progressive people excelling in all the arts of civilized life.

The apex of the Northwestern triangle points to the east; two of its sides face the Atlantic slope; but causes now to be pointed out made the Ohio River the seat of the earliest settlements.

The census-takers of 1790 found in the United States a population of 3,929,214 souls, and the number was not much less in 1788. All of this population, save about five per cent., was distributed along the seaboard from Maine to Georgia, presenting an average depth of settlement, in a direction at right angles to the coast, of two hundred and fifty-five miles. This was the population that the Northwest was first to draw upon; for the days of European emigration had not then dawned.

General Walker, the superintendent of the tenth census, has pointed out that, in the early census-years, population moved westward along four main lines: (1) Through Central New York, following the valley of the Mohawk River; (2) across Southern Pennsylvania, Western Maryland, and Northern Virginia, parallel to and along the course of the Upper Potomac; (3) southward down the Valley of Virginia, and through the mountain-gaps into Tennessee and Kentucky; (4) around the southern end of the mountains, through Georgia and Alabama.[1] These movements were along the original lines of communication, surveyed by Nature ages before man appeared on the continent. The Great Lakes lie in the first of these directions, and they afterward became a main thoroughfare of emigration; but, at the time of which we write, no road had been cut through the wilderness of Western New York to Lake Erie, and as late as 1796 the surveyors of the Connecticut Land Company reached that lake by the Wood Creek portage, Lake Ontario, and the Niagara portage.

---

[1] Statistics of the Population of the United States at the Tenth Census, June 30, 1880, xiii.

Nor had population then advanced on this line west of the interior New York lakes. Besides, the country above the head of Lake Erie was in the possession of England, and her garrison at Detroit would have turned back adventurous pioneers as promptly as Du Lhut turned back the Dutch traders at the close of the seventeenth century. Furthermore, the Lake Basin was thought less inviting than the Ohio Valley. On the second line, the situation was very different. In the French War two practicable roads were built over the mountains: The Braddock Road, cut through from the Upper Potomac in 1755, and the Forbes Road of 1758. These two roads connected the Ohio with tide-water, one at Philadelphia and the other at Alexandria. Accordingly, when the adventurer or the pioneer had once reached the Monongahela or the Alleghany, the whole West lay open before him, and he had but to descend the "beautiful Ohio" to his chosen destination. Then, in the years just preceding the Revolution, Finley, Harrod, and Boone had discovered the natural highway leading from the mountain-gaps near the southern line of Virginia to the fairest region of Kentucky. Moreover, the relations of the Ohio Valley to the country east and south were such that it necessarily received the full streams of population which the second and third of these channels soon began to discharge. In fact, settlers moving west by these two roads had reached the bank of the Ohio River at points as distant as the Forks and the mouth of the Kentucky before the Massachusetts men had thought of an Ohio colony at all.

The five per cent. of the total population of 1790 not found on the Atlantic Plain was distributed in little islands almost lost in the wilderness-ocean of the West. Four of these islands lay on the border of the new Territory. The first, containing 63,218 people, was in Southwestern Pennsylvania; the second and third, containing together 55,873, were in Western Virginia, clustered around Wheeling and the mouth of the Kanawha; the fourth was in Kentucky, below the Licking

River, and contained 73,677 souls. From the close of King George's War, when the colonies began to awaken to their Western interests, the Virginians had surpassed all their competitors in Western enterprise; but they were closely followed by the Marylanders and Pennsylvanians on the north and the Carolinians on the south. These causes together explain the sources of the four clusters of settlements found south of the Ohio River in 1790. Nearly all of the settlers, excluding those born on the soil, came from those parts of the country east of the mountains, south of New York and north of South Carolina. A man living in 1787, possessing all these facts, and also observing the great relative disadvantage of New England in the Western competition, growing out of her remoteness from the scene of operations and of the indisposition of her orderly population to fall into the channels of emigration, should have been able to indicate the principal sources of the population that, in the first period of its history, flowed into the country beyond the River Ohio. We shall soon find the facts of history justifying the prophecy that this remark implies.

In one sense the whole Northwest below the head of Lake Erie was open to the Ohio Company of Associates in 1787, but, practically, only the Ohio Valley. It made choice of lands on both sides of the Muskingum, but mainly below that stream. Three men appear to have controlled the location. In 1785 General Benjamin Tupper, one of the State surveyors under the land-ordinance of that year, came west as far as Pittsburg, where he was stopped by the Indian hostilities then raging. But he had caught a glimpse of the Western vision, and he returned to New England, his imagination filled with pictures of Western possibilities. The same year General Samuel Holden Parsons, a Revolutionary veteran, descended the Ohio to the Falls; he, also, returned on fire with Western enthusiasm. The reports made to their old comrades in the East by Tupper and Parsons furnished much of the motive power that kept the new-colony enterprise moving, as well as tended to fix its seat on the Ohio rather than on Lake Erie. Thomas Hutchins, the Geographer of the United States, who probably had a more definite knowledge of the West than any other man living at the time, determined its precise location. He advised Cutler, to whom he was introduced in New York, to choose the Muskingum, which he considered the most favorable location in the West for the purposes of the company, and his advice was decisive. The choice was the more fortunate for'the reason that Fort Harmar—a fort large enough to receive a garrison a regiment strong, built at the confluence of the two streams to protect passengers on the Ohio, to overawe the Indians, and to furnish armed escorts for the surveyors at work on the seven ranges—had been completed in the spring of 1786. The contract, signed by Samuel Osgood and Arthur Lee, of the Board of Treasury, for the United States, and by Manasseh Cutler and Winthrop Sargent for the company, bounded the purchase, east by the seventh range of townships, south by the Ohio, west by the eighteenth range, and north by an east and west line far enough back from the Ohio to include 1,500,000 acres of land. Five hundred thousand dollars was paid at the date of the contract. The company not being able to pay the second moiety, further legislation was had, which reduced the quantity of land actually patented, not including reservations, to 1,064,285 acres.[1]

How well matured were the plans of the Associates is shown by the fact that the advanced guard of the colony reached the Youghiogheny, January 23, and the second division, February 14, 1788. Here they built boats for descending the Ohio on the opening of navigation in the spring. From the deck of a row-galley, appropriately named the Mayflower, General Rufus Putnam, a hero of two wars and one of the prominent promoters of the colony, stepped to the bank of the Muskingum, April 7, 1788. Forty-seven other sons of

---

[1] Andrews: Washington County and the Early Settlement of Ohio, 16-18.

New England landed at the same time. Felling trees, building houses, laying out a city, and the erection of a stockade, called "Campus Martius," began at once. In the course of the year one hundred and thirty-two men, including fifteen families, arrived. This was a modest and unpretentious beginning, but, with the pressure of General Putnam's foot on this new soil, the present order of things in the old Northwest began.

Meantime, the steps necessary to the setting up of the new government were being taken. On October 5, 1787, Congress elected General Arthur St. Clair governor, and Winthrop Sargent secretary, of the new Territory; afterward Samuel Holden Parsons, James M. Varnum, and John Cleves Symmes were chosen judges. St. Clair was a veteran soldier of both the French and Revolutionary Wars, a trained civilian and an accomplished gentleman, a sterling patriot, a friend of Washington, and president of Congress at the passage of the Ordinance. A Scotchman by birth, he had come out an officer in one of the British regiments in the time of the French War; he was a lieutenant under Wolfe at Quebec; and made Western Pennsylvania his home soon after the coming of peace. We have already met him in that region in the troublous times that preceded the Revolution. Secretary Sargent was from Massachusetts, and a man of many abilities and accomplishments; soldier, civilian, a member of learned societies, and a poet. Parsons was from Connecticut, and Varnum from Rhode Island; both were distinguished soldiers and able lawyers. Judge Symmes was Chief Justice of New Jersey at the time of his appointment. Parsons and Varnum soon died, and their places were taken by George Turner and Rufus Putnam.

Independence Day was duly celebrated at the mouth of the Muskingum; and the expectant state of the colony, as well as the grandiose eloquence sometimes indulged in by the Revolutionary orators, is well illustrated by this extract from the oration delivered by Judge Varnum:

"We mutually lament that the absence of his Excellency will not permit us, upon this joyous occasion, to make those grateful assurances of sincere attachments, which bind us to him by the noblest motives that can animate an enlightened people. May he soon arrive. Thou gently flowing Ohio, whose surface, as conscious of thy unequaled majesty, reflecteth no images but the grandeur of the impending heaven, bear him, oh, bear him safely to this anxious spot! And thou, beautiful, transparent Muskingum, swell at the moment of his approach, and reflect no objects but of pleasure and delight." [1]

Governor St. Clair landed at the Muskingum bank, July 9th, and was received with appropriate civic and military honors; the 15th of the same month, attended by Secretary Sargent and Judges Parsons and Varnum, he made his public entry at the bower, in the city, where he was received by General Putnam, at the head of the citizens, "with the most sincere and universal congratulations." The Governor made a short address; Secretary Sargent read the Ordinance and the commissions of the officers. The Governor then made a longer address. The citizens applauded, the concourse broke up, the wheels of government began to revolve, and civil life began.

On July 26th the Governor created Washington County, the oldest county in the Northwest; and a little later appointed magistrates and established a Court of Quarter Sessions. The Judiciary was formally inaugurated, September 2d, with impressive ceremonies. A procession marched from Fort Harmar to one of the block-houses of Campus Martius, where the judges took their seats on the high bench; Dr. Manasseh Cutler, who was on a visit to the colony, offered a fitting prayer; the commissions of the judges and officers of the court were read; and then, with the sheriff's proclamation, "O, yes! a court is open for the administration of even-handed justice to the poor and the rich, to the guilty and

---

[1] St. Clair Papers, I., 139.

the innocent, without respect of persons; none to be punished without trial by their peers, and then in pursuance of the laws and evidence in the case"—the judicial history of the Territory began. Paul Fearing was admitted as an attorney, the first lawyer in the Northwest.

Such, briefly told, is the story of the founding of Marietta, named for the unfortunate Marie Antoinette, and the institution of civil government in the Northwest Territory. Not even the Pilgrim colony of 1620 was made up of better elements. At the distance of a century, no fitter eulogy upon the men who constituted it can be given than Washington's: "No colony in America was ever settled under such favorable auspices as that which has just commenced at the Muskingum. Information, property, and strength will be its characteristics. I know many of the settlers personally, and there were never men better calculated to promote the welfare of such a community."[1] The difference between French and American colonization in the Northwest is strikingly shown by two simple facts: On April 7, 1788, the village of Saut Ste Marie was one hundred and twenty years old; Marietta will not have reached a century until April 7, 1888.

Another land-purchase, second only to that of the Ohio Company, was made in 1787—the Miami purchase or Symmes Tract of one million acres, lying on the north bank of the Ohio between the two Miami Rivers.[2] Three colonies were planted in this tract in the year 1788: Columbia, at the mouth of the Little Miami; Losantiville, opposite the mouth of the Licking River; and North Bend, at the farthest northern sweep of the Ohio west of the Kanawha. For a time every one of these settlements aspired to the leadership; but the second, founded December 24, 1788, having been chosen as the seat of a military post, and also as the county seat of Hamilton County, rebaptized by St. Clair Cincinnati, a name borrowed

---

[1] Sparks: Writings of Washington, IX., 385.
[2] The tract was not paid for, and only about one-third was patented.

from the celebrated society of Revolutionary officers of which he was a prominent member, soon outstripped both its competitors. Here lived the Governor, and here sat the first Territorial Legislature. Still, its growth was slow; and when Judge Burnet first saw it, in 1796, it gave faint promise of becoming what it now is in name, and what it long was in fact, the Queen City of the West. The buildings were few and poor; the population, including the garrison, was about six hundred; and the social habits of the place anything but commendable.[1]

Those philosophers who trace all historical phenomena to physical causes may read a suggestive lesson in the history of the Miami purchase. The location of North Bend is as favorable as that of Cincinnati. It was the home of Judge Symmes, and the first station of the troops detailed by General Harmar to protect the Miami pioneers. Unfortunately, before a permanent fortification was constructed the commanding officer of the troops became enamored of the black-eyed wife of one of the settlers. The jealous husband's removal to Cincinnati led to the prompt discovery, on the part of the officer, of the superior military advantages of that location; whence resulted not the walls of lofty Rome, but the walls of Fort Washington and the ascendancy of the town named for the Cincinnati.

As in the case of the Muskingum colony, a very large number of the Miami settlers had seen service in the War of Independence. They were from no single locality, but Middle States men seem to have predominated—some of the most prominent from New Jersey. The Virginia Military District, embracing six thousand five hundred and seventy square miles of the fairest part of Ohio, became the seat of a third group of settlements, the founders of which came from Virginia. These were later, mainly owing to the Indian War, than the settlements of the Ohio and Miami purchases. Gen-

---

[1] Burnet: Notes on the Settlement of the Northwest Territory, 35 et seq.

eral Nathaniel Massie and Duncan McArthur, afterward Governor of Ohio, laid out the town of Chillicothe, soon made the capital of Ross County, on the west bank of the Scioto, in 1796. These Virginia colonies drew to themselves numbers of very able men, and they exercised a marked influence upon the nascent society of the Northwest, and particularly of Ohio.

The Virginia Military District is often mentioned in connection with the Connecticut Western Reserve. Beyond the fact that both were reservations, they have no points of likeness and many of unlikeness; Virginia's reservation was conditional and special, Connecticut's absolute and general.

Virginia voted her soldiers upon continental and State establishment liberal land-bounties. She also set apart for this purpose the lands bounded by Green River, Cumberland Mountains, the Tennessee line and Tennessee River, and the Ohio. In her act and deed of cession of the Northwest, Virginia stipulated that, in case these lands should prove insufficient for the purpose, the deficiency should be made up to the said troops in good lands, to be laid off between the Rivers Scioto and Little Miami. The Cumberland lands did prove insufficient for the purpose. Congress having been apprised of this fact, it passed a law in 1790 directing the Secretary of War to make return to the Governor of Virginia of the names of the Virginia officers and men entitled to bounty-lands, and the amount in acres due them. The same act authorized the agents of the said troops to locate and survey for their use, between the two rivers, apparently in the old Virginia fashion, such a number of acres of land as, together with the number already located on the waters of the Cumberland, would make the amount to which they were entitled; these locations and surveys to be recorded, together with the names of those for whom they were made, in the office of the Secretary of State. The President was then directed to issue letters patent for these lands to the persons entitled to them, for their use or the use of their heirs, assigns, or legal representatives. The Secretary

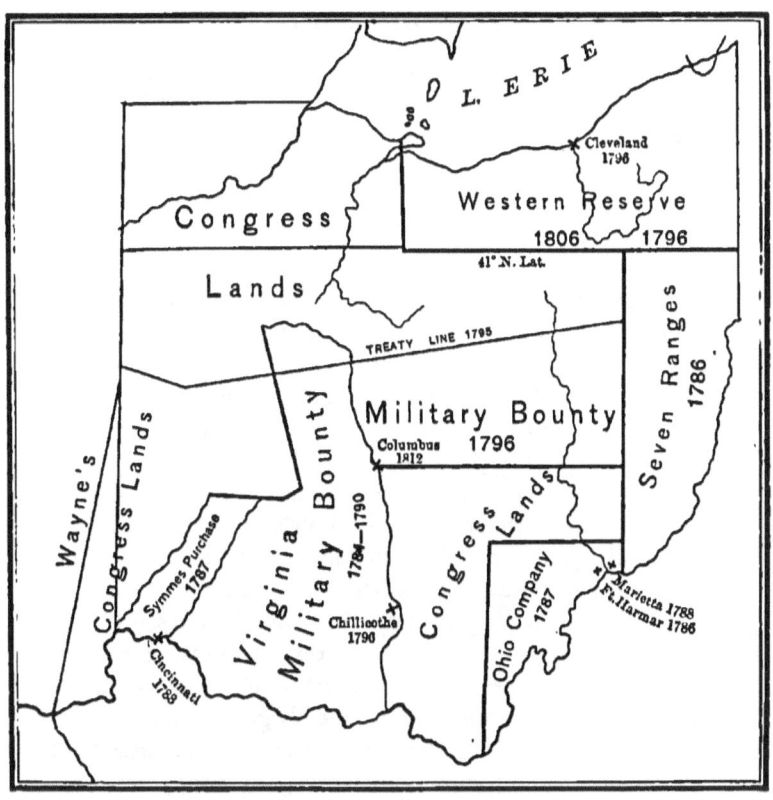

MAP ILLUSTRATING LAND SURVEYS IN OHIO,
WITH EARLY POSTS AND SETTLEMENTS.

*Adapted from Colonel Charles Whittlesey's Tract No. 61, Western Reserve
and Northern Ohio Historical Society.*

of State should forward these deeds to the Executive of Virginia, to be delivered to the proper persons. It will be seen that the national Government issued the deeds, but did not make the surveys. It is not surprising, therefore, that Dr. Andrews should speak of the " no system " surveys of the Virginia Military District, and that Colonel Whittlesey should characterize the private surveys as "so loose as to be entirely useless for geographical purposes." Early in the history of the locations and surveys a dispute arose as to the Western boundary of the Virginia District. The United States held that it should be the Little Miami and a line drawn from the source of that stream to the source of the Scioto; Virginia contended for a straight line drawn from the mouth of the one river to the source of the other. The first is called " Roberts's line ; " the second, " Ludlow's line." Roberts's line was virtually established by a decision of the Supreme Court in 1824. No question of jurisdiction concerning this District ever arose between Virginia and the United States. In 1852 Virginia released to the United States all lands in the District not already located, in consideration of Congress having provided other lands for such of the Virginia claims as were not yet satisfied. In 1871 Congress ceded such of these lands as remained unappropriated, amounting to 76,735 acres, appraised at $74,287, to the State of Ohio, and the State, in turn, ceded them to the State University.[1]

In fulfilment of its promises made in the course of the war, the national Government set apart a large tract for land-bounties lying south of Wayne's treaty line, west of the seven ranges, and east of the Scioto River. This tract, known as the United States Bounty Lands, embraces about four thousand square miles.

As a separate chapter will be devoted to the Western Reserve, it will not be noticed here, beyond the remark that it was the fourth centre of early colonization within the limits

---

[1] Donaldson: The Public Domain, 233, 234.

of Ohio. Passing by some small tracts dedicated to various objects, the remaining lands within the present limits of Ohio were known as "Congress lands," because surveyed and sold under its authority.

In Indiana and Illinois the French towns were the centres of the new settlements. Kentucky and Ohio were at first naturally preferred by emigrants, and the growth of the two States beyond them was for many years exceedingly slow. Governor Reynolds, who made his home in Illinois in 1800, found in that State a white population of two thousand persons, one thousand two hundred *habitants* and eight hundred Americans.[1] These people were scattered along the Mississippi River from Kaskaskia to Cahokia, with a few about Peoria. Moreover, the emigration to Indiana and Illinois, in the first period, was almost wholly from the South. They lay not only within the current of emigration that poured down the Ohio Valley, but also within the stream of the one which passed through the gaps of the Cumberland Mountains and swept northwestward across the States of Tennessee and Kentucky. Many of these emigrants were native Tennesseeans and Kentuckians. Mr. Washburne tells us that the Kentucky emigration was by far the best, and that the North Carolinians who came to Illinois were mostly "poor whites."[2]

In the winter and spring of 1790 Governor St. Clair made a lengthy visit to the *habitants* of the Wabash and the Mississippi. Writing to the Secretary of War from Cahokia, May 1st, he tells a moving tale of their condition. "They are the most ignorant people in the world;" "there is not a fiftieth man that can either read or write;" though ignorant, they are the gentlest and best disposed people that can be imagined; the distress at Vincennes and on the Mississippi is extreme."[3] In a long and very interesting report to the President, the

---

[1] My Own Times, 20.   [2] Sketch of Edward Coles, 69.
[3] St. Clair Papers, II., 136-140.

Governor describes their situation still more fully. With great cheerfulness the people had furnished Clark's command with everything they could spare, "and often with much more than they could spare with any convenience to themselves;" "most of the certificates for these supplies are still in their hands, unliquidated and unpaid;" following the conquest, "a set of men pretending the authority of Virginia embodied themselves, and a scene of general depredation and plunder ensued;" "to this succeeded three successive and extraordinary inundations from the Mississippi, which either swept away their crops or prevented their being planted;" all this was followed by the decline of the Indian trade, hostile Indian incursions, and the loss of the last corn crop by an untimely frost. That the terms of the Virginia Cession might be kept, and the public domain also be protected, Congress had directed surveys of the Kaskaskia and Vincennes lands to be made at the expense of the claimants, a charge the Governor found them ill able to meet.[1] Father Gibault, who had rendered the American cause such great services in the days of the invasion, laid before St. Clair a memorial in behalf of his people that arouses one's pity.

Since 1763, and even since the time of Clark's arrival in the Illinois, the settlements had materially declined. The character of the government in the Virginia period is plainly hinted by St. Clair; while in the six years following the cession, although the people kept calling upon Congress for relief, there was no government at all. It was found very difficult to adjust these decaying French communities—mere patches of the Middle Ages—to the aggressive life that ultimately overwhelmed them. For example they had, from the first settlement of the country, enclosed their small farms by common fences. There was great lack of surveys and records, and so of titles. The accumulated difficulties that grew out of such arrangements were in time referred to the Terri-

---

[1] St. Clair Papers, II., 164 et seq.

torial Legislature for settlement; and we can well believe Judge Burnet when he tells us it was no easy matter to devise a remedy for a case so complex. "A plan, however, was devised, and made obligatory on all concerned, by an act which regulated the enclosing and cultivating of common fields, and which gave general satisfaction."[1]

The picture of the Detroit *habitants* given by Burnet lacks the elements of picturesque beauty found in the chapters of Mr. Hubbard referring to a period forty years later. Burnet presents them as extremely ignorant and strongly superstitious; treading the footsteps of their fathers, imitative, not seeming to know that improvements had been made in agriculture since Noah planted his vineyard; raising the same crops without variation, exhausting fields by poor tillage and then abandoning them; throwing the barn and stable litter, so much needed by the hungry soil, into the river; and, withal, conscientiously exact in the performance of their religious duties, regularly paying their tithes to the priest with cheerfulness, and constant in attendance at church.[2] No doubt the man who would form a correct conception of this French civilization must take the two accounts together.

It is impossible to follow carefully the development of the majestic civil life that has its springing point in the Marietta settlement. Attention will, however, be drawn to some of the principal questions that arose in the Territorial period.

The question whether the Old Congress could successfully manage the Territory, keeping it in due relation to the Confederacy and erecting the new States when the time should come, was happily adjourned by the adoption of the National Constitution. A brief act passed at the first session of the first Congress sufficed to effect the necessary adjustments of the Ordinance to the new government. This act put the Territorial officers, as respects their appointment and commissions, upon the same footing as the officers provided for by the Con-

---

[1] Burnet: Notes, 307.　　　[2] Ibid., 281 et seq.

stitution—nomination by the President and confirmation by the Senate. Afterward Congress authorized the Governor and Judges to repeal laws that they had once adopted, a power that the Ordinance had not conferred.

One of the first duties with which Governor St. Clair was charged was the negotiation of a treaty of peace with the Indians. All the Western Indians repudiated the second Treaty of Fort Stanwix, 1784; and the majority of them the Treaty of Fort McIntosh, of the following year. In 1789 St. Clair concluded the Treaty of Fort Harmar with the Wyandots, Delawares, and several other tribes, whereby the tribes confirmed the Treaty of Fort McIntosh, and relinquished to the United States all lands, so far as they had a right to the same, east, south, and west of these lines: The Cuyahoga and Tuscarawas Rivers, and the portage between them from Lake Erie to the forks above Fort Laurens; a straight line west from the forks to Loramie's on the Big Miami; and a line from Loramie's to the Maumee, and then down the Maumee to the Lake. But the larger number of the Indians interested refused to be bound by this agreement. The Indians demanded that the whites should retire beyond the Ohio; and the long war that had devastated the frontier almost without cessation since 1755 continued to lengthen out the years. Harmar's, St. Clair's, and Wayne's invasions of the Indian country are told in every book of Indian warfare, and do not fall within the compass of the present work. The power of the Indians was broken for the time by Wayne's victory on the Maumee in 1794; and, by the Treaty of Fort Greenville, entered into in 1795, they relinquished all the lands east and south of this series of lines: The Cuyahoga and Tuscarawas Rivers from the Lake to the forks above Fort Laurens; a straight line drawn from this point to Loramie's; thence to Fort Recovery on the Wabash; and thence southwest to the Ohio opposite the mouth of the Kentucky River. This victory gave the Northwest peace until the days when, just before the War of 1812, the Indians made, under the leadership of

Tecumseh and the Prophet, another effort to stay the tide of invasion. The fondness of the Indians for this noble domain is shown by the long and determined stand that they made to retain it; as the desire of the whites to possess it is, by their suffering and sacrifices in the long conflict. It is said that, in the seven years closing with 1790, one thousand five hundred and twenty men, women, and children, in Kentucky alone, were massacred by the Indians or carried away into slavery.[1]

The Indian War materially retarded population, and also influenced its distribution. In 1795 Governor St. Clair, who had given careful attention to the subject, estimated the population under his jurisdiction at only fifteen thousand souls. The census-takers of 1800 reported finding, in the whole Northwest, 51,006 people. Kentucky, however, increased from 73,679 in 1790 to 220,955 in 1800. The geographical relations of the Territory to the East, to the Middle States, and to the South rendered a mixed population a foregone conclusion. The New Englanders took the initiative, making their way across the Hudson and the Delaware, and through Pennsylvania, to the Forks of the Ohio. For a time the Indian War almost stopped the flow of emigration from New England; and by the time that it began to move again the Western Reserve had been thrown upon the market in part, and thenceforth that region absorbed the larger number of the New Englanders who made their homes west of New York. But, even then, the Pennsylvania road by Pittsburg was preferred by many of the emigrants to the New York road by Buffalo. Had it not been for the renewed ferocity with which the war was waged after the Marietta settlement was made, New England would no doubt have contributed a much larger relative number to the first population of the Ohio Valley. It should be mentioned, to the great credit of the Ohio Company, that it contributed largely of its means

---

[1] Cooley : Michigan, 31.

to defend the infant settlements on the Ohio against the Indians.[1]

The Ordinance of 1787 made the Governor and Judges a temporary legislature, empowered not to enact laws but to "adopt and publish such laws of the original States" as they deemed necessary and fit, etc., reporting them to Congress from time to time; said laws to continue in force until the organization of the general assembly, "unless disapproved by Congress." This method of legislation was followed in constituting all the territories carved out of the old Northwest except Wisconsin, organized in 1836, and also in the act of 1790 for the Territory South of the Ohio. Immediately this legislature set to work to provide a code of laws for the Territory, giving its attention, first of all, as was natural, to a militia law; but the history of its work will not be followed, except to point out two or three interesting features.

First, the Governor and Judges did not confine themselves to adopting and publishing laws of the original States, but legislated *de novo*. This course they defended on the ground of necessity; they could not find laws suited to all the wants of the Territory in the State statute-books. As Congress did not formally disapprove these laws, with one or two exceptions they continued in operation until set aside by the Territorial authorities. There being no proper capital, the legislature promulgated laws at various places, as Marietta, Cincinnati, and Vincennes. In June, 1795, the legislature took up the problem of a "complete system of statutory jurisprudence, by adoption from the laws of the original States, in strict conformity to the provisions of the Ordinance." By adopting an old Virginia statute of the colonial period "the common law of England, and all general statutes in aid of the common law prior to the fourth year of James I.," were

---

[1] See Services of the Ohio Company in Defending the United States Frontier from Invasion, an article by W. P. Cutler, in the Ohio Archæological and Historical Quarterly, I., 293 et seq.

put in force in the Territory. "The other laws of 1795 were principally derived from the statute-book of Pennsylvania. The system thus adopted," continues Mr. Chase, whom we are here following, "was not without many imperfections and blemishes, but it may be doubted whether any colony at so early a period after its first establishment ever had one so good."[1] Another difficulty was a difference of opinion between the Governor and the Judges as to their respective legislative functions. Was the Governor simply one member of the legislature? or was he a constituent part of it, having equal authority with the Judges as a whole? The Governor vetoed drafts of laws submitted to him; the Judges called his attention to the words "or a majority of them" in the clause of the Ordinance relating to the adoption of laws, and he retorted, with no little force, that wherever the law-expounders are also the law-makers, the result is a tyranny. On this issue St. Clair had his way; on another one he was less successful.

The Ordinance gave the Governor power to appoint "such magistrates and other civil officers, in each county or township, as he should find necessary," thus giving him, by implication, the power to erect counties. The Governor, therefore, proceeded to constitute counties. While these counties were not as large as those that Virginia had bounded on the west by the South Sea, or even by the Mississippi River, they were still of truly imperial proportions. Washington County, for example, reached from the Ohio to Lake Erie, and from the Pennsylvania line to the Cuyahoga-Tuscarawas line and the Scioto. St. Clair County embraced all Southern Illinois. But Wayne County, organized in 1796, was the most extensive of all, including all the territory within the following limits: North by the international boundary line, east by the Cuyahoga, the portage-path, and the Tuscarawas; south by a line reaching from the forks above Fort Laurens west and northwest to the head of the Miami of the Ohio; thence north-

---

[1] Preliminary Sketch of the History of Ohio, in Statutes of Ohio, I., 26, 27.

west to the portage between the Miami of the Lake and the Wabash, where Fort Wayne now is, and thence northwest to the head of Lake Michigan; and west by a line running north to the international boundary, including all the lands in Wisconsin draining eastward to the same lake. The original counties had to be divided into smaller ones, and the General Assembly, after 1799, claimed the power to make the subdivision. The Governor denied the Assembly's claim, and vetoed its bills erecting new counties, the result being a controversy that was finally carried to Congress, and decided against him. Much of the bitterness of this controversy is said to have been due to land-speculators, anxious to influence the erection of counties and the location of county towns, who found Governor St. Clair standing in their way.

The mingling of elements from all parts of the Atlantic slope in the new population, and particularly the appointment of New England and Middle State men in about equal numbers to Territorial offices, decided the character of the local institutions now found in Ohio. Two radically different types of local government are found in the old States—the town system and the county system. As the names indicate, the first assigns the major part of political power to town or township officers, the second to county officers. These systems are traceable to England. The founders of New England came from towns and cities, and they naturally set up municipal institutions; the founders of Virginia came from the English counties, and as naturally set up county institutions. That the one would be more congenial to a civic democracy, the other to a landed gentry, goes without the saying. As is well known, Mr. Jefferson strove to introduce the New England system into Virginia, and made it the subject of frequent eulogy. "These wards, called townships in New England," he said, in 1816, "are the vital principle of their governments, and have proved themselves the wisest invention ever devised by the wit of man for the perfect exercise of self-government and for its preservation." Again, in

1810 he speaks of "the large lubberly division into counties," of the Middle, Southern, and Western States "which can never be assembled."¹ Local government in the Middle States is a compromise of the town and county systems; the county is more than in New England, and the town more than in the South. Governor St. Clair was from Pennsylvania, Judge Symmes from New Jersey, General Putnam from Massachusetts; and the three established in the Territory local institutions that are a sort of cross on the compromise and town systems.²

Very serious evils grew out of the first land-policy that was adopted. The effect of that policy was the sale of the lands in large tracts to first purchasers, to be resold to settlers in lots suitable to their convenience. About one-half the State of Ohio was made up of large blocks of land ranging from the 1,000,000 acres of the Symmes purchase to the 4,209,800 acres of the Virginia Military District. In its undivided form the Virginia District, as well as the United States Bounty Lands, belonged to a large number of persons; but, through the sale and purchase of rights, the lands in both of them tended to work into the hands of large holders. In 1800 Governor St. Clair called the attention of the legislature to this state of things. He said in his address that the lands had generally been held by a few individuals in large quantities, who had sold them out in small parcels on credit; that in some of the counties the majority of the people, unable in the midst of the general poverty to meet their engagements, were debtors to the proprietors; and that this state of things gave creditors a dangerous power over the votes of debtors. He therefore suggested whether the substitution of election by ballot for election *viva voce* would not be "the best way of guarding against that not improbable evil."³ No attention was paid to this suggestion until the year 1802,

---
[1] Jefferson: Works, VII., 13; V., 525.
[2] Andrews: Washington County, 32.
[3] St. Clair Papers, II., 501 et seq.

when it was adopted in the Ohio Constitution; but competition and the inability of the great land-owners to hold their tracts tended to diminish the danger that the Governor had pointed out.

But there were practical evils of a serious character connected with the land-system. At first Congress did not itself propose to sell lands save in large tracts, like the Ohio and Symmes purchases. The Land Ordinance of 1785 created a very complicated machinery for effecting sales. It authorized the Loan Commissioners of the several States to sell at public vendue lands in townships of 23,040 acres, and in sections of 640 acres, in equal quantities; it made no provision for land-offices in the Western country; and it fixed the minimum price at one dollar an acre and the cost of survey, in specie or its equivalent. Under the Constitution successive acts of legislation corrected the evils growing out of these features of the Ordinance of 1785 so effectually as to create other evils of the opposite character almost equally great. The survey and sale of half-sections, quarter-sections, and then of smaller lots were authorized. In 1800 the minimum price of lands was advanced to $2 an acre on a long credit, or $1.64 in cash. Land-offices were established and multiplied. No doubt the credit system facilitated settlements, but it led to great abuses and much suffering. In 1820, if we may trust Judge Burnet, more than half of the men Northwest of the Ohio River were in debt to the Government; and it was feared that an attempt to enforce payment, by a forfeiture of the land, under the laws of Congress, would produce resistance, and probably terminate in a civil war. A similar state of things existed in the Southwest. In response to a perfect snow-storm of memorials calling for relief, Congress, in 1821, by enacting that purchasers indebted to the Government might relinquish lands they could not pay for, receiving credit on lands not relinquished for moneys actually paid in, relieved the general distress. That act paid more than $20,000,000 of debts; while the sore experience that led to it caused Congress to reduce the price of lands to $1.25 an acre, with payment in advance.[1]

When Judge Burnet began to practise law in the Territory the General Court, which consisted of the three judges provided for by the Ordinance, who received each a salary of $800, sat in four places: Marietta, Cincinnati, Vincennes, and Kaskaskia. Soon after, Detroit was included within the circuit. This court had power to review and to revise the decisions of all inferior tribunals, but from its own decisions there was no appeal, not even to the Supreme Court of the United States. The Judges spent about as much time in the saddle as on the bench. Court and bar travelled through the wilderness, five or six together, sometimes seven or eight days on a single journey, with a pack-horse to transport the supplies that they could not carry on their own horses or purchase by the way. When purchasing a horse, one of the first questions was whether he was a good swimmer.[2] But that was the day when the mail was a week in going and coming between Marietta and Zanesville; when the Postmaster-General sometimes filled up mail schedules and contracts with his own hand; and when the principal means of transportation on the Ohio was the "Ark," invented by one Krudger on the Juniata River—a square, flat-bottomed vessel, forty feet in length by fifteen in breadth, six feet deep, covered with a roof of thin boards, accommodated with a fireplace, and carrying from two hundred to four hundred barrels of flour.[3]

For a number of years the Territory was not vexed by party politics; but in due time men began to divide along the line separating the two nascent political parties in the old States. In general, New England men tended to the Federal party and Southern men to the Republican party, while Middle State men were divided more equally. The facts of emigration already pointed out gave the party led by Mr.

---

[1] Burnet: Notes, 450–454; Sumner: Andrew Jackson, 184.
[2] Burnet: Notes, 63–65.   [3] Harris: The Journal of a Tour, etc., 30, 31.

Jefferson a considerable advantage, and the democratizing influences of the time, and particularly of the West, increased that advantage more and more. In searching for an explanation of the final triumph of the Republicans over the Federalists, Mr. Hildreth says the second "had their strength in those narrow districts where a concentrated population had produced and contributed to maintain that complexity of institutions and that reverence for social order which, in proportion as men are brought into contiguity, become more absolutely necessaries of existence." These conditions existed at the close of the last century in New England, New Jersey, Maryland, Delaware, and tide-water South Carolina; and here he finds represented "the experience, the prudence, the practical wisdom, the discipline, the conservative reason and instincts of the country." "The ultra-democratical ideas of the opposition"—that expressed the country's wishes, hopes, and especially theories, its passions, sympathies, antipathies, and its impatience of restraint—"prevailed in all that more extensive region in which the dispersion of population, and the despotic authority vested in individuals over families of slaves, kept society in a state of immaturity, and made legal restraints the more irksome in proportion as their necessity was the less felt." These conditions were best represented by Virginia, the head and front of the Republican party. North Carolina, Georgia, Tennessee, and Kentucky followed Virginia; and "the rapidly increasing backwoods settlements of all these States constantly added new strength to the opposition." The decision depended ultimately "on the two great and growing States of Pennsylvania and New York; and from the very fact that they were growing, that both of them had an extensive backwoods frontier . . . they both inclined more and more to the Republican side."[1] Perhaps these most suggestive remarks do not accurately state the case be-

---

[1] History, V., 415, 416.

tween the two parties at the close of Mr. Adams's administration; but there is no question that the rapid growth of the new settlements, whether in the old States or in the West, from 1790 on, was a material cause of the final complete annihilation of the Federal party. The democratizing influences were less strong in the region that soon became Ohio than in the slave-holding States south of the river; but they were strong enough to give the Virginia party a decided ascendancy for a full generation. The fact is—and a very important fact, too—that the political temper of Western society, even north of the Ohio, was far more like that of the South than that of New England.

As soon as the new political yeast began to work, men began to complain bitterly of the centralization of the government provided by the Ordinance, and of the Governor's administration. St. Clair's sense of justice, eminent public services, social qualities, and weight of character had made him a popular officer as long as there was no politics in the district; but henceforth his popularity continues to wane. He was a gentleman of the old school, and a Federalist; his manners were those of cultivated circles; he could not be, and did not wish to be, a Democrat; he stood stoutly for the dignity and prerogatives of his office; he did not trim his sails to the breeze that was now blowing stiffly from Virginia; he committed indiscretions of power, and incurred personal enmities, as a matter of course; besides, and in consequence of the foregoing, on the exciting questions now coming to the front, he took the unpopular side.

In 1798 it was ascertained that the Territory had the five thousand free male inhabitants that the Ordinance had made the condition of the second stage of government. That stage it accordingly entered upon, the following year. The General Assembly first met for the transaction of business at Cincinnati, September 24, 1799. The Lower House consisted of twenty-two members representing nine counties. Seven of the number came from the four counties containing the old French settlements in Michigan, Indiana, and Illinois, fifteen from the five Ohio counties. Hamilton County alone, eleven years old, had the same number of representatives as the four French counties, more than a century old. Four of the five members of the Council were from Ohio counties, and one from Vincennes. William Henry Harrison, who had succeeded Mr. Sargent in the secretaryship, was chosen delegate to Congress, where he rendered his constituents much good service, particularly in procuring needed legislation on the subject of lands. The new order of things was quite different from the old. The Governor was no longer part of the legislature, but he had an unquestioned veto that he freely exercised, particularly in legislation relating to counties. His power was materially strengthened by the change, and his troubles proportionally increased. Moreover, the appearance of a legislature and a delegate in Congress greatly stimulated political activity, and from this time on to the admission of Ohio to the Union, events became more and more exciting. Section 1 of the Ordinance reserved to Congress the right, which it would have had otherwise, since it was not a subject of compact, to divide the Northwest into two territories whenever circumstances might render it expedient. At the session of 1799–1800 the House of Representatives referred the subject to a committee, of which Delegate Harrison was chairman. In a letter to Harrison, dated February 17, 1800, St. Clair recommended the formation of three territories, the dividing lines to be the Scioto River, and a meridian line drawn through the mouth of the Kentucky River, with Marietta, Cincinnati, and Vincennes as capitals. This scheme, which was to continue only until the new States were formed, he supported with many plausible arguments. The vision of a new State in the eastern part of the Territory was now rising full-orbed upon the sight of national statesmen and Territorial politicians, and, as in many another similar case, both statesmen and politicians were anxious that the State should come into the Union with the right kind of politics. It was objected to St. Clair's scheme that it would postpone the formation of the State, which was true enough, and that his purpose was to carve out a territory of which he could be governor for life, which was absurd. His scheme failed to command the support of Mr. Harrison, who was a State man, and of Congress, but it did not fail to add to St. Clair's growing unpopularity. On May 7, 1800, an act was approved constituting all that part of the Northwest lying west of the treaty-line of 1795, from the Ohio to Fort Recovery, and a line drawn from the fort to the international boundary, a separate territory, to be called Indiana Territory. The act made Chillicothe and Vincennes the two capitals, until otherwise ordained by the respective legislatures; and said, whenever the territory east of the meridian of the mouth of the Great Miami River should become an independent State, thenceforth said meridian should be the boundary between the new territory and such State.

The Virginia colony of Ross County were very influential in bringing about this legislation. In fact, the original scheme of the Chillicothe managers was much more extensive, embracing these features: (1) The appointment of William Henry Harrison as Governor of the Indiana Territory; (2) the establishment of the permanent seat of government for the Eastern district at Chillicothe ; and (3) such alterations in the form of the Territorial Government as should vacate the offices.[1] Of course, the programme included the retirement of St. Clair. Harrison did become the governor of the new territory, and Chillicothe the temporary capital of the Eastern district; but, owing to the opposition of the Senate, the act of May 7th contained an express prohibition of change in the government of the old Territory other than its limitation in extent. Henceforth, until its final disappearance from the map, on February 19, 1803, the name Northwest Territory is limited to the eastern of the two territories. The striking

---

[1] St. Clair Papers, I., 236.

features of its history are the agitation of the State question and the growing embarrassments of Governor St. Clair. The census of 1800 reported a population of 45,916 in the Territory, thus distributed by counties: Adams, 3,432; Hamilton, 14,692; Jefferson, 8,766; Ross, 8,540; Trumbull, 1,302; Wayne, 3,757.

Toward the close of his long administration there was a total want of agreement between the Governor and a majority of the people of the Territory in political ideas and temper. He was a pronounced Federalist; they were pronounced Republicans. So extreme was he in his opinions that he wrote and published a pamphlet in defence of the Alien and Sedition Laws, which President Adams said was "masterly," written "in the style and manner of a gentleman, and seasoned with no more than was useful and agreeable of Attic salt."[1] If seasoned to Adams's taste, it must have been pungent indeed. At this time the Federalists were taking those extreme measures which conclusively showed that they did not understand the popular temper, and the Republicans were seeking to rescue the country from evils and dangers which they described in the most exaggerated language. To this extent, the strife in the Valley of the Ohio was simply a part of the bitter political controversy then going on in all the old States. Then some of the Governor's personal qualities were a source of criticism. Judge Burnet, who was an admirer of St. Clair, and a member of the same political party, says he placed too high an estimate on his own powers of mind, and, although modest and unassuming in society, very rarely yielded an opinion that he had once deliberately formed.[2] St. Clair was a Scotchman and a Federalist, holding a position of great power and responsibility in a young American democracy west of the Ohio River. Naturally, he became less yielding as he grew older, and assaults upon him became more frequent and bitter. But St. Clair's Federalism and obnoxious

---

[1] St. Clair Papers, I., 234. [2] Burnet: Notes, 378–381.

personal qualities alone would not have caused the opposition that he encountered. The question of a new State in the Eastern district of the Northwest was now coloring—and deeply coloring—all Territorial questions. Generally speaking, Federalists and Republicans divided on this subject. A resolution unanimously adopted by a delegate convention of the County of Washington, held at Marietta in June, 1801, expressed the common view of the one party, viz. : " That in our opinion, it would be highly impolitic, and very injurious to the inhabitants of this Territory, to enter into a state government at this time."[1] The Republican view, as expressed by a writer in the *Scioto Gazette*, was that such a change would be like opening the floodgates to a mill ; wealth would flow in, improvements would spring up, the streams would " roll along " food to thousands suffering from want, and arrangements for education would be perfected ; plains covered with herds and farms with crops would gladden the owners' hearts, and the government, like the tree of liberty, would extend its benign branches over the citizens, sheltering them from tyranny and oppression.[2] One side objected that a State government would be costly, that the people could not pay the taxes, and that it was far better to allow the United States to pay the expenses of government than to impose them upon the citizens ; and the other side replied that the salaries now paid by Congress to the Governor and Judges amounted to only $5,500, that a State government would not cost more than $15,400 per annum, while the people were able to pay taxes amounting to $27,926.90 for the year 1801. Those were days of small things, in more senses than one. But beneath all these petty arguments was the great question of national politics. The elder Meigs said the Federalists opposed a new State because it meant three more Republican presidential electors and two more Republican Senators ; if he had added that the Republicans favored it for the same reason, as well

---

[1] Andrews : Washington County, 27.   [2] St. Clair Papers, I., 225, 226.

as because there would be a number of State offices to be distributed among the active politicians, he would then have told an equal amount of truth about both sides. St. Clair was the head and front of the Federal party. What Mr. Smith[1] calls the "junto" had plenty of reasons for desiring to break down the Governor's influence or to drive him from the Territory. Men of to-day who have been taught by historians that Arthur St. Clair was a thorough patriot, and by jurists that the Ordinance of 1787 was a paragon of political wisdom, would find it hard to explain the language in which the extreme Republicans of the Territory habitually spoke of both, were they not also instructed in the capabilities for detraction of heated political partisans. Thomas Worthington, afterward Governor of Ohio, called St. Clair "Arthur the First," and spoke of the efforts to thwart him as efforts "to curb a tyrant." General Darlington, speaking of the formation of the new State, said the people of Adams County "congratulated themselves on the prospect of having it soon in their power to shake off the iron fetters of aristocracy and in the downfall of the Tory party in this Territory."[2] These "aristocrats" and "Tories" were Arthur St. Clair and the leading citizens of Marietta. The writer in the *Scioto Gazette*, already quoted, speaks of "the utter impossibility of a government conducive to national happiness in this enlightened day being administered under" the Ordinance, "unless by a person more than mortal," adding: "This government, now so oppressive, was prescribed by the United States at a time when civil liberty was not so well understood as at present, and when it could not be contemplated but for the government of a few." Judge Symmes, one of the Governor's most determined foes, declared, "We shall never have fair play while Arthur and his Knights of the Round Table sit at the head."[3] In some respects the best places to study the clash between the old political *régime*

---

[1] The editor of the St. Clair Papers.
[2] Andrews: Washington County, 28. [3] St. Clair Papers, I., 242.

and the democratizing movement headed by Jefferson are the new communities of the West.

Postponing the State question to the next chapter, we shall now rapidly follow St. Clair's fortunes to the end.

A determined but ineffectual effort was made to induce President Adams not to reappoint him on the expiration of his fourth term. No sooner was President Jefferson established in the chair than a still more determined effort was made to effect his removal. An indictment almost as formidable as the one preferred against George III. by the Continental Congress was drawn up and forwarded to Washington. The principal charges contained in this paper, as formulated by General Massie and revised by General Worthington, are usurpations of legislative power, the abuse of the veto, receiving unlawful fees, attempting to dismember the Territory, to destroy its constitutional boundaries and so to prevent the formation of a State, endeavoring to influence the judiciary, obstructing the organization and disciplining of the militia for the defence of the Territory, and hostility to the form and substance of republican government.[1] Fragments of St. Clair's private conversation, taken down and duly authenticated by affidavits, were also sent to Washington. But Mr. Jefferson refused to move until St. Clair, by a characteristic act of indiscretion, himself gave a reasonable pretext for so doing. On November 1st the convention elected to frame a constitution for the State of Ohio sat, and on the 3d, in reluctant response to his own request, the Governor was permitted to address that body. Burnet says the address was "sensible and conciliatory;" but no man reading it now, understanding the temper of the times and of the convention, would be apt to think it conciliatory. This is the bolt that answered the Governor's unfortunate speech:

---

[1] St. Clair Papers, II., 566, 567.

"DEPARTMENT OF STATE,
"WASHINGTON, November 12, 1802.
"ARTHUR ST. CLAIR, ESQ.

"SIR: The President observing, in an address lately delivered by you to the convention held at Chillicothe, an intemperance and indecorum of language toward the Legislature of the United States, and a disorganizing spirit and tendency of very evil example, and grossly violating the rules of conduct enjoined by your public station, determines that your commission of Governor of the Northwestern Territory shall cease on the receipt of this notification.

"I am, etc.,
"JAMES MADISON."[1]

And then, as though removal were not punishment enough, the Secretary of State sent this letter enclosed in one to Secretary Byrd, one of St. Clair's strongest enemies, directing that officer to assume the duties of the governor's office. Thomas Jefferson would have shown himself a larger man if he had overlooked the indiscretion of the Chillicothe speech and permitted the venerable Governor to remain at the head of the Territory the few weeks yet to elapse before it ceased to exist.

St. Clair now retired to the home that he had made near Ligonier, Pennsylvania, in the interval between the French War and the Revolution. He had spent more than a quarter of a century in the continuous service of the country. He was sixty-eight years old. His private affairs had been sadly neglected in his devotion to public business. He had incurred liabilities for the Government that the Government now refused to pay. What of his once considerable fortune remained was swept away by his creditors. The handsome "Hermitage" that he had built and furnished in the days of his prosperity went with the rest, and he spent the remainder of his days in dignified poverty with his beloved daughter Louisa in a log-house standing beside the road leading to the

---

[1] St. Clair Papers, I., 244–246.

great Territory with which his name will ever be identified. The tardy pension voted him by Congress passed directly from the treasury to one of his creditors. Pathetic in the extreme are the glimpses that we have of his last years. Hon. Lewis Cass, who had known him in happier days, found the old soldier and civilian in his rude cabin eking out a livelihood by selling supplies to the wagoners on the road, and he described the scene as "one of the most striking instances of the mutations which chequer life." Hon. Elisha Whittlesey, who visited him in 1815, was profoundly impressed by the dignity and benignity of his character. "I never was in the presence of a man that caused me to feel the same degree of esteem and veneration. . . . Poverty did not cause him to lose his self-respect, and were he now living, his personal appearance would attract universal attention."[1]

St. Clair died, August 31, 1818, in consequence of being thrown from a wagon while going to a neighboring village. To him who is acquainted with St. Clair's history, the name always suggests a striking example of the ingratitude of men and of republics.

The independent existence of Indiana Territory began July 4, 1800. At first it included all that part of the old Territory lying west of the treaty-line of 1795 from the Ohio River to Fort Recovery, and of the meridian of the fort to the national limits. The act creating the Territory plainly contemplated the creation of only three States in the Northwest, for it provided that, whenever the part of it east of the meridian passing through the mouth of the Great Miami, from the Ohio to the territorial line, should be admitted to the Union as an independent State, "thenceforth said line shall become and remain permanently the boundary-line between such State and the Indiana Territory." But the Enabling Act for Ohio, 1802, bounded that State on the north by a due east and west line,

---

[1] St. Clair Papers, I., 253.

from the Miami meridian to the international boundary, drawn through the southerly extreme of Lake Michigan, and added all territory north of such line, as well as between the meridian and the line of 1800, to Indiana. Again, in 1804 Louisiana, extending from parallel thirty-three degrees north to the British dominions, and from the Mississippi River to the Rocky Mountains, was annexed to Indiana, but the next year was created an independent territory. The act of 1800 continued the form of government created by the Ordinance of 1787, and guaranteed to the people all the rights and privileges that the Ordinance secured to them. Vincennes was the capital, and William Henry Harrison the first governor, of the territory. The population was five thousand six hundred and forty-one. It entered on the second stage of government in 1805.

Michigan Territory was created January 11, 1805. It was bounded on the south by the parallel passing through the southerly extreme of Lake Michigan; west by a line extending from the same extreme through the middle of the said lake to its northern extremity, and thence north to the national limits; and north and east by the international boundary. The act creating the Territory continued all the governmental features of the Ordinance. Detroit was the seat of government, and General William Hull, the same who seven years later surrendered Michigan to the British arms, was appointed governor. The population reported in 1800 was two thousand seven hundred and fifty-seven. The Territory entered on the second stage partially in 1823, and fully in 1827.

The next step in this process of territorial evolution was the creation of the Territory of Illinois. The act of February 3, 1809, separated it from Indiana Territory by the Wabash River from its mouth to Vincennes, and a due north line from that point to the territorial line between the United States and Canada. The form of government was that prescribed in the Ordinance, save in one feature; a General Assembly might be organized whenever satisfactory evidence should be given to the governor that such was the wish of a majority of the free-holders, "notwithstanding there may not be therein five thousand free male inhabitants of the age of twenty-one years and upwards." Ninian Edwards, at the time of his appointment Chief Justice of Kentucky, was the first governor; Kaskaskia was the capital; the population, in 1810, was twelve thousand two hundred and eighty-two. The Territory entered on the second stage in 1812. We must now return to Michigan.

The Enabling Act for Indiana, April 19, 1816, bounded that State on the north by an east and west line ten miles north of the southerly extreme of Lake Michigan. The Enabling Act for Illinois, April 18, 1818, made the northern boundary of that State parallel of latitude 42° 30′ north. The act also attached all that part of the Territory of Illinois lying north of this line to Michigan. An act, approved June 28, 1834, attached to Michigan all the country extending west of the Mississippi to the Missouri and White Earth Rivers, and from the State of Missouri to the national boundary. Thus at its greatest extent the Territory reached from Lake Huron and the Detroit River to the Missouri, and from the States of Ohio, Indiana, Illinois, and Missouri to Canada.

The Territory of Wisconsin, created April 20, 1836, contained what was left of the Territory of Michigan after the State of that name was constituted. It embraced the region extending from a line drawn through the middle of Lake Michigan to the Missouri and White Earth Rivers, and from Illinois and Missouri to the British possessions. A much greater innovation than that in the case of Illinois was now made in the form of government. The peculiar features of the Ordinance of 1787 were all abandoned, and a new and very elaborate model established, the first of its kind: A governor, a secretary, judges, etc., appointed by the President by and with the consent of the Senate; a legislature, consisting of a council and house of representatives elected by the qualified electors of the Territory; and a delegate to the national House of Representatives, elected in the same way. At the same time, Section 12 enacted that the inhabitants of the Territory should be entitled to all the rights secured to the people of the Territory of the United States Northwest of the River Ohio by the articles of compact contained in the Ordinance of 1787, and should be subject to all the conditions and restrictions in said articles imposed upon the people of the said Territory. The act approved June 12, 1838, constituting the Territory of Iowa, limited Wisconsin on the west by the Mississippi River and a line drawn from its sources to the territorial line, but guaranteed to the new Territory all the rights, privileges, and immunities that the old one had enjoyed.

Such, in outline, is the history of the first territory, and the most important territory, that the Government of the United States ever organized.

NOTE.—Perhaps as wide a deduction from Article V. of compact of the Ordinance of 1787 as could have been dreamed of at the time is one made in the discussion of the Dakota question. It has been seriously contended that the compact, reaffirmed by five successive acts of Congress, guaranteed absolutely and inviolably " to Dakota the right to found a permanent constitution and State government whenever said Territory should contain sixty thousand free inhabitants." The guarantee quoted above from the Wisconsin Act of 1836 is one of the five "successive acts." This claim is pressed to the extent of holding that the people have this right " in their primary and sovereign capacity," without any enabling act whatever. See " The State : How it may be Formed from the Territory," Hugh J. Campbell, United States Attorney of Dakota Territory.

XVII.

THE ADMISSION OF THE NORTHWESTERN STATES TO THE UNION.

THE "pioneer thought" that Maryland laid before Congress in 1777 was the proposition that the Western territory should ultimately be divided into new States, to be admitted to the Union on an equal footing with the original States, under the superintendence and jurisdiction of Congress. Such was the promise of the resolution of 1780, such one of the conditions of the Virginia deed of cession of 1784, and, so far as the Northwest was concerned, such the guarantee of the Ordinance of 1787. Kentucky and Tennessee had already been admitted, in pursuance of that general line of policy. The population of the Eastern division of the Northwest Territory had not reached the minimum established in 1787 by many thousands when, in 1802, the chiefs of the Democratic-Republican party at Washington, as well as in the Territory, decided that the time had come to bring in the State of Ohio.

I. OHIO.

This decision was hastened by a bill passed by the Territorial Legislature at the session beginning November 23, 1801, declaring the assent of the Territory to the following modification of the Ordinance respecting the boundaries of the States when they should be formed: The eastern State to be bounded on the west by the Scioto River and a line drawn from the intersection of the river with the Indian boundary as fixed in 1795 to the western limit of the Western Reserve; the middle State to be bounded on the west by a line drawn from the lower extremity of George Rogers Clark's grant at the Falls of the Ohio to the head of Chicago River, and that river and Lake Michigan; the third to be bounded west by the Mississippi.[1] This was a Federal plan, and it incurred very serious resistance in the Lower House. Taking alarm at this move, General Worthington hastened to Washington, where he succeeded in giving matters a very different shaping.

Soon after the legislature adjourned, in January, 1802, a census was taken which found 45,028 persons of both sexes and all ages in the Territory. The next step was for the friends of the measure to petition Congress for admission. The special committee to which this petition was referred reported favorably thereon. The Houses promptly passed the appropriate bill, which received the President's approval and became a law, April 30th. These are the main features of this act : (1) The inhabitants of the Eastern division of the Territory were authorized to form a constitution and State government, assuming such name as they deemed proper, said State to be admitted to the Union on the same footing as the original States in all respects. (2) The boundaries of the State should be: East, the Pennsylvania line; south, the Ohio River; west, the meridian of the mouth of the Great Miami; north, a due east and west line drawn through the southern extreme of Lake Michigan, and the international boundary-line. Congress, however, reserved the right to annex to this State that portion of Michigan included within the territorial lines of 1800—that is, about one-half the lower peninsula—or to dispose of it otherwise. (3) All territory included within the limits of 1800, that these lines did not embrace, was annexed to Indiana Territory. (4) All male citizens residing in the Territory, having certain prescribed qualifications, were authorized to choose representatives to form a convention in designated numbers, county by county, on the second

---

[1] Chase : Preliminary Sketch, 30.

Tuesday of October ensuing. (5) The representatives thus chosen were authorized to meet in convention at Chillicothe the first Monday of November, 1802; which convention should determine, by a majority of its whole number, whether it were now expedient to form a constitution and government, and, if so, to form them, but if not, then to provide by ordinance for calling a second convention for that purpose; said constitution, in either case, to be republican and not repugnant to the Ordinance. (6) Until the next census the new State should be entitled to one member in the House of Representatives. (7) Three propositions were submitted to the convention which, if accepted, should bind the United States: The grant to the State of section No. 16 in every township for the use of schools, the grant of certain salt-springs, and the grant of one-twentieth part of the net proceeds of all lands sold by Congress within the State, to be applied to building roads connecting the Eastern and the Western waters; provided, the State would exempt from taxation all such lands for the term of five years from the date of sale.

This was the first "enabling act," so called, ever enacted by Congress. It was, however, the model of many succeeding acts of a similar nature. It is, therefore, a curious question, and one that cannot be very satisfactorily answered, how far its leading features were due to a statesmanlike study of the subject, and how far to political exigencies. The act did not contain a gleam of what was afterward called "popular sovereignty." The Territorial Legislature was wholly ignored. Neither the legislature nor the people themselves were asked to pass upon the question of entering into a State government. The sole function of the electors was to vote for members of the convention, in the manner prescribed by Congress. The opposition did not fail to put these points very strongly, as the bill was on its way through the House of Representatives. Mr. Griswold, of Connecticut, declared that the bill "went to a consolidation and destruction of all the States;" that the districting of the Territory and the apportionment of the members was arbitrary and unjust; that the whole scheme was beyond the power of Congress and an invasion of popular rights; and that the next thing would be a similar dictation to the States already in the Union. In the Territory, the opponents of the measure said these features of the bill were due to the fear of the party managers that the legislature and the people could not be trusted. There is probably some truth in this charge; but the framers of the Ordinance had created a centralized government, and the feeling was still strong, notwithstanding the complaint that Western Democrats made of their "colonial government," that there was a very wide difference between a territory and a State, even when the time came to frame a constitution. "Popular sovereignty" was due to that progress of democratic ideas which the peopling of the West did so much to facilitate.

Other objections were strongly urged. Mr. Fearing, the Territorial delegate, said Congress had exhausted its power when it consented to the admission of the State before its population reached sixty thousand. He argued, also, that Congress could not divide the district, admitting part at one time and part at another; that the division proposed would throw Lake Erie out of the State; and that the great distance of the Michigan people from Vincennes would make their annexation to Indiana exceedingly inconvenient. Mr. Bayard, of Delaware, urged that the population of the State, as bounded, would not exceed thirty-nine thousand; that this was a smaller number than any State in the Union then had; and that Wayne County should come in with the rest of the district, subject to the reserved right of Congress to alter the boundary afterward. Mr. Griswold said that not less than $40,000 would be devoted to roads, a "sum too large to be withdrawn from the national treasury and devoted to local objects;" but Mr. Fearing thought one-half the proceeds of the lands should be given to build roads within the Territory, and a proposition to that effect actually commanded twenty-five votes. It was also objected that Mr. Gallatin, the Secretary of the Treasury, owned lands that would be benefited by these improvements. The friends of the bill replied to these arguments as best they could. Mr. Giles, of Virginia, made the very just observation that a glance at the map sufficed to show that the boundary of 1800, running from the Ohio to the Straits of Mackinaw, was necessarily temporary, and that the State as bounded by the bill was one of the most compact and convenient in the Union. An analysis of the vote in the House of Representatives shows the sources of the anxiety to bring the State into the Union at an early day. The 47 affirmative votes came: Twenty-six from the South, 14 from the Middle States, and 9 from New England; the 29 negative votes came: Nine from the South, 5 from the Middle States, and 15 from New England. Virginia gave 15 votes for and one against the bill; Massachusetts, 5 for and 5 against; Connecticut, none for and 5 against. This vote is one of many proofs that, at the opening of the century, the Middle and Southern States were far more at touch with the West than New England. The vote of Dr. Manasseh Cutler, then a member of the House from Massachusetts, is registered in the negative.

The battle fought in the House of Representatives was fought over again with the same weapons in the Territory. The exclusion of Wayne County caused the deepest dissatisfaction to all Federalists, and particularly to the people of the county, most of whom were Federalists. A letter written to Judge Burnet by Mr. Solomon Sibley, of Detroit, August 2, 1802, puts the case very strongly. Annexation to Indiana will be the "eternal ruin" of the county; but the ruin of five thousand people is of little consequence to the half-dozen political aspirants who have brought things to the present pass. The exclusion of the county was due to Judges Symmes and Meigs, and "Sir Thomas," as he calls General Worthington, who foresaw that its people would be "a dead weight against them."[1] Politics may have been the cause of the peculiar grievance of the people of Detroit, which was, no doubt, a considerable one for a time; but in the end it was most fortunate that the five-State plan was adopted rather than the three-State plan. Still more, the grief of the Wayne County people was of short duration. The political character of the population points to the conclusion that those interested in such questions were few in number; and Burnet tells us that the project of a new territory north of the Ordinance line, having Detroit as a capital, with the accompanying offices, promised to the leaders of opinion, if they came out promptly and decidedly in favor of the new State on the plan proposed by Congress, effectually won these few over to the popular side.[2]

The flanks of those who opposed a new State, or favored bounding it on the west by the Scioto, had been completely turned. At first they talked about a further effort to postpone the issue. A public meeting of citizens of Dayton and vicinity, held September 26th, unanimously passed a resolution denouncing the enabling act as a usurpation of power, bearing a "striking resemblance" to the course of Great Britain in regard to the colonies; expressing deep sympathy with their fellow-citizens of Wayne County, and calling upon the Territorial Legislature to assert itself by causing a new census to be taken and by calling a convention to frame a constitution. But these plans came to nothing. The members of the convention were duly elected, and on November 1, 1802, they came together in Chillicothe, and organized for business. In his unfortunate address to the convention, Governor St. Clair stated, in very strong terms, the ordinary Federalist objections to the Enabling act. He affirmed that no act of Congress was necessary to enable the Territory to form a State government, as the right was secured to them by the Ordinance; declared that the people of Wayne County had been

---

[1] Burnet: Notes, 494 et seq.   [2] Notes, 337, 338.

"bartered away like sheep in a market;" and urged the formation of a convention for the whole Territory and a demand for admission to the Union. "If we submit to the degradation [imposed by the Enabling act] we should be trodden upon, and, what is worse, we should deserve to be trodden upon."[1]

The convention had first to decide whether it would itself form a constitution or call a second convention to do that work. This could hardly have been a doubtful question, no matter what the political antecedents of the members. The opposition totally collapsed, Judge Ephraim Cutler, of Marietta, being the only man who voted to refer the matter to a second convention. The convention proceeded with such expedition that it adjourned, November 29th, having completed its task.

Attention can here be drawn to only one feature of the constitution that the convention framed; others will be mentioned in future connections.

And first, the Chillicothe convention planted the seed of controversies that affected the boundaries of three States. The fifth compact of 1787 ordained that there should be not less than three States, nor more than five, in the territory beyond the Ohio; if three, the lines of division should be the meridian of the mouth of the Great Miami, and the Wabash and the meridian of Vincennes, from the Ohio River to the international line; if four or five, then the lower States should be separated from the upper one or ones by the parallel passing through the southern bend or extreme of Lake Michigan. North of this parallel the whole subject was left to the discretion of Congress. No legislation could be more binding than this east and west line; it was forever unalterable, except by common consent, and yet it was eventually set aside throughout its entire length from Lake Erie to the Mississippi River. The act of 1800 dividing the Territory seems to have assumed that the three-State plan would be followed; but the Enabling

---

[1] St. Clair Papers, II., 592 et seq.

Act for Ohio, of two years later, proceeded on the other theory. That act bounded the new State in the northwest by the line of 1787, thus reaffirming the Ordinance. But the convention, and this is the seed planted at Chillicothe, inserted a proviso in the Constitution of Ohio that, in case the line should be found not to intersect Lake Erie, or to intersect it east of the mouth of the Maumee River, then, with the consent of Congress, the boundary should be a straight line running from the southerly extreme of the Lake to the most northerly cape of Maumee Bay, from its intersection with the Miami meridian to the international boundary-line. Judge Burnet says the understanding had always been that the Ordinance line would cross the strait connecting the two lakes between Detroit and the River Raisin; but that, while the convention of 1802 was in progress, an old hunter, familiar with the region, appeared in Chillicothe, and imparted to some of the members the information that the head of Lake Michigan was much farther south than had been supposed.[1] Whether this hunter's story was true or not, and whether it was the cause of the boundary-proviso, as Burnet states, it well illustrates the state of geographical knowledge touching the Northwest at that time, and the sources of information upon which men conducting grave public business were sometimes compelled to draw. The act of 1803 recognizing Ohio said not a word about this proviso; but the act of 1805 creating the Territory of Michigan reaffirmed the Ordinance line.

Ohio was never, in set terms, admitted to the Union; but an act entitled "An Act to provide for the execution of the laws of the United States within the State of Ohio" was equivalent to the customary act of admission, and the date of its approval, February 19, 1803, is the proper date of admission.[2]

---

[1] Burnet: Notes, 360, 361.

[2] The date of the admission of Ohio is the subject of much controversy, and has given rise to a considerable literature. As many as seven dates have been assigned, but of these only three are worthy of mention: April 30, 1802, the date of the enabling act; November 29, 1802, the date of the adjournment of the

ADMISSION OF THE NORTHWESTERN STATES. 325

The act of 1802 assigned the thirty-five members of the convention to the counties as follows: Trumbull two, Jefferson five, Belmont two, Washington four, Ross five, Fairfield two, Adams three, Hamilton ten, and Clermont two. The counties bearing these names in 1802 were much larger than the counties bearing the same names to-day; but as the names have remained with the original settlements, a glance at the map of 1887 will show where the people lived for whom the constitution was immediately made. Save only the two from Trumbull County, the thirty-five delegates all came from the Southern part of the State, and the large majority from a narrow strip of territory fringing the Ohio River. Excluding the small beginnings made on the Western Reserve, the Ohio of 1802 lay within the sweep of the Pennsylvania-Virginia current of emigration to the West. Of the twelve members of the convention whose previous history I have been able to trace, six came from Virginia, two from Massachusetts, and one each from Pennsylvania, North Carolina, Maryland, and Connecticut. Still further, thirty-three of the forty-seven men who represented the State in Congress from 1803 to 1829 came: Nine from Pennsylvania, six each from Virginia, Connecticut, and New Jersey, three from New York, and one each from New Hampshire, Massachusetts, and Kentucky. The others are unknown. Judge Jacob Burnet, who rendered Ohio and the Northwest most valuable services as a member of the Territorial Council, as Judge of the Supreme Court, and as Senator, as well as author of the "Notes," was from New Jersey. These facts, in connection with those of a similar nature found in the last chapter, plainly indicate the origin of the forces that shaped the early destinies of Ohio.

Chillicothe convention; February 19, 1803, the date of the act of recognition mentioned above. Dr. I. W. Andrews has proved very conclusively that this last is the proper date. See "Kentucky, Tennessee, Ohio—their Admission into the Union," in Magazine of American History for October, 1887. Still, the act of February 19, 1803, after recapitulating the history, says: "Whereby the said State has become one of the United States of America."

II. INDIANA.

The admission of Indiana was effected so quietly as scarcely to cause a ripple on the surface of public affairs. In response to a petition from the Territorial Legislature, Congress passed the requisite enabling act, which was approved, April 19, 1816. The second section of this act bounded the State, east, by the boundary line of Ohio; south, by the Ohio; west, by the middle of the Wabash from its mouth to a point where a due north line drawn from Vincennes would last touch the northwestern shore of said river, and from thence by said due-north line; and north, by an east and west line drawn through a point ten miles north of the southern extreme of Lake Michigan. The convention was required to ratify these boundaries. This last line deprived Michigan of a strip of territory ten miles wide across the whole northern end of Indiana, that had been solemnly guaranteed to her by the Ordinance of 1787; but I have not discovered traces of remonstrance then or afterward. The act was justified at the time on the ground that the State should have a lake-frontage, which the line of 1787 would not give. A convention elected in pursuance of this act sat at Corydon, June 10–29, and framed a constitution. Indiana was formally admitted to the Union, December 11, 1816. At the close of the previous year the population was 68,897.[1] The petition of the legislature praying for admission said the inhabitants were principally composed of emigrants from every part of the Union; but the names of the counties and the facts of emigration show that a large majority of them came from the Middle and Southern States.

III. ILLINOIS.

The Enabling Act for Illinois, which bears the date, April 18, 1818, bounded the State on the east by the Indiana line

---

[1] Dillon: History of Indiana, 555.

ADMISSION OF THE NORTHWESTERN STATES. 327

as fixed two years before, on the south and west by the Ohio and Mississippi Rivers, and on the north by the parallel 42° 30' north latitude. This last was a much more serious infraction of the Ordinance than the Indiana line, and it deserves more than a passing allusion.

The enabling act, as originally introduced into the House of Representatives by Mr. Pope, the Territorial delegate, adhered strictly to the Ordinance line; but that statesman, thinking better of the matter, moved, April 3d, the line of 42° 30' as an amendment. He urged that the State, lying between the Mississippi Valley and the Lake Basin, and resting upon both, should be brought into relation with the States east by way of the lakes as well as the States south by way of the river; said if the mouth of the Chicago River were included within her limits, the State would be interested in a canal connecting the two systems of waters and in improving the harbor on the lake; insisted upon the State's right to a lake-frontage; and also used an argument that, from 1789 to 1861, was made to do duty in almost every kind of political emergency. If shut out from the Northern waters, then, in case of national disruption, the interests of the State would be to join a Southern and Western Confederacy; but if a large portion of it could be made dependent upon the commerce and navigation of the Northern Lakes, connected as they were with the Eastern States, a rival interest would be created to check the wish for a Western or Southern confederacy; and her interests would then be balanced, and her inclinations turned to the North. This reasoning was convincing to the South and the North alike, apparently, for the House adopted the amendment without a division. The consent of the people of Wisconsin was not asked, or the preference of those living in the district consulted. As the line of 1787 is in latitude 41° 37' 07.9" north, the tract of territory that Congress thus generously gave to Illinois, at the expense of Wisconsin, and in utter disregard of the Ordinance, is 52' 52.1" of latitude, or a little more than sixty-one miles, in width, and in length, from the lake to the river; it contains 8,500 square miles of as good soil as exists in the Northwest, as well as many fine streams and the sites of such cities as Chicago, Rockford, Freeport, Galena, and Dixon, not to mention smaller ones.

The Illinois State Convention sat at Kaskaskia, completing its work, August 26, 1818. The resolution of Congress declaring the admission of the State to the Union bears the date, December 3d, of the same year. A severe struggle on the practical recognition of slavery will be noticed in a future chapter. The population, which was mostly found in the Southern part of the State, was less than that required by the Ordinance. The census of 1810 assigns 12,282, the census of 1820, 55,162, people to Illinois.

IV. MICHIGAN.

We come again to Michigan, the first part of the Northwest visited by civilized men, and the last, except Wisconsin, to receive a permanent form of government. No other part of the United States has seen so many changes of national and local jurisdiction. It has belonged to France, to England, and to the United States; from 1796 to 1803 it was part of the Northwest Territory, from 1803 to 1805 a part of Indiana, and then an independent territory until its admission to the Union in 1837. Judge Cooley has appropriately sketched its history as a "history of governments"[1] No other name of an organized territory east of the Rocky Mountains has stood so long upon the map. Moreover, the growth of population was for a long time exceedingly slow. In explaining this fact, Judge Cooley mentions the late day at which the Indian titles to the soil were eased, the fur-trade within the Territory, the 'false ideas of Michigan geography, and the want of roads; but, plainly, these are only proximate causes, and merely another way of saying that civ-

---

[1] Preface to Michigan, in Commonwealth Series.

ilization was slow in taking possession of the beautiful peninsula.

Some of the main causes of the early discovery and exploration of the regions of the Upper Lakes also contributed to their late development. What were the opportunities of the French, and what use they made of them, has been shown in earlier chapters. Beyond discovery, exploration, and a feeble colonial life that was eventually extinguished, they did nothing for the Northwest. Had the St. Lawrence fallen to England that country would not have been so promptly explored, but it would have been more promptly peopled. It is easy to conceive a contingency in which the shores of the Lakes would have become the seats of civilization much earlier than the banks of the Ohio. As things turned, however, Michigan drew her emigrants by the northern channel of emigration, from the Northern part of the Atlantic Plain. But here she was at a great disadvantage as compared with Ohio, particularly the Southern part. Emigration moved less promptly by this channel than by those farther south, and when it did move it was for many years absorbed by Western New York and Northern Ohio. It was not until the appearance of steam-boats on the Lakes, in 1818, the opening of the Erie Canal in 1825, and the partial filling up of the inviting fields of emigration farther to the east, that the period of active settlement in Michigan began. While the population of Michigan merely doubled from 1800 to 1820, the population of Ohio increased twelve-fold.

But political development was slow from another cause. It was many years before the inertia given to the community by the *habitants* could be overcome. Mr. Sibley wrote to Judge Burnet in 1802: "Nothing frightens the Canadians like taxes. They would prefer to be treated like dogs, and kenneled under the whip of a tyrant, than contribute to the support of a free government." In 1818, under the belief that the Territory had the requisite population, the question of entering on the second stage of government provided for by the Ordinance was submitted to the people, but was lost by a decided majority, and it was not until 1827 that that end was fully consummated. Plainly, the old *régime* had done its work as thoroughly as Colbert could have desired.

But in time steps forward began to be taken. In 1832 the people, at a popular election, cast a large majority vote in favor of entering into a State government. In 1834 a census showed that between the two lakes and north of the line of 1787 there was a population of 87,278. Proceeding upon the theory held by St. Clair and other Federalists in 1802, that no enabling act was needed, the Territorial Legislature, January 26, 1835, passed an act calling a convention to frame a State constitution, and appointing April 4th the day for the election of delegates. This election was duly held; the convention sat in Detroit, May 11th to June 29th; the people ratified the constitution framed, at an election held November 2d; President Jackson laid it before Congress in a special message, December 9th, and the State would, no doubt, have been promptly admitted had it not encountered a series of adverse influences that render "the Michigan case" one of the most remarkable in the history of the admission of new States. The first and most formidable of these was a boundary-quarrel with Ohio.

The Constitution for Michigan framed at Detroit assumed in its preamble the boundaries of the Territory as established in 1805, viz.: The Ordinance line on the south; a line drawn through the middle of Lake Michigan to its northerly extremity, and a line due north from that point on the west; and the international boundary on the north and east. This was overlapping Indiana as bounded in 1816, and the provisional boundary of Ohio adopted in 1802. The Indiana and Illinois boundaries did not touch the Ohio-Michigan controversy that we are now to sketch, save as they tended to destroy the authority of the Ordinance.

Between 1802 and 1835 some history was made on the Northwestern Ohio frontier. In 1817 a Government surveyor laid down the boundary in conformity with the Chillicothe idea, and a little later another ran the line in conformity with the Michigan idea. These lines are called the "Harris" and "Fulton" lines, from the names of the two surveyors. In 1812 Amos Spafford, collector of the port of Miami, wrote to Governor Meigs, saying the fifty families comprising that settlement desired to have the laws of Ohio extended over them; that the few who objected were office-holders under the Governor of Michigan, who were determined to enforce the Michigan laws; that the people regarded this a great usurpation, and that he anticipated serious trouble unless the matter was adjusted. In 1823 Dr. Horatio Conant, of Fort Meigs, wrote to Ethan Allen Brown, Senator from Ohio, that the Michigan jurisdiction was extended to the territory between the Harris and Fulton lines, with the decided approbation of the inhabitants, which "makes it impossible for the State officers of Ohio to interfere without exciting disturbance."[1] The territory was in possession of Michigan all this time; it had been organized into a township, and roads had been cut at her expense. The letters of Spafford and Conant show that the people sometimes inclined to one side and sometimes to the other; which was not unnatural, considering that they were settlers in a wilderness who had formed no jurisdictional attachments, and that sometimes their interests seemed to incline them to Columbus, and then again to Detroit. But now there came a change. The city of Toledo was founded in 1832; and the inhabitants desired to belong to Ohio and not to Michigan. Especially were they anxious to secure the full advantage of the Miami Canal, then in course of construction from Cincinnati to the mouth of the Maumee. The strip of disputed land extended from Indiana to Lake Erie, eight miles wide at one end and five at the other, containing four hundred and sixty-eight square miles. The land was rich and

---

[1] The two letters are found in Knapp's History of the Maumee Valley, 242, 243.

fertile, but the prizes in the contest that opened in 1835 were the mouth of the Maumee and the young but promising city of Toledo. Evidently, the Ordinance line did not well suit territorial relations. It excluded Indiana and Illinois from Lake Michigan, and cut the people of the Maumee off from their natural connections. To be sure, these business arguments have no weight to the mind of a jurist in 1887; but they had great *weight* with the forceful people of the Northwest in 1816, 1818, and 1835. They would naturally demand: "Why should a line established in ignorance of geography and in advance of territorial development be suffered to stand in the way of our convenience?"

In 1835 Governor Lucas brought the boundary-question before the Ohio Legislature. That body promptly extended the contiguous Ohio counties over the disputed tract, and directed the Governor to appoint three commissioners to survey and re-mark the Harris line. At the end of March, Governor Lucas, attended by his staff and the boundary commissioners, arrived at Perrysburg to carry out the directions of the Legislature. As resistance was expected, General Bell and some six hundred Ohio militia were called into the field. These went into camp at the same place. Governor Mason of Michigan, attended by General Brown at the head of about one thousand Michigan militia, took possession of Toledo. At this juncture Richard Rush, of Philadelphia, and B. C. Howard, of Baltimore, arrived in the tented valley of the Maumee, sent by President Jackson as messengers of peace. Their efforts to effect a compromise until Congress could settle the dispute accomplished nothing more than the disbanding of the militia. What is variously known as "Governor Lucas's War," the "Toledo War," etc., came to a sudden end. It was a bloodless war; it had some serious and many comic aspects, and long furnished material for merriment in both Ohio and Michigan. The further local incidents of the controversy, such as the attempt of Ohio to run the Harris line and the seizure of some of the surveying

ADMISSION OF THE NORTHWESTERN STATES. 333

party by Michigan officers; the special session of the Ohio Legislature, at which it enacted a law to prevent the forcible abduction of the citizens of Ohio, created Lucas County, extending to the Harris line, appropriated $300,000 out of the treasury to carry into effect the laws in relation to the northern boundary, and authorized the Governor to borrow as much more on the credit of the State; the arrest and imprisonment by Michigan officers of citizens of Ohio; the excitement in both the State and the Territory; the disturbed state of affairs at Toledo—these and other incidents of local interest must be passed by. The quarrel was settled by politicians at Washington, and not by militia generals and sheriffs on the banks of the Maumee.

Strictly speaking, the quarrel was between Ohio and the United States. The Attorney-General gave President Jackson an opinion that, until Congress should change the law, the land between the Harris and Fulton lines belonged to Michigan; and this opinion was properly binding on the President as long as Mr. Butler continued his law adviser. But the President was in a strait. A presidential election would occur the next year, and he was deeply interested in the candidacy of Martin Van Buren. Indiana and Illinois, both of which States had profited by the disregard of the line of 1787, sympathized with Ohio; and the three States together had a large number of votes to be given to either the Democratic or the Whig candidate. Michigan stood alone, only a territory. John Quincy Adams thus defined the situation: "Never in the course of my life have I known a controversy of which all the right was so clearly on one side and all the power so overwhelmingly on the other; never a case where the temptation was so intense to take the strongest side and the duty of taking the weakest was so thankless."[1] Very naturally, the President counselled both sides to keep the peace, but he was understood to lean to the Ohio side.

---

[1] Cooley: Michigan, 219.

But this was not all the politics involved in the case. The State of Arkansas also stood at the door of the Union knocking for admission. The administration party was anxious that both the States be admitted in time to vote at the ensuing presidential election, for it was expected that both would be Democratic; but Michigan was a free State, Arkansas a slave State, and although it was understood that, in this scale, one would balance the other, there was yet an anxiety on either side lest the other should get the advantage.

Besides, a State government had been organized. A member of the House of Representatives, as well as legislative and executive officers, had been elected, and judges had been appointed. The legislature had met and chosen the national Senators. President Jackson, displeased at the activity of Governor Mason on the boundary-controversy, appointed a new Territorial governor to succeed him, whom the people would not receive, and whom they soon joked and laughed across Lake Michigan into Wisconsin, which was still a part of Michigan Territory. This was the local situation: Theoretically, the Territorial government was in force, but practically, the State government. Obviously, such a state of things could not long continue in an Anglo-Saxon country.

Acts for the admission of the two States were finally approved, June 15, 1836. The one admitted Arkansas unconditionally, the other Michigan with a very serious condition, that is hinted by the very title of the law: "An Act to establish the northern boundary line of the State of Ohio, and to provide for the admission of the State of Michigan into the Union," etc. Section 1 gave the district in dispute to Ohio; but Section 2 made Michigan a territorial compensation in the Upper Peninsula, drawing the line separating her from Wisconsin through Green Bay, the Menomonee River, Lake of the Desert, and Montreal River. These arrangements Michigan was required to assent to by a delegate convention elected for that sole purpose, before she could take her place in the family of States. A convention that sat at Ann Arbor on the fourth Monday of September rejected this overture by a very decided majority, and for a time it seemed that nothing had been concluded.

But now the politicians came again upon the scene. Arguments in favor of the State's yielding were put in circulation. Political arithmeticians at Washington figured out how much the five per cent. on the public lands sold within the State would yield, affirming that it would all be lost. The Senators and Representatives were desirous of taking their seats in Congress. President Jackson and his partisans exerted a steady pressure on the same side. The edge of disappointment becoming somewhat dulled, the people of the State, with characteristic American good humor, began to look on the bright side, and before the end of October Democratic county conventions were calling for a second State convention to pass upon the terms of admission. The State Governor replied that there was no time to call a second convention, and that he had no authority to call one, but hinted that the Government at Washington might, possibly, recognize a popular convention. Accordingly, five citizens, "in the name of the people in their primary capacity," called a convention to meet in Ann Arbor, December 14th. This was in pursuance of a scheme worked out in the Democratic caucuses. Although the elections of delegates were much ridiculed, they were still held, and although the convention was stigmatized as the "frost-bitten convention," it still sat, and did the work for which it had been called—that is, "assented" to the terms of the act of admission, having no more authority to do so than the crew of a Detroit schooner or a lumberman's camp in the Valley of Grand River. Still further, and most astounding of all, the two Houses of Congress, by large majorities, passed an act, approved January 26, 1837, accepting this convention as meeting the requirements of the act of admission, and so declared Michigan one of the United States. The electoral vote, however, was not counted.

Judge Campbell says the State was recognized when admitted as having existed since November, 1835.[1] As one closes the history of the admission of Michigan, he wonders whether the people learned to accent the first word in the Territorial motto: *Tandem fit surculus arbor.*

The Upper Peninsula is about three hundred miles in length, and from thirty to one hundred and sixty in breadth. It contains about twenty-two thousand six hundred square miles of area. It has considerable agricultural resources; its copper and iron mines are among the richest in the world; its fisheries are the finest on the Lakes; it contains excellent harbors, and it commands the outlets of both Lake Michigan and Lake Superior; and yet Michigan was unwilling to accept this rich peninsula for a few hundred square miles of corn-lands on the Ohio border. She protested again and again that she did not wish to extend beyond the boundaries assigned her in 1805. The tip of the Northern Peninsula she strove for when Wisconsin sought to wrest it from her, because of its relations to the two straits, and because of the ancient commercial connection between Detroit and the upper posts; but she wished nothing more. Mr. Lyon, the Territorial delegate, said, in 1834, "that for a great part of the year nature had separated the Upper and Lower peninsulas by impassable barriers, and that there never could be any identity of interest or community of feeling between them." However, when we remember that the copper mines first became productive in historic times in 1845, although they had been worked by the Mound Builders, and been known to white men since the days of Brulé and Joliet, and that the whole peninsula a half-century ago seemed a sterile waste, we need not be surprised at Michigan's preference for the mouth of the Maumee.

---

[1] Political History of Michigan, 478.

V. WISCONSIN.

The Ordinance of 1787 left to the discretion of Congress the question whether the Northwest should be divided into three, four, or five States. No man, looking at the map, can doubt that the five-State plan was far better than either of the others. States extending from the Ohio River to the national boundary would have been of over-size, as well as ill-shapen; while Michigan and Wisconsin are both too large and too widely separated to constitute one State. These facts were perceived as early as 1802 and 1805. Furthermore, it was perceived at the same time that the Upper Peninsula belongs geographically to Wisconsin. Accordingly, in 1805 the dividing line between them was drawn from the southern bend of Lake Michigan through the middle of that lake to its extremity, that is, the Straits of Mackinaw, where historical causes turned it due north on the Miami meridian to the national limit. The addition of Wisconsin to Michigan for purposes of government, in 1818, subject to the future disposition of Congress, confirmed this line. Nor was any other thought entertained until a territorial compensation to Michigan for the lands that the course of events required her to surrender to Ohio was proposed. The plan of giving her the Upper Peninsula appears to have been first suggested by Mr. Preston, of South Carolina, when the Ohio-Michigan boundary was before the Judiciary Committee of the Senate. He thought the region beyond the Lake too large for one State, and he appears to have thought the peninsula an island. Mr. Preston said in the Senate: "Whatever disadvantage may arise from connecting with Michigan a portion of the country west or north of the Lake is, we think, not to be weighed with the inconvenience of subjecting, forever after, to the jurisdiction of a single State all the inhabitants who may reside in the region west and north of the Lake."[1]

---

[1] In preparing this account of the controversy touching the Wisconsin boundaries, the author acknowledges his indebtedness to two articles entitled The

Wisconsin, more unwilling to part with the peninsula than Michigan was to receive it, made a valiant effort for its retention. The connection of the two regions under the law of 1818 proved little more than nominal, and the people beyond the Lake made repeated efforts, beginning as early as 1829, to secure the organization of an independent territory, called, at different times, "Chippewau," "Wiskonsan," and "Huron," that should include the whole peninsula to the very tip. The act of April 20, 1836, creating the Territory, bounded it on the northeast by the line of the Michigan Enabling Act. A survey of that line made in 1840 and 1841 disclosed the fact that Congress had assumed a state of things that did not exist, and that the line was an impossible one. Wisconsin took advantage of this discovery to bring forward her original claim, pleading the Ordinance of 1787, which did not touch the issue (since in the northern tier of States everything was left to the discretion of Congress), and the acts of 1805 and 1818, which was more to the purpose; but she expressed a willingness to accept a "compensation" in the shape of extensive and valuable internal improvements. The legislative committee that uttered these views recommended that the Territory insist upon her "ancient boundaries," to the extent, if necessary, of forming a "*State out of the Union*," "*the sovereign, independent State of Wisconsin*," and then of appealing to the Supreme Arbiter of Nations to adjust all difficulties that might arise. A most belligerent address to Congress, adopted about the same time, declared that Wisconsin would never "lose sight of the principle that, whatever may be the sacrifice, the integrity of her boundaries must be observed."[1] It is needless, perhaps, to say that this is the familiar voice of South Carolina in the days before the Civil War. But this note of secession, sounded among the woods and lakes of the

---

Boundaries of Wisconsin, by R. G. Thwaits, in Magazine of Western History, September and October, 1887.

[1] Magazine of Western History, VI., 504, 529.

Northwest, made no impression on the course of events. Having compelled Michigan to accept what she did not want, Congress now compelled Wisconsin to surrender what she wished to retain. The Enabling act approved August 6, 1846, followed the Menomonee-Montreal line with some slight modifications.[1] In both the conventions held under it, attempts were made to win back the ancient northeastern boundary, but without success.

The act of 1836, creating the Territory of Wisconsin, made the line 42° 30′ the southern boundary. Three years later, and twenty-one years after the admission of the State of Illinois, the Territorial Legislature adopted resolutions declaring that Congress had violated the Ordinance of 1787 in fixing the northern boundary of Illinois, and requesting the people of the Territory, and also those living between the line of 1787 and parallel 42° 30′, to vote at the next general election upon the question of forming a State government that should embrace the whole of ancient Wisconsin. Strange to say, this proposition was received with more favor by the people of Northern Illinois than by the people of Wisconsin proper. Public meetings held in various Illinois towns adopted resolutions in favor of the Wisconsin claim; and a convention held at Rockford, July 6, 1840, declared that the fourteen northern counties of Illinois belonged to Wisconsin, and recommended the people to elect delegates to a convention to be held at Madison in November, for the purpose of adopting such lawful and constitutional measures as may seem to be necessary and proper for the early adjustment of the southern boundary.[2] Public sentiment ran very strong in many of these counties in favor of the northern claim. But the boundary was complicated with the formation of a State government, which the people at the north thought prema-

---

[1] Mr. Thwaits contends that the seeds of future controversies lie thick along this line.

[2] Magazine of Western History, VI., 538, 539.

ture, and the total vote cast in favor of the proposition of 1839 was small. In 1842 the Territorial Governor sent an official communication to the Governor of Illinois, informing him that the Illinois jurisdiction over the frontier counties was "accidental and temporary." The Enabling act of 1846 followed the Illinois line on the south, as it followed the Michigan line on the northeast, and again Wisconsin submitted. In the first constitutional convention a vigorous but unsuccessful attempt was made to secure a clause referring all disputes as to boundary to the Supreme Court of the United States, the State to come in with boundaries undetermined. Here, again, politics intervened; the failure of this plan is said to have been due, in part, to the jealousy of the Northern Illinois politicians entertained by those of Wisconsin. Nor is it unlikely that political ambition had something to do with the fondness of the Illinois counties for a northern State connection.

As Wisconsin was the last of the five Northwestern States to enter the Union, it was not, perhaps, surprising that her geographical and historical boundaries should be invaded on the south and northeast; but it would appear surprising that on the farther or northwestern side, she should have suffered more heavily than on any other side. The explanation consists of facts of geography and of history.

After the rectification of the northwestern boundary by the treaty of 1818, the meridian of the northwesternmost point of the Lake of the Woods, from its intersection with the Mississippi to parallel 49°, was considered the farther boundary of the Northwest Territory; but the act of 1838, creating the Territory of Iowa, drew a line due north from the head-waters or sources of the Mississippi to that parallel, and this line Wisconsin henceforth called her "ancient boundary" in that quarter. The second of these lines falls somewhat farther to the west than the first one. Again, the population that planted the early settlements on the upper waters of the Mississippi reached their destination by ascending the river, and not by an overland journey from Lake Michigan; moreover, all their natural connections, industrial, commercial, political, and social, were with the river valley rather than with the lake basin. In these circumstances originated the idea of a "sixth State," to consist either wholly of territory belonging to the old Northwest, or partly of such territory and partly of territory acquired of France in 1803.

The Enabling Act for Wisconsin, approved August 6, 1846, departed from the "ancient boundary," adopting the following in its stead: The main channel of the St. Louis River to the first rapids in the same (above the Indian village, according to Nicollet's map); thence due south to the main branch of the River St. Croix; thence down the main channel of said river to the Mississippi. In the debate the extension of "the ancient boundary" beyond the limits of the original territory, the great size of Wisconsin unless limited, and the desirability of a State that should lie on both sides of the great river and encompass its farther sources, were urged in favor of this line. In the constitutional convention which sat at Madison, October 5th, this boundary received far more attention than any other. The people of the St. Croix Valley, who were left in Wisconsin, wished to go with their neighbors across the river. At the end of a long contest, by a vote of 49 ayes to 38 nays, the convention adopted a proviso that would have thrown the basin of the St. Croix into the State beyond. The principal champion of this measure favored a State extending from the Mississippi to the Saut Ste. Marie and Green Bay, to be called "Superior." On March 3, 1847, Congress assented to this proviso, but a month later the people, at a popular election, rejected the constitution on grounds wholly distinct from boundaries.

In the second constitutional convention, convened at Madison, December 15, 1847, this ground was all fought over again with equal pertinacity. The Lake Michigan side of the State now proved to be stronger than the Mississippi side; and the convention adopted a proviso that the boundary should be drawn from the rapids of the St. Louis southward to the mouth of the Rum River, which is some twenty miles above the Falls of St. Anthony, thus giving a large tract that now belongs to Minnesota, including St. Paul and the eastern side of Minneapolis, to Wisconsin. This proviso brought out the full strength of the Upper Mississippi settlements in opposition. The people of the St. Croix Valley and about Fort Snelling sent a strong memorial to Washington, urging, among other things, that "the Chippeway and St. Croix valleys are closely connected in geographical position with the upper Mississippi, while they are widely separated from the settled posts of Wisconsin, not only by hundreds of miles of mostly waste and barren lands, which must remain uncultivated for ages, but equally so by a diversity of interests and character in the population."[1] This memorial suggested a line drawn due south from Cheqaumegon Bay, on Lake Superior, to the main Chippeway River, and thence down that stream to the Mississippi. This memorial, seconded by a vigorous lobby, defeated the Rum River proviso, but did not secure the Chippeway line. Wisconsin came into the Union with the limits of the Enabling act. No man who studies the geography of the Upper Mississippi, and its material and political interests, will question the practical wisdom of the limitation on the western side, whatever he may think of its legality. He will also be apt to think, with the memorialists of 1848, that the Chippeway would have been a better boundary than the St. Croix.

In all, Wisconsin lost about fifty-seven thousand square miles of territory originally intended for her,[2] but she remains the third of the Northwestern States in size, falling only 1,490 square miles behind Illinois, and 2,527 square miles behind Michigan.

After a very animated contest, the first Wisconsin Consti-

---

[1] Magazine of Western History.
[2] Viz., 8,500 to Illinois, 22,600 to Michigan, and 26,000 to Minnesota.

tution was rejected by a majority of 6,112 votes in a total of 34,450. The people of the Territory, in common with the people of the West generally, had suffered many evils from reckless and irresponsible banking. These evils, together with the extreme Democratic opinions relating to banks and paper money, led the convention to deny all legal authority to banks. The constitution declared it not lawful for any corporation, institution, person or persons within the State, to make or issue paper money, or any evidence of debt intended to circulate as money; forbade any corporation to carry on any of the other functions of banking institutions; prohibited the establishment of any branch or agency of a banking institution existing without the State; and made it illegal to circulate, after 1849, bank-notes of a less denomination than $20. Deposit, discount, and exchange banking were left wholly to private enterprise. The convention had presumed too far upon the popular hostility to banks. The Whigs opposed the constitution to a man, and many of the Democrats as well. Serious objections were also made to other features that will not be particularized. The second convention followed, for the most part, the paths marked out by its predecessor. But it empowered the legislature to submit to the voters, at any general election, the question of "bank or no bank;" also to grant bank charters, or to pass a general banking law, provided a majority of all the votes cast on this subject should be in favor of banks. This constitution was ratified by a majority of over 10,000 in a vote of 23,000. Wisconsin was admitted to the Union May 29, 1848. The State received its emigration by the great northern current, and accordingly had to wait until Michigan was partially peopled, as Michigan had been obliged to wait for Western New York and Northern Ohio. The population was only 30,945 in 1840, but it made the astonishing advance to 305,391 in the ten years following.

Minnesota, the half-sister of the five Northwestern States, was admitted to the Union May 11, 1858.

The five noble commonwealths formed out of the Territory Northwest of the River Ohio, with their twelve or thirteen millions of population; their material, intellectual, and moral resources; their vast wealth of achievements and still vaster wealth of possibilities, are the grandest testimonial to the Ordinance of 1787, to the men who framed it, and to the pioneers who laid their foundations.

XVIII.

SLAVERY IN THE NORTHWEST.

THE surprise that historians still continue to express at the ease and celerity with which the Ordinance of 1787 was enacted culminates when they come to the sixth article of compact. A few words touching that article will serve as a fitting introduction to an account of slavery in the Territory Northwest of the River Ohio.

At the close of the Revolutionary War slavery existed in nearly all the States of the Union, but was far stronger in the South than in the North. In the one section the causes were already at work that ere long brought about its abolishment; in the other, the causes had not yet begun to operate that, in the end, practically united all the people in defence of slavery. In the sense of later controversies, the one section was not anti-slavery nor the other pro-slavery. The Northern States tended toward anti-slavery views, but not in the aggressive spirit of later times; the Southern States, toward pro-slavery views, but not with such unanimity as to preclude a great amount of strong and even fervid anti-slavery sentiment, and particularly in Virginia. The average opinion South and North was that slavery could not be violently uprooted; that it must be tolerated and protected for the time; but that it was an evil the peaceful death of which every real well-wisher of his country would be glad to hasten. This was the opinion that declared itself in the slavery compromises of the Constitution, and in the sixth article of compact of the Ordinance of the same year, which is also a compromise, as anyone must see the moment he looks at the two clauses of the article balanced on the word "provided." The long and fierce contest over the extension of slavery, which did not begin until many years afterward, gave to that prohibition an importance which no one dreamed of according to it at the time of its enactment. The fact is, the article was not of the substance of the Ordinance. It was not even a part of the original draft, but was brought forward by Mr. Dane on the second reading. There is no reason to suppose that Mr. Lee, of Virginia, changed his views on the subject of slavery in the interval, but he voted against the prohibition of 1784, and for the prohibition of 1787. The Ohio Associates desired the exclusion of slavery from the region where they proposed to purchase lands, and probably would have declined to purchase them without it;[1]

---

[1] This was a point that the New England men always insisted upon. The "Proposition for settling a new State by such officers and soldiers of the Federal Army as should associate for that purpose," drawn up by Colonel Timothy Pickering, early in 1783, which was an important link in the history of the Ohio Company, when told at length, contained this language: "The total exclusion of slavery from the State to form an essential and irrevocable part of the Constitution." The editors of the "Life of Rev. Manasseh Cutler" present convincing evidence that Dr. Cutler was the author of the sections of the Ordinance of 1787 relating to religion, education, and slavery (I., 342-344). Judge Ephraim Cutler, mentioned in the text, says his father asked him, in 1804-1805, whether he had prepared the prohibition of slavery inserted in the Ohio Constitution. On receiving an affirmative answer, the doctor said it was a singular coincidence, as he had himself prepared Article VI. of the Ordinance, while he was in New York negotiating the Ohio purchase. The doctor further said he acted in that matter for associates, friends, and neighbors who would not embark in the enterprise unless the principles in relation to religion, education, and slavery were unalterably fixed. Dr. Cutler's editors also bring out with much force, as partially explaining the singular interest that the Virginia members of Congress took in the Ohio purchase and the Ordinance, that settlements on the further banks of the Ohio would be a screen for the Virginia and Kentucky settlements on the south bank against the Indians. They say further: "Virginia, under the leadership of Washington, had entered upon a wise and comprehensive policy of internal improvement, designed to secure the trade of the Ohio Valley and the Northwest to Virginia seaports. Additional value would also be imparted to her bountylands lying between the Scioto and Little Miami. Add to these the personal sympathy of Washington for the success of his old associates, as well as his own landed interests in the Ohio Valley, and we find plain business considerations

but their attitude toward its extension was very different from that of David Wilmot and Abraham Lincoln. Accordingly, the sixth compact was regarded neither as an anti-slavery victory nor as a pro-slavery defeat; it was simply a feature, though an important one, of the frame of government provided for the Northwest. The tremendous consequences flowing from it no man then living was wise enough to foretell. Still the article was of great immediate advantage to freedom; for when the real battle with slavery in the Northwest was joined, it proved a rock of defence that was never successfully assaulted.

Negro slaves were introduced into the Mississippi Valley early in the eighteenth century. Throughout the French period pecuniary ability and personal desire were the only limitations on the number of such slaves that a colonist might own. Accordingly, as the *habitants* of the Northwest increased in substance and were brought into closer commercial relations with Louisiana and the West Indies, they imported them in considerable numbers. The number continued to grow, both by natural increase and by later importations. Judge Breese quotes a Jesuit missionary who found 1,100 whites, 300 blacks, and 60 "red slaves of the savages" in five Illinois villages in 1750.[1] But this slavery was of the old patriarchal rather than the modern commercial type. Breese gives a pleasing picture of the male slaves working side by side in the fields with their masters, and of the females going with their mistresses "in neat attire" to matins and vespers; both "unmindful of the fetters with which a wicked policy had bound them."[2] Monette gives an equally pleasing picture of the festive enjoyments of the *habitants*, in which the slaves freely mingled.[3] An ordinance of Louis XV., issued in

---

that controlled at that time this most important decision. And all evidence points to Rev. Manasseh Cutler as the agent who carefully, skilfully, and successfully conducted these negotiations and brought about their results" (L, 352).

[1] Early History of Illinois, 194.   [2] Ibid., 199, 200.
[3] History of the Valley of the Mississippi, I., 186, 187.

1724, enjoined that all slaves in the French colonies should "be educated in the Apostolic Roman Catholic religion, and be baptized," enjoining their owners to have these matters attended to within a reasonable time, under pain of an arbitrary fine.[1] Negro slaves were relatively numerous in the Northwest in 1763. Governor Reynolds, who says the first importation was one of five hundred made from San Domingo in 1726, by Philip Renault, to work the mines, reports that there were 168 slaves in Illinois in 1810, 917 in 1820, and 746 in 1830.[2] Negro slaves are also heard of at Green Bay in Wisconsin.[3]

The Western Indians were slave-holders. They followed the ancient and honorable custom of selling captives taken in war into slavery, often as the alternative of putting them to death; and among their best customers, from the early days of French colonization, were the white men, who often bought, it must be added, as acts of humanity. So many of these red slaves belonged to a single tribe that Pawnee, or "Pani" as the French wrote it, came to be the common word for slave irrespective of race, thus repeating the history of the word "Slav" itself.

The transfer of the Northwest to England in no way disturbed the relation of master and slave; for the capitulation of 1760 and the treaty of 1763 guaranteed the full protection of all the property of the people who were transferred. Moreover, such Englishmen as made their way into the country enjoyed the same privileges as the old residents, and some of them promptly improved this opportunity. As a consequence, the Northwest came to the United States with a slave dowery; and although the treaty of 1783 did not repeat the guarantee of the treaty of 1763, no one thought that the dowery would in any way be interfered with, for slavery was then, practically, co-extensive with the Union. The

---

[1] Dillon: History of Indiana, 32. [2] My Own Times, 28, 132.
[3] Strong: History of the Territory of Wisconsin, 67.

Northwest was slave territory all through the Virginia period, reaching from 1778 to 1784; and when that State made her cession she stipulated, in terms: "That the French and Canadian inhabitants and other settlers . . . who have professed themselves citizens of Virginia, shall have their possessions and titles confirmed to them, and be protected in the enjoyment of their rights and liberties;" and this stipulation, no doubt, included slaves. Furthermore, the United States Government recognized the existence of slavery in the Territory. The Ordinance of 1784 mentions "free males of full age" and free inhabitants; and, by allowing the people "to adopt the constitution and laws of any one of the original States," gave full scope for the continuance of slavery. It has even been contended that the expression, "free male inhabitants," found in the great Ordinance, assumes tacitly that such slavery as then existed in the Territory should not be disturbed. And, finally, Jay's Treaty, negotiated in 1794, in the article providing for the evacuation of the Western posts on June 1, 1796, guaranteed to all settlers and traders within the precincts or jurisdiction of the said posts all their property of every kind and protection therein, which applied to slaves as well as to other property.

In his very entertaining account of life at Detroit in the years following the extension of the American authority over that town, Judge Burnet, after bearing testimony to the "excellence of their hirelings and domestics," adds: "But their best servants were the Pawnee Indians, and their descendants, who were held and disposed of as slaves, under the French and English governments—a species of slavery which existed to a considerable extent in Upper Canada. . . . That relation existed when the country was delivered up to the United States; though the practice of purchasing Indian captives as slaves, by the white people, had ceased before the surrender; and consequently, the principal part, if not all, the Indians then in slavery were the descendants of enslaved captives."[1] Judge Cooley divides the slaves in the Northwest, in 1796, " as regards the legal questions affecting their liberty," into three classes: (1) "Those who were in servitude to French owners previous to the cession of jurisdiction to England, and who were still claimed as property in which the owners were protected under the treaty of cession," 1763. (2) " Those who were held by British owners at the time of Jay's treaty and claimed afterward as property under its protection." (3) " Those who since the Territory had come under American customs had been brought into it from the States in which slavery was lawful."[2]

When the *habitants* of Vincennes and the Illinois, alarmed by the sixth article of compact, called upon Governor St. Clair to explain its meaning, he promptly replied that it was not retroactive but prospective; "a declaration of a principle which was to govern the legislature in all acts respecting that matter, and the courts of justice in their decisions in cases arising after the date of the Ordinance." He argued that had Congress intended to emancipate the slaves in the Territory, compensation would have been made to their owners. Congress had "the right to determine that property of that kind afterwards acquired should not be protected in future, and that slaves imported into the Territory after that declaration might reclaim their freedom."[3] This was the theory on which the various Territorial governments of the Northwest appear to have been administered. For example, the revenue laws of the Territory of Illinois levied a tax upon slaves; and Congress, that had the power of revising all such laws, in this case never exercised its power. However, in one instance a court of law materially limited this ground. The Chief Justice of the Territory of Michigan, in a case that arose at Detroit in 1807, held that the sixth article was absolute, save as modified by Jay's Treaty. These are his words: " A right

---

[1] Notes, 283.
[2] Michigan, 131, 132.
[3] St. Clair Papers, I., 205, 206.

of property in the human species cannot exist in this Territory except as to persons in the actual possession of British settlers in the Territory on June 1, 1796, and that every other man coming into this Territory is by the law of the land a freeman, unless he be a fugitive from lawful labor and service in some other American State or territory."[1] Chief Justice Woodbridge accordingly refused to return to their owners fugitive slaves from Canada escaping into Michigan, thereby causing no little bad blood. In 1807, it may be remarked, the guarantee given the French slave-owners by England was more than forty years old, and had no other than an historical interest.

Under the operation of the Ordinance such slavery as existed in 1787 slowly but surely died out. However, black slaves were still found in Illinois as late as 1846 or 1847; and men of middle age now living have seen in Detroit an ancient "Pani" who had been a slave in his earlier life.[2]

The active and dangerous championship of slavery in the Northwest did not come from the French inhabitants. The New England and Middle State emigrants were generally opposed to slavery; but the larger number of the emigrants from Virginia, the Carolinas, and Kentucky, accustomed to slaves, and finding in the Ohio Valley physical conditions very similar to those they left behind them, not unnaturally desired its introduction. Accordingly, they united with the slaveholders already on the ground in a series of attempts permanently to break down or temporarily to set aside the inhibition. A petition asking the suspension of Article VI. was met by an adverse report in the House of Representatives in May, 1796.

In 1799, officers of the Virginia line, desiring to remove with their slaves to the Virginia Military District, between the

---

[1] Cooley: Michigan, 137.
[2] Edwards: History of Illinois, 180, 184; and Campbell: Political History of Michigan, 246, 247.

Scioto and Miami Rivers, petitioned the Territorial Legislature for permission to do so; but the peremptory language of the Ordinance gave that body no such discretion and the petition was refused. The granting of the petition would have brought into the Territory, says Burnet, "a great accession of wealth, strength, and intelligence; yet the public feeling, on the subject of admitting slavery into the Territory, was such, that the request would have been denied by a unanimous vote if the legislature had possessed the power of granting it. They were not only opposed to slavery on the ground of its being a moral evil, in violation of personal right, but were of opinion that, whatever might be its immediate advantages it would ultimately retard the settlement and check the prosperity of the Territory, by making labor less reputable and creating feelings and habits unfriendly to the simplicity and industry they desired to encourage and perpetuate."[1] But it is impossible to harmonize such a unanimous and decided anti-slavery sentiment as this with the admitted facts of history.

In December, 1802, a delegate convention held at Vincennes, the capital of the new Territory of Indiana, called and presided over by Governor William Henry Harrison, again memorialized Congress to set aside the sixth compact; and in the following March, John Randolph, as chairman of a special committee to which the memorial and a letter of the same tenor from Governor Harrison had been referred, reported it inexpedient to grant the prayer. The argument of the report is in these words:

"The rapid population of the State of Ohio sufficiently evinces, in the opinion of your committee, that the labor of slaves is not necessary to promote the growth and settlement of colonies in that region; that this labor, demonstrably the dearest of any, can only be employed in the cultivation of products more valuable than any known to that quarter of the United States; that the committee deem it highly dangerous and in-

---

[1] Notes, 306, 307.

expedient to impair a provision wisely calculated to promote the happiness and prosperity of the Northwestern country, and to give strength and security to that extensive frontier. In the salutary operation of this sagacious and benevolent restraint, it is believed that the inhabitants of Indiana will, at no very.distant day, find ample remuneration for a temporary privation of labor and of emigration."

However, the people of Indiana, refusing to accept Mr. Randolph's view of the case, continued to call upon Congress for the suspension of the obnoxious article. In every one of the years 1804, 1806, 1807, committees of the House of Representatives reported favorably to their wishes, but the House, for some reason now unknown, never acted on the reports. Governor Harrison and the Indiana Legislature now took their cause to the Senate, where they encountered an adverse report from a special committee that ended attempts to induce the new Congress to undo what the old one, with such solemnity, had done.[1] But it must not be supposed that the people of Indiana were unanimous in desiring the introduction of slavery. The citizens of Clark County, for example, sent a vigorous counter-memorial to Congress in November, 1807. These citizens say: "When we take into consideration the vast emigration into this Territory—and of citizens, too, decidedly opposed to the measure—we feel satisfied that, at all events, Congress will suspend any legislative act on this subject until we shall, by the Constitution, be admitted into the Union, and have a right to adopt such a constitution, in this respect, as may comport with the wishes of a majority of the citizens."[2]

In 1807 the Indiana Legislature passed an act authorizing the owners of negroes and mulattoes more than fifteen years of age to bring them into the Territory, and to have them bound to service by indenture for such time as the master and

---

[1] St. Clair Papers, I., 120-122.
[2] Dillon: History of Indiana, 410-414.

slave might agree upon. If within thirty days of the time he was brought into the Territory the slave would not consent to be indentured, then his owner should have sixty days in which to remove him into any State where slavery existed. The law also permitted any person to bring slaves under fifteen years of age into the Territory, and to hold them to service—the males until the age of thirty-five, the females until the age of thirty-two years. Male children, born in the Territory of a parent of color owing service by indenture, should serve the master until the age of thirty years, female children until the age of twenty-eight years. This act continued in force until 1810. On the Territorial Statute Book are also found very repressive acts concerning servants. This act was continued in force by the Illinois Legislature after the division of the Territory. In 1814 the same legislature passed a law providing that slaves might, with consent of their owners, hire themselves in the Territory for a term not exceeding one year; and that such act should not in any way affect the master's right of property in them in the State or territory where they belonged. The preamble of this act assigns as reasons for its provisions that mills cannot be erected or other needed improvements made, for want of laborers; and, particularly, that the manufacture of salt, the supply of which should be abundant and the price low, cannot be carried on by means of white men. Still further, an act passed in 1812 forbade the emigration of free negroes to the Territory of Illinois under severe penalties; and enjoined free negroes already there to register themselves and their children in the office of the Clerk of the County Court, also under severe penalties.

When one remembers that the Northwest was covered on two sides by slave territory, from which it was separated only by the Ohio and Mississippi Rivers, he appreciates the facilities that such enactments as the foregoing gave for evading the intent of the sixth compact of the Ordinance. Comment is not needed to show that the ingenuity here displayed could have invented a system of enforced labor not at all inferior to that devised by some of the Southern States under President Johnson's reconstruction scheme. Moreover, these enactments explain certain provisions respecting indentures in the first Constitutions of Ohio, Indiana, and Illinois that would otherwise be inexplicable.

The constitutional conventions of the three divisions of the Territory lying on the Ohio River offered opportunities for attacking the integrity of the Ordinance that in two instances were improved.

Judge Burnet's "Notes" and Mr. William Henry Smith's "Life of St. Clair" do not convey the impression that an issue was really drawn in the Ohio Convention of 1802. But Judge Ephraim Cutler's journal conveys that impression very distinctly. Those favorable to slavery took the ground that, however it might be with the Territory, the Ordinance could not bind a State unless the State herself, as a party to a compact, assented to it; and they accordingly advocated a "modified form" of servitude. Judge Cutler was a son of Dr. Manasseh Cutler, was one of the Washington County delegates to frame the constitution, and a member of the committee charged with framing the bill of rights, of which John W. Brown was chairman. Cutler's journal gives this account of proceedings in the committee:

"An exciting subject was of course immediately brought before the committee, the subject of admitting or excluding slavery. Mr. Brown produced a section which defined the subject, in effect, thus: No person shall be held in slavery if a male, after he is thirty-five years of age; and if a female, after twenty-five years of age. I observed to the committee that those who had elected me to represent them there were desirous of having this matter clearly understood, and I must move to have the section laid upon the table until our next meeting, and to avoid any warmth of feeling, I hoped that each member of the committee would prepare a section which should express his views fully on this important subject. The committee met the next morning, and I was called on for what I had proposed the last evening. I then read to them the section as it now stands in the constitution. Mr. Brown observed that what he had introduced was thought by the greatest men in the nation to be, if established in our constitution, obtaining a great step toward a general emancipation of slavery, and was, in his opinion, greatly to be preferred to what I had offered."

The section that Cutler prepared prohibited slavery in the very words of the Ordinance; it forbade the holding, as a servant, under pretence of indenture or otherwise, any male person twenty-one years of age, or female person eighteen years of age, unless such person had entered into the indenture while in a state of perfect freedom, and on condition of a *bona fide* consideration, received or to be received, for the service; closing with the clause: "Nor shall any indenture of any negro or mulatto, hereafter made and executed out of this State, or, if made in the State, where the term of service exceeds one year, be of the least validity, except those given in the case of apprenticeships."

After a sharp discussion in the committee, the section was adopted by a majority of one, five votes to four. It now went to the convention, where "several attempts were made to weaken or obscure the sense of the section on its passage." In committee of the whole, a material change was introduced. Cutler was unwell, and so absent at the time. "I went to the convention," he continues, "and moved to strike out the obnoxious matter and made my objections as forcible as I was able, and when the vote was called Mr. Milligan changed his vote and we succeeded in placing it in its original state." Thus by a majority of only one, first in the committee and afterward in the convention itself, was the attempt to fasten a modified slavery upon the State of Ohio defeated.

Judge Cutler understood President Jefferson to be the author of the proposition which he so effectually opposed, and the "one of the greatest men in the nation" referred to by

Mr. Brown. He gives as evidence for this opinion a conversation with Governor Worthington in Washington at the time Congress passed the law authorizing the convention, in which Worthington told him that Mr. Jefferson "had expressed to him that such, or a similar article, might be introduced into the constitution, and he hoped there would not be any effort made for anything farther for the exclusion of slavery, as it would operate against the interests of those who wished to emigrate from the slave States to Ohio."[1]

Judge Burnet says "much warmth of feeling" was manifested in the convention on the different propositions which were offered relating to the people of color then residing in the Territory, amounting probably to one or two hundred. These propositions, found in the "Journal of the Convention," were finally abandoned, in the fear that the feeling excited by them might defeat the object for which the convention was called. The judge says: "A few of the members were disposed to declare them citizens, to the full extent of that term; while others contended against allowing them any other privilege than the protection of the laws, and exemption from taxes and militia duty. Propositions were made to declare them ineligible to any office, civil or military; also

---

[1] The facts stated above in regard to the Ohio Convention are drawn from A Funeral Discourse on the occasion of the death of Hon. Ephraim Cutler, delivered at Warren, Washington County, O., July 24, 1853, by Professor E. B. Andrews of Marietta College, Marietta, O., 1854. In this discourse Professor Andrews also calls Governor Morrow as a witness that Mr. Jefferson favored the admission of slavery, for a limited period, into Ohio. The editors of the "Life of Rev. Manasseh Cutler" say: "This effort was supported by Jefferson's favorite theory of States rights. The advocates of the measure claimed that, as soon as the State assumed its own autonomy and became a sovereign among others, it had the right to decide upon the provisions of an ordinance which was the act of only one party, the general government. The central and southern portions of the State then had a majority of the population, and the labor of slaves would have suited the interests of their fertile valleys, while the political prospects of the new and rising 'States' rights democracy would have been advanced by holding out such a premium for emigration from Virginia and Kentucky" (I., 348).

to exclude them from being examined as witnesses in courts of justice against white persons."[1] Colored men were excluded from the basis of representation and from the suffrage. The sentiments of hostility to negroes that appeared in the Convention afterward ripened in the infamous "Black Laws" of Ohio, the last vestiges of which were not swept from the statute-book until 1887.

There was a decided change of sentiment on the slavery question in Indiana between the years 1807 and 1816. At least, I have not been able to find evidence of a slavery controversy in the constitutional convention. The constitution prohibited slavery in the words of Article VI. of the compacts of 1787, and coupled with it this clause: "Nor shall any indenture of any negro or mulatto, hereafter made and executed out of the bounds of the State, be of any validity within the State."

In no one of the three States bordering the Ohio was there such a determined effort made to nullify the sixth compact as in Illinois. This was partly due to the geographical position of the State, and partly to the character of the population. The lower part of the State projects, wedge-like, into what was then slave territory. It was as well adapted to slave labor as Kentucky on the one side or Missouri on the other. Its commercial connections, in 1818, were with the down-the-river country. Here was the stronghold of slavery in the day of French domination. Here came the first emigrants in the new *régime*. Long before the New Englanders and Middle State men had reached the Central and Northern parts of the State, Kentuckians, Tennesseeans, Carolinians, and Virginians made their way by the Ohio and its affluents into this new "Egypt." Nearly all these people were accustomed to slavery; many of them were "poor whites," and were intensely eager to acquire that badge of distinction in the States from which they came, the ownership of slaves;

---

[1] Notes, 354, 355.

many of them, too, were very ignorant, and nearly all were strongly prejudiced against the "Yankees," as they called all people from the free States. In a word, early Illinois was homogeneous with Kentucky or Tennessee in many features, including devotion to slavery. No attempt was made in the convention that framed the constitution of 1818 to abrogate the Ordinance in terms, but the provisions now to be mentioned subverted its substance.

In room of a prohibition of slavery we find the following: "Neither slavery nor involuntary servitude shall hereafter be introduced into this State, otherwise than for the punishment of crimes whereof the party shall have been duly convicted;" a plain, practical recognition of the slavery already existing. The Ohio clauses in regard to indentures were copied word for word. Slaves holden in other States should not be hired to labor in Illinois save in the salt-works tract near Shawneetown; nor hired for a longer time than one year, or after the year 1825. The last of the three sections devoted to the subject legalized the contracts and indentures already existing in virtue of the laws of Illinois Territory, but provided that the children hereafter born of such indentured persons, negroes or mulattoes, should become free, the males at the age of twenty-one, the females at the age of eighteen years.

When the resolution declaring the admission of Illinois to the Union was on its passage through the House of Representatives, Mr. Tallmadge, of New York, opposed its adoption on the ground that it contravened the sixth article of the Ordinance. He felt himself constrained to come to the conclusion that the sections of the constitution described above embraced a complete recognition of existing slavery, if not providing for its future introduction and toleration. He contrasted the Illinois and the Indiana Constitutions, to the disadvantage of the former. Thirty-four votes were registered in the House against the resolution.

But the real battle in Illinois followed the constitution. In 1822 Edward Coles was elected Governor of Illinois over three competitors. There were no proper political parties or issues in the State at the time, and elections turned largely on local questions and personal preferences; there was a strong tendency to divide along the slavery-line, but this line was not so tightly drawn as to prevent two pro-slavery candidates from entering the field. Coles was well understood to be an anti-slavery man. The pro-slavery candidates together had 5,302 votes, to 3,332 for all others, and Coles was elected by a plurality of only 50. In his speech to the legislature the Governor spoke of the existence of slavery in the State as a violation of the Ordinance of 1787, and strongly recommended its abolition. He also advised a general revisal of the Black Code of the State. These recommendations led to action very different from what the Governor desired.

Up to this point the pro-slavery men had proceeded upon the theory that the Ordinance must be formally observed until the State was fairly in the Union. They now invented a new theory, or perhaps extended the old one. As developed by a committee of the legislature, this theory was "that the people of Illinois have now the same right to alter their constitution as the people of the State of Virginia, or any other of the original States, and may make any disposition of negro slaves they choose, without any breach of faith or violation of compact, ordinances, or acts of Congress."[1] The slave-owners in the State held their slaves by the various titles that have been described. In 1818 these had been thought sufficient; but now the Governor's bold challenge, and the increase of the "Yankee" population, began to shake their confidence and drive them to the conclusion that nothing short of a constitution sanctioning slavery would make them perfectly safe. Accordingly, the pro-slavery men in the legislature, by resorting to the most flagrant breaches of parliamentary law and of common justice, carried a proposition, by the requisite two-thirds vote of both Houses, to sub-

---

[1] Washburne: Sketch of Edward Coles, 68.

mit the question of a constitutional convention to the people. This proposition was adopted at the winter session, 1822–23; but, fortunately, it could not be voted on until August, 1824. We can glance at only two or three features of the remarkable contest that now followed.

The men who passed through this struggle could hardly find, in after years, language strong enough to describe its violence and bitterness. "Men, women, and children entered the arena of party warfare and strife;" "families and neighborhoods were so divided and furious and bitter against one another, that it seemed a regular civil war might be the result;" "many personal combats were indulged in;" "the press teemed with publications;" "stump orators were invoked;" "the pulpit thundered;" "old friendships were sundered;" "threats of personal violence were frequent;" "pistols and dirks were in great demand;" "the whole people, for the space of months, did scarcely anything but read newspapers, handbills, and pamphlets, quarrel, wrangle, and argue with each other whenever they met together to hear the violent harangues of their orators"—these are excerpts from the accounts that have come down to us. On the pro-slavery side, especially, the campaign was marked by violence, passion, appeals to ignorance and subterfuge, partially relieved by those half-true arguments that have so often done duty in defence of slavery. The social and industrial condition of the State gave that side a great advantage.

"The times were hard. The farmer could find no market for his abundant crops. Manufactures languished, improvements were at a standstill, and the mechanic was without work. The country was cursed by a fluctuating and irredeemable paper currency, which had driven all *real* money out of circulation. The flow of emigration to the State had in a great measure ceased, but a great emigration passed through the State to Missouri. Great numbers of well-to-do emigrants from the slave States, taking with them their slaves, were then leaving their homes to find new ones west of the Mississippi.

When passing through Illinois to their destination, with their well equipped emigrant wagons, drawn by splendid horses, with their retinue of slaves, and with all the lordly airs of that class of slave-holders, they avowed that their only reason for not settling in Illinois was that they could not hold their slaves. This fact had a very great influence, particularly in that part of the State through which the emigration passed, and people denounced the unwise provision of the constitution prohibiting slavery, and thus preventing a great influx of population, to add to the wealth of the State."[1]

From the first, the propagandists fought a losing battle. When the end was finally reached, the vote stood : For a convention, 4,950; against a convention, 6,822—being a majority of 1,872 in a total vote of 11,772. In view of this large majority, the subsequent political history of Illinois for thirty years is very remarkable. The State passed almost at once into the hands of a powerful and violent pro-slavery party, and thus remained until the repeal of the Missouri Compromise brought about a new combination of political forces. But the attempt to enthrone slavery in the citadel of the State Constitution was not renewed.

Generally speaking, the leading free-State men in this extraordinary contest were from the North, the slave-State men from the South. The one shining exception on the free-State side was the incomparable leader, Edward Coles. Born in Albemarle County, Va., in 1784, Governor Coles was one of those gentlemen of cultivation and fortune of whom the Old Dominion, in the last century, produced so many, who profoundly believed American slavery to be an economical mistake, a political evil, and a moral wrong. He belonged to the Virginia school of politics, and saw much public service before removing to the West. Popular in his manners, calm in his judgment and temper, strong in his political and social connections, able and polished in his addresses to his fellow-citizens,

---

[1] Washburne : Sketch of Edward Coles, 132, 133.

easy in his fortune, which he freely used for the public good, making his appeal to the popular reason and conscience rather than to ignorance and passion, the governor of the State, and residing at the capital, where he could make his influence felt—he was the very leader who was needed. To him has always been adjudged the honor of defeating the scheme to make Illinois a slave State. But the further fact must be told, that this statesman and benefactor was the object of an unrelenting persecution from the day that he communicated his views on slavery to the legislature until, shaking the Illinois dust from his feet, he removed to Philadelphia, in 1833. Mr. Coles removed from Virginia to Illinois, because he would not longer consent to live in a slave State. He emancipated his slaves, because he would not longer consent to be the owner of property in man. He took his negroes with him to his new home, taking good care to make suitable provision for their material well-being. In executing this benevolent purpose, he failed to conform to the terms of a law, that had never been published and the existence of which was not commonly known, regulating the residence of free negroes in the State. For this offence he was harassed with litigation, and adjudged to pay a fine of $2,000, which, however, was finally remitted. All in all, it does not seem extravagant to say that Mr. Coles's arrival in the State, in 1819, was more important in its results than the arrival of any other man since Clark summoned Kaskaskia to surrender in 1778.

The slavery struggle in the Northwestern States was watched with keen interest by statesmen at a distance. Albert Gallatin wrote to his Genevan friend Badollet, who had become a citizen of that State : " If you have had a share in preventing the establishment of slavery in Indiana, you will have done more to that part of the country at least than commonly falls to the share of man."[1] And W. H. Crawford of Georgia, himself a slave-holder, cheered the heart of Gov-

---

[1] Cooley: Michigan, 135.

ernor Coles in the Illinois contest with the words: "Is it possible that your convention is intended to introduce slavery into the State? I acknowledge, if I were a citizen, I should oppose it with great earnestness; where it has ever been introduced it is extremely difficult to get rid of and ought to be treated with great delicacy."[1] Other reasons for calling a convention were assigned in the controversy, but slavery was the only real issue.

The attentive reader of the preceding history will not fail to see several places where events might easily have taken some other direction. Nor will he fail to ask, "With what final results?" What if Ohio had formed a slave-State constitution in 1802? What if Illinois had actually made the proposed change in 1824? What would Congress and the Supreme Court, possibly, have done with the hard questions that would have arisen in such a contingency? And if one or both of those States had become slave States, what then? What would have happened if slave-State men had been in a majority in Ohio, Indiana, and Illinois no one can do more than conjecture. Fortunately, at the decisive tests the free-State men were in the majority. Moreover, the Ordinance helped to create that majority as well as to protect it against assault. Governor Reynolds, who had lived in Illinois since 1800 and who was a slave-State man in 1824, although he afterward rejoiced at his own defeat, said, in 1855: "This Act of Congress was the great sheet-anchor that secured the States of Ohio, Indiana, and Illinois from slavery. I never had any doubt but slavery would now exist in Illinois, if it had not been prevented by this famous Ordinance."[2] Never, perhaps, in the history of political controversy was the advantage of winning the victory before the battle was fought more happily illustrated.

In the sixty-two years following the adoption of the National Constitution, eighteen new States were brought into

---

[1] Washburne: Sketch of Governor Coles, 131. [2] My Own Times.

the American Union—nine free and nine slave States. Not only were the numbers of free and slave States equal, but in several instances one of each kind came in together, or nearly so, as though they had been born twins. It has long been the habit, at least in the Northern States, to attribute these so-called "double births" to the management of statesmen, and particularly Southern statesmen, determined to perpetuate the balance of freedom and slavery in the Senate and, as far as possible, in the electoral colleges and in the House of Representatives. It is true that, from the first, there were men who were interested, on general principles, in preserving this balance; true that the Slave Power, after it came upon the scene with distinct ideas and purposes of its own, had no greater interest in any political subject than in this one; also true that, when it became demonstrably apparent, as it did about 1850, that this balance could not be maintained, the more ultra-Southerners began to take new interest in the idea of an independent slave republic. But it is important to observe that the coming of the Slave Power upon the scene with such ideas and purposes was later than the majority of men, prone to carry too far backward the facts with which they are personally familiar, suppose. To fix definitely its arrival may be difficult, or impossible. Certainly, the annexation neither of Louisiana nor of Florida, although the South profited by both, was a Southern measure. Everything considered, the fittest time to fix upon is the demand for the annexation of Texas. But that annexation was as largely the result of Manifest Destiny as of slavery aggression. It is also important to observe that, until the Northern States, like the "frozen North" in the first centuries, burst their barriers, and poured their floods of population into the Lake Basin and the upper parts of the Mississippi Valley, which followed the opening of the great thoroughfares to the West, of which the Erie Canal was the first, the West and the South were much more homogeneous in thought, in temper, and in manners than the West and New England; and, even after that flow began in large volume, the terms "East" and "West" had more political significance than the terms "North" and "South." What was really Western, or, at most, Southern-Western, sentiment has often been taken for the distinct and peculiar sentiment of the South. It is really worth remembering that, when disunion was first heard of, the dividing line proposed ran along the Alleghany Mountains. Witness the letter written by Washington to Governor Harrison in 1784, already quoted from.

The creation of the new free and slave States was due to causes far more powerful than state-craft. In 1787 the Atlantic Plain and the West marched together from the Gulf of Mexico to the Northern Lakes. The northern half of the Plain was free, the southern half slave, soil. The Southern population was inferior in numbers to the Northern population, but it had the advantage of position. As a whole, it was much nearer to the West. Two of the four channels of Western emigration headed within the limits of the South. A third channel, and for a time the most important of all, belonged to the South in common with the North. As a consequence, the two kinds of population, taking a term of years together, reached the Western country in about equal numbers, moving mainly along parallels of latitude. Still further, the line separating free-labor and slave-labor productions, the economical and political consequences of which Professor J. E. Cairnes so clearly pointed out in his "Slave Power," divides the West, as it divides the East, into two nearly equal parts. In this respect, therefore, freedom and slavery had about equal advantages. A still further consideration is, that the cotton-gin and other mechanical inventions enormously increased the demand for cotton about the time that the new lands were laid open to settlement. He who considers all these things, in connection with the facts of Western geography, must see that the expansion of the areas of freedom and of slavery in the United States was due to natural causes, and particularly that the organization and admission of States according to programme, were as much beyond the ken and power of statesmen as the regulation of the tides and eclipses is beyond the power of natural philosophers. There were cases when the admission of States was hastened or retarded somewhat by political management growing out of slavery. But the "balance" theory is wholly at variance with the facts pertaining to the admission of the earlier States. For example, Kentucky came into the Union in 1792, and Tennessee in 1796, each having a population of seventy-five thousand or more. Ohio was admitted in 1803, Indiana in 1816, and Illinois in 1818, each with a population of about forty-five thousand.[1] The reconciliation of the case of Ohio with the "balance" theory, in particular, would require the reversal of all the most important facts connected with its admission.

---

[1] The population of Kentucky in 1790 was 73,677; of Tennessee, in 1790, 35,691; in 1800, 105,602; Ohio, including Michigan, in 1800, 45,365; of Indiana, in 1810, 24,520; in 1820, 147,178; of Illinois, in 1820, 55,162.

XIX.

THE CONNECTICUT WESTERN RESERVE.

ONE effect of the release and cession of Western lands that Connecticut made, September 14, 1786, was to leave her in possession of the territory bounded north by the line of 42° 2', or, rather, the international line, east by the western boundary of Pennsylvania, south by the forty-first parallel, and west by a line parallel with the eastern boundary and distant from it one hundred and twenty miles—supposed, at the time, to be equal in extent to the Susquehanna tract given to Pennsylvania, 1782. Connecticut's claim included both the soil and the jurisdiction. If the territory belonged to her at all, it belonged to her in a sense as full and absolute as any town or county within her present limits. This territory Connecticut was said "to reserve," and it soon came to be called "The Connecticut Western Reserve," "The Western Reserve," etc. These names were popular in their origin, but they were not long in making their way into legal and historical documents. The disposition to be made of these lands became at once an interesting State question.

In October, 1786, a month after the cession, the General Assembly determined to offer the lands lying east of the Cuyahoga and Tuscarawas Rivers for sale. It accordingly directed that they be surveyed into townships six miles square, fixed terms of sale, dedicated five hundred acres in every township to the support of schools and the same quantity to the support of the Gospel, promised two hundred and forty acres, in fee simple, in every township, to the first minister who should settle in it, and guaranteed peace and good order to the settlers under the jurisdiction of the State until it should resign its jurisdiction to Congress and local government be established. Beyond the Salt-springs Tract of 24,000 acres, lying in the Mahoming Valley, sold to General S. H. Parsons, which was not surveyed or settled until many years afterward, nothing was done in pursuance of this legislation.

On May 11, 1792, the General Assembly quit-claimed to the inhabitants of several Connecticut towns who had lost property in consequence of the incursions into the State made by the British troops in the Revolution, or their legal representatives when they were dead, and to their heirs and assigns, forever, 500,000 acres lying across the western end of the Reserve, bounded north by the lake shore, said lands to be divided among the grantees in proportion to their respective losses as found and reported by a committee previously appointed by the assembly. The total number of sufferers, as reported, was 1,870, and the aggregate losses, £161,548 11s. 6½d. The grant was of the soil only. These lands are known in Connecticut history as "The Sufferers' Lands," in Ohio history as "The Fire Lands." In 1796 the Sufferers were incorporated in Connecticut, and in 1803 in Ohio, under the title, "The Proprietors of the Half-million Acres of Land lying south of Lake Erie." In due time the lands were surveyed into one hundred and twenty tracts, each tract being one-fourth of a township, or about four thousand acres.[1] Next, the share-holders were arranged in "classifications," 1, 2, 3, 4, etc., up to 120; each "classification" footing up one one-hundred and twentieth part of the whole stock, or £1,343 7s. The tracts of land were now apportioned to the "classifications" by lot, and a careful registration made of the results. Nothing remained for the share-holders making up a "classification" to do, but to dispose of the tract of land that they had drawn, in any manner agreeable to themselves: To sell it in an

---

[1] There were also some broken tracts that were subdivided, and then added to the 120 to "equalize" them.

undivided form, to divide it among themselves by agreement, or to resort to the courts for proceedings in partition. Connecticut gave no deed to the Fire Lands other than the act of the legislature making the appropriation; and this act, the "classifications," and the record of "drawings," all recorded and made legal evidence by the State, are the ultimate title. An abstract of title, therefore, in Huron or Erie County, O., always begins with a statement of the historical circumstances now recounted. The drawings of the Fire Lands were made November 9, 1808, and their settlement began soon after.

In May, 1793, the Connecticut Assembly offered the remaining part of the Reserve for sale; and in October following it enacted that the moneys received should be a perpetual fund, the interest of which should be appropriated to the several ecclesiastical societies or churches of all denominations in the State, to be by them applied to the support of their respective ministers and schools of education. This legislation caused a profound agitation throughout the State that finally led to its repeal.

In May, 1795, the General Assembly the third time offered the lands for sale. It fixed terms and conditions, appointed a committee to negotiate the sale, and set apart the proceeds as a perpetual fund, the interest of which should be appropriated to the support of schools.[1] In the September

---

[1] The Connecticut School Fund, which amounts to something more than two million dollars, consists wholly of the proceeds of those lands and of capitalized interest. Hon. C. D. Hine, the Secretary of the State Board of Education, questions the current opinion that this fund has promoted the cause of public education. He says:

"The School Fund derived from the sale of Western lands yielded an income last year of $120,855, which amounts to 80 cents for each person of the school-age. The average expense of educating each of these persons throughout the State is $10.31, so that the fund now furnishes about eight per cent. of the total cost. In those towns and cities where the people insist upon good schools, no reliance is placed upon these permanent funds. Indeed, the history of our State shows conclusively that at the time when the fund was most productive, yielding $1.40 or $1.50 for each person of the school-age, and when towns depended upon it,

following this legislation the committee sold the lands in a body, without survey or measurement, to thirty-five purchasers, who severally agreed to pay stipulated sums that, together, made up twelve hundred thousand dollars, the price of the tract agreed upon. The committee made as many deeds as there were purchasers. The deed granted to the purchaser, in behalf of the State of Connecticut, and to his heirs forever, all right, title, and interest, "juridical and territorial," in and to a certain number of twelve hundred-thousandths of the lands described, to be held by the said purchaser as tenant in common of said whole tract or territory with the other purchasers, and not in severalty. The number of undivided shares that each purchaser received was the same as the number of dollars that he had agreed to pay toward the purchase-money. The term "purchaser" is here used in the legal sense; the number of persons interested in the purchase being much larger than the number of purchasers. The sale was made on credit; the purchasers at the time gave their bonds for the amount of the several contracts, with personal security, but afterward they gave mortgages on the lands.

Such are some of the more important facts pertaining to the largest land-sale, so far as the quantity of land sold is concerned, ever made in the State of Ohio. It was a large transaction of any kind for the time. Moreover, it was fol-

---

as they generally did, for the support of their schools, the schools themselves were poor and short. In fact, this was the darkest period of our educational experience. A very striking deterioration took place as soon as the fund became productive and the income began to be distributed. Before that period schools had been maintained at least six months, and at most nearly the whole year, according to the size of the district. After, and not long after, this new source of income was opened, the usual length of schools was reduced to only three months, or just the time that this fund would maintain the schools. The sums which came as gratuities relieved the people of responsibility and deadened their interest, until the schools were continued only so long as the charity lasted. Happily, the danger from this direction is passed and cannot return. The fund has probably reached its greatest productiveness, and the per capita will constantly decrease. The public schools must draw their sustenance from the people who are directly or indirectly benefited by them."—The Nation, No. 1076.

lowed at once by events of far more than a temporary or local interest.

The purchasers of the Reserve, most of them belonging to Connecticut, but some to Massachusetts and New York, were men desirous of trying their fortunes in Western lands. Oliver Phelps, perhaps the greatest land-speculator of the time, was at their head. September 5, 1795, they adopted articles of agreement and association, constituting themselves the Connecticut Land Company. The company was never incorporated, but was what is called to-day a "syndicate." They divided the stock into four hundred shares of $3,000 each. They determined to survey the lands into townships of five miles square. They appointed seven directors and three trustees, with defined powers and functions. In April, 1796, the company adopted a very elaborate method of partitioning the lands. Six townships should be offered for sale for the benefit of the company as such. Four townships should be surveyed into four hundred tracts of one hundred and sixty acres each, to be distributed among the share-holders by lot. The remaining lands should be divided into "equalized" parcels, to be distributed in the same way: (1) A certain number of the best townships should be set apart as standard townships; (2) certain other townships and parts of townships should be cut up into tracts, to be added (3) to the remaining townships to equalize them with the best ones.

In the spring of the same year the directors sent out the first party of surveyors, consisting, all told, of fifty persons. The party assembled at Schenectady, and ascended the Mohawk to Fort Stanwix, whence most of them passed, with the boats and stores, over the portage to Wood Creek, and then down that stream, Oneida Lake, and Oswego River to Lake Ontario; but some made their way by Canandaigua, then the Western outpost of civilization on that route, to Buffalo Creek. The British garrison holding Fort Oswego caused those who went by that route some inconvenience, calling out from one of the surveyors the observation: "Such are the effects of allowing the British Government to exist on the continent of America."[1] At Buffalo the agent bought of the Indians their remaining claim to the lands east of the Cuyahoga River for £500, New York currency in trade, two beef cattle, and one hundred gallons of whiskey. From Buffalo the surveyors made their way westward along the south shore of the lake, reaching the mouth of Conneaut Creek, where they fixed their base of operations, July 4th. Here their first act was to celebrate the twentieth anniversary of American Independence, which they did with much enthusiasm. Two of the toasts ran thus:

"May the Port of Independence [as they christened the place], and the fifty sons and daughters who have entered it this day, be successful and prosperous." "May these sons and daughters multiply in sixteen years sixteen times fifty."[2]

The settlement of the Western Reserve properly dates from this celebration. General Moses Cleaveland, the agent in charge, with a few companions, soon moved on to the west, reaching the mouth of the Cuyahoga River, July 22d, from which day there have always been white men on the site of the city that takes its name from him.[3]

The western boundary of Pennsylvania, as run ten years before, and the parallel forty-one degrees north, now run for the first time, were the base-lines of the survey.[4] The courses

---

[1] Whittlesey: Early History of Cleveland, 174.

[2] Whittlesey: Early History of Cleveland, 182. In 1810 the population of the Reserve was 16,092.

[3] "It was in 1830 that a newspaper called The Cleveland Advertiser was established. In preparing to issue the first number, the editor discovered that the heading was too long to fit the form, and so, in order to adjust it, he dropped out the letter 'a' in the first syllable of the word 'Cleaveland,' and made it read 'Cleveland.' The public at once accepted this change in orthography."—Rice: Sketches of Western Life, 23.

[4] The western boundary of Pennsylvania has an interesting history. As early as the troubles with Virginia, the question arose, "From what point on the Delaware shall the five degrees of longitude be measured?" A glance at the map will show that different answers to this question would materially affect the State's westward extension. Messrs. Tilghman and Allen, the Pennsylvania

north and south were called "ranges;" east and west, "townships." Cleveland is in No. 7 in range 12; that is, the seventh township counting from the southern boundary, and the twelfth counting from the eastern one. It was several years before the surveys were finished. The lands and other property of the company were drawn in four drafts—in 1798, 1802, 1807, and 1809. The trustees, to whom all the lands had been deeded by the share-holders, in trust, in 1795, made the deeds; and with the last draft the company was dissolved, having been in existence fourteen years.

As a land-speculation, the purchase of the Reserve was unfortunate. In 1795 the ideas concerning the southern shore of Lake Erie, dating from the old French days, had not been corrected; and the company supposed they were buying 4,000,000 acres of land. The survey proved that they had bought less than 3,000,000 acres.[1] Instead of thirty

---

commissioners sent to Williamsburg in 1774, proposed that Mason and Dixon's line be run to a point five degrees from the river, and that from this point a series of zigzag lines be run northward, "similar to the courses of the Delaware." Lord Dunmore replied that the Crown could not have intended such a boundary as this, because it was so "very inconvenient." The agreement of 1779 provided that Mason and Dixon's line should be run west five degrees from the river, and that a meridian line drawn from this point should be the western boundary of Pennsylvania. This meridian line was run in 1785 and 1786, Andrew Ellicott being the chief engineer. The line between Ohio and Pennsylvania was re-run and re-marked by a joint State commission, beginning in 1878. Virginia really fought the battle of Ohio against Pennsylvania. If the "zigzag" plan had been adopted, or if a meridian boundary had been run five degrees west of the westernmost point of the Delaware, Ohio would have shown very differently upon the map from what it does. The survey of parallel forty-one degrees was not completed till 1806. The line departs slightly from the true parallel as it runs westward; but the Surveyor-General advised in 1810 that it be not disturbed. See Chapman: The French in the Alleghany Valley, 197 et seq. Report of the joint commission appointed by the States of Pennsylvania and Ohio to ascertain and re-mark the boundary-line between said States. Whittlesey: Western Reserve Historical Society, Tract No. 61. Historical Collections of the Mahoning Valley, I., 517 et seq.

[1] The precise quantity of land in the purchase is matter of dispute. Perhaps 2,837,109 acres is the best estimate. The same authority makes the whole Reserve consist of 3,333,699 acres. Whittlesey, 258, 259.

cents an acre, they had paid more than forty cents. The expenses of the survey were much heavier than the company anticipated. And, finally, a jurisdictional question, having its origin in the charter of 1662, caused them much vexation and pecuniary loss, and even threatened to deprive them of the property altogether.

The troubles of the Land Company began almost with its existence. It will be remembered that the State had sold to the company the juridical and territorial right, as well as the soil, of the tract. For a State to alienate the jurisdiction of one-half its territory to a company of land-speculators that never rose to the dignity of a body corporate and politic was certainly a remarkable proceeding. Whether the subject attracted much attention at the time, and, if so, what was the current theory of jurisdiction, are questions very difficult to answer. Colonel Charles Whittlesey, who studied the early history of the Western Reserve with great care, and who was himself a part of that history, remarks, touching this feature of the transaction: "So little was known at this time of the respective powers of the State and of the United States, under the Constitution of 1787, that many of the parties thought the Land Company had received political authority, and could found here a new State. They imagined themselves, like William Penn, to be proprietors, coupled with the rights of self-government." He says, also, that both parties to the transaction "imagined that the deed of Connecticut conveyed powers of civil government to the company, and that the grantees might organize a new State;" but adds that "the United States objected to this mode of setting up States." Whittlesey also speaks as though the establishment of a new State by the company was, at one time, a settled purpose. New Connecticut was to be governed from Hartford, as New England had been by the Council of Plymouth, in England.[1]

---

[1] Early History of Cleveland, 167, 168; Early Civil Jurisdiction on the South Shore of Lake Erie, 4.

A new State was certainly in the air in 1796. The second of the toasts drunk, in "several pails of grog," at the Conneaut celebration of the Fourth of July was: "The State of New Connecticut." But what part the company expected to play in establishing the new State is not very clear. If it ever imagined itself clothed with juridical and territorial powers, it soon dismissed such a thought.

By 1800 as many as twenty or thirty settlements had been begun on the Reserve. The census of that year reports a population of 1,302 souls. These facts point to a society, young and small, indeed, but active and growing, transacting the business incident to their condition, and accustomed, withal, to the forms and machinery of legal government. Lands were bought and sold; contracts relating to personal services were entered into; marriages were solemnized in various places. But there was no government whatever; no laws or records, no magistrates or police. The people were thoroughly trained in civil obedience; they were orderly and fully competent to govern themselves; and yet, in those three or four years, the need of civil institutions began to be severely felt. The lack of records, in particular, was a source of much embarrassment.

It is impossible to state whether the relation of the Connecticut Reserve to the Territory Northwest of the River Ohio was considered in 1787 or not; but Governor St. Clair included all that part of it lying east of the Cuyahoga River in Washington County, organized July 26, 1788. In 1796 he included the whole Reserve in Wayne County, the county seat of which was Detroit. Once more, July 29, 1797, he included the eastern part in Jefferson County. St. Clair proceeded upon the theory that his jurisdiction extended over lands that had not been ceded to the United States, as well as over lands that had been ceded; and perhaps this was the natural view for him to take, since the Ordinance of 1787 made no discrimination. But it was a view that necessarily brought on a collision with the Reserve settlers. The erection of Jefferson County coincided with the arrival of settlers on the soil, and so became the occasion of the collision.

General Parsons caused his deed of the Salt-springs Tract to be recorded at Marietta. Some of those who bought parts of the tract from him did the same. A few deeds were also recorded at Steubenville, the county seat of Jefferson County. But the people of the Reserve, with practical unanimity, denied the Territorial jurisdiction. The Jefferson County authorities sent an agent to inquire into the matter of taxation; but the settlers laughed at him, and he returned to Steubenville no richer and no wiser than he came. The laughter showered upon the unfortunate tax-gatherer signified much more than the familiar disposition to avoid the payment of taxes. No further attempt was made to extend the Territorial jurisdiction over the Reserve until some very important legislation had been enacted in Philadelphia and in Hartford.

The settlers resisted the authority of the Territory, and so of the United States, in the name of the State of Connecticut. Ostensibly, they were defending the right and dignity of that ancient commonwealth. But the State herself was indifferent to the controversy. She even refused to assert her jurisdiction when the Land Company importuned her to do so. Having divested herself of the territory, she apparently took little further interest in the subject.

On January 27, 1797, only a few days after the first party of surveyors returned from the Reserve, the stockholders of the company, at a meeting held in Hartford, instructed the directors and trustees to make application to the General Assembly at the next ensuing session for an act erecting the Western Reserve into an entire and distinct county, "with proper and suitable laws, to regulate the internal policy of said territory for a limited term of time, and the same to be administered at the sole expense of proprietors."[1] Presumably, such an application was made, but the

---

[1] The quotations from the proceedings of the stock-holders are made from The Book of Drafts, in the records of Trumbull County, Ohio.

General Assembly took no such action. It did not care to repeat, upon a more distant field, the Westmoreland experiment. This was the first of several distinct calls that the Land Company made upon the State to exercise the juridical and territorial right that she had formally laid aside.

In October, 1797, the stock-holders gave the directors and trustees "full authority to pursue such measures as they deemed best calculated to procure legal and practical government over the territory belonging to the company." A new tack was now taken. The Connecticut Assembly passed an act authorizing its Senators in Congress to execute, in the name of the State, a deed releasing to the United States the jurisdiction of the Reserve. On January 12, 1798, Mr. Tracy moved, in the Senate, the appointment of a committee to take into consideration the acceptance of such a cession. At the next session of Congress the Senate, after mature deliberation, passed a bill to that effect, but the House of Representatives postponed it, and the measure fell.

Meantime the company was calling for help more and more loudly. On January 22, 1798, the stock-holders voted that if Congress should agree to accept from the company their juridical right to the Western Reserve, then application should be made to Governor St. Clair to erect all that part of it to which the Indian title had been extinguished into an entire and distinct county in the Northwest Territory. At the next meeting, held in October, 1798, the stock-holders instructed the directors to appoint an agent "to proceed on Philadelphia" to facilitate the acceptance of the jurisdiction. They voted, also, that in case the application to Congress should fail, then the directors should "pursue the petition of the company now pending before the General Assembly of the State, at their next session." In May, 1799, the stock-holders spoke again, and more distinctly than ever.

"Voted, that the trustees and directors be authorized, and they are hereby requested, to make out and lay before the

General Assembly of the State, now in session, a statement in writing of the measures taken by the Company before Congress at their last session in endeavoring to obtain an acceptance of the cession of the jurisdiction of the Western Reserve. Also a statement of the sums of money actually expended by the Company in surveying lands, cutting roads, and erecting mills. Also the probable sums disbursed by individuals in making improvements in different parts of the Reserve the last and present years. Also state the difficulty of making any sales of the lands by the proprietors and enforcing a payment of sales already made arising from the want of government in and over the territory."

And at still another meeting the directors were instructed to represent to the assembly the ill success of the application to Congress, the continued embarrassed situation of the stockholders' property, the difficulty of raising money out of the land, and to pray the assembly to extend government over the territory until Congress should accept the cession of jurisdiction, or to grant such other relief as they should think proper.

Nothing could mark the desperation of the Land Company's situation more distinctly than these votes. The stockholders fly from the assembly to Congress, and from Congress to the assembly. Men desiring Western lands would hesitate to purchase in a district where there was no government, and particularly where the right to govern was in dispute. Men owning lands would hesitate to sell so long as payment could not be enforced. But all this time there was an authority standing ready to extend itself, at a moment's notice, over the Reserve. All that the Land Company and the settlers had to do was to let their wants be known to Governor St. Clair. Connecticut did not restrain them in the least. Perhaps the company and the settlers would have applied to him for relief had it not been for a question that is never for a moment admitted into the minutes of the company's proceedings, but that the man attempting to write the civil history of the Western Reserve must bring into the foreground, viz., the insufficiency of the Connecticut title to the soil and its relation to the jurisdiction.

The history of the Northwestern cessions need not be again recited at length. But it is important to observe that the validity of all the Western land-claims had been by many denied; that the lands ceded and the lands reserved by Connecticut had all been claimed by New York and Virginia; that the acceptance of the partial cession made by Connecticut in 1786 had been strongly opposed in Congress, on the ground that such acceptance would be a guarantee of the reservation; and that, in consequence, a cloud rested on the title to the Reserve. The situation was perfectly understood at the time the sale and purchase were made. The State only quit-claimed to the Land Company her own right and title to the territory, and received a consideration from the company that was graduated with reference to the title. The change of owners excited new doubts rather than allayed old ones. The survey of the lands, the inflow of population, and the attempt to embrace the Reserve in the Territorial jurisdiction kept the subject before men's minds. Thus, the original doubt as to the title tended to cast a shadow on every land-transaction within the district. These facts do not appear in the minutes of the stock-holders' meetings; but the question whether the company could make valid titles caused as much difficulty in making sales of lands as the want of a government to protect society and to enforce contracts. Furthermore, Connecticut held the soil before 1795 by the same title that she held the jurisdiction; and if the jurisdiction was in the United States after 1786, then the ownership of the soil was there too. Accordingly, the extension of the Territorial Government over the Reserve was a real, though not an intended, menace to the Connecticut title that the company and the settlers alike could do no less than resist. The company's situation was, therefore, much more serious than the resolutions quoted above imply. It needed to have the question of ownership settled as much as it needed to have a government established.

What the terms of the Senate bill of 1798-99 were is known only inferentially. The title shows that it authorized the acceptance by the United States, from the State of Connecticut, of a cession of the jurisdiction over the Reserve. It must also have contained a cession by the United States to the State of Connecticut of the soil of the Reserve. Without such a guarantee, the position of the company as to titles would have been weakened rather than strengthened, and perhaps subverted altogether.

On February 18, 1800, Mr. Brace, of Connecticut, offered in the House of Representatives a resolution creating a committee to take into consideration the expediency of accepting the cession of jurisdiction. A few days later such a committee was appointed, with John Marshall, of Virginia, soon afterward made Chief Justice of the United States, as chairman. Marshall's report covers five of the ample pages of the "State Papers."[1] More than three-fourths of this report is a mere transcript of one made to the Senate the year before by Mr. Reed; but, since it had Marshall's approval and was the basis of the subsequent action of Congress, it is the most authoritative paper ever devoted to the discussion of Connecticut's title to the lands within her charter-limits west of Pennsylvania. It recites the history of the charters from 1606 to 1664; considers the controversy between England and France, closed by the treaty of 1763; mentions the Quebec Act; recounts the boundary-disputes between Connecticut and New York, and Connecticut and Pennsylvania; relates the history of the cessions, followed by the acts of the Connecticut Legislature pertaining to the Reserve, and the sale to the Land Company. The company have paid $100,000 of interest on the purchase-money, and expended $80,000 on the survey and various improvements. Thirty-five settlements have been

---

[1] Public Lands, I., 94.

made, containing a population of about a thousand people. The dilemma of the company is stated in a single sentence: " As the purchasers of the land commonly called the Connecticut Reserve hold their title under the State of Connecticut, they cannot submit to the government established by the United States in the Northwestern Territory, without endangering their titles, and the jurisdiction of Connecticut could not be extended over them without much inconvenience." The report closes with the declaration that, in the opinion of the committee, the offer of the jurisdiction ought to be accepted on the terms and conditions specified in the accompanying bill. The aim throughout is to establish the validity of the Connecticut title. Connecticut is seized of the jurisdiction; she could set up a government on the Reserve if she chose to do so; it is far better to merge the jurisdiction in the Northwest Territory—such is the logic of the report.

The bill as passed authorized the President, in the name and in behalf of the United States, to execute and deliver to the Governor of Connecticut letters patent whereby the right, title, interest, and estate of the United States to the territory commonly called the Western Reserve should be released and conveyed to the said Governor and his successors in office, " for the purpose of quieting the grantees and purchasers under said State of Connecticut, and confirming their titles to the soil of the said tract of land;" *provided, however*, that Connecticut should, within eight months from the passage of the act, by a legislative act, renounce forever all territorial and jurisdictional claims whatever to the soil and jurisdiction of any and all lands lying westward, southwestward, and northwestward of the eastern line of the State of New York, as ascertained by the agreement of 1733 between New York and Connecticut, excepting from such renunciation only the Western Reserve; *provided, further*, that the State of Connecticut should also, within eight months, execute and deliver to the President a deed expressly releasing to the United States the jurisdictional claim of the said State of Connecticut to the Reserve; *provided, also,* that this act shall not " be construed to pledge the United States for extinguishment of the Indian title to the said lands, or further than merely to pass the title of the United States thereto." Another proviso was added, on motion of Mr. Gallatin, that the act should not be construed in any manner to question the conclusive settlement of the dispute between Pennsylvania and Connecticut by the Federal Court at Trenton in 1782.

This bill was vehemently opposed in both Houses of Congress. Mr. Cooper, of New York, first moved to postpone it until the next session, and then to amend it in such a way as to make it obnoxious to the Pennsylvania members. Mr. Elmendorf, of the same State, also moved an amendment in the spirit of obstruction. Mr. Marshall made a lengthy speech in favor of the bill and against the Elmendorf amendment. Mr. Randolph and Mr. Nicholas, both of Virginia, made long speeches against the "principle of the bill." Elmendorf argued at great length against the validity of Connecticut's claim to the lands, and Mr. Bird, of New York, and Mr. Randolph followed on the same side. The bill passed the House —ayes, 54; nays, 36. In the Senate an amendment to make the execution and delivery of the letters patent contingent upon a decision by the Supreme Court of the United States affirming the validity of the Connecticut claim, was lost—ayes, 10; nays, 15. The bill passed the Senate—ayes, 15; nays, 10. President Adams's approval, given April 28, 1800, made the bill a law.

The questions arise: "Why such a determined opposition to this measure?" "What objection could be urged against a bill that seems so reasonable and so necessary?" Not a scrap of the speeches made on either side has been preserved, and the entries in the "Journals" and the "Annals" are always brief, and often obscure. At the same time, there is no difficulty in reading between the lines the general grounds of objection.

There was no reason why the surrender and acceptance

of the jurisdiction should provoke opposition; nor did it. It was the release and conveyance to Connecticut of the right, title, interest, and estate of the United States that made all the trouble. Marshall's report was written to establish the validity of Connecticut's claim, and the bill proposed, virtually, to guarantee that claim. It could be argued, in opposition, that the lands in question belonged to the United States: (1) Because the British Crown had ceded them in 1783; or (2) because New York had ceded them in 1781; or (3) because Virginia had ceded them in 1784. A certain temptation to deny the Connecticut title, and to hold that the lands were a part of the national domain, arose from their commercial value. Then an objector might argue that, since the cession and the reservation of 1786 were final, and since both the soil and the jurisdiction belonged to Connecticut, Congress had nothing to do with the matter; and that the State, the Land Company, and the settlers must get out of their troubles the best way they could. It could also be objected that the passing of a title from the Nation to the State was unnecessary, because if Connecticut owned the jurisdiction she also owned the soil. Marshall's report and the accompanying bill were not logically consistent. The more cogently Marshall reasoned to show the validity of the Connecticut title, the more conclusively did he prove that it was unnecessary for Congress to release the soil. If the United States owned the soil she also owned the jurisdiction, and if Connecticut owned the jurisdiction she, or those to whom she had released it, also owned the soil. The Land Company's resolutions speak of surrendering the jurisdiction and of the establishment of government; the quieting act proposes to surrender the title of the United States to the soil on certain terms and conditions, one of which is the surrender of jurisdiction. Moreover, Congress, by releasing its right and title to Connecticut, would, by implication, deny that either New York or Virginia had ceded the Reserve, and so deny that either of them had any right or title to it previous to its cession. Furthermore, since New York's title was later than Connecticut's, this, in effect, would be holding that New York's whole Western claim, from the Lakes to the Cumberland Mountains, had been baseless. New York and Virginia had now no more pecuniary interest in the question at issue than any other States, but they would naturally resent any action on the part of Congress that threatened to invalidate their historical position. A denial of New York's claim to the Western Reserve would be a denial of her claim to all the Western lands whatsoever. Moreover, such denial would really extend as far east as the Delaware River, for that river was the eastern boundary of the original Western claims of Massachusetts and Connecticut. Such denials could indeed no longer have any practical bearing, since these points of controversy had been adjusted, but it would still be a reflection upon New York's original title that her representatives would be apt to repel. Then the guarantee of the Reserve to Connecticut would be very galling to Virginia; for the Old Congress had stubbornly refused to guarantee her claims southeast of the Ohio River. And, finally, the bill was based on a new principle; hitherto Congress had never, in a single instance, strengthened the Western title of a State growing out of the old charters.

Within the compass of the foregoing remarks, no doubt, the objections to the quieting act of 1800 lay.[1]

---

[1] The quieting act had been anticipated. On the day that Congress accepted the Connecticut cession, Mr. Wilson, of Pennsylvania, made a motion, that was lost, declaring that Congress could not accept it, since to do so would be a ratification of the part not ceded but reserved, and closing with this resolution, which once more stirs the embers of old controversies :

"*Resolved*, . . . that when the State of Connecticut shall cede and release to the United States, and to the States of New York and Pennsylvania, respectively, all the claim of the said State of Connecticut to jurisdiction and property of territory westward of the eastern boundary of the State of New York, the United States in Congress assembled will thereupon grant, release and confirm to the State of Connecticut, the property, but not the jurisdiction of the territory and tract or land described as follows" [then describing the reservation].

The geographical distribution of the opposition to this act throws light upon its animus. The attacks upon the bill in the House of Representatives were made by Bird, Cooper, and Elmendorf, of New York; and by John Nicholas and John Randolph, of Virginia. Of New York's ten votes eight were thrown against the bill, and none for it. Of the twelve Virginia votes the bill received but three. Pennsylvania gave ten of her twelve votes for the bill, and none against it. But Pennsylvania had never been a claimant State, and had no State dignity to uphold. It might, perhaps, be expected that Massachusetts would be disinclined to see the seal of congressional approval set on the Connecticut claim, but she had never claimed the Reserve, or any part of it, as both the other States had done. Many of her people were seeking homes on the Reserve, some members of the Land Company were Massachusetts men, and she would naturally be influenced more or less by good neighborhood. Massachusetts gave fourteen votes for the bill. In the Senate, not a vote for the measure came from either New York or Virginia.

Finally, it is not impossible that there was a partisan animus in the opposition; Connecticut was strongly Federalist in politics, while most of the opposition belonged to the Jeffersonian school.

The General Assembly of Connecticut promptly complied with the conditions of the quieting act. It passed an act renouncing the State's claims to all lands lying west of the boundary-line between Connecticut and New York as agreed upon in 1733, except the Reserve, both soil and jurisdiction, and authorizing and directing the Governor of the State to execute and deliver to the President of the United States a deed conveying to the United States the jurisdiction of the Reserve. On May 30, 1800, Governor Trumbull performed this duty, and soon after President Adams executed and delivered letters patent releasing all the right, claim, and interest of the United States to the soil. The renunciation of the State's claim to all lands west of the line of 1733, except the Reserve, was a surrender of the "Gore" to New York, and it brought to a sudden end the suits that holders of the Ward and Halsey titles had brought in the Circuit Court of the United States to eject the occupants with New York titles. Such was the solution of the last puzzle growing out of the from-sea-to-sea charters.

The longer one looks into the situation of the Connecticut Land Company from 1797 to 1800 the more trying he sees it to have been. The interest was running on their obligations, but they could not effect sales, or could effect but few. Then, when the subject was finally brought forward in Congress, there was abundant opportunity for constitutional metaphysics and legal hair-splitting. Logically inconsistent as were the two principles of the quieting act, and reversing as that act did the policy of the Old Congress, it gave the State of Connecticut, the Land Company, and the people of the Reserve, a happy escape from difficulties that were already serious, and that threatened grave disaster. The act is a good example of the Anglo-Saxon habit of disregarding logical refinements and legal technicalities and of pursuing the direct common-sense road to a just end. It could have been successfully defended on broad grounds of public policy. The foremost champion of the act was John Marshall; and when we recall that he was a Virginian, and that he had great influence in the House of Representatives, particularly on legal questions, it does not seem too much to say that the Western Reserve is indebted to him for the institution of civil government and for a perfect system of land-titles. At all events, Marshall's name is connected with its history in an interesting way.

On July 10, 1800, Governor St. Clair issued a proclamation constituting the whole Reserve a county, with the name of Trumbull. Rather, he bounded the county on the north by the parallel 42° 2' north latitude, which was carrying it some distance beyond the international boundary-line and invading the British dominions. Next, the Governor appointed a probate judge and justices of the quorum for the new county. The first Court of Quarter Sessions sat at Warren, the county seat, on the fourth Monday of August, 1800, at which time the county was organized. The first election was held at the same place on the second Tuesday of October, when the electors of the county, by thirty-eight votes out of forty-two, chose a representative in the Territorial Legislature. Civil government on the Western Reserve was at last established. The first act in the long series leading to its establishment was performed at Whitehall, in 1662, by the third Stuart; the last act, at Warren, O., in 1800, by the forty-two backwoods electors.

The development of the Western Reserve has been as gratifying as its beginning was discouraging. Its area is about five thousand square miles, its population about six hundred thousand souls. It is a trifle larger than Connecticut, but has a somewhat smaller population.[1] No other five thousand square miles of territory in the United States, lying in a body outside of New England, ever had, to begin with, so pure a New England population. No similar territory west of the Alleghany Mountains has so impressed the brain and conscience of the country. No other district gives so fine an opportunity to study the development of the New England character under Western conditions. In externals, the colonists, a majority of whom came from Connecticut, reproduced New England in Northeastern Ohio. It has long been remarked that, in some respects, the Western Reserve is more New England than New England herself. Mr. John Fiske found the illustration that he wanted of an early feature of English life in Euclid Avenue, Cleveland.[2] There is also an undeniable continuity of intellectual and moral life. But the southern shore of Lake Erie is not the northern

---

[1] The population of the Reserve in 1880 was 536,832; of Connecticut, 622,700.
[2] American Political Ideas, 22.

shore of Long Island Sound; New Connecticut is not a reproduction of Old Connecticut.

The position of Connecticut in history is a most honorable one, quite disproportionate to her territorial area, or to the numbers of her population. Far should it be from a man of Connecticut descent to speak slightingly of the commonwealth of his fathers. But the Connecticut of 1796 was dominated by class influences and ideas; a heavy mass of political and religious dogma rested upon society; an inveterate conservatism fettered both the actions and the thoughts of men. The church and the town were but different sides of the same thing. The town was a close corporation; and the man who did not belong to it, either by birth or formal naturalization, could be a resident of it only on sufferance. The yearly inauguration of the governor is said to have been "an occasion of solemn import and unusual magnificence." Connecticut Federalism was the most ironclad variety anywhere to be found, unless in Delaware. In 1804 the General Court impeached several justices of the peace who had the temerity to attend a Jeffersonian convention in New Haven. Mechanics were accounted "vulgar;" farming was the "respectable" calling; "leading men" had an extraordinary influence; and "old families" were the pride and the weakness of their respective localities. The militia captain and the deacon were local magnates. Congregationalism was an established religion; and how restive the Episcopalians, the Baptists, the Sandemanians, the Methodists, and other dissenting churches, and men of no church, were, under its reign, a glance through a file of old Connecticut newspapers will show. For years the General Assembly refused to charter Episcopalian and Methodist colleges. President Quincy paints this picture of a Sabbath morning in Andover, Mass.:

"The whole space before the meeting house was filled with a waiting, respectful, and expecting multitude. At the moment of service, the pastor issued from his mansion, with Bible and manuscript sermon under his arm, with his wife leaning on one arm, flanked by his negro man on his side, as his wife was by her negro woman, the little negroes being distributed, according to their sex, by the side of their respective parents. Then followed every other member of the family according to age and rank, making often, with family visitants, somewhat of a formidable procession. As soon as it appeared, the congregation, as if led by one spirit, began to move towards the door of the church, and before the procession reached it all were in their places. As soon as the pastor entered, the whole congregation rose and stood until he was in the pulpit and his family were seated. At the close of the service the congregation stood until he and his family had left the church. Forenoon and afternoon the same course of proceeding was had."[1]

Of course, such magnificence as this was unusual; but the passage well marks the awful consequence with which the New England mind, in that period, invested the parson. All the conservatism of Connecticut rallied around the venerable charter of 1662, holding it as sacred as the Trojans ever held the Palladium; and the party which broke down the charter and set up the constitution of 1818 were called "The Tolerationists."

It is plain that at the close of the last century Connecticut had shelled over. While a desire to break through this shell was the motive that sent many a man and family to the West, the whole emigration still brought much of the old conservatism and dogma to Ohio. But these people had not been long in their new home before they began to feel the throbbings of a new life, and they soon began to do things that in their old home they would never have dreamed of doing. As early as 1832, President Storrs and his assistants in the faculty of Western Reserve College were preaching and lecturing against slavery, at Hudson. Those sermons and lectures were the real beginning of anti-slavery propa-

---

[1] North American Review, No. CCL., 13, 14.

gandism in Northern Ohio. How much the anti-slavery men of the East counted upon Storrs's co-operation is shown by Whittier's pathetic elegy written on Storrs's too early death. Early in its history, the name of Oberlin became synonymous with Abolitionism throughout the country. Giddings upheld anti-slavery principles in Congress when there was none but John Quincy Adams to support him. Full fifty years ago the Reserve had a more definite anti-slavery character than any other equal extent of territory in the United States. A liberalizing tendency may also be traced in religion. The Calvinistic rigidity of the churches was softened. The new theology sounded out from Oberlin, while that seat of learning was still hidden in the woods, was even more hateful to New England orthodoxy than the new theology sounded out from Andover is to-day. Dissenting bodies, as they would have been in Connecticut—Baptists, Methodists, and Disciples—gained a foothold and multiplied in numbers. And the same in education. Men on whom the awful shadow of Yale and Harvard had fallen, begun at Oberlin the first collegiate co-education experiment tried in the world. Both at Oberlin and at Hudson the finality of the old educational rubrics was denied, and new studies were introduced into the curricula. The common school, the academy, the college, the church, the newspaper, the debating society, and the platform stimulated the mental and moral life of the people to the utmost. The Reserve came to have a character all its own. Men with "new ideas" hastened to it as to a seed-bed. Men with "reforms" and "causes" to advocate found a willing audience. Later years have brought new elements; but to-day the mail clerks on the Lake Shore Railroad are compelled to quicken their motions the moment they enter its borders from either east or west. Adapting the language that General J. D. Cox once used, there are in Northeastern Ohio the straits in a great moral Gulf Stream. Between Lake Erie and the Ohio, from Pittsburg to Chicago, has been compressed a human tide fed by the overflow of New England, the Middle

States, and Europe. Beyond Lake Michigan this stream widens out, fan-like, northwest and southwest, from Manitoba to the Arkansas River; and breaks over the ridges of the Rocky Mountains in streams that reach the Pacific Coast. Wherever it has gone this stream has carried the thought-seeds gathered from the banks of the straits through which it rushes.[1] But the Reserve has been conservative as well as radical. Since Elisha Whittlesey took his seat, in 1828, the Nineteenth Ohio Congressional District has been represented in Congress by but five men. In 1872 the greatest of these five men, in addressing the convention that had just nominated him for the sixth time, said for more than half a century the people of the district had held and expressed bold and independent opinions on all public questions, yet they had never asked their representative to be the mere echo of the party voice. They supported and defended their representative in maintaining an independent position in the National Legislature, and whenever he acted with honest and intelligent courage in the interests of truth, they generously sustained him even when he differed from them in minor matters of opinion and policy.[2] The old charge of "'isms" and "extravagance" cannot be wholly denied; but, on the whole, the plain people, while throwing much of the New England ballast overboard, and crowding their canvas, have held the rudder so true as to avoid dangerous extremes. The historian finds small occasion to defend them on the ground that somewhat of folly and fanaticism always attend a people's emancipation.

---

[1] The Oberlin Jubilee, 290, 291.
[2] Garfield: Works, IL, 30, 31.

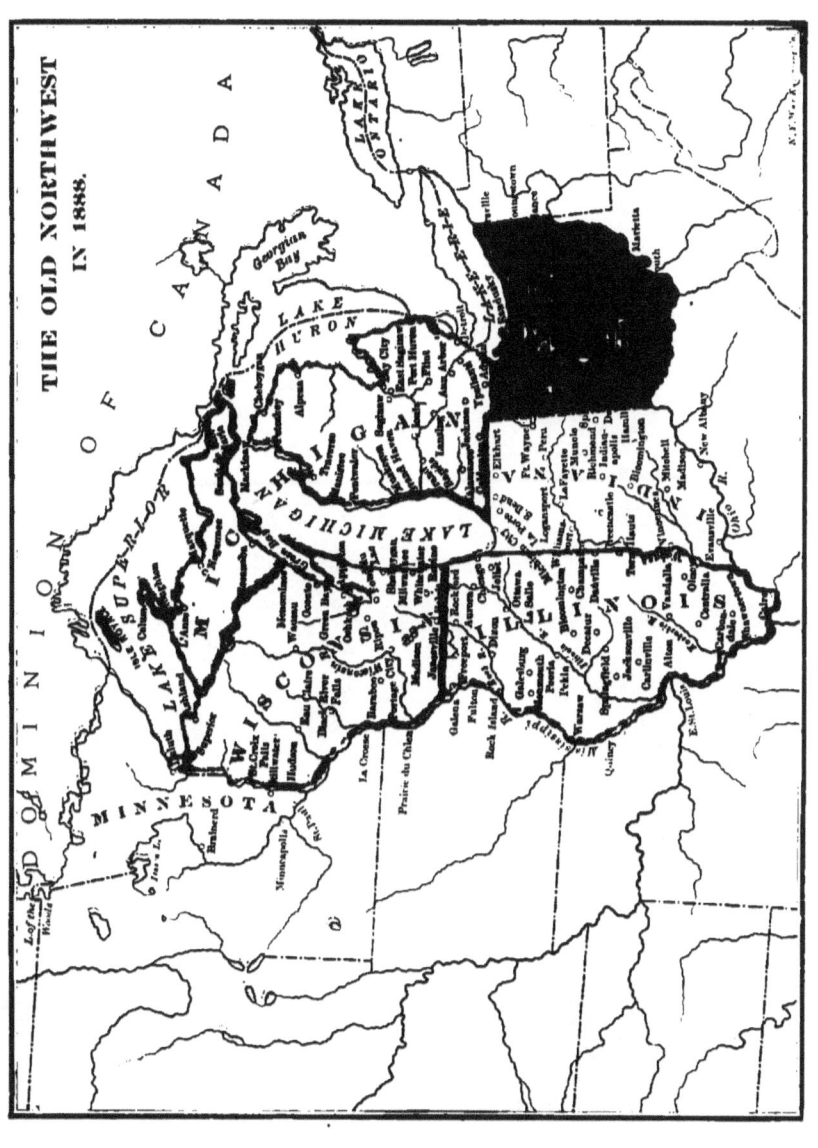

XX.
A CENTURY OF PROGRESS.

CHARLES SUMNER once gathered, in a celebrated article, some of the happier prophecies concerning America.[1] He might have made a similar collection of the less happy ones, that would have been quite as instructive and more curious. Had he done so, he might have come upon some of the following about the Great West.

Few of Dr. Franklin's contemporaries had his grasp of the Western question. But even Franklin's prescience was not equal to his subject. He saw that east of the Mississippi and south of the Lake and the St. Lawrence there was room enough for a hundred millions of people; "but this must take some centuries to fulfil." When the question of fixing a permanent seat of government was under discussion in Congress, in 1789, much was said of the centre of population. Mr. Goodhue, of Massachusetts, said he believed this centre "would not vary considerably for ages yet to come, because he supposed it would constantly increase more toward the Eastern and manufacturing States than toward the Southern and agricultural ones," not taking the West into account at all. At that time the centre of population was twenty-five miles east of Baltimore; and little did the men who took part in that debate dream that it would move steadily westward along the thirty-ninth parallel at the nearly uniform rate of five miles a year, and that, in a century, it would be much nearer the Mississippi River than the Alleghany Mountains. Fisher Ames said, in the same debate, that when "the

---

[1] Prophetic Voices about America, the Atlantic Monthly, XX., 275.

almost immeasurable wilderness" of the Ohio would be settled, or how it could possibly be governed, was "past calculation;" that it was "romantic" to make the decision of the capital question turn upon that circumstance; and that it would be near a century before the people of that region would be considerable. In 1825 Mr. Dickerson, of New Jersey, discussing in the Senate the occupation of Oregon, said the territory could never be a State in the Union, and went into an elaborate calculation to prove the physical impossibility of a man's representing the Valley of the Columbia in Congress, since he would be the whole year, travelling at the rate of thirty miles a day, making the overland journey to Washington and back; and affirmed that it would be more expeditious to double Cape Horn or to pass through the Arctic Ocean. "It is true," he added, "this passage is not yet discovered, except upon our maps, but it will be as soon as Oregon shall be a State." If any man had a large conception of the West, it was Henry Clay, yet Mr. Clay said, in 1832: "We may anticipate that long, if not centuries, after the present day, the representatives of our children's children may be deliberating in the halls of Congress on laws relating to the public lands." Even men who have lived in an age of wonders often think that wonders will cease with them. Defending the Treaty of Washington, in 1846, Daniel Webster said: "We have heard a vast deal lately of the commercial value of the River Columbia and its occupation; but I will undertake to say that for all purposes of human use the St. Johns is worth a hundred times as much as the Columbia is, or ever will be." We wonder at such feeble prophecies; but, although we have seen the progress that so far outran the highest anticipations of our fathers—a progress each decade of which has been a new morn risen on high noon—our own visions of the next century may fall as far short of the reality. The possibilities of the United States, and particularly of the Great West, under a free and stable government, in an age of stupendous material development, defied the forecast of the wisest statesmen.

A CENTURY OF PROGRESS.

TABLE SHOWING THE POPULATION OF THE NORTHWESTERN STATES, THE PER CENT. OF INCREASE, THEIR RANK AMONG THE STATES OF THE UNION, AND THE NUMBER OF PEOPLE TO A SQUARE MILE, FOR THE CENSUS YEARS 1800-1880.

	Ohio.	Indiana.	Illinois.	Michigan.	Wisconsin.	Total of five States.	Total, United States.
1800.							
Population	42,161	2,517	2,457	3,757	115	51,007	5,308,483
Per cent. of increase							
Rank	18	21	22				
Number per square mile	1.1						
1810.							
Population	230,760	24,520	12,282	4,762		272,324	7,289,884
Per cent. of increase	408.6	339.6					
Rank	13	21	24	25			
Number per square mile	5.7	.7	.2				
1820.							
Population	581,295	197,178	55,162	8,765		842,400	9,633,822
Per cent. of increase	151.9	502.2	349.1	84			
Rank	5	18	24	27			
Number per square mile	14.3	4.1	1	.1			
1830.							
Population	937,903	343,031	157,445	31,639		1,470,018	12,866,020
Per cent. of increase	61.3	133	185.4	260.9			
Rank	4	13	20	27			
Number per square mile	23	9.6	2.8	.6			
1840.							
Population	1,519,467	685,866	476,183	212,267	30,945	2,924,728	17,069,453
Per cent. of increase	62	99.9	202.4	570.9			
Rank	3	10	14	23	30		
Number per square mile	37.3	18.1	8.5	3.7	.6		
1850.							
Population	1,980,329	988,416	851,470	397,654	305,391	4,523,260	23,191,867
Per cent. of increase	30.3	44.1	78.8	87.3	886.8		
Rank	3	7	11	20	24		
Number per square mile	48.6	27.5	15.2	6.9	5.6		
1860.							
Population	2,339,511	1,350,428	1,711,951	749,113	775,881	6,926,884	31,443,321
Per cent. of increase	18.1	36.6	101	88.3	154		
Rank	3	6	4	16	15		
Number per square mile	57.4	37.6	30.6	13	14.2		
1870.							
Population	2,665,260	1,680,637	2,539,891	1,184,059	1,054,670	9,124,517	38,588,371
Per cent. of increase	13.9	24.4	48.3	58	35.9		
Rank	3	6	4	13	15		
Number per square mile	65.3	47	45.3	20.6	19.3		
1880.							
Population	3,198,062	1,978,301	3,077,871	1,636,937	1,315,497	11,206,668	50,155,783
Per cent. of increase	19.9	17.7	21.1	38.2	24.7		
Rank	3	6	4	9	16		
Number per square mile	78.5	55.1	55	28.5	24.2		
1887.[1]							
Population	3,600,000	2,200,000	3,350,000	2,000,000	1,650,000	12,800,000	60,602,000

[1] Fisher: The Essentials of Geography for the School Year 1887-88.

North America is the marvel of human progress; the old Northwest the marvel of North America. No other region of equal size ever made such progress in one hundred years. The theme requires a volume; nothing more can here be done than to state the results that have been reached in some principal lines of development. Population comes first.

One of the interesting features of this table is the great strides with which Ohio made her way to the third rank among the States in the Union.

The population of the five States in 1880 consisted of 5,758,244 males, and 5,453,464 females. Ohio had the largest proportion of females, 98,152 to 100,000 males; and Michigan the smallest, 89,821—the ratio in the whole country being 96,544 to 100,000. The native population was 9,290,038; the foreign-born, 1,916,630. The foreign-born to 100,000 natives were, in Ohio, 14,089; Indiana, 7,860; Illinois, 23,396; Michigan, 31,119; Wisconsin, 44,584. The ratio in the United States was 15,368 foreign-born to 100,000 natives. In Michigan the greater number of the foreign-born were British Americans, of whom this State had a larger proportion than any other in the Union. The large foreign element in Illinois and Wisconsin is principally due to the attraction of their agricultural advantages for German and Scandinavian emigrants.

The census-maps showing in five degrees of density the distribution of the population of the United States at the census-years, illustrates in a striking manner what has been said in previous chapters concerning Western emigration and development, and particularly concerning the early superior advantages of the Ohio Valley as compared with the Lake region. In 1790 the island of color lying in Southwestern Pennsylvania extends its edge across the Ohio River below Pittsburg. Pin-points of color appear at the mouth of the Muskingum, on the Wabash, and in the Illinois. In 1800 the patches of color on the white surface have increased in size, and some of them have deepened. Chillicothe, Cincinnati, Conneaut, Cleveland, and Detroit appear. In 1810 two-thirds of Ohio is colored, some of the color representing a population of from eighteen to forty-five and some from six to eighteen, but the larger part from two to six to the square mile. The Vincennes settlements extend to the Ohio River, and a belt of population appears along the eastern line of Indiana, one-half the length of the State. The Illinois population has extended over a larger area, both up and down the river and back from it. A stroke of color extends along the western side of the Detroit River, and specks appear at Mackinaw, at the Saut, at Green Bay, and at the mouth of the Wisconsin. In 1820 all of Ohio but the northwestern quarter, the southern third of Indiana, the southern fourth of Illinois are settled more or less densely. A line of light color curves around the head of Lake Erie from the mouth of the Cuyahoga to the head of Lake St. Clair. In 1830 a white patch, of considerable size, appears in Northwestern Ohio. The northern third of Indiana is white, with a colored island at Fort Wayne. In Illinois the settlements have extended north from the Ohio and east from the Mississippi, covering about one-half the State. A red spot appears in the Northwest, in the region of the lead mines, and crosses the boundary into Wisconsin. The Detroit settlements have grown in every direction, and a considerable population has appeared in the southwestern part of Michigan, extending into Northern Indiana. In 1840 not a white spot is left in Ohio. Nearly all Indiana and Illinois are colored. Michigan and Wisconsin are crossed by varying bands of color as high as the latitude of Port Huron and Madison. Beginnings have been made at the head of Lake Superior, and in the Valley of the St. Croix. From 1840 to 1850 the northern frontier of these two States is slightly crowded back; the density of the old population increases; and beginnings are made in the great lumber and mining regions of the North, particularly on the southern shore of Lake Superior. A similar description will apply to 1860 and to 1870. The map of 1880 shows the whole of the Northwest inhabited, except a small interior island in the northern part of the lower peninsula of Michigan, about one-half of the upper peninsula, and a large tract in Northern Wisconsin. To each of these two States is assigned an unsettled area of 10,200 square miles.

The census of 1880 reported an urban population of 2,689,081, and a rural population of 8,516,880 souls; the first found in 158 centres of 4,000 people and upward. The per cents. of the urban to the total population ranged from seventeen in Indiana to twenty-eight in Ohio. Eighteen of the one hundred principal cities of the Union were within the five States, and ten more upon their immediate borders.

In 1860 Mr. Seward called Chicago "the last and most wonderful of all the marvellous creations of civilization in North America." What would he say of Chicago in 1887?

TABLE SHOWING THE NUMBER OF PEOPLE EMPLOYED IN THE DIFFERENT GAINFUL OCCUPATIONS.

	Agriculture.	Professional and Personal Services.	Trade and Transportation.	Manufactures and Mechanical and Mining Industries.	Total.
Ohio	397,495	250,371	104,315	242,294	994,475
Indiana	331,240	137,281	56,432	110,127	635,080
Illinois	436,371	229,467	128,372	205,570	999,780
Michigan	240,319	143,249	54,723	130,913	569,204
Wisconsin	195,901	97,494	37,550	86,510	417,455
Total	1,601,326	857,862	381,392	775,414	3,615,994

Agriculture leads the column of the Northwestern industries. The following table will show the total number of farms in the five States, their aggregate size, their value, the value of farm-products, the value of live stock, the value of farms per acre, and the per cent. of the States' area in farms:

	Number of Farms.	Total Acreage in Farms.	Per Cent. of Area in Farms.	Value of Farms.	Value per Acre.	Value of Products.	Value of Live Stock.
Ohio	247,189	24,529,226	94.0	$1,127,497,353	$46.37	$156,777,152	$103,707,730
Indiana	194,013	20,420,983	88.9	635,236,111	31.11	114,707,082	71,068,785
Illinois	255,741	31,673,645	88.4	1,009,594,580	31.56	203,980,137	132,437,762
Michigan	154,008	13,807,240	37.6	499,103,181	36.15	91,150,858	55,720,113
Wisconsin	134,322	15,353,118	44.1	357,709,507	23.30	72,779,496	46,508,643
Total	985,273	105,784,212		$3,629,140,732		$639,403,725	$409,443,033

No other States in the Union have so large per cents. of area in farms as Ohio, Indiana, and Illinois. Ohio surpasses all the other States in the amount of capital invested in farms, and Illinois all others in farm-products and in live stock.

This table will show the capital invested in manufactures, the value of manufactured products, the aggregate wealth of the States, the wealth *per capita*, and the taxation for State purposes, all for the year 1880:

	Capital invested in Manufactures	Value of Products.	Total Wealth.	Wealth per Capita.	Taxation.
Ohio	$188,939,614	$436,298,390	$3,301,000.000	$1,032 19	$25,756,658
Indiana	65,742,962	148,006,411	1,499,000,000	752 72	12,343,630
Illinois	140,652,066	414,864,673	3,092,000,000	1,004 59	24,586,018
Michigan	92,930,959	150,715,025	1,370,000,000	836 93	8,627,949
Wisconsin	73,821,802	128,225,480	969,000,000	636 60	7,588,325
Total	$562,087,403	$1,278,109,79	$10,231,000,000		$78,962,580

On no line of progress has the human race made greater strides than in means of travel and transportation; and the whole sweep of this progress, from the most primitive to the most improved methods, can be studied in the history of the old Northwest.

The men who first entered it from the East followed the paths that the deer and the buffalo had made, called by the hunters "streets" or "buffalo-roads." Next the white man followed the Indians' trail, which, marked and widened by the axe, became the "trace." The trader who followed the waters borrowed of the Indian his canoe, or of the Frenchman his *bateau;* the trader who kept to the land introduced the pack-saddle and the train of pack-horses. When the day came to move passengers in numbers and freight in quantities, the "keel-boat" and the "ark" appeared. The movement of passengers and freight was mostly westward, owing as well to the current of the streams as to the necessities of emigration. Boatmen who descended to New Orleans commonly broke up their craft and sold them for lumber; those who came from the Upper Ohio returning by sea to Baltimore, or Alexandria and thence over the mountains; those who came from below the Muskingum marching homeward through the wilderness by Natchez and Nashville in companies of fifteen or twenty. Then came steam-boats, the first of which on the Ohio appeared in 1811, and on the Northern Lakes in 1818. On land regular roads and wheeled vehicles succeeded the "trace" and the pack-saddle, and in due time came canals and railroads. In 1788 Dr. Manasseh Cutler did twenty-nine days of hard travelling in reaching Marietta from Hamilton, Mass. We read that "on January 11, 1794, a line of two keel-boats, with bullet-proof covers and port-holes, and provided with cannon and small arms, was established between Cincinnati and Pittsburg, each making a trip once in four weeks." Mr. Carnegie tells us that in 1884 the trade of the same river was valued at $800,000,000, and that transportation upon it is the cheapest in the world—coal, coke, and other bulky articles being transported at the rate of one-twentieth of a cent per ton per mile.[1] The colossal proportions to which land travel and transportation have grown are shown by the following statistics of railroads in 1886:

	Ohio.	Indiana.	Illinois.	Michigan.	Wisconsin.	Total.
Miles of railroad	9,246	5,641	14,708	5,201	7,084	41,880
Engines and cars	99,087	39,908	89,169	26,480	28,416	283,060
Capital stock	$386,440,877	$147,652,448	$332,725,395	$95,916,518	$92,162,661	$1,054,897,889
Cost	$703,011,783	$278,883,884	$638,501,557	$203,826,163	$240,142,885	$2,063,866,292
Bonded debt	$338,010,901	$167,045,609	$330,737,889	$95,300,654	$147,500,000	$1,078,655,062
Passengers carried	24,099,140	7,446,993	30,564,801	8,116,614	6,160,601	76,408,158
Tons of freight moved	57,592,145	20,521,625	40,939,396	15,873,494	9,141,461	144,068,125
Gross earnings	$71,196,610	$33,547,289	$97,685,889	$27,114,912	$28,174,270	$257,718,913

The canal around the Saut Rapids, at the foot of which St. Lusson stood in 1671 when he took possession of the Northwestern lakes and rivers, islands and countries, in the

---

[1] Triumphant Democracy, 309.

name of the Redoubtable Monarch Louis XIV., of France, has become one of the great commercial thoroughfares of the world. In 1886, 7,428 passages of vessels of all descriptions were made through this canal, conveying 4,527,759 tons of freight. In the table of this commerce we find such items as these: 1,009,999 tons of coal; 1,759,365 barrels of flour; 18,991,485 bushels of wheat; 38,627 tons of copper; 2,087,809 tons of iron ore; 138,688,000 feet of lumber. This tonnage, which already surpasses that of the Suez Canal for the number of days per year that the two are open to navigation, in connection with the undeveloped capabilities of the country beyond Lake Superior, stretching to the Pacific Ocean, mocks one's power to predict the extent and value of the future commerce of this artificial water-way. Nor is this all. When the Cascade Mountains have been tunnelled, New York, by this Northwestern route, will be brought within ten thousand five hundred miles of Canton, China, which is only one-half the distance, by the Isthmus of Suez or the Cape of Good Hope; while the English and Dutch commercial cities are distant not less than eighteen thousand miles.

The Ordinance of 1787 declared: "Religion, morality, and knowledge being necessary to good government and the happiness of mankind, schools and the means of education shall forever be encouraged." The moral significance of statistics is commonly lost; nevertheless, some figures will help us to understand how Congress and the Northwest have kept this educational compact.

The Land Ordinance of 1785 provided that, wherever it operated, "there shall be reserved from sale the lot No. 16 of every township for the maintenance of common schools within the said township." From that day the policy of setting apart for this purpose one thirty-sixth part of the land in every new State has been uniformly followed. Besides, other large grants have been made, from time to time, for educational purposes. These educational land-grants would be a very prominent feature of any adequate history of education in the Northwest. Here attention can be drawn to only two or three points.

The total amount of the grants under the Ordinance of 1785 is 4,865,917, of which 4,293,989 acres were sold previous to 1884. In addition to these grants, one-half of the five per cent. of the sales of public lands in Illinois, that the State was entitled to in accordance with the policy inaugurated in 1802 of giving the State five per cent. of such sales for some purpose, was devoted to schools, and in Wisconsin the whole of it was so devoted. In 1884 the aggregate school funds of the five States arising from these two sources, principal and capitalized interest, was $16,418,477, which yielded a yearly income of $1,406,801.

The five States received from the Agricultural and Mechanical College grant of 1863, 1,980,000 acres of land and land-scrip. In 1884 the present funds, resulting from the sale of 1,800,862 acres of these lands, was $1,864,514, which produced a yearly income of $108,172.

Previous to the same year, the National Government had patented to the five States, under the legislation of Congress, 11,461,000 acres of swamp lands, of which Ohio, Indiana, and Illinois appropriated the whole, and Michigan and Wisconsin fifty per cent. to education. The appropriations have produced educational funds amounting to $2,541,115.

Ninety-three thousand three hundred and thirty-six acres of saline lands dedicated to education have produced $327,986.

The University lands, amounting to 345,716 acres, yielding a total fund of $1,136,245 and an annual income of $78,801, closes the list of educational land-grants in the old Northwest.

Here are educational endowments amounting to more than twenty million acres of lands.[1] The practical management of these enormous endowments by the States has been marked by short-sightedness and wastefulness fully propor-

---

[1] These statistics are given on the authority of Prof. George W. Knight: History and Management of Land Grants for Education in the Northwest Territory, 170-172.

tional to the liberality of Congress in making them. The annual funds arising from these endowments are but a small per cent. of the vast sums that the Northwestern people raise by taxation for educational purposes; but they have still served a noble educational purpose in the past, and will be of considerable value in years to come.

The following table exhibits the more important public-school statistics for the school-year 1884–85:

	Ohio.	Indiana.	Illinois.	Michigan.	Wiscon'n.	Total.
Number of school-youth...	1,095,469	722,851	1,077,302	595,687	544,976	4,036,285
Number enrolled in schools	774,660	501,142	738,787	411,954	321,718	2,748,261
Public-school houses.....	12,674	9,664	12,076	7,164	6,033	47,611
Number of teachers......	24,628	13,312	20,619	15,358	10,866	84,783
Expenditures for Public Schools	$10,094,000	$4,660,000	$10,199,000	$4,729,000	$3,300,000	$32,982,000
Value of public-school property	$27,970,000	$13,619,000	$22,340,000	$11,267,000	$6,132,000	$81,328,000
School Fund	$3,534,000	$9,339,000	$9,450,000	$3,839,000	$4,646,000	$30,808,000

From the report of the National Commissioner of Education for the same year these items concerning superior instruction have been gathered:

Colleges and universities reporting..	90
Instructors in them	889
Students...	8,594
Value of buildings, grounds, and apparatus..	$9,588,000
Productive funds	8,091,000
Value of college-property reported..	$17,679,000

The number of newspapers and periodicals published in the five States the year of the last census, with the aggregate circulation per issue, was as follows:

	Newspapers and Periodicals.	Circulation.
Ohio...	774	3,093,931
Indiana...	467	661,111
Illinois	1,017	2,421,275
Michigan	464	620,974
Wisconsin...	340	436,576
Total..	3,062	7,233,867

The school-master has been abroad in the Northwest since 1788; but that he still has plenty of work to do is shown by this exhibit of the number of persons in 1880, ten years of age or more, unable to write:

Ohio	131,847
Indiana	110,761
Illinois	145,397
Michigan	63,723
Wisconsin	55,558
Total	507,286

The educational influence and results of opening the territory northwest of the Ohio River to civilization may be treated in a narrower and in a broader way. The narrower treatment would embrace school-lands, school-laws, and school-systems, with all that these imply; the broader treatment would deal with the general forces and conditions that have wrought out the peculiar character of the Northwestern people, and, through them, have acted upon the national life. But no better example of the broadening and liberalizing influence of the Northwest can be given than that furnished by the history of education in the specific sense. Here, as elsewhere, it has much crudeness and shallowness to answer for. The "fresh-water college" and the American "university" have had a rank growth. Perhaps, too, the Northwest has not always looked with sufficient reverence upon the old educational rubrics. But if she had not been free from an undue conservatism, she would never have done what she has for education, either directly at home or by reaction upon the East. The best contributions of the five States to educational progress are these: The flexibility of their educational systems, and their adaptation to existing conditions; the extent to which they have carried the public-school superintendency; the prominence that they have accorded to the State University; the range and scope that they have given to the principle of election in higher education; the measurable adjustment of the high school to the college; the readiness with which the coeducation of the sexes has been taken up and developed; and the faith, energy, and enthusiasm of teachers. We have heard a great deal about what the East has done for the West, as respects education and other matters; the time has come for drawing attention to what the West has done for the East. Particular attention may be drawn to the coeducation of the sexes. In the five States are 95 institutions that rank as colleges; 68 of these admit women to their halls. Of the 27 non-coeducational colleges, 21 are Protestant and 6 Roman Catholic. In this respect the new Northwest follows the example of the old Northwest. Forty-one coeducation and 17 non-coeducation colleges are found in the States of Minnesota, Iowa, Kansas, Nebraska, Colorado, California, and Oregon. Besides, the largest, the most flourishing, and the most influential colleges throw open their doors to men and to women on equal terms.

The influence of the country beyond the Alleghany Mountains on the population that occupies it, its reaction on the Atlantic Plain, and its effect on the national life, character, and government are themes demanding fuller investigation than they have ever received. Here originated many of the crude theories and vicious arts that blot our history and disfigure our civilization. The West perfected, if she did not invent, "wild-cat" banking; she crowned the "spoils system" king of politics; she brought forth "manifest destiny;" she furnished the forces and the conditions that have produced Mormonism. Mr. Levermore says a full revelation of the connection between the growth of a State banking system in the West and sundry prevalent financial doctrines about the powers of Congress is essential to a satisfactory constitutional history of the United States;[1] and Professor W. G. Sumner points out with great clearness the vast influence on national politics of certain Western financial views in the old day of the United States Bank.[2] What a change had taken place

---

[1] The Republic of New Haven, Introduction.
[2] Andrew Jackson, in Statesmen Series 119 et seq.

in the country when General Jackson, the first Western President, ascended the President's chair in 1829. That the American system was not shattered to pieces by the admission to it of the West, before 1840, is proof of its elasticity and power second only to the Civil War. But the West has also contributed incomparably valuable elements to American civilization. Mention may be made of her all-abounding vitality, her inexhaustible spirits, her unconquerable courage, her largeness of views, her freedom from tradition, her power of initiative, her unfailing faith in the Republic, and her confidence in her own destiny. As a group, these topics cannot be here considered; but this work may fitly close with a rapid view of the trend of political thought in the old Northwest.

There are two colonial periods in the history of the United States. The first saw the English colonies established on the Atlantic slope between the Kennebec and Savannah Rivers; the second saw the American colonies in the Mississippi Valley. The first planting was mainly the work of the seventeenth century; the second began before the Revolutionary War, but its success was not assured until at Paris, in 1782, the American Commissioners thwarted the purpose of the three powers to shut us up between the Appalachian Mountains and the Atlantic Ocean, and secured the Mississippi River as our western boundary. It is no exaggeration to say that the immediate effect of the first planting on the Englishman was small, compared with the immediate effect of the second on the American. For example, in the period that lies before the Revolution constitutional monarchy was developed into conservative republicanism, while in the period since the Revolution conservative republicanism has been developed into democracy. How thoroughly English the fathers of the Revolution were, in political ideas and temper, is conclusively shown by all their constructive political work, including the Ordinance of 1787.

In some respects this is the most interesting document that the Revolutionary era produced. All the constitutions of that era, and particularly the National Constitution, were largely the result of compromise; but the framers of the Ordinance legislated for the wilderness, and so were not compelled to consult facts accomplished; they were free to put into their work their best ideas of what a charter of free government should be. And no man can read the Ordinance without seeing that the men who drafted it shrank from conclusions that are commonly accepted now; witness, for example, the provisions relating to the qualifications of the governor, the representative, and especially the elector. But these rules express the average republicanism of 1787. Similar rules are found in many of the State constitutions, and they stand as landmarks from which we may measure how far the American people have marched on the democratic road in a century. In fact, the interval between the constitutional monarchy of 1690 and the federal republicanism of 1790 is less than the interval between the federal republicanism of 1787 and the democracy of 1887. The progress of democratic ideas is well illustrated by the study of constitutional provisions relating to the suffrage, to the powers assigned to the legislative and executive branches of government, to the appointment and tenure of the judges, and to the length of official terms.

In 1787 most of the States conditioned the elective franchise upon a property qualification. Notwithstanding the sore experience of the colonies with the veto power, as wielded by the colonial governors and the Crown, the States still left that important power in the hands of their governors. In twelve of the States the judges held office during good behavior, and in all of them they were appointed—in one by the governor alone, in one by the council alone, in five by the legislature, and in the others by the governor by and with the consent of a confirming body.[1] These are the facts commonly

---

[1] Hitchcock: American State Constitutions, 48.

referred to by the Jeffersonian politicians when, a few years later, they denounce the "monarchical" ideas and tendencies of the Federalists.

The Constitutions of Kentucky, 1792, and Tennessee, 1796, mark a distinct advance of democratical opinions. The first one gave the suffrage to all free male citizens twenty-one years of age having a two years residence in the State; the second, to every freeman of the same age having a six months residence. The first imposed no property qualification upon office-holders; the second required that members of the assembly should own freeholds of two hundred acres each, and the governor a freehold of five hundred acres. The Kentucky judges were appointed by the governor, to hold office during good behavior; the Tennessee judges, by the legislature, for seven years. In Kentucky members of the House of Representatives were chosen annually by the qualified electors; the senators and governor every four years, by electors chosen by the people; the senators to be "men of the most wisdom, experience, and virtue above twenty-seven years of age." In Tennessee the same officers were chosen every two years at the popular elections. The Governor of Kentucky was clothed with the veto power, but the Governor of Tennessee was not so clothed. Neither of these constitutions was submitted to the people for their approval.

Mr. Jefferson pronounced the Constitution of Tennessee "the most republican yet framed in America." He must have been equally well satisfied with that of Ohio. This constitution permitted all white male inhabitants, twenty-one years of age, who had resided in the State one year preceding, and who also paid or were charged with a State or county tax, to vote at all elections. No property qualification was required of officers. The judges were chosen by the legislature on joint ballot of the two houses, "to hold their offices for the term of seven years if so long they behaved well." The secretary of state, the auditor, and treasurer, as well as the superior militia officers, were also appointed by the assembly. The governor had no veto, but he might temporarily fill vacancies in the offices, regularly filled by the legislature, occurring in the recesses of that body. Members of the legislature and the governor were elected for two years by the people. The common explanation of the extreme limitation of the executive power and of the unusual powers given to the General Assembly is found in the frequent collisions that occurred between Governor St. Clair and the Territorial Legislature. This was no doubt one cause of the limitation; but it is probable that the Jeffersonian theory of government was a more potent cause.[1] The Chief Magistrate of Ohio has always been an officer of dignity rather than of power.

The Constitution of Ohio was not submitted to the people. A resolution making provision for such submission was lost by a decided vote—ayes, 7; nays, 27. Sometimes this refusal has been ascribed to the supposed fear of the leaders of the convention that the people would not approve the constitution that had been framed, and sometimes to an undue anxiety to get the new government in motion. At that time, however, the practice of submitting constitutions to the people for their approval had not become thoroughly established. The Federalists of the State thought the failure to submit a serious grievance; and it is certainly true that the State was brought into the Union in a manner little in accord with those democratical principles which the State party so loudly proclaimed.

The Constitutions of Indiana, 1816; of Michigan, 1837; and of Wisconsin, 1848, conferred the suffrage upon white

---

[1] This is Mr. J. C. Hamilton's explanation. Commenting upon the great political change that occurred in 1800, he says: "The Constitution of Ohio shows the democratical opinions prevalent on the Western frontier. It reduced the executive power almost to a nonentity, elevating and enlarging that of the legislature, giving to it the election of the judges to hold office for a short term of years, thus destroying their independence, and that of all the other officers, with the exception of sheriffs and coroners, who, with the governor, were to be chosen by the suffrages of all the people, residents for a year, and who had been charged with a tax."—Life of Alexander Hamilton, VII, 602.

male citizens, twenty-one years of age, having a short residence in the State; that of Illinois, 1818, upon all white male inhabitants similarly qualified. No property-qualification was imposed upon office-holders in any one of them. Michigan and Wisconsin gave their governors the veto; Indiana and Illinois did not; Indiana and Michigan made the judges' tenure seven years; Illinois and Wisconsin made it good behavior. In Indiana the superior judges were appointed by the governor, with the Senate's approval, the inferior ones by the legislature; in Michigan, the superior judges were appointed as in Indiana, but the inferior ones were elected by the people. In Illinois all judges were appointed by the governor, with the consent of the Senate. By 1848 the tide in favor of an elective judiciary had attained its full volume, and we are not surprised to find, therefore, the Constitution of Wisconsin providing that all judges should be chosen by the qualified electors of their several circuits or counties. In Indiana the governor's term was made three years; in Illinois, four; in Michigan and Wisconsin, two. The Constitutions of the first two States were not submitted to the people; those of the last two were submitted.

Another gauge of the trend of political opinion in the Northwest is furnished by the history of political parties.

The overthrow of the Federal party and the admission of Ohio to the Union came practically at the same time. But even if the Federalists could have maintained themselves in the old States, there is not the smallest probability that they could have imposed their ideas upon a single one of the Northwestern States. Three things that run into one another, and are yet separable, are contemporaneous with the colonization of the Northwest: The establishment of the American Republic, the increased energy of the democratizing movement considered as a tone of thought or stream of tendency, and the organization of the Democratic-Republican party. These causes, together with the powerful democratical stimulus of backwoods life, were more than sufficient to establish the party of Jefferson in the States of Ohio, Indiana, and Illinois. The people of these States favored the acquisition of Louisiana and the War of 1812, and were opposed to a national bank. Ohio was so strongly Democratic, and the legislature was so all-powerful, that in 1810 some of the judges who had declared State laws unconstitutional were impeached, and in 1820 an attempt was made to nullify the law chartering the United States Bank. Ohio voted for all the Democratic-Republican Presidents: Jefferson, Madison, and Monroe. Clay received the electoral vote in 1824, but Adams received the State's vote in the House of Representatives. From this time on Mr. Clay had a numerous and ardent following in the State. This was due partly to growing interest in a protective tariff and in internal improvements, partly to Mr. Clay's political history and personal character, and partly to the fact that he was a Western man. General Jackson carried the State in 1828 and in 1832; Harrison, in 1836 and 1840; Clay, in 1844; Cass, in 1848; and Pierce, in 1852. From 1828 to 1856 the governors were about equally divided between the two parties. In Indiana the Democratic-Republican and Democratic parties elected the presidential electors from 1816 to 1860, save in 1836 and 1840, when the Whigs carried the State. Illinois gave her electoral votes to the same parties down to 1860, but her vote in the House of Representatives was cast for Adams in 1824. Michigan's electoral vote was cast for Van Buren in 1836, but was not counted; for Harrison in 1840, and for the Democratic candidates in 1844, in 1848, and in 1852.

In 1848 the five States all voted for General Cass, giving him an aggregate plurality over Taylor of 37,707; in 1852 they all voted for General Pierce, giving him an aggregate plurality over Scott of 66,216. The Democratic pluralities had much more than kept pace with the growth of population. The national Democratic party felt proud and confident in the strength of its position in 1852; but political insight could then discern, what history soon proved to be the fact, that only an occasion was wanting to effect a combination of elements that would drive that party from power. A large majority of Northern Whigs were at heart opposed to the further extension of slavery. The Democratic party in the North also contained a large anti-slavery element. Then there was the Liberty party, or Free-soilers, who gave Birney 62,300 votes in 1844; Van Buren, 291,263 in 1848; and Hale, 155,825 in 1852. In the Northwest Birney's vote was 17,358; Van Buren's, 80,035; and Hale's, 64,619. Nor did the falling off in the Free-soil vote from 1848 to 1852 indicate a decline of the party strength; a large part of Van Buren's vote represented Democratic disaffection rather than anti-slavery principle. Obviously, here were the elements of a formidable new political party, if they could be united.

Their overwhelming defeat in 1852 convinced Northern Whigs that the usefulness of the Whig organization was a thing of the past. Their great victory of the same year made the Democrats more blind and confident than ever; and two years later they repealed the Missouri Compromise, thereby reopening the question of slavery north of 36° 30′ beyond the State of Missouri. This act brought the anti-slavery elements of the North together in a new political organization with a rapidity and success unexampled in the history of the country.

An anti-Nebraska convention held in Michigan in June, 1854, baptized the new party Republican. In Wisconsin the new party was organized with equal promptness. Since that time neither one of these States has ever failed to elect Republican presidential electors. Michigan gave Frémont 71,762 votes; Buchanan, 52,136; Wisconsin gave them 66,090 and 52,843, respectively. However, the great change of the vote from 1852 in both of these States was not wholly due to change of opinion, but partly to emigration. The Republicans of Ohio elected Mr. Chase governor in 1855, and since that year they have never failed to return a Republican electoral college. Frémont received 187,497 votes; Buchanan, 170,874. In

Indiana and Illinois the elements that coalesced in the Republican party were weaker than in the other Northwestern States. The old national pike has been aptly called "a sort of Mason and Dixon's line," since it formerly separated the Republican counties of Ohio, Indiana, and Illinois from the Democratic counties. South of this line the two States were fully settled in 1850; north of it there were still unsettled tracts of territory. Population was also more dense South than North. Besides, the Southern-born population of Indiana was twenty per cent. of the whole population; the Southern-born population of Illinois sixteen per cent. of the whole. The two States, respectively, gave Buchanan 118,670 and 105,348 votes, and Frémont 94,375 and 96,189 votes. In the years following 1856 the Republican party increased in strength throughout the country. In the two States, besides changes of opinion, emigration told powerfully on the Republican side. By 1870 the Southern-born population of Indiana had fallen to ten per cent., of Illinois to nine per cent., of the whole. In 1860 both States gave Lincoln large majorities over Douglas; and since that year they have uniformly returned Republican electors, except that Indiana gave her vote to Mr. Tilden in 1876 and Mr. Cleveland in 1884. Space will not be taken to enumerate the Republican leaders that the Northwest has furnished; but it is a noteworthy fact that four of the party's six presidential candidates, and all the successful ones, have been Northwestern men. The Northwest decided the constitutional contest between freedom and slavery. Mr. Seward said, at Madison, Wisconsin, in 1860: "It seems almost as if it was providential that these new States of the Northwest, the State of Michigan, the State of Wisconsin, the State of Iowa, the State of Ohio, founded on this reservation for freedom that had been made in the year 1787, matured just in the critical moment to interpose, to rally the free States of the Atlantic coast, to call them back to their ancient principles, to nerve them to sustain them in the contest at the Capitol, and to send their noble and true sons and daughters to the plains of Kansas, to defend, at the peril of their homes, and even their lives, if need were, the precious soil which had been abandoned by the Government to slavery, from the intrusion of that, the greatest evil that has ever befallen our land."[1]

In the United States political changes are quite as rapid and extreme as any others. The history of the last thirty years is full of the profoundest lessons for the statesman and the moralist. Externally the political situation, after the presidential election of 1852, was exceedingly deceptive. No political party ever felt more confidence in its position than the Democratic party in 1853. No political party was ever more thoroughly divided and broken than the same party eight years later. No political party ever accomplished its original object more quickly and effectually than the Republican party after 1861. So completely was that object secured, and everything logically involved in it; so entirely have its original aspirations become matters of history; so different are the specific party doctrines in 1887 from what they were in 1857, that it is not superfluous to state that the original Republican platform contained but one "plank" on which all the members of the party stood. This was the declaration of the right and duty of Congress to prohibit slavery in the territories. It was the sixth compact of 1787 become a political creed. This creed the Northwest embraced with the more alacrity because her own history and daily life were evidence of its truth and value.

The Northwest opposed secession with much more unanimity than she opposed the spread of slavery. In all the Northwestern States there was more or less opposition or indifference to the Union cause; in those that extended to the Ohio River, and particularly in Indiana and Illinois, by reason of their large Southern-born population, there was some actual disloyalty and overt treason; but no other part of the

---

[1] Works, IV., 325.

Union has greater reason for thinking of the part it played in the great contest with satisfaction and pride. The President, the great finance and war ministers, the foremost generals, were Northwestern men; while she furnished one-third of the total physical force that suppressed the Rebellion.[1]

The Northwest has shared to the full Western faith in the West. What this is is best shown on a background of Eastern narrowness and jealousy. That the annexation of Louisiana in 1803 was in the line of providence will hardly be denied to-day by any man who believes in providence at all; but it was vigorously opposed at the time, on the ground that it would subtract from the weight and influence of the old States, particularly New England. Josiah Quincy avowed the sentiment of great numbers of Eastern people when in 1811 he declared, on the floor of the House of Representatives, that the admission of the Territory of Orleans as a State to the Union would be its dissolution; that it would free the States from their moral obligations to each other; and that it would, in that event, be the duty of some States, as it would be the right of all, definitely to prepare for a separation, amicably if they could, violently if they must. Daniel Webster was a man too large to share the small views of his Eastern neighbors; but Daniel Webster *did* say in the

---

[1] TABLE SHOWING NUMBER OF MEN CALLED FOR BY THE PRESIDENT OF THE UNITED STATES, AND FURNISHED BY THE NORTHWESTERN STATES, DURING THE WAR OF THE REBELLION. (This table is compiled from Phisterer: Statistical Record of the Armies of the United States, 10.)

	Quota.	Total Furnished.	Number reduced to Three Years' Standard.
Ohio	306,322	313,180	240,514
Indiana	199,788	196,363	153,576
Illinois	244,496	259,092	214,133
Michigan	95,007	87,364	80,111
Wisconsin	109,080	91,327	79,260
Total	954,693	947,326	767,594
Total for the United States	2,763,670	2,859,132	2,320,272

Senate, in 1846, that the St. Johns was worth a hundred times as much as the Columbia was or ever would be. The speech of the Revolution was continental; there was the "Continental Congress," the "Continental Money," the "Continental Army;" but the ideas of the Revolution were not continental. It is one of the achievements of the West to have taught the East the continental lesson.

Her geographical position and relations have always caused the Northwest to take a deep interest in the territorial expansion and integrity of the Union, and particularly in the use and ownership of the Mississippi River. First and last, that river has presented five distinct questions to the American people.

The question of 1782 was: "Shall the United States extend to the Mississippi, or shall the country beyond the mountains be left to England or Spain, or to the two powers together?" The answer given to this question was the boundaries of 1783.

The second question was: " Shall the United States, and particularly the West, be allowed that use and benefit of the river to which their position fairly entitles them, or shall Spain be suffered to exclude them from its waters?" This question first arose when Mr. Jay was sent to the Spanish Court to negotiate a treaty of alliance. Nothing was concluded at Madrid or at Paris touching this question; so far from it, the concession by England of the independence of the States, with their rightful boundaries, led at once to new complications. As these were a sequel to the discussions at Madrid and Paris, they will be traced somewhat at length.

The treaty of 1763 made a line running along the middle of the Mississippi from its source to the River Iberville, and thence along the middle of the Iberville, and Lakes Maurepas and Pontchartrain, the boundary between the possessions of England and Spain. England immediately divided Florida into two provinces, separated by the Appalachicola River. On the north their boundaries were, at first, the thirty-first parallel of north latitude from the Mississippi to the Appalachicola, thence down that river to its junction with the Flint, thence by a straight line to the head of the St. Marys River, and thence by the St. Marys to the ocean. But the next year, she carried West Florida one hundred and ten miles farther north, making the northern boundary of that province a due east and west line extending from the mouth of the Yazoo to the Appalachicola. The northern boundary of Florida, as established in 1763, became the southern boundary of the United States in 1783. But by a treaty signed the same day as the American treaty of 1783, England ceded the Floridas to Spain, mentioning no boundaries whatever. An immediate conflict between the United States and Spain was the result. The United States claimed down to the thirty-first parallel ; Spain claimed the Floridas, with the boundaries that they had when England ceded them. In other words, the block of land lying north of parallel 31° and south of an east and west line running through the mouth of the Yazoo, between the Mississippi and the Appalachicola, was in dispute. The United States certainly had a good title, and Spain could say much in defence of hers. Moreover, it must be remembered that Spain had captured the British posts in West Florida, and was in possession of them at the close of the war. Instead of surrendering the territory that she held falling within the limits of the United States, Spain began to strengthen herself in West Florida, building new forts and re-enforcing old ones. She controlled the river as far as the mouth of the Ohio on both sides, and beyond that point on the west side. She made treaties with the Indians residing in the district, they recognizing the Spanish title and agreeing to defend it. For the time, the Republic was no more able to drive the Spanish garrisons from the Southwest than she was to drive the British garrisons from the Northwest. So the issue was left to diplomacy and the logic of events. And, however it might be with diplomacy, the logic of events worked more and more on the American side.

The preliminary treaty of 1782 between the United States and His Britannic Majesty contained a secret article to the effect " that in case Great Britain, at the conclusion of the present war, shall recover or be put in possession of West Florida, the line of north boundary between the said province and the United States shall be a line drawn from the mouth of the River Yazoo, where it unites with the Mississippi, due east to the River Appalachicola." As Great Britain did not " recover," and was not " put in possession of " West Florida, this article fell ; but its existence soon became known to His Catholic Majesty and gave him mortal offence. Again the treaty of 1783, by an article which was not secret, declared that " the navigation of the river Mississippi, from its source to the ocean, shall forever remain free and open to the subjects of Great Britain and the citizens of the United States." This provision seems strange, to say the least. Great Britain, according to the terms of the two treaties, no longer touched the Mississippi at a single point, although the sources of that river were supposed to be within her territories; moreover, from the thirty-first parallel to the Gulf the river lay wholly within the Spanish possessions. How, then, since it is a rule of public law that the owner of the mouth of a river controls it, granting ingress and egress as he sees fit, could the two powers agree to such a stipulation ? No answer to this question is apparent, except this, that the treaty merely ceded the right of navigation so far as the United States were concerned. Finally, His Catholic Majesty saw very clearly that an American republic, in the free use of the Mississippi River, foreboded disaster to the Floridas, to Louisiana, and to Mexico. All in all, it was most natural that he should be offended at the American treaty, that he should discover every day a new reason why the States should have been confined to the Atlantic shore, and that he should stoutly maintain his right to the territory lying below the Yazoo. From 1784 onward the Mississippi River was a " burning question " in our politics. No man can do justice to it who does not encompass the social, industrial, and political life of the nascent society then forming in the valleys of the streams flowing into the Mississippi on its eastern side.

All through the Revolution, and still more afterward, population west of the mountains was increasing. Scattered through the valleys of the Ohio and of the streams falling into it; cut off from the east by the high mountain-wall that had so long been a barrier to emigration; bound to the old States by feeble ties; having no means but the Mississippi of reaching the markets of the world with their constantly increasing products; bold, hardy, adventurous, with plenty of lawless and reckless characters—it is not strange that this population chafed and grew restive under the restraints which the King of Spain imposed upon the great river. The national authority was too weak either to expel the Spaniard from the disputed district or to compel, at New Orleans, commercial concessions. This, however, the West could but poorly understand. Again, those States that did not run over the mountains evinced an almost total inability to understand this nascent society, its commercial necessities, and the drift of its political tendencies. In fact, large numbers of people in these States looked askance upon the growing West, and cared little or nothing whether it had any outlet to the world or not. The hesitation of Congress to admit Kentucky to the Union, and the breakdown of the State of Franklin, added to the growing irritation. It was a time of upheavals in both worlds; Revolution was in the air, and the peculiar conditions of Western life invited reckless and desperate schemers. Minister Genet fomented Western hatred of the Spaniard; George Rogers Clark organized a formidable expedition to descend the river, and seize its mouth; and Senator Blount, of Tennessee, was expelled from the United States Senate because he tried to induce England to send an army from Canada, by Lake Michigan and the Mississippi, to Louisiana and the Floridas. Boatloads of Kentucky products were confiscated and the boats broken up; but, generally, a trade more or less open, more or less clandestine, was carried on. The times were rife with intrigue, rascality, and corruption. James Wilkinson, who moved to Kentucky in 1784, found there a home that gave full scope to his remarkable talents for speculation and intrigue. Spanish agents constantly travelled on various errands through the Valley of the Ohio. American speculators and informers as constantly visited New Orleans. At one time there seemed a probability that the Western people would detach themselves from the States and form a union with the Spaniards, and at another there was a probability that they would secede from the Union, swallow up the Spaniards in the Southwest, and create a Mississippi Valley nation. Indian wars in the Western country, a discontented and almost rebellious population in the valley, the whiskey-insurrection in Pennsylvania, England refusing to carry out her treaty-stipulations, France fomenting domestic troubles and trying to commit the United States to a foreign war, and England and Spain trying to detach the West, first from the Confederacy and afterward from the Union—surely the Republic was sorely vexed. Then it was that the first disunion scheme was broached, antedating Aaron Burr's plans as well as nullification and secession : namely, a scheme to divide the country by a north and south line drawn along the Alleghany Mountains. How imminent separation was, at least an attempt at separation, was not appreciated at the time;[1] nor has history yet done full justice to

---

[1] "I need not remark to you, Sir, that the flanks and rear of the United States are possessed by other powers, and formidable ones too; nor how necessary it is to apply the ament of interest to bind all parts of the Union together by indissoluble bonds, especially that part of it which lies immediately west of us, with the Middle States. For what ties, let me ask, should we have upon those people? How entirely unconnected with them shall we be, and what troubles may we not apprehend, if the Spaniards on their right, and Great Britain on their left, instead of throwing stumbling-blocks in their way, as they now do, should hold out lines for their trade and alliance? What, when they get strength, which will be sooner than most people conceive (from the emigration of foreigners, who will have no particular predilection towards us, as well as from the removal of our own citi-

the subject. It is pertinent to remark that, had the New England Federalists, who had small sympathy with the West, had their way, it is not improbable that the West would have been lost; not, indeed, through formal excision, but through failure to strengthen its connections with the Union. Certain it is that the Virginia statesmen of the Republican school, who understood the Western problem much better than the New Englanders, on account of their closer connection with the Western people, then rendered the cause of American union and nationality an invaluable service.

Almost always the history of the Mississippi question has been written from what may be called a Kentucky standpoint. Great stress has been laid on the unreasonable and arbitrary course taken by the Spaniard; small allowance has been made for his fears, rights, and jealousies. Spain was weak, torpid, almost effete; but the Mississippi controversy touched her, as Mr. McMaster has well stated, on the one point which still remained exquisitely sensitive. "Whoever touched her there, touched her to the quick. Her treasury might be empty, her finances might be in frightful disorder, her army a rabble, her ships lie rotting at the docks. A horde of pirates might exact from her a yearly tribute, competition might drive her merchants from the sea, and she might in European politics exert far less influence than the single city of Amsterdam, or the little State of Denmark. All this could be borne. But the slightest encroachment on her American domains had more than once proved sufficient to rouse her from her lethargy and to strengthen her feeble nerves."[1] Hence the alarm with which she viewed the

---

zens), will be the consequence of their having formed close connections with both or either of those powers, in a commercial way? It needs not, in my opinion, the gift of prophecy to foretell. The Western States (I speak now from my own observation) stand, as it were, upon a pivot. The touch of a feather would turn them any way."—Washington to Governor Harrison of Va., in 1784. Writings, IX., 62, 63.

[1] History of the People of the United States, I., 372.

growth of the Western settlements; her attempt, in 1782, to confine the States to the Atlantic shore; her determination to hold the territory between the mouth of the Yazoo and the thirty-first parallel; and the feeble-forcible policy that she pursued to the very last in reference to the Mississippi, sometimes threatening and sometimes wheedling her terrible neighbors to the north. It must be remembered, too, that the people of New Orleans were French, and that the Spanish Governor ruled over foreigners. Mr. Cable has told the story from the stand-point of New Orleans. How "the Spanish occupation never became more than a conquest;" how, in 1793, when Spain and France were at war, the governor "found he was only holding a town of the enemy;" how the Creole sang "The Marseillaise" in the theatre; how the city was fortified against its own inhabitants, as well as an outside foe; how, again, "the enemy looked for from without was the pioneers of Kentucky and Georgia;" how "Spain intrigued, Congress menaced, and oppressions, concessions, deceptions and corruptions lengthened out the years;" how there came to the governor "commissioners from the State of Georgia demanding liberty to extend her boundary to the Mississippi, as granted in the Treaty of Paris;" how "Orleens," as the Westerners called it, was "to Spain the key to her possessions," "to the West the only possible breathing-hole of its commerce;" how, by 1786, "the flatboat fleets that came floating out of the Ohio and Cumberland, seeking on the lower Mississippi a market and port for their hay and bacon and flour and corn, began to be challenged from the banks, halted, seized and confiscated;" how "the exasperated Kentuckians openly threatened and even planned to descend in flatboats full of long rifles instead of bread stuffs, and make an end of controversy by the capture of New Orleans;" how the security of the city was thought essential to the security of all Louisiana, the Floridas, and even Mexico; and how the authorities sometimes received the pioneers who swarmed down to their border, not as invaders but as emigrants, yielding allegiance to Spain, and sometimes did their utmost to foment a revolt against Congress and the secession of the West—all this, and much more, has Mr. Cable told in his own admirable manner.[1]

Sometimes the port of New Orleans was open, sometimes closed; and sometimes, as Mr. Cable says, "neither closed nor open," by which he means that it was legally closed but practically open, at least to preferred traders who were in collusion with the Spanish authorities. In 1785-86 Mr. Jay, Secretary of State for Foreign Affairs, conducted a long and tedious negotiation with Gardoqui, the Spanish minister, touching the issues between the two countries. But the negotiation came to nothing beyond alarming and angering the West, since Mr. Jay, as well as several States voting in Congress, had declared a willingness, for the sake of peace and amity, to yield the claim to the free use of the Mississippi for a term of years. In 1793, when the Creole was singing "The Marseillaise," Spain conceded to the United States open commerce with her colonies, and then, as soon as the song ceased, she withdrew the concession. Governor Carondolet wrote: "Since my taking possession of the government, this province has not ceased to be threatened by the ambitious designs of the Americans." Evidently, fear of the gaunt Kentuckian was again in the ascendant. But, finally, the two powers concluded at Madrid, in October, 1795, a treaty intended to compose all their difficulties.

Article 2 of this treaty confirmed the boundary given to the United States by England in 1783. The same article provided for the withdrawal of any troops, garrisons, or settlements that either party might have within the territory of the other party, said withdrawal to be made within six months after the ratification of the treaty, and sooner, if possible. Article 3 made provision for a commission to survey and mark the boundary from the Mississippi to the sea. Article 4 de-

---

[1] The Creoles of Louisiana, XVI, XVII.

clared the middle of the channel of the Mississippi the western boundary of the States, from their northern boundary to the thirty-first parallel of north latitude. Article 4 also declared: "And His Catholic Majesty has likewise agreed that the navigation of the said river, in its whole breadth from its source to the ocean, shall be free only to his subjects and the citizens of the United States, unless he should extend this privilege to the subjects of other powers by special convention." Article 22 permitted the citizens of the United States, for three years, to deposit their merchandise in the port of New Orleans, and reship the same without other duty or charge than a fair price for storage, and declared that His Catholic Majesty would either extend this right of deposit beyond the three years or would assign the Americans some other place of deposit on the bank of the river.

Perhaps the United States fondly expected that the Treaty of Madrid would end all troubles. Far from it. The concessions that it contained were extorted from Spain by fears growing out of the state of Continental affairs, and there is only too much reason to think that she regarded them only as diplomatic manœuvres, to serve a temporary purpose. Certain it is that Spanish procrastination and intrigue delayed carrying into effect the promise in regard to withdrawing troops and garrisons; and it was not until March, 1798, that the Spanish Governor stealthily abandoned rather than formally surrendered the territory above the thirty-first parallel. Then, on the expiration of the three years, the Spanish Intendant at New Orleans denied the longer right of deposit at that port, and failed to designate, as the Treaty of Madrid provided, an "equivalent establishment." This act set the West all in a ferment again, and war between the two nations seemed imminent. Alarmed at the prospect of war, Spain reopened the port, but only to close it again in 1802, just as Louisiana was slipping from the hand of His Catholic Majesty into the hand of First Consul Bonaparte.

Such was the answer to the second Mississippi question.

The third question was: "Shall the United States or France own and control the mouth of the river?" It really involved the ownership of the Western half of the great valley. The natural boundary of the United States in 1783 was the Mississippi; they could not safely stop short of that limit—they need not extend beyond it; but in 1803 it was as important for them to control the river absolutely as it had been for them twenty years before to extend to its middle line. In 1800 Spain, having been in possession for thirty-seven years, agreed to retrocede Louisiana to France; and this agreement, as soon as known on this side of the ocean, brought the new question immediately to the front. In April, 1802, President Jefferson wrote to Robert R. Livingston, the American minister at Paris: "There is on the globe one single spot the possessor of which is our natural and habitual enemy. It is New Orleans, through which the produce of three-eighths of our territory must pass to market, and from its fertility it will ere long yield more than one-half of our whole produce, and contain more than half our inhabitants."[1] In February, 1803, he wrote to M. Dupont: "The suspension of the right of deposit at New Orleans, ceded to us by our treaty with Spain, threw our whole country into such a ferment as immediately threatened its peace. This, however, was believed to be the act of the Intendant unauthorized by his government. But it showed the necessity of making effectual arrangements to secure the peace of the two countries against the indiscreet acts of subordinate agents. . . . The occlusion of the Mississippi is a state of things in which we cannot exist. . . . Our circumstances are so imperious as to admit of no delay as to our course, and the use of the Mississippi so indispensable that we cannot hesitate one moment to hazard our existence for its maintenance"[2] How urgent the case was is apparent from the rapid growth of population on what were then called "the Western waters," the boundless capabilities of the country that they

---

[1] Works, IV., 432.   [2] Works, IV., 457.

occupied, and their absolute dependence upon the Mississippi as a means of reaching the markets of the world. Exclusive of Western Pennsylvania, the over-mountain population was 166,641 in 1790, 469,397 in 1800, and 1,162,939 in 1810. What was less than five per cent. of the total population of the Union grew in twenty years to be more than sixteen per cent. The annexation of Louisiana by purchase in 1803 was the answer that the Republic made to the third Mississippi question. It reunited, politically and historically, the great valley, divided since 1763. Mr. Madison in 1802 said "the Mississippi was everything to the Western people; the Hudson, the Delaware, the Potomac, and all the navigable streams of the Atlantic States formed into one stream."

The transfer of Louisiana to the United States filled the Court of Spain with fresh alarm and anger. It confirmed the worst fears that she had entertained in 1782; it removed the screen heretofore interposed between the United States and Mexico; and it immediately gave rise to the fourth question: "Shall the United States reap all the advantages naturally flowing from the purchase—shall the act of 1803 stand in its full integrity?" Practically, it assumed the form: "What are the extent and boundaries of the purchase?" The treaty answered: "The colony or province of Louisiana with the same extent that it now has in the hands of Spain, and that it had when France possessed it, and such as it should be after the treaties subsequently entered into between Spain and other States."[1] History alone could tell what this language meant, and the two powers could not agree as to her answer. After a long controversy that more than once threatened to involve them in war, in 1819 they came to an agreement. Florida became a possession of the United States by purchase, thus ending the dispute as to the eastern extension of Louisiana; and the Sabine, the Red River, the one-hundredth me-

---

[1] Spain was still in actual possession of the province when the treaty was signed. She delivered it to France, November 30, 1803, and France to the United States a month later.

ridian, the Arkansas, and the forty-second parallel of North latitude were made the boundary between the United States and Mexico, thus practically excluding the Spaniard from the Mississippi Valley.

The fifth and last Mississippi question came with the Civil War. "Shall the Father of Waters flow all the way from his remotest sources to the sea through the territory of the United States, or shall he, below latitude 36° 30″, roll his floods through a foreign country?" This question involved all that had gone before it. The Southern leaders thought the river so indispensable to the Northwest that, threatened with its loss, it would rather cleave to the South and part company with the East. These leaders did not miscalculate the estimate that the people of the Northwest set upon the river. But they wofully miscalculated the terms upon which they were willing to possess it. How thoroughly the Northwestern people comprehended the issue, and the means by which it must be reached, is shown by the heroic part which they sustained in the long and arduous effort to reopen the Mississippi after it had been closed by the Confederacy. Still, the Northwestern troops have not the exclusive glory of winning back to the Union this great national highway. President Lincoln thus distributed the honor of this glorious achievement in August, 1863: "The Father of Waters again goes unvexed to the sea. Thanks to the great Northwest for it; nor yet wholly to them. Three hundred miles up they met New England, Empire, Keystone, and Jersey hewing their way right and left. The sunny South, too, in more colors than one also lent a helping hand. On the spot, their part of the history was jotted down in black and white. The job was a great national one, and let none be slighted who bore an honorable part in it."[1] The maintenance of the Union was the answer to the last Mississippi question.

---

[1] Raymond: Life and Public Services of Abraham Lincoln, 442.

AUTHORITIES CITED.

Adams, H. B. : Maryland's Influence on Western Land Cessions to the United States. Baltimore, 1885.
Andrews, E. B. : Funeral Discourse on the Death of Hon. Ephraim Cutler. Marietta, 1855.
Andrews, I. W. : Washington County and the Early Settlement of Ohio. Cincinnati, 1877. Ohio Archæological and Historical Quarterly. Columbus, 1887. Magazine of American History, 1887.
Annual Register, The : 1763, 1774. London.
Baldwin, C. C. : The Geographical History of Ohio, and a Centennial Lawsuit. Tracts 63 and 35 of the Western Reserve and Northern Ohio Historical Society. Cleveland.
Bancroft, George : History of the United States. Boston, 1876, and New York, 1885.
Bigelow, John : Works of Franklin. New York.
Book of Drafts, The : Records of Trumbull County, Ohio.
Breese, Sidney : The Early History of Illinois. Chicago, 1884.
Browne, W. H. : Maryland, in the Commonwealth Series. Boston.
Burnet, Jacob : Notes on the Early Settlement of the Northwestern Territory. New York and Cincinnati, 1847.
Butterfield, C. W. : The Washington-Crawford Letters. Cincinnati, 1877. Crawford's Expedition against Sandusky. Cincinnati, 1873.
Cable, G. W.: The Creoles of Louisiana. New York, 1884.
Campbell, H. J. : The State, etc.
Campbell, J. V. : Political History of Michigan. Detroit, 1876.
Carnegie, Andrew : Triumphant Democracy. New York, 1887.
Chalmers, George : A Collection of Treaties between Great Britain and other Powers. London, 1790.
Chapman, T. J. : The French in the Alleghany Valley. Cleveland, 1887.
Chase, S. P. : Statutes of Ohio and of the Northwestern Territory. Cincinnati, 1833.

Clark's Campaign in the Illinois, in Ohio Valley Historical Series. Cincinnati, 1869.
Cooke, E. H. : Virginia, in the Commonwealth Series. Boston.
Cooley, T. M. : Michigan, in the Commonwealth Series. Boston.
Cox, J. D. : On Country between the Ohio River and the Lakes, Oberlin Jubilee. Oberlin, 1883.
Curtis, G. T. : History of the Constitution of the United States. New York, 1865.
Cutler, Wm. P. and Julia P. : Life, Journals, and Correspondence of Rev. Manasseh Cutler, LL.D. Cincinnati, 1888.
Cutler, W. P. : Services of the Ohio Company in Defending the United States Frontier from Invasion, Ohio Archæological and Historical Quarterly. Columbus, O., 1888.
Dillon, J. B. : History of Indiana to the Year 1816. Indianapolis, 1857.
Donaldson, Thomas : The Public Domain. Washington, 1884.
Edwards, Ninian W. : History of Illinois, and Life of Ninian Edwards. Springfield, Ill., 1870.
Eliot, Jonathan : Debates, etc. Washington, 1836.
Fiske, John : American Political Ideas. New York, 1885.
Fitzmaurice, Lord : Life of William, Earl of Shelburne. London, 1875, 1876.
Gannett, Henry : Boundaries of the United States and of the Several States and Territories, etc. Washington, 1885.
Garfield, J. A. : Works of. Boston, 1883.
Grattan, P. R. : Reports of Cases Decided in the Supreme Court of Appeals and General Court of Virginia. Richmond, 1847.
Green, J. R. : History of the English People. New York, 1878, 1880.
Hamilton, J. C. : Life of Alexander Hamilton.
Harris, T. M. : The Journal of a Tour into the Territory Northwest of the Alleghany Mountains, made in the Spring of the Year 1803. Boston, 1805.
Hening's Statutes of Virginia, X.
Hildreth, Richard : History of the United States of America. New York, 1882.
Hillsborough, Lord : Report of, in Sparks's Works of Franklin.
Hine, C. D. : Connecticut School Fund, The Nation, No. 1076.
Historical Collections of the Mahoning Valley. Youngstown, 1876.
Hitchcock, Henry : American State Constitutions. New York, 1887.
Hoyt, H. M. : Brief of a Title in the Seventeen Townships in the County of Luzerne. Harrisburg, 1879.
Hubbard, Bela : Memorials of a Half Century. New York, 1887.
Jefferson, Thomas : Writings of. New York, 1853.

AUTHORITIES CITED. 431

Johnston, Alexander : Connecticut, in the Commonwealth Series, and A Century of the Constitution, The New Princeton Review, September, 1887.

Journals of the American Congress from 1774 to 1788. Washington, 1823.

Journals, Secret, of the Acts and Proceedings of Congress, etc. Boston, 1821.

Knapp, H. S. : History of the Maumee Valley. Toledo, 1872.

Knight, G. W. : History and Management of Land Grants for Education in the Northwest Territory. New York, 1885.

Labberton, R. H. : New Historical Atlas and General History. New York, 1886.

Larned, Ellen D. : History of Windham County, Conn. Worcester, Mass., 1874, 1880.

Levermore, C. H. : The Republic of New Haven. Baltimore, 1886.

Lyman, Theodore : Diplomacy of the United States. Boston, 1826.

Madison, James : Papers of. Washington, 1840.

McMaster, J. B. : A History of the People of the United States. New York, 1883, 1885.

Monette, J. W. : History of the Discovery and Settlement of the Valley of the Mississippi. New York, 1846.

Morse, J. T. : John Quincy Adams, in American Statesmen Series. Boston.

Parkman, Francis : The Pioneers of France in the New World ; The Jesuits in North America ; La Salle and the Discovery of the Great West ; Count Frontenac and New France ; The Old Regime in Canada ; Montcalm and Wolfe. Boston.

Phisterer, Frederick : Statistical Record of the Armies of the United States. New York, 1883.

Poole, W. F. : Dr. Cutler and the Ordinance of 1787, North American Review.

Poore, Ben. Perley : Charters and Constitutions of the United States, etc. Washington, 1878.

Quincy, President Josiah : On Sabbath in Andover, North American Review.

Raymond, H. J. : The Life and Public Services of Abraham Lincoln. New York, 1865.

Report of the Joint Commission Appointed by the States of Pennsylvania and Ohio to Ascertain and Re-mark the Boundary Line between said States. Columbus, 1883.

Reynolds, John : My Own Times. Chicago, 1879.

Rice, Harvey : Sketches of Western Life. Boston, 1887.

Roberts, E. H. : New York, in the Commonwealth Series. Boston.
Robinson, H. M. : The Great Fur Land. New York, 1879.
Scaife, W. B. : Boundary Dispute between Maryland and Pennsylvania, The Pennsylvania Magazine of History, 1885.
Seeley, J. R. : The Expansion of England. Boston, 1883.
Seward, W. H. : Works of, Vol. IV. Boston, 1884.
Shaler, N. S. : Kentucky, in the Commonwealth Series. Boston. Physiography of North America, Narrative and Critical History of America, Vol. IV. Boston.
Smith, W. H. : The Saint Clair Papers. Cincinnati, 1882.
Sparks, Dr. Jared : The Works of Benjamin Franklin. Chicago, 1882. The Writings of George Washington. Boston, 1835. Diplomatic Correspondence of the American Revolution. Boston, 1829.
Speed, Thomas : The Wilderness Road, etc. Louisville, 1886.
State Papers, The. Washington, 1823.
Strong, Moses M. : History of the Territory of Wisconsin from 1836 to 1848. Madison, Wis., 1885.
Sumner, Charles : Prophetic Voices about America, Atlantic Monthly.
Sumner, W. G. : Andrew Jackson as a Public Man, in American Statesmen Series. Boston.
Thwaits, R. G. : The Boundaries of Wisconsin, Magazine of Western History. 1887.
Tyler, M. C. : Patrick Henry, in American Statesmen Series. Boston.
Vinton, Samuel F. : Argument in Garner's Case, Report of Ohio State Fish Commission. Columbus, O., 1877.
Waddell, J. A. : Annals of Augusta County, Va. Richmond, 1886.
Walker, C. I. : The Northwest during the Revolution, Michigan Pioneer Collections, Vol. III. Lansing, 1881.
Walker, Francis A. : Statistics of the Population of the United States at the Tenth Census. Washington, 1884.
Washburne, E. B. : Sketch of Edward Coles. Chicago, 1882.
Wheaton, Henry : Reports, etc., Vol. V. Philadelphia, 1833.
Whittlesey, Charles : Early History of Cleveland, Ohio. Cleveland, 1867. Tracts Published by Western Reserve and Northern Ohio Historical Society.
Winsor, Justin : Narrative and Critical History of America. Boston.

INDEX.

ACADIA ceded to England, 66
Adams, John, 167
Adams, J. Q., opinion on Ohio and Michigan boundary question, 333
Admission of Northwestern States, 317
Aix-la-Chapelle, terms of treaty of, 57
Albany Congress, 125, 201
Alleghany Valley, first occupied by French, 47
Allen, 107
Allen, Ethan, 116
Amendments on land questions, 206
Anglo-French war, character of, 55
Anti-slavery views, in Ohio, 390
Aranda, Count de, negotiations with Jay, 175
Ark, The, 303
Arkansas, influence of, on admission of Michigan, 334
Articles of Confederation, 222
Arthur the First, 310
Augusta County, Va., 104
Ayllon, explorer and settler, 6

BALTIMORE, LORD, 78
Banks, hostility to, in Wisconsin, 343
Berkeley, Lord John, buys New Jersey, 95
Bienville, report on Ohio Valley, 61
Bird, Captain, 158
Blanca, Count Florida, 172
Boone, Daniel, 265
Boundary lines, difficulty of defining, 20
  disputes between Connecticut and New York, 94
  of the United States, 121, 180, 165, 187
Brandt, 115
British, Government, Western land policy of, 120
  occupation of West after the Revolution, 184
Brulé, Etienne, discovers copper, 25
Bunch of Grapes, 268
Burke, Edmund, on America, 145
Butler, 115

Butler, Captain Zebulon, in Wyoming Valley, 112

CABOT, JOHN, discovers America, 12
Cabot, Sebastian, visits America, 12
Cadillac, La Motte, 47
Cahokia, 293
Campus Martius, 286
Canada, taken by Cartier, 10
  ceded to England, 66
  Pamphlet, 127
  Franklin's view concerning, 128
  proposed cession to U. S., 169
  refugees, lands reserved for, 259
Cape Breton Island ceded to England, 66
Carroll, Daniel, 222
Carolina grant, 80
Carteret, Sir George, 95
Cartier, James, 9
Centre of population, 393
Cessions, Maryland's influence upon, 216
  by New York, 229, 237
  by Virginia, 244
  by Massachusetts, 246
  by Connecticut, 247
  dangers of, to the Republic, 251
Champlain, Samuel de, 10, 22, 23
Charles I., grant to Lord Baltimore, 78
Charles II., grant of Carolina, 80
  charters Connecticut Co., 87
  charters Rhode Island, 88
  grants New England to Duke of York, 92
Charter, to Sir Walter Raleigh, 71
  to Lord Baltimore, 78
  to Carolina, 80
  to Connecticut Company, 87
  to Rhode Island, 88
  to Penn, 98
Chase, Chief Justice, on claims of United States to Western lands, 250
Chicago, 398
Chippewas cede lands, 256
Choate, Rufus, on colonial boundaries, 90
Christian Indians, 259

Church lands, 276
Cincinnati, Society of, 288
Cincinnati, early name of, 288
Clark, George Rogers, the conquest of country west of the Ohio, 153, 183
  instructions from Patrick Henry, 154
Clarendon, Earl of, sells Plymouth grant, 82
Cleaveland, General Moses, 373
Coeducation in Northwest, 405
Colbert represses Canadian political life, 52
Coles, Edward, influence on Black Laws of Illinois, 360, 363
Colonial periods, 406
Colonies, French and English, contrasted, 38, 39
  extent of the Thirteen in 1776, 164
College statistics in Northwest, 403
Color line in Ohio Constitution, 357
Columbia, 288
Columbia River, Webster's view of, 394
Committee on Northwestern land claims, 224, 226
Conception River, 31
Confederacy, fear of Western and Southern, governs northern boundary of Illinois, 327
Confederation, articles of, 207
Congress, land policy of, 205, 219
Connecticut, how originally constituted, 87
  Company chartered, 87
  and New Haven consolidated, 88
  disputes with Massachusetts, 89
  disputes with New York, 94
  quarrel with William Penn, 110
  Westward emigration, 112
  in Pennsylvania, 114
  claim to Western lands, 199
  cedes her Western lands to Congress, 247
  Western Reserve, 368
  School Fund of, 370
  Land Company, 372
  resigns jurisdiction of Western Reserve, 378
  influence on Western Reserve, 388
Connolly, Dr. John, 106, 152
Continental Army at close of Revolution, 267
Coronada explores Mississippi Valley, 7
Coureurs des bois, *i.e.*, French bushrangers, character of, 41
Court in early territorial days, 303

Culpepper, Lord, 79
Currituck River, 80
Cutler, Dr. Manasseh, 268, 275, 346
Crawford, Colonel William, 198
Crawford, W. H., on slavery, 363
Croghan, report of, 48, 49
Crozat, Anthony, 51

DAKOTA construction of Ordinance of 1787, 316
Delaware, bought by Penn, 99
  Company, 112
  becomes independent, 103
Delawares cede lands, 256
De Narvaez, expedition of, 7
Denonville, Governor of Canada in 1685, 40
De Soto, 7
De Tret, Fort, 47
Detroit, founded, 27
  Straits occupied by French, 42
  population in 1765, 48
  in the Revolution, 150
  importance of, 156
De Vaca, 7
Dickerson on State of Oregon, 394
Dinwiddie, Governor, 104
Dixon, of Mason and Dixon, 103
Dongan gains Western land for New York, 41
Duane, 221
Du Lhut, 36, 42
Dunmore, Governor, controversy with Penn, 107
  ignores Quebec Act, 144
Duquesne seizes northeast branches of the Ohio, 61
Dutch, trading posts in New York, 39
  discoveries, 90
  claims ignored by the English, 91

EARLY representatives of Ohio, 325
Education in Northwest, 402–404
Educational features of Ordinance of 1787, 401
Edwards, Ninian, Governor of Illinois Territory, 315
Electors, qualifications of, in Northwest Territory, 270
Elizabeth, Queen, 71
Elliot, 150
Emigration, paths of Western, 329
Enabling Act, 319, 321
England's claim to North America, 12
  yields Western posts, 185
English, on the Atlantic plain, 12

INDEX. 435

English, treaties with Indians, 60
Entails, erasure of, 269
Erie, City founded, 47
    Lake, discovered, 26

FAIRFAX, LORD, 79
Fallen Timbers, victory of, 184
Father Marquette, 30
Fearing, Paul, first lawyer in Northwest, 288
Federal, character of the United States, 165
    theory of Government, 251
Federalist views on admission of Ohio, 308, 309
Fire Lands, allotment of the, 369
Five Nations, 57
Five State Plan, 321
Florida, ceded to England, 68
    East and West constituted, 121
    boundary dispute, 417
    purchased, 426
Floyd, 221
Fort, Crèvecœur, 35
    Duquesne built, 62
    Harmar built, 285
    Le Bœuf, 61
    McIntosh, 256
    Stanwix, 134, 256
    St. Louis, 43
    Venango, 61
Franklin, Benjamin, his plan for settling Western colonies, 126
    the Canada Pamphlet, 127
    reply to Lord Hillsborough, 135
    arguments for the Grand Company, 136
    Commissioner to Paris in 1779, 169
    demands Mississippi for Western limits of the United States, 174
    outwits the French minister, 181
Franquelin, 51
French, in Valley of the St. Lawrence, 9
    discoverers in the Northwest, 21
    settlements kindly disposed toward Americans, 159
    settlers, their character, 52, 161
    alliance, 162, 177
French and Indian War, 62, 65, 66, 68
Frontenac, Count, sends Joliet to discover the Mississippi, 30
    policy of, 46
Fulton and Harris lines, 331
Fur Trade, 40

GALISSONIÈRE, 161
Galinée, first map of the Lakes, 27

Galvez, 173
Gates, grant from James I., 72
Georgia founded, 81
Genesee Valley surrendered to Massachusetts, 119
Gerard, 172
Gibault, Father Pierre, 155
Girty Brothers, 150
Gist, Christopher, 58
Gladstone, description of West, 186
Gore, The, 118
Gorges, Sir Ferdinando, 85
Grand Company, 133
Grayson, arguments for Western Reserve, 248
Griffin, The, 32
Grosselliers visits country beyond Lake Superior, 26
Guadaloupe preferred to Canada, 130

HABITANTS, history of, from 1763 to Revolution, 150
Hakluyt, Richard, 119
Haldman, General, 184
Halsey and Ward, 118
Hamilton, Governor, adopts Indian warfare, 149
    civil and military head of Northwest, 150
Hanson, John, 222
Harris and Fulton lines, 331
Harrison, William Henry, delegate to Congress, 306
    Governor of Indiana, 314
Heights of Abraham, 69
Hennepin with La Salle, 34
Henry, Patrick, instructions to Clark, 154
    views on Detroit, 158
Hillsborough, objections to the Walpole Company, 134
Hopton's grant, 79
Hudson Bay restored to England, 56
Hudson, Henry, 90
Hull, William, Governor of Michigan Territory, 314
Huron, Lake, discovered, 23, 24
Hutchins, Thomas, author of United States plan of survey, 262

ILLINOIS, separated from Louisiana, 52
    County, 159
    River seized by Spain, 174
    County claims, 229
    settlement of, under Virginia rule, 293, 294

Illinois as a territory, 314, 315
  admitted as a State, 315, 328
  northern State boundary, 327
  dispute with Wisconsin, 330
  slavery regulations in, 354
  character of immigrants, 358
  census of 1880, 396
Independence, Port of, 373
Indentures of slaves in Indiana and Illinois, 354
Indian, position in French plan of colonization, 22
  land titles, 59
  allies of the English, 149
  in War of the Revolution, 184
  treaties, 256
  slaveholders, 348
  slaves, 349
Indiana, claim, 229; settlement of, 293
  Territory formed, 307
  admitted as a State, 326
  prohibits slavery, 358
  census of 1880, 396
Industries of Western settlements, 50
Ingles-Draper settlement, 58
Iowa Territory, 340
Iroquois, destroy the Hurons, 24
  influence on our national history, 25
  convey their lands in trust to England, 39
  cede Western land to New York, 41
  cede land formerly of the Hurons to England, 46
  conquests claimed by England, 65
  title to Ohio lands, 137

JACKSON'S position in regard to Ohio boundary, 333
Jamestown founded, 6, 12
James I., grant to Sir Thomas Gates and Sir George Somers, 72
Jay, John, envoy to Madrid, 171, 174
  treats with Count de Aranda, 175
  saves the West to his country, 182
  his treaty, 184, 190
Jefferson, Thomas, views on Virginia land claims, 234
  plan of government for Western territories, 266
  views on town systems, 300
Jesuit College at Kaskaskia, 50
Johnson, Sir William, negotiations with Six Nations, 132
Johnston, Alexander, on provisions for new States, 223

Joliet, explores Lake Erie, 26
  discovers the Mississippi River, 31

KALM, 129
Kaskaskia, population of, 48
  surrenders to Americans, 154
Kentucky, land litigation in, 261
King George's War, 57
King, Rufus, 190
King William's War, 46, 56
Knights of the Golden Horseshoe, 17
Kirk, David, 56

LA CLEDE founds St. Louis, 151
Lake Erie, how reached in 1796, 282
Lake of the Woods controversy settled, 190, 191
Land, cessions, Madison's views upon, 231-234
  litigation, causes of, 260
  Ordinance of 1785, 255, 263
  policy in Ohio, 301
  system of the Government, 302
Langlade, Captain de, 152
Lansdowne, Marquis of, 182
La Salle, meets Joliet near Grand River, 30
  schemes of, 32, 43
  explores Lower Michigan, 34
  builds Fort Crèvecœur, 35
  takes possession of mouth of the Mississippi, 35
  establishes Fort St. Louis, 43
  death of, 43
Le Caron, missionary to the Hurons, 23
Livingston, Robert R., gains Louisiana, 190
  views on importance of New Orleans to the United States, 425
London Company, 72, 77, 190
Long Island attached to New York, 93
Lomax, opinion on Virginia Western claims, 196
Losantiville, now Cincinnati, 288
Louisiana, the first geographical, 51
  reserved to France, 67
  invites settlers, 151
  ceded to the United States, 190
  annexation of, 426
  annexed to Indiana, 314
Louisville, 171
Lucas's, Governor, war, 332
Lucke Island, 80
Ludlow's line, 292

MCARTHUR, DUNCAN, 290

INDEX. 437

McComas, opinion on Virginia Western claims, 195
McDougal, 221
McGee, 150

MADISON, JAMES, gives rule for territorial limits, 165
   letter to Pendleton, 231
   letters on land cessions, 231–234
   on admission of Vermont, 237
   on acceptance of Northwestern cessions, 238
   on revenue plan, 238
   on policy of land companies, 243
Maine, bought by Massachusetts, 85, 93
Marietta, 276, 286
Marquette, Father, 30, 31, 32
Marshall, John, views on Western land titles, 252
   influence on government of Western Reserve, 381, 387
Maryland, named, 78
   disputes concerning boundaries of, 100, 102, 103
   resistance to Articles of Confederation, 213
   remonstrates with Virginia, 214
   ratifies Articles of Confederation, 220
Mason and Dixon, 103
Mason, Captain John, grant in New England bounded, 84
Mass first celebrated in Canada, 23
Massachusetts, Bay Colony, 83, 85
   disputes with Connecticut, 89
   disputes with New York, 94
   surrenders Western claims to New York, 118
   claim to Western land, 199
   cedes her Western land to Congress, 246
Massie, General Nathaniel, lays out Chillicothe, 290
"Mer Douce" discovered, 23
Miami Purchase, 288, 289
Michigan, Lake, discovered, 25
   Territory, 314, 315
   influence of habitants on, 328
   Constitution formed, 330
   boundary quarrel with Ohio, 330
   controversy over admission of, as a State, 335
   Upper Peninsular, objections to, 336; resources of, 336
   census of 1880, 396
Michilimacinac, mission of, 38

Minnesota admitted, 343
Mississippi River, discovered by De Soto, 7
   by Joliet and Marquette, 31
   taken possession of by La Salle, 35
   called St. Louis River, 51
   natural western boundary after the Revolution, 169
   control of the navigation on, 418
   navigation fixed by treaty, 423
Mississippi Valley, why abandoned by Spain, 8
   French occupation planned, 32
Missouri River, called St. Philip, 51
Mohawk Valley, its important part in American history, 4, 15
Monroe gains Louisiana, 190
Montcalm, principles represented by, 68
Morgan, George, memorial for Western land claimants, 212
Morgan, Colonel George, 242

NANTUCKET, 92
National capital, location of, 393
Neutrality belt of Indian Territory proposed between United States and Canada, 145
New Albion, 95
New Ceaserea, 95
New Connecticut, 97, 375
New England, 13, 16, 85
New Hampshire Grant, 84
   annexed to Massachusetts, 85
   becomes Royal Colony, 85
   becomes independent, 85
   boundary difficulties, 86
   Grants, 96
New Haven Colony, 87, 88, 110
New Jersey bounded, 95
   objections to Articles of Confederation, 207
New Netherlands, its limits, 90, 92
Newport, Captain, portable barge of, 14
New Scotland, Lordship and Barony of, 82
Newspaper statistics in Northwest, 403
New York possibly a part of New England, 91
   western claims of, 198
   plan to promote adoptions of Articles of Confederation, 216
   cession accepted, 229, 237
Niagara, Fort, built, 47
Nicolet, Jean, discovers Lake Michigan, 25
North Bend, 288

438 INDEX.

Northwest Territory wrested from France, 55
  in Revolution, 147
  land claims, 192
  lands the means of defraying war expenses, 230
  First General Assembly of, 305
  boundary of Ohio, how fixed, 324
Nova Scotia ceded to England, 66
  refuses lands reserved for, 259

OBERLIN, 391
Oglethorpe, James, 81
Ohio, first maps of, 28, 291
  Company formed, 58
  River, difficulty of fortifying, 60
  Company of Associates, 267
  Purchase, 275
  University, endowment, 276, 292
  Valley, how related to country east and south, 283
  Indians in, 296
  admission as State, 267, 306, 318, 322, 324
  First Constitutional Convention, 325
  anti-slavery discussion in, 355
  population in census of 1880, 396
  trade of, 400
  Constitution of, 408
Old National Pike, 413
Ontario, Lake, discovered, 24
Ordinance governing western territory, terms of, 269
  of 1787, 315, 364
Oswald, British Commissioner, 169, 179
Ottawa River, 27
Ottawas cede lands, 256
Ouabache River, 52

PAN HANDLE, 109
Pani, 348
Parallel of 36° 30', 80
Parsons, General S. H., 269, 284, 286, 369
Parties, growth of, in Northwest, 304
Pemaquid, 93
Penn, William, charter, 98
  buys Delaware, 99
  quarrel with Connecticut, 110
Pennamite and Yankee war, 112, 116
Pennsylvania, disputes concerning boundaries, 99, 101, 102, 103, 109, 373
Perry's victory, 185
Pickawillany, 59

Pierce, John, 82
Pitt, William, policy, 63
Pittsburgh surveyed, 105
Plonden, Sir Edmund, 95
Plan of Union, 125, 126
Plough and the Harrow, 269
Plunket, Colonel, 114
Plymouth Colony, boundaries of, 83
  Company, 72, 75
  Council, 84, 85
Political parties in Canada, 52
  parties in Northwest, 406, 410, 414
Pontiacs conspiracy, 148
Popular Sovereignty ignored in Enabling Act, 320
Population, of New France and British Colonies in 1754, 69
  of United States in 1787, 282
  of Western Territory in 1800, 297
  of Western Reserve, 395
Portages, 46
Pownall, Governor Thomas, 264
Presque Isle, 47
Products of Northwest, 399
Providence Plantation, 88
Pro-slavery arguments in Illinois, 358, 361
Public Domain not a source of revenue, 211, 264
Public Land System, 302
Public school, statistics for, 403
Purre, Don Eugenio, 173
Putnam, General Rufus, leads colony to the Muskingum, 285

QUEBEC established, 10
  boundaries of, in 1763, 121
  Act, 141
Queen Anne's War, 56
Quincy, Josiah, on secession of Eastern States, 415

RADISSON visits Superior country, 26
Raleigh, Sir Walter, 71
Randolph, John, on slavery in Indiana, 352
Rayneval's conciliatory line, 176, 177
Report of Committee on Western Boundaries, 166
Republican Party, its birth, 412, 414
  views on admission of Ohio, 301
Resolutions of Albany Congress, 1754, 122, 201
Revenue plans in connection with land claims, 238
Rhode Island settlements, 88

INDEX. 439

River of the Holy Spirit, 6
  St. Louis, 51
Roberts's Line, 292
Robertson, James, 265
Rockford, Boundary Convention at, 339
Ross County, influence on division of Northwest Territory, 307
Roswell, Sir Henry, 83
Roving Patent granted the Pilgrims, 82
Rutledge Committee, 239, 240
Ryswick, treaty of, 46, 156

SAFFORY AND WOODWARD, 89
Sante Claire Lake, origin of name, 33
Sante Esprite, mission of, 29
Salt Springs, 377
Saltonstall, 110
Saydys, administration of, 77
Sargent, Winthrop, 286
Saut, Saint Marie, 26, 29, 38, 401
School, provisions in land, 259, 262
  fund of Connecticut, 370
Schuyler, Philip, 217
Secession in the Northwest, 414
  of Eastern States advocated, 415
Seven Cities of Cibola, 7
Seven Years' War, 66
Sevier, John, 265
Seward on political influence of Northwest, 413
Shaler, Professor, disadvantages of French colonists, 51
Shelburne, Earl of, 178, 182
Sioux, first discovered, 26
Six Nations, first discovered, 26
  aid England, 39
  their territory claimed by Virginia and New York, 198
  treaty with, 256
Slavery, in ordinance of 1787, 272
  views of, at close of Revolution, 345
  in Northwest, 345, 347, 348, 349, 351, 352, 355, 365
Soldiers furnished by the Northwest, 415
Somers' Grant from James I., 72
Southampton, administration of London Company, 77
Spain, in the Gulf of Mexico, 6
  in French and Indian Wars, 68
  claims the Mississippi River, 170
  refuses to receive Mr. Jay, 172
  seizes post St. Joseph, 173
  disputes Florida boundary, 417
  opposes treaty of 1783, 418
  views on Louisiana question, 421

Spain withdraws from Louisiana, 424
  excluded from Mississippi Valley, 426
Spotswood, Governor, 16, 17
Starved Rock, 43
St. Augustine, key to Spanish possessions, 9
St. Clair, Arthur, 106
  appointed Governor of Marietta, 286
  treats with Indians for Ohio, 296
  waning popularity, 305
  indictment against, 311
  last years, 313
  explains anti-slavery clause of ordinance of 1787, 350
  conflict with Western Reserve, 376
  County, 299
  Lake, origin of name, 33
St. Croix Valley, 342
Steamboats on Ohio and Lakes, 400
Steuben, Baron, 184
Stirling, Earl of, grant of New England, 82
St. Jerome River, 52
St. Joseph, Fort, 42, 173
St. Lawrence, 9, 11
St. Louis, 43, 151
St. Philip's River, 51
Strachy assists Oswald, 178
Stuart, negotiations with Cherokees, 132
Sufferers' Lands, 369
Suffrage in Northwest, 408
Superior State proposed, 341
Surveys, methods, 257, 260
Susquehanna an outlet of Lake Erie, 26
  Company, 111
Symmes, John Clives, 286
  Purchase, 288
  Tract, 288

TECUMSEH, 185
Tilghman, 107
Titles to Land, 70, 380, 382
Toledo War, 332
  City, 331
Tonty, 35
Township, size decreed, 258
Territorial claims, 19, 167, 280
Territory of Northwest, 280, 281
Transportation in Northwest, 399
Treaty of Ghent, 185
  Greenville, 184
  Paris, 182, 187
Trent, William, 213

440 INDEX.

Trenton Decision, 116
Tupper, General Benjamin, 284
Turner, George, 286
Trumbull County organized, 387
Trumbull, Governor of Connecticut, 117

UNITED STATES wrests Northwest from England, 162
   original boundaries, 186
   jurisdiction on western rivers, 384
Utrecht, treaty of, 56

VAN BUREN'S election, 333
Vandalia, 133
   memorial, 213
   grant, 229
Varnum, James M., 286
Venango, Fort, 61
   views on Spain's demands, 176
Vermont, in War of Independence, 97
   influence on land questions, 235
   admission to the Union, 235
Verazzano, 9
Vincennes, 44, 155
Vincent's Port, 44
Vinton, Samuel F., on Ohio and Virginia boundaries, 193
Virginia, early map of, 13
   treaty with Iroquois, 59
   ceded to Raleigh, 71
   ceded to Gates and Somers, 72
   named, 72
   boundaries in 1609, 73
   governors commissioned, 77
   resists Lord Baltimore's grant, 79
   releases Maryland, Pennsylvania, North and South Carolina, 110, 192
   organizes Illinois County, 158
   claims to Ohio, 194
   western counties of, 197
   prepares to sell western lands, 212
   denies jurisdiction of Congress, 215
   cessions not recommended, 228
   terms of cession, 243
   vote on ordinance of 1787, 277
   military district of, 290

WABASH COUNTY Claims, 229
Walker, Dr. Thomas, 58
Walpole Colony, 133, 134, 139
War, French and Indian, 62
War Claims settled by land, 258
Ward and Halsey Titles, 118, 387
Warren, Ohio, First Court sits at, 388

Washington, George, on Western settlements, 266
   on separation of Western States, 420
   against the Walpole grant, 140
Washington County, Ohio, created, 287, 299
Water-ways of the continent, 2, 3
Wayne, General, 184
Wayne, County, 299, 321
Webster, Ashburton Treaty, 191
   on Columbia River, 394
Western Colonial boundaries, 124
   government decided upon, 269
   prophecies, 393
   question, three phases of, 148
   territory, government of, 266
Western Reserve, mistaken area of, 28
   description of, 117, 247
   what might have been, 186
   possibility of falling to England, 189
   government of, 266
   how different from Virginia Military District, 290
   sale of, 371
   need of a government, 379
   land titles, 380, 382
   made into Trumbull County, 387
   character of settlers in, 388
Whig Party in Northwest, 412
Whitfield, Rev. George, 126
Whittlesey, Colonel Charles, on Western Reserve Land Company, 375
Wilderness Road, 15
Williams, Roger, 188
Windsor planted, 87
Wisconsin Territory, 315
   contends for Upper Peninsula, 338
   threatens to form an independent State, 338
   boundary dispute with Illinois, 339
   boundaries fixed by Congress, 341
   admitted as a State, 343
   population of, 343
Woodward and Saffary, 89
Wolfe, principles represented by, 68
Wyandots cede land, 256
Wyoming Valley Massacre, 112, 115
Wyonoak Creek, 80

XAVIER, ST. FRANCIS, mission founded, 44

YORK, DUKE OF, 82

www.ingramcontent.com/pod-product-compliance
Lightning Source LLC
Chambersburg PA
CBHW022112300426
44117CB00007B/684